The Cambridge Companion to Oscar Wilde is an essential introduction to one of the theatre's most important and enigmatic writers. Although a general overview, these newly commissioned essays also offer some of the latest thinking on the dramatist and his impact on the twentieth century.

Part one places Wilde's work within the cultural and historical context of his time and includes an opening essay by Wilde's grandson, Merlin Holland. Further chapters also examine Wilde and the Victorians and his image as a dandy. Part two looks at Wilde's essential work as playwright and general writer, including his poetry, critiques and fiction, and provides detailed analyses of such key works as *Salome* and *The Importance of Being Earnest*, among others. The third group of essays examines the themes and factors which shaped Wilde's work and includes Wilde and his view of the Victorian woman, Wilde's sexual identities and interpreting Wilde on stage.

The volume also contains a detailed chronology of Wilde's work, a guide to further reading and illustrations from important productions.

THE CAMBRIDGE
COMPANION TO
OSCAR WILDE

CAMBRIDGE COMPANIONS TO LITERATURE

THE CAMBRIDGE
COMPANION TO
OSCAR WILDE

EDITED BY
PETER RABY
Homerton College, Cambridge

CAMBRIDGE
UNIVERSITY PRESS

PUBLISHED BY THE PRESS SYNDICATE OF THE UNIVERSITY OF CAMBRIDGE
The Pitt Building, Trumpington Street, Cambridge CB2 1RP, United Kingdom

CAMBRIDGE UNIVERSITY PRESS
The Edinburgh Building, Cambridge CB2 2RU, United Kingdom
40 West 20th Street, New York, NY 10011–4211, USA
10 Stamford Road, Oakleigh, Melbourne 3166, Australia

First published 1997
Reprinted 1998

Printed in the United Kingdom at the University Press, Cambridge

Typeset in Sabon 10/13

A catalogue record for this book is available from the British Library

Library of Congress cataloguing in publication data

The Cambridge companion to Oscar Wilde / edited by Peter Raby.
p.   cm. – (Cambridge companions to literature)
Includes bibliographical references and index.
ISBN 0 521 47471 X (hardback). ISBN 0 521 47987 8 (paperback)
1. Wilde, Oscar, 1854–1900 – Criticism and interpretation.
I. Raby, Peter. II. Series.
PR5824.C36   1997
828'.809–dc21 96–37705 CIP

ISBN 0 521 47471 X hardback
ISBN 0 521 47987 8 paperback

CE

CONTENTS

ILLUSTRATIONS

CONTRIBUTORS

KARL BECKSON, Professor of English at Brooklyn College, City University of New York, is the author or editor of eleven books on various figures of the 1890s, among them *Oscar Wilde: The Critical Heritage* (1970); *London in the 1890s: A Cultural History* (1993); and *The Oscar Wilde Encyclopedia* (1997). He is the co-editor (with Bobby Fong) of *Poems and Poems in Prose*, volume 4 of *The Complete Works of Oscar Wilde* (forthcoming).

JOSEPH BRISTOW is Professor of English at the University of California, Los Angeles. His most recent books include *Effeminate England: Homoerotic Writing after 1885* (1995) and *Sexuality, New Critical Idiom* (1996). He has edited several volumes, including (with Isobel Armstrong and Cath Sharrock), *Nineteenth-Century Women Poets: An Oxford Anthology* (1996).

STEPHEN CALLOWAY is an Associate Curator in the Prints, Drawings and Paintings Department at the Victoria and Albert Museum, London. He divides his time between writing, lecturing, broadcasting, and designing and consulting on films and the care of historic interiors. His books include *Twentieth Century Decoration* (1988), *The Elements of Style* (1994), and most recently *Baroque Baroque: The Culture of Excess* (1996). He selected and catalogued the V & A Exhibition *High Art and Low Life: The Studio and the Fin-de-siècle*, and is the Curator of the 1998 Aubrey Beardsley Centenary Exhibition.

RICHARD ALLEN CAVE is Professor of Drama and Theatre Arts at Royal Holloway in the University of London. He has written extensively on Renaissance, nineteenth-century and modern theatre, and in particular on Anglo-Irish drama. He has edited Yeats's plays and his essays on drama for Penguin. As a director he has staged productions of plays by Lady Gregory, Yeats and Brian Friel, and is Joint Artistic Director of Border Crossings Theatre Company.

LAWRENCE DANSON is Professor of English at Princeton University. He is the author of *Wilde's Intentions: The Artist in his Criticism* (1997) and *Max Beerbohm and the Act of Writing* (1989), as well as books and essays on Shakespeare and Renaissance drama. He is preparing *Intentions* and *The*

xi

Portrait of Mr W. H. for the forthcoming Oxford English Texts edition of *The Complete Works of Oscar Wilde*, and writing *Shakespeare and the Kinds of Drama* for the Oxford Shakespeare Library.

JOSEPH DONOHUE, Professor of English at the University of Massachusetts, Amherst, is author of *Dramatic Character in the English Romantic Age* (1970) and *Theatre in the Age of Kean* (1975) and, more recently, editor with Ruth Berggren of *Oscar Wilde's 'The Importance of Being Earnest': A Reconstructive Critical Edition of the Text of the First Production* (1995). Former editor (1986–96) of the journal *Nineteenth Century Theatre*, he is General Editor of *The London Stage 1800–1900: A Documentary Record and Calendar of Performances*.

BOBBY FONG is Professor of English and Dean of the Faculty at Hamilton College (Clinton, New York). Author of essays on Wilde's poetry, he is textual editor of volume 4, *Poems and Poems in Prose* (co-edited with Karl Beckson) in the forthcoming Oxford edition of *The Complete Works of Oscar Wilde*.

REGENIA GAGNIER is Professor of English at the University of Exeter. Her books include *Idylls of the Marketplace: Oscar Wilde and the Victorian Public* (1986), *Subjectivities: A History of Self-Representation in Britain, 1832–1920* (1991) and an edited collection, *Critical Essays on Oscar Wilde* (1992). Most recently she has published essays on the histories of economics and aesthetics in market society.

MERLIN HOLLAND, Oscar Wilde's grandson, writes, lectures and broadcasts on all aspects of Wilde's life and works. For twenty-five years he has been in the unique position, through administering the remaining copyrights in Wilde's writings, of being in close touch with the latest academic research while also presenting his grandfather to a wider audience.

RUSSELL JACKSON is Deputy Director of the Shakespeare Institute, the University of Birmingham's graduate school of Shakespeare studies in Stratford-upon-Avon. His publications include *Victorian Theatre: A New Mermaid Sourcebook* (1989), and critical editions of *The Importance of Being Earnest* (1980) and *An Ideal Husband* (1993). He is co-ordinating editor of *Theatre Notebook*, the journal of the Society for Theatre Research.

JOEL KAPLAN is Professor of Drama and Chair of the Department of Drama and Theatre Arts at the University of Birmingham. He has recently edited *Edwardian Theatre: Essays on Performance and the Stage* (1996), and is currently preparing new texts of Wilde's Society plays for the Oxford edition of *The Complete Works of Oscar Wilde*. He is co-author with Sheila Stowell of *Theatre and Fashion: Oscar Wilde to the Suffragettes* (1994) and *Wilde on Stage: A Cultural and Performance History* (forthcoming).

DECLAN KIBERD was educated at Trinity College, Dublin where he took a degree in English and Irish. He took a doctorate at Oxford under Richard Ellmann and this was subsequently published as *Synge and the Irish Language* (1979, second edition 1993). Among his other books are *Men and Feminism in Modern Literature* (1985), *Idir Dha Chultur* (1993), and *Inventing Ireland: The Literature of the Modern Nation* (1995). He has lectured on Irish topics in more than twenty countries and is a former Director of the Yeats International Summer School. He writes regularly in Irish newspapers. He is Professor of Anglo-Irish Literature and Drama at University College, Dublin.

JERUSHA MCCORMACK lectures in the Department of Modern English and American Literature at University College, Dublin. She has written the definitive biography of the man said to be 'the original of Dorian' in *John Gray: Poet, Dandy and Priest* (1991) as well as producing an edition of his *Selected Prose* (1992). She has just completed a book about Wilde and Ireland.

KERRY POWELL is Professor of English and Director of Graduate Study at Miami University, Oxford, Ohio. He is the author of *Oscar Wilde and the Theatre of the 1890s* (1990) and of *Gender and Theatre in the Victorian Period* (1997). His essays on Wilde have appeared in a wide range of journals, including a collection of essays on the Salome legend to be published by the University of Chicago Press in 1997.

PETER RABY is head of the Drama Department at Homerton College, Cambridge. He has written an introductory study of Wilde (1992) and edited Wilde's plays for the World's Classics series. He is the author of biographies of Harriet Smithson Berlioz and Samuel Butler, and a study of Victorian scientific travellers, *Bright Paradise* (1996). His writing for the stage includes the book for a new musical of *The Three Musketeers*.

JOHN STOKES is Professor in the Department of English at King's College, London. He has written widely on the culture of the *fin de siècle* and is the author of *In the Nineties* (1989) and *Oscar Wilde: Myths, Miracles and Imitations* (1996).

PREFACE

Wilde has been the subject of increasing critical attention over the last decade. Most notable, perhaps, was the publication of Richard Ellmann's biography in 1987, which has itself come under scrutiny. Wilde's works for the theatre have been given a series of successful and sometimes innovative productions, so that his distinctive exploration of the stage has been widely experienced in all its breadth; and the performance dimension itself has been minutely discussed and analysed. His radical position as a critic has been re-evaluated. He has been identified as a key figure within gay criticism. He is now recognised as a highly professional writer, acutely aware of his readership at a variety of levels, and also one who deliberately and systematically explored the oral dimension. His position as an Irish writer gives him status in the context of postcolonial criticism. The centenary of his trial, and the approaching centenary of his death as we approach our own *fin de siècle*, gives him a special contemporary relevance. In defiance of what might seem critical overkill, Wilde, both as writer and individual, remains as elusive as ever.

What also needs to be recognised is that, throughout the inevitable variations on the academic index, Wilde has retained his interest for the wider reading and theatre-going public. Few writers have succeeded in so many forms: *The Picture of Dorian Gray*, stories such as 'The Happy Prince' and 'The Selfish Giant', the high farce of *The Importance of Being Earnest*, the scenario of Strauss's *Salome*, the tragic *Ballad of Reading Gaol*, are only five examples of Wilde's mastery of different genres.

This collection of essays is organised in three parts: the first aims to give some context, beginning with Merlin Holland's review of the variety of attempts to recreate a sense of Wilde himself. The second places the focus on Wilde's achievements in most of the major kinds of writing he practised. The third part contains essays which track him across those boundaries, and assess his impact on aspects of the culture and society which succeeded him. Inevitably, in a book of this length, there are omissions, which are perhaps the more inevitable when the subject's life and personality are so intricately entwined with his work, and when the subject experimented so widely. There is, for example, no explicit commentary on *De Profundis*, itself a good example of the elusive nature of a Wilde text: a 'private' letter from prison to Douglas which the authorities did not allow to be sent, apparently written for one person, later published in edited form with a title supplied by Ross, and only issued in a complete version sixty-five years later. But this extraordinary retrospective autobiography inevitably surfaces in a number of these chapters. Other texts, for example 'The Portrait of Mr W. H.' or 'The Decay of Lying', are discussed in a number of essays. Wilde's work is full of self-reference, and the index to this book is a virtual adjunct to the table of contents. Choices have had to be made, and priority given to the public sphere of the theatre, where Wilde's major works were so prominent both at the height of his own career, and in the last decades of the twentieth century. As Wilde wrote, 'I took the drama, the most objective form known to art, and made it as personal a mode of expression as the lyric or the sonnet . . .' (*CW* 1017).

A book of this kind is heavily dependent on goodwill. I would like to thank all the contributors for their courtesy and patience, and for their easy co-operation. A special thanks to Joel Kaplan and Merlin Holland for generous assistance with the illustrations, to the commissioning editor at Cambridge University Press, Victoria Cooper, for her enthusiastic support and the occasional hint of steel in her discriminating comments and to Brian Ridgers and Alan Finch for their editorial assistance. As should be the case with Wilde, pleasure has dominated.

ACKNOWLEDGEMENTS

The quotation from Brendan Behan in Declan Kiberd's essay is printed by kind permission of the author and The Gallery Press from *Poems and a Play in Irish* (1981); the translation is printed by kind permission of Mr Ulick O'Connor.

NOTE ON REFERENCES

The references placed within the text are as follows:

CW   *Complete Works of Oscar Wilde*, introduction by Merlin Holland (London: HarperCollins, 1994).

E   Richard Ellmann, *Oscar Wilde* (London: Hamish Hamilton, 1987).

L   Rupert Hart-Davis (ed.), *The Letters of Oscar Wilde* (London: Hart-Davis, 1962).

Any variations on this practice are explained in the endnotes to particular chapters, notably in John Stokes's essay on Wilde's journalism and in Russell Jackson's essay on *The Importance of Being Earnest*.

CHRONOLOGY

1854   *16 October*   Oscar Fingal O'Flahertie Wills Wilde born at 21 Westland Road, Dublin, the second son of oculist and ear-surgeon Sir William Wilde, and Jane Francesca Elgee, Lady Wilde, who wrote under the name 'Speranza'.

1855   Family moves to 1 Merrion Square North.

1864–71   Attends Portora Royal School, Enniskillen.

1871–4   Undergraduate at Trinity College, Dublin, where he wins many prizes, including the Berkeley Gold Medal for Greek.

1874   *October*   Enters Magdalen College, Oxford, with a scholarship.

1875   *June*   Travels in Italy with Mahaffy, Professor of Ancient History at Trinity College, Dublin.

1876   *19 April*   Death of Sir William Wilde.

1877   *March–April*   Travels in Greece and Italy with Mahaffy.

1878   *June*   Wins Newdigate Prize with poem 'Ravenna'.
          July   Completes his degree with a First in Greats.

1879   *Autumn*   Takes rooms in London with Frank Miles.

1880   *August*   Moves with Miles to Keats House, Tite Street, Chelsea.
          September   Wilde's first play, *Vera; or the Nihilists*, is printed privately.

1881   *23 April*   Gilbert and Sullivan's *Patience* – Bunthorne, the Fleshly Poet, is associated with Wilde.
          June   *Poems* published.

17 December   *Vera*, scheduled for performance at the Adelphi Theatre, is withdrawn.
24 December   Wilde sails to New York for a lecture tour arranged to coincide with the New York production of *Patience*.

1882   Carries out an extensive tour of the USA and Canada, lecturing principally on 'The English Renaissance' and 'Decorative Art in America'.

1883   *January–May*   In Paris, where he completes his verse play *The Duchess of Padua*.
August–September   Visits New York for the first production of *Vera*.
September   Lectures in UK, an activity which continues sporadically for a year.
26 November   Becomes engaged to Constance Lloyd.

1884   *29 May*   Oscar Wilde and Constance Lloyd are married in London.

1885   *1 January*   The Wildes move into 16 Tite Street, Chelsea.
May   'The Truth of Masks' published in the *Nineteenth Century* as 'Shakespeare and Stage Costume'.
5 June   First son, Cyril, is born.
Wilde begins to be active in journalism, writing both signed and unsigned articles, in periodicals such as the *Pall Mall Gazette* and *Dramatic Review*.

1886   Meets Robert Ross.
5 June   Younger son, Vyvyan, is born.

1887   Accepts the editorship of the *Woman's World*.

1888   *May*   *The Happy Prince and Other Tales* is published, illustrated by Walter Crane and Jacomb Hood.

1889   *July*   'The Portrait of Mr W. H.' is published (in *Blackwood's Magazine*).

1890   *June*   *The Picture of Dorian Gray* is published (in *Lippincott's Magazine*).

1891   Meets Lord Alfred Douglas.
January   *The Duchess of Padua* – 'Guido Ferranti' – is produced in New York.
February   'The Soul of Man under Socialism' is published in the *Fortnightly Review*.

April   The extended version of *The Picture of Dorian Gray* is published, the title-page and binding designed by Charles Ricketts.
May   *Intentions* is published.
July   *Lord Arthur Savile's Crime and Other Stories* is published.
November   *A House of Pomegranates* is published, designed and decorated by Ricketts and Charles Shannon.
November–December   Wilde visits Paris, where he writes *Salomé*.

1892   *20 February*   *Lady Windermere's Fan* opens at the St James's Theatre, produced by George Alexander.
June   *Salomé* is in rehearsal, with Sarah Bernhardt in the title role, when it is banned by the Lord Chamberlain.
August–September   Wilde works on *A Woman of No Importance* in Norfolk.

1893   *February*   Publication of *Salomé* in French.
19 April   *A Woman of No Importance* opens at the Theatre Royal, Haymarket, produced by Sir Herbert Beerbohm Tree.
November   *Lady Windermere's Fan* is published; Shannon designs the binding for this and subsequent comedies.

1894   *February*   *Salome* published in English, illustrated by Aubrey Beardsley.
June   Poem *The Sphinx* published, designed by Ricketts.
May   Wilde visits Florence with Douglas.
August–September   Writes *The Importance of Being Earnest* at Worthing, Sussex.
October   *A Woman of No Importance* published.

1895   *3 January*   *An Ideal Husband* opens at the Theatre Royal, Haymarket, produced by Lewis Waller.
January–February   Wilde travels to Algiers with Douglas, where he meets André Gide.
14 February   *The Importance of Being Earnest* opens at the St James's Theatre, produced by George Alexander.
28 February   Wilde finds the Marquess of Queensberry's card, 'To Oscar Wilde, posing [as a] Somdomite' [*sic*] at the Albemarle Club. He applies for a warrant for Queensberry's arrest, for publishing a libel.
5 April   Queensberry is acquitted, and Wilde is arrested.
26 April   The first trial opens. On 1 May, the jury disagree, and a new trial is ordered.
25 May   Wilde is convicted of indecency, and sentenced to two years' imprisonment with hard labour; imprisoned first at Newgate, and then in Pentonville. In July, he is transferred to Wandsworth, and in November, after being declared bankrupt, to Reading Gaol.

1896   *3 February*   Death of his mother, Lady Wilde.
11 February   *Salomé* is produced by Lugné-Poe at the Théâtre de l'Œuvre, Paris.
19 February   Constance visits Wilde in Reading Gaol, to break the news to him of his mother's death. It is their last meeting.

1897   *January–March*   Writes his long letter to Douglas, later published as *De Profundis*.
19 May   Wilde is released from prison. He crosses on the night ferry to Dieppe, and lives abroad – in France, Italy, Switzerland – until his death.
May–September   Lives mostly at Berneval-sur-Mer, near Dieppe.
September   Travels to Naples, where he meets Douglas.

1898   *February*   *The Ballad of Reading Goal* is published.
7 April   Death of Constance Wilde.

1899   *February*   *The Importance of Being Earnest* published.
July   *An Ideal Husband* published.

1900   *30 November*   After being received into the Roman Catholic Church, Wilde dies in the Hôtel d'Alsace, Paris.

I
CONTEXT

I

MERLIN HOLLAND

Biography and the art of lying

Three days before he died in the Hôtel d'Alsace, Oscar Wilde was asked by the proprietor Jean Dupoirier about his life in London. 'Some said my life was a lie but I always knew it to be the truth; for like the truth it was rarely pure and never simple', he replied, echoing Algy Moncrieff, paradoxical as always and never one to lose the opportunity of recycling a well-turned phrase.[1] Biographers ever since have been by turn delighted at the rich pickings and exasperated by the contradictions. The duality of Wilde in all aspects fascinates, confuses: the Anglo-Irishman with Nationalist sympathies; the Protestant with life-long Catholic leanings; the married homosexual; the musician of words and painter of language who confessed to André Gide that writing bored him;[2] the artist astride not two but three cultures, an Anglo-Francophile and a Celt at heart. And overlaid on it all is the question of which facets of the Wildean dichotomy were real and involuntary and which were artificial and contrived for effect.

For the biographer it becomes important to find out, but for Wilde, who confessed that he lived in permanent fear of not being misunderstood, it becomes equally important that he should not. What is one to make of Wilde's response to the New York reporter who asked whether he had indeed walked down Piccadilly with a lily in his hand? 'To have done it was nothing, but to make people think one had done it was a triumph.'[3] Wilde blurs the edges and hides behind a non-alignment with his own utterances:

> Not that I agree with everything that I have said in this essay. There is much with which I entirely disagree. The essay simply represents an artistic standpoint, and in aesthetic criticism attitude is everything. For in art there is no such thing as a universal truth. A Truth in art is that whose contradictory is also true. (CW 1173)

Equivocality is maintained by both man and artist, and the biographer's nightmare continues. Some who have tried to pin him down have found that he turns to quicksilver in their fingers. The shimmering whole suddenly

Figure 1   Oscar Wilde with his friends at Magdalen College, Oxford; it seems likely that the bust in the foreground was the one of Augustus bequeathed by Dr Daubeny to the first Member of Magdalen after his death to win the Newdigate Prize Poem

divides momentarily, not into fragments, but into a myriad smaller globes, each different and complete in itself, and just as suddenly re-forms leaving no trace of the parts. Others have attempted to fit him into moulds of their own making and, on discovering that he overlaps the edges in a tiresomely uncooperative way, have simply trimmed off the surplus.

Yet for all the contradictions there is a strange consistency about Wilde's story. There is a Faustian element about this classical scholar who thirsted for sensation and experience. In Reading Gaol he was to reflect on the conflicting patterns of his past:

> I remember when I was at Oxford saying to one of my friends – as we were strolling round Magdalen's narrow bird-haunted walks one morning in the June before I took my degree – that I wanted to eat of the fruit of all the trees in the garden of the world, and that I was going out into the world with that passion in my soul ... I don't regret for a single moment having lived for pleasure ... There was no pleasure I did not experience ... Tired of being on the heights I deliberately went to the depths for new sensations.   (CW 1026)

It is simply not a life which can tolerate an either/or approach with logical conclusions, but demands the flexibility of a both/and treatment, often raising questions for which there are no answers. Few of Wilde's biographers have been able to tackle it satisfactorily. Too many have come to him with an agenda of their own or a depth of personal feeling which limits their view and somehow dilutes the richness of his character. Peel the onion and you separate it into its component parts; slice it down the middle and you reveal the intricate relationship between all the layers yet still retain the form. Richard Ellmann's blade was certainly sharp enough but his untimely death prevented the follow-through of a clean cut. His predecessors, with the notable exception of Hesketh Pearson, for the most part took rough aim with a meat-cleaver.

If this sounds unduly harsh, it should be remembered that most of them did not even have access to the whole onion, let alone the proper implements. For ten years after his death Wilde's reputation was cloaked in what Christopher Millard called 'a vague fog of obscenity'. Letters were destroyed lest they implied guilt or even sympathy by association – Oscar's letters to his wife Constance, especially from the weeks after prison, being among the worst casualties. Those friends who could have given balanced and reliable (even if strongly personal) accounts, the likes of Robert Ross, Reggie Turner, Carlos Blacker and More Adey, did not, except in letters which only surfaced in private archives decades afterwards. Others, Robert Sherard and Frank Harris, journalists both, wrote vividly if with questionable accuracy about their friendship with Wilde. Those who had known him less well found that by 1920 the connection was more beneficial than harmful and slipped a few paragraphs or even a chapter into their memoirs. But the view of his life was fragmentary, even impressionistic, and books for the most part alluded to his downfall in veiled terms. In England between the wars homosexuality was tolerated in artistic circles with a knowing wink and a nudge but with little approaching understanding. Even as late as 1948 when Montgomery Hyde published his reconstruction of Wilde's trials it was not intended for the general reader but rather for lawyers and a 'specialist' market, as it was then called. Wilde's collected letters were only published in 1962, and even then with severe misgivings from my father, Wilde's only surviving son, since they were quite explicit in places about his sexuality. There was an inherent irony in having to separate the man from his work in order to gain public approval for him. At the time the British could not have accepted him otherwise, but the approach was sadly misguided, and assessments of his life and literature both suffered in consequence. My father's misgivings, however, were totally unfounded as it turned out. Publication of the letters gave an entirely new impetus to Wilde studies and a much greater understanding of the complexities of his character. They also, most importantly, helped to corroborate or disprove certain facts and statements about him made posthumously by his friends and contemporaries.

Ironically it was this 'monstrous worship of facts', as Wilde once called it, which has led to an unfortunate and fashionable trend: to regard many of Oscar Wilde's early biographers with a good deal of suspicion, even to dismiss some of them outright as self-seeking liars. In retrospect it is hardly surprising since the majority of what was published in English had been written by those whose public squabbles about the 'truth' of his life had, until the 1940s, assumed all the elements of a sort of boulevard theatre. Each had needed to tell the story from an intensely personal point of view. If most ('Bosie' Douglas being the notable exception) were coloured with deep affection for the subject on the one hand, on the other there was inevitably a tendency for the authors to present themselves in the best possible light. This combined with varying degrees of journalistic if not poetic licence led to almost farcical exchanges of the 'Oh yes I did! – Oh no you didn't!' variety. Stories with the same pay-off had a curious way of changing the supporting cast around Oscar's lead, often to include the author of the memoir. A half-remembered snatch of conversation or a memorable witticism had hung, suspended in time's cupboard, waiting for the full scenario to bring it back to life, but when two or even three claimed the right to authenticity, it became suspect – even unusable – to later writers.

For example the well-known story of Wilde envying a Whistler *bon mot*, wishing out loud that he had said it and being cut down by the latter's 'You will, Oscar, you will' appears in several guises. Herbert Vivian recalls it in 1889 occurring at a dinner after Wilde had delivered his lecture on art to the students of the Royal Academy at which Whistler was present; in 1915 Douglas Sladen remembers it from a party of Louise Jopling's when the original remark which Wilde envied had not been made by Whistler at all; Frank Harris tells it in 1916 as taking place at an exhibition of Whistler's pictures when the artist had a witty exchange with Humphry Ward, art critic of *The Times*.[4] Hesketh Pearson repeats Harris's story in 1946 and Richard Ellmann repeats Pearson rather than Harris which gives the anecdote more credibility since Harris is 'known' to be utterly unreliable. Indeed, in his bibliography Pearson says of Harris's *Oscar Wilde: His Life and Confessions* 'This work is nowhere reliable' but quotes the story nonetheless, immune from accusations of inconsistency since he himself cites no sources.

Harris was a journalist, and journalists live by writing for a sensation-hungry public. He may have been a braggart and occasionally a liar but his life of Wilde is long overdue for re-evaluation. It first appeared in America in 1916 published privately, one suspects, because he discussed far more openly than anyone had before him Wilde's homosexuality as well as Douglas's role in Wilde's downfall. Douglas had already been to court in

1913 over Arthur Ransome's fairly circumspect study of Wilde which, he complained, had libelled him, so Harris's far more outspoken approach only infuriated him further. Douglas threatened legal action if so much as one copy were sold in England. In 1925, however, he visited Harris in Nice and, on the strength of new 'evidence' from Douglas, together they wrote the *New Preface to 'The Life and Confessions of Oscar Wilde'*. It was intended to correct Harris's misstatements and allow his life of Wilde to be sold without further hindrance from Douglas. Within days of Douglas's departure Harris found out, as he wrote to my father, that he had been told 'one truth and twenty lies' and insisted that the piece be rewritten.[5] Douglas, realising that their joint preface was tantamount to a retraction and an apology by Harris, refused to allow it to be changed and published it as a separate work.

Harris was also taken to task by Robert Sherard, whose friendship with Wilde had started in Paris in 1883 and lasted until the latter's death seventeen years later. He had already published two accounts of Wilde's life before Harris's book appeared and one shortly after: *The Story of an Unhappy Friendship* (1902), *The Life of Oscar Wilde* (1906) and *The Real Oscar Wilde* (1917), in which his spaniel-like devotion to Wilde's memory is at times an embarrassment. He attempts to explain Wilde's homosexual behaviour as a form of epilepsy or madness brought on by excessive indulgence in food and drink, and seems incapable of accepting that Wilde was perfectly well aware of what he was doing. Also, in a memorably ignorant passage, he entirely overlooks Wilde's subterfuges and begging letters during the last years in Paris, for which the 1962 *Letters* provide ample and pathetic testimony: 'Not on one single occasion in the whole of his life – even in the starveling years after his release from prison – did he obtain or attempt to obtain resources by any means unworthy of proper pride, of self-respect, of delicacy.'[6]

Harris's blunt but curiously sympathetic account of Wilde's life, given the imprimatur from its second edition by Bernard Shaw, so incensed Sherard that he was even prepared to associate himself with Douglas in order to discredit Harris. The result was an entire volume *Bernard Shaw, Frank Harris & Oscar Wilde* (1937) attempting to expose Harris as a liar. Unfortunately Sherard's method is largely one of nitpicking over details, and he inflicts as much damage on himself as on Harris with his own inaccuracies when attempting to show Harris in the wrong. Wilde, for instance, did not, as Sherard claims, return to England from America in September 1882; nor was he late in delivering the script of *The Duchess of Padua* to Mary Anderson.[7] Once again the *Letters* provide cast-iron evidence.

Sherard's own biographies are filled with factual errors: Wilde was not initially imprisoned in, nor released from, Wandsworth Gaol; he was not born in Merrion Square; he did not translate Barbey d'Aurevilly; and the conjecture that his hopelessness at mathematics while at Portora School was responsible for his life-long extravagance is almost worthy of Harris as depicted by Sherard.[8]

Alfred Douglas's attempt at biography was worse. His impotent scream of rage at discovering that *De Profundis* had been addressed to him, but had been deposited out of his destructive reach for fifty years in the British Museum, found its voice in *Oscar Wilde and Myself* (1914), largely written for him by T. W. H. Crosland. It was full of inaccuracies, untruths and attempts at self-justification, even going to the extent of denying that he knew Wilde was homosexual until the trials, though he later had the sense to repudiate the book and express his regret over publishing it.[9]

As for Harris there are unquestionably parts of his life of Wilde which are Harris exaggerations; his total recall of Wilde's words twenty years after the event is quite clearly an impossibility. At one time he even plunders the 1912 transcript of the trials for material and incorporates it in the form of a conversation which was supposed to have taken place between Wilde and himself. In another fictitious exchange he uses one of Wilde's letters to Ross in which he asks for certain books on his release; and Frank Harris not Robbie Ross becomes the generous provider.[10] The bare facts are respected but the journalist feels they are more readable in fancy dress.

But for all their faults these early biographers of Wilde knew the man in person. Without Sherard we would know only half of what we do about Wilde's various stays in France from the start of their friendship in 1883 to the poignant sketch of their last meeting in Paris at the Hôtel d'Alsace. The writing of *The Duchess of Padua*, Mary Anderson's rejection of it, Wilde's disappointment, Sherard's consolation dinner (and many other evenings spent in each other's company) – all would have been lost; we would not have had the astute observations of Wilde's effect on the French literary scene of the 1890s, trying too hard to impress at first but coming into his own as Wilde the natural *raconteur*;[11] and a host of anecdotes which have the clear ring of truth about them and which bring to life, for instance, Oscar's relationships with his mother and his brother Willie.

Despite Douglas's belittling of Wilde's abilities and achievements (understandable if not forgivable when you had lived nearly twenty years in his shadow), there is the odd valuable character sketch both in his disgraceful 1914 book and his *Autobiography* published in 1929. Wilde, he maintained, was something of a social snob. This fits in with Douglas's overall arrogant criticism of his friend and could easily be dismissed were it not corroborated by the three most unlikely sources, namely Harris, Sherard and Shaw. Their view was more gentle and sympathetic, noting Wilde's almost childlike pleasure in the grandeur of historic names: 'Surely everyone prefers Norfolk, Hamilton and Buckingham to Smith or Jones or Robinson', he is supposed to have remarked to Frank Harris.[12] The truth probably lies somewhere between the two – a fascination rather than an obsession with the aristocracy. More important, though, are Douglas's claims about his financial support of Wilde. It is generally assumed that he lied about or at best exaggerated the extent of his support during Wilde's libel case against his father and later when they were together in Naples, but what seems indisputable, and backed by evidence from his bank, is that during the last ten months of Wilde's life in Paris he gave him £332 in cheques quite apart from the occasional cash handout.[13] This is in direct contradiction to all that Wilde says in his letters about Bosie's meanness and raises the more serious problem of how much we can trust anything that Wilde says at that time about his finances. He writes to Robbie Ross on one occasion, saying that he needs money because an innkeeper at Nogent was about to sell his clothes for an unpaid bill and then openly admits his fib: 'I am so sorry about my excuse. I had forgotten I had used Nogent before. It shows the utter collapse of my imagination and rather distresses me' (L 763). This manipulation of the truth for financial advantage needs to be considered carefully by biographers before using Wilde's post-prison letters at face value. At the end of 1898, Frank Harris invited Wilde to spend three months on the Riviera. In his 1916 biography he describes their train journey from Paris a week before Christmas and their first days at Napoule. Ten days later Wilde writes to Ross asking for money and saying that Harris did not come to Napoule after all. Harris, 'always unreliable', must have been inventing again and yet a letter to him from Wilde later in February states quite clearly '. . . since our arrival nine weeks ago' (L 780).

Harris's sin would appear to be embellishment rather than outright fabrication. Shaw called his biography 'the best literary portrait of Wilde in existence', continued to say so for over twenty years and explained why in his preface to the first 'permitted' English edition of 1938. He would hardly have made such an endorsement had Harris been a total charlatan. Robert Ross was sent a copy in 1916 and wrote to Harris: 'I am delighted to hear that the "Life" has caught on well in America', and provided a list of corrections which Harris included as an appendix in later editions. 'I do not, of course, agree with all you say or your estimate and criticism of various incidents', he continued, 'but I would not suggest altering anything materially. The point of the book is that it is *your* view.'[14]

All these early accounts by Wilde's friends are essentially impressionistic personal views. They are the technicolour elements in a grey world of facts. To Sherard, Shaw, Douglas and Harris must be added the shorter studies of Ada Leverson, Charles Ricketts, André Gide and Vincent O'Sullivan, each in their way bringing Wilde briefly back to life as they saw him, each more or less flawed by modern standards but even the flaws adding a dimension to the picture.

Thirty-eight years after his death two of Oscar Wilde's friends were corresponding about his life. 'I don't suppose', wrote Reggie Turner to Robert Sherard, 'any book will ever be published on that limitless subject [Oscar] which will be entirely satisfactory to everybody "in the know" or will be free from inaccuracies, mostly unimportant enough, and the future historian or compiler will be puzzled to get at the most probable straight path and is sure to stray sometimes and somewhere. All these books have told me that no biography is quite to be trusted.'[15]

Exactly so, but there is much which is unique in these personal appraisals. Treated with caution, weeded of self-interest, they remain an invaluable source which modern critics, obsessed with factual accuracy, are too often ready to condemn out of hand.

Another sixty years have passed. All those who knew Wilde are long since dead. A few memoirs, notably Douglas's 'The Wilde Myth' and Sherard's 'Ultima Verba', remain unpublished and the flow of unrecorded letters both by and about Wilde has been reduced to a mere trickle.[16] The likelihood of sensational new source material passing through the sale-rooms is slight and biographers have had to content themselves with reassessing the available material rather than springing dramatic new discoveries about Wilde on the public – at least in theory. In practice Wilde is not Wilde without the whiff of scandal and, stale scandals being as interesting as cold mutton, new books need fresh ones. And if they don't exist, they can be invented.

When Richard Ellmann's biography of Wilde was published in 1987, among the illustrations was one captioned 'Wilde in costume as Salome'. The photograph looked vaguely like a decadently soft-fleshed Wilde as one imagines him to have been in the 1890s and it was credited to a French photo archive. Originally it had illustrated a book review in Le Monde a few weeks before Ellmann's death. It was picked up by his editor who was in Paris at the time and who sent it to England. The publishers, sensing something of a literary scoop, included it in the book without further ado. Naturally it appeared in many of the reviews as a previously unpublished photograph of Wilde, depicting previously unsuspected transvestism and gradually found its way into half-a-dozen works wholly or partly concerned with Wilde. Photographs are seldom reproduced with corroborative evidence or footnotes. On condition they resemble their captions, they pass

Figure 2   The Hungarian opera singer Alice Guszalewicz as Salome, Cologne, 1906; featured
in Richard Ellmann's biography as 'Wilde in costume as Salome'

unquestioned. Nobody asked whether this was likely behaviour on Wilde's part or whether, if he had been in the habit of cross-dressing, he would have posed for a photograph. From what we know it would seem to have been entirely out of character, but few people did any more than express uncertainty. Such was Ellmann's reputation as a scholar that no one thought to check out its provenance. That was unwise. In 1994 an article appeared in the *Times Literary Supplement* proving beyond doubt that the 'Salome' in the photograph was in fact a Hungarian opera singer, Alice Guszalewicz, photographed in Cologne in 1906.[17] It had become separated from its caption in the photo archive, and, after Ellmann's book had appeared, the archive had even redescribed it as Wilde according to 'the latest research'. To give Ellmann his due he was terminally ill and was in no position to verify its pedigree, and the lure of sensation to a commercial publisher was stronger than considerations of scholarly exactitude. It was subtly reinforced as an image by reproducing on the previous page a drawing by Alfred Bryan entitled 'Caricature of Wilde dressed as a woman'. Put properly into context it is a caricature of Wilde dressed as Lady Windermere, carrying a fan and smoking, and was a comment on his author's curtain call at the first night of *Lady Windermere's Fan* when he defied social convention by appearing on stage with a cigarette. Another Wilde myth was born and, had it survived, might have become undisputed fact.

Less excusable, because certain facts were manipulated to fit the theory and others blatantly ignored, was Ellmann's insistence on Wilde's death from syphilis. That it might have been the cause of death was first suggested in Arthur Ransome's 1912 biography of Wilde where it appeared in the form 'His death ... was directly due to meningitis, the legacy of an attack of tertiary syphilis', already a medically suspect statement since tertiary syphilis does not come in 'attacks' and syphilitic meningitis is principally associated with the secondary stage of the disease.[18] Shortly after publication Douglas sued Ransome for suggesting that he had contributed to Wilde's downfall. He lost the case but Ransome still removed the offending passages from the second edition as well as the reference to syphilis. For this he was commended by Sherard who said that in the seventeen years that he had known Wilde, he never once saw any signs of the disease.[19] Various biographers (mostly foreign) picked up Ransome's statement and repeated it in the 1920s but in 1934, after an exchange of letters with Reggie Turner, who was with Wilde when he died, Sherard suddenly performed the most extraordinary volte-face in order to give weight to a pamphlet which he published attacking what he called the lies of André Gide, G. J. Renier and Frank Harris about Wilde. He gave Wilde a double dose of syphilis, the first inherited from his 'libertine father' and the second acquired while at Oxford.[20] The statement from Turner which must have changed Sherard's view was: 'The ear trouble, which I believe began in prison, was only shortly before his death diagnosed as a tertiary symptom of an infection he had contracted when he was twenty.'[21] On the basis of that alone, for there is nothing else in the correspondence which could have justified it, Sherard recreated the how, when and where, as pure conjecture, and started to correspond on the subject with other biographers with all the authority of a primary witness. The doctors' diagnosis has survived in written form; it refers only to cerebral meningitis and is quite at odds with Turner's recollections anyway. That is the extent of the available 'evidence'.[22]

Ellmann, however, takes Sherard's conjecture that Wilde must have been infected by an Oxford prostitute and, without further documentation, establishes it as a fact. He offers Turner's letter to Sherard as evidence of the death-by-syphilis theory but conveniently ignores the next sentence: 'The doctor told him that he would live many years if he took care of himself ...' which is totally inconsistent with a diagnosis of terminal syphilis, as well as a later letter in which Turner says: 'Nor was there ever any question at the real mode and cause of his death. He died of meningitis and was practically "fuori di se" some days before.'[23] Ransome's original statement suddenly appears as a direct quotation from Robert Ross, but the fact that Ransome dedicated the book to Ross and acknowledges his help in verifying certain details is surely no justification for Ellmann to put the words into Ross's mouth in an attempt to give them more authority, particularly since they disappear altogether in the second edition. Basing conjectural theories on a balance of probabilities is a perfectly respectable tool of the biographer, but not when a foot is slid surreptitiously under the scale to tip it in your favour.

In order to back up the Oxford prostitute story, Ellmann sees Wilde's last-minute withdrawal from Catholic conversion in April 1878 and Father Sebastian Bowden's letter to him referring to a 'temporal misfortune' as having sexual origins, whereas it seems much more likely that it had to do with his half-brother's will under whose terms he inherited far less than expected and would lose even that if he converted.

Since the publication of Ellmann's biography a number of scientific papers have been published on Wilde's last illness and death which have been unanimous in their scepticism about its syphilitic origins. Perhaps most conclusive of all was that of Dr Macdonald Critchley which revealed that the French doctor who attended Wilde and signed the diagnosis, Paul Claisse, had previously written papers on skin disorders, meningitis and tertiary syphilis, all conditions which are alleged to have contributed to his death. One may confidently assume that his diagnosis of meningitis was correct.[24]

If Wilde did not die of syphilis, Sherard's recreation of his syphilitic history no longer has any proper foundation. Indeed by 1938 Sherard himself is having doubts: 'As to the cause of his death, I am even today as uncertain of how his happy release came as were Ross and Reggie Turner

... and were I writing his life anew, I could with an easy conscience towards my public omit all reference to a disease [syphilis] which is still looked upon by the hypocritical and the ignorant as a proof of depraved character.' Relying so heavily as he did on Sherard's fabrications in the matter, and having made extensive use of the collection in which this typescript is to be found, it is regrettable that Ellmann did not take notice of this 'last word' by Sherard.[25]

Informed discussion post-Ellmann does not seem to have deterred the more persistent sensationalists intent on discovering new skeletons in the Wilde cupboard. A recent 'psychoanalytic biography' of Wilde by Melissa Knox bows before the weight of medical opinion and accepts that he did not die from the disease but attempts to make a case for a syphilitically determined life largely from the Sherard conjectures, which themselves relied on the false premise of his death from syphilis as a starting-point. Even allowing for this hiccup in logic, she overlooks the fact that Sherard's information was all second-hand; that he espoused the syphilis cause principally to attack Harris, Gide and Renier; and that as a convert he is a fanatic and a totally unreliable source as his 1934 pamphlet shows. The Knox strain is nothing if not contagious; by the end of the book 'possibly, even probably' Wilde's two sons have it, his wife has died of it, and the Canterville Ghost has it by implication. The only one to escape, curiously, is Bosie Douglas.

Trying to establish when Oscar Wilde's first homosexual encounter took place, preferably before his marriage, has become another of the new sensationalist pursuits. In 1993 Christie's, the auctioneers, sold two of Wilde's letters together with an inscribed photograph, all of which had been addressed to a young man called Philip Griffiths.[26] The first was an effusive but otherwise innocent letter and the second asked Griffiths to keep himself free for Wednesday night, the Wildes' 'At Home' day. With a blatant disregard for accuracy (and for the date stamps on their envelopes) the letters were catalogued in reverse order in an attempt to show a growing intimacy between the two men. The photograph was signed in one ink and inscribed 'To Philip Griffiths' in another, suggesting that it had been presigned as a publicity photo for the Midlands lecture tour Wilde was on when they met – hardly a way to treat your lover. In order to give the sale of these items more significance than they deserved, a press release, a mixture of ignorance and shoddy research, was issued trumpeting 'Oscar Wilde's secret love letters'. They sold for three times their estimated price and will doubtless support a 'first male lover' claim sometime in the future.

Nor could Ellmann resist joining in this game. He recounts the story of Wilde shopping with his wife at Swan & Edgar, the Piccadilly department store. At the sight of what Ellmann calls 'the painted boys on the pavement' Wilde says: 'Something clutched at my heart like ice.' The story was originally told to Ada Leverson in 1930 by a friend of Wilde's, almost certainly Reggie Turner. 'A curious, very young, but hard-eyed creature appeared, looked at him, gave a sort of laugh, and passed on. He felt, he said, "as if an icy hand had clutched his heart". He had a sudden presentiment. He saw a vision of folly, misery and ruin.' Given Wilde's strong belief in portents and the supernatural the sex of the 'creature' seems immaterial. The point being made was this person knew, or seemed to know, something about Wilde's future that he himself didn't – hence the feeling of terror. Pearson in 1946 picks up the story and turns the creature into a woman, if only because Piccadilly in the 1880s was the haunt of prostitutes. In Stanley Weintraub's biography of Turner in 1965 the creature moves inside and is transformed into young male shop assistants. And finally Ellmann brings them back outside again and turns them unequivocally into rent-boys.[27] Another myth? But wait; what have we here? An academic footnote. The matter will be solved once and for all.

Thank goodness for the age of the footnoted biography. Footnotes give a stamp of authenticity to conjecture and a pedigree to knowledge. So much has it become the norm that without them we are even a touch disoriented; we have less inclination to believe what we are told; we become suspicious of the sources and at best accuse the author quietly to ourselves of mislaying his references; at worst of suppressing them as untrustworthy but important to his argument. Give us our footnotes, though, and we feel that we can trust what is served up on the page. Unfortunately the general reader has neither time nor motive to check them out, which he would have been well advised to do in this case. The document exists (a letter from Turner to A. J. A. Symons) in which Wilde's early homosexuality and possible seduction by Robbie Ross is discussed but no 'painted boys'. Nor do they appear in any other letter from Turner to Symons. The phantom footnote joins the ranks of other biographical misdemeanours.[28]

Ninety-seven years after his death, the arguments about Wilde's life and works continue. The individuals who claimed him have become groups and the weapons of dispute have become less crude. One part of academia insists that he was simply a passing socio-cultural phenomenon and the author of lightweight popular works; another that he was a modern thinker, bridging two centuries, an astute critic and commentator, a 'conformist rebel' as one German critic aptly called him. The moderate gay community holds him up as a martyr and the militant wing accuses him of setting back 'the cause' by seventy years for not speaking out more forcefully. The British read his stories to their children and flock to see his plays, tut-tut or shake their heads sympathetically over his scandal which could not be openly discussed forty years ago, yet most of them still feel deeply uncomfortable about his homosexuality. The French, who for decades have treated him as *un écrivain sérieux* because they know him through his essays, *De Profundis* and *Dorian Gray*, are suddenly discovering his plays which they stage in the fashion of Feydeau farces. As a delicious final irony the playwright who died disgraced and bankrupt in Paris has just saved the Théâtre Antoine from closing its doors for good with a sixteen month run of *Un mari idéal*.[29]

Biographers now have access to such a wealth of material that Wilde's private and public lives may be picked over like few others'. Paradoxically (what else) this makes Wilde's life more contradictory and complicated than ever. The inherent duality lives on, now more of a plurality. Will the real Oscar Wilde please stand up? Half-a-dozen figures oblige. Biographers, said Wilde, 'are the body-snatchers of literature. The dust is given to one and the ashes to the other and the soul is out of their reach' (*CW* 1109). It will remain so until we accept that our view of Wilde must always be a multicoloured kaleidoscope of apparent contradictions in need not of resolution but of appreciation.

NOTES

1 From Dupoirier's own account, the typescript of which was given to Thelma Holland, my mother, by Dupoirier's daughter in November 1950 on the 50th anniversary of Wilde's death when Robert Ross's ashes were placed in his tomb at Père Lachaise cemetery (TS Holland).

2 André Gide, *Oscar Wilde: In Memoriam* (Paris: Mercure de France, 1910) p. 32n.

3 *New York World*, 8 Jan. 1882.

4 Herbert Vivian, 'The Reminiscences of a Short Life', *The Sun*, 17 Nov. 1889; Douglas Sladen, *Twenty Years of My Life* (London: Constable, 1915) p. 65; Frank Harris, *Oscar Wilde: His Life and Confessions* (New York: Frank Harris, 1916) p. 64.

5 Frank Harris letter to Vyvyan Holland, 1 Mar. 1926 (MS Holland).

6 Robert Sherard, *Life of Oscar Wilde* (London: T. Werner Laurie, 1906), p.282.

7 Robert Sherard, *Bernard Shaw, Frank Harris & Oscar Wilde* (London: T. Werner Laurie; New York: Greystone Press, 1937) pp. 98–9.

8 Robert Sherard, *Oscar Wilde: The Story of an Unhappy Friendship* (London: privately printed, 1902), pp. 201, 228, 264; Sherard, *Life*, pp. 87, 104.

9 Lord Alfred Douglas, *The Autobiography of Lord Alfred Douglas* (London: Martin Secker, 1929), *passim* but p. 13 in particular.

10 Harris, *Oscar Wilde*, pp. 185–9, 357–8; *L* 521.

11 Sherard, *Life*, p. 288–93.

12 Harris, *Oscar Wilde*, p. 113.

13 Douglas, *Autobiography*, p. 323.
14 Robert Ross letter to Frank Harris, 1 Feb. 1917 (MS Clark).
15 Reginald Turner letter to Robert Sherard, 21 June 1938 (MS Reading).
16 The page proofs of 'The Wilde Myth' are in the Harry Ransom Humanities Research Center at the University of Texas, Austin; the typescript of Sherard's 'Ultima Verba' is in a private collection in the US.
17 'Wilde as Salome?', in *TLS*, 22 July 1994; see also Horst Schroeder, *Alice in Wildeland* (Braunschweig: Privately published, 1994).
18 Arthur Ransome, *Oscar Wilde* (London: Martin Secker, 1912) p. 199.
19 Ransome, *Oscar Wilde* (2nd edn 1913) p. 217; Robert Sherard, *The Real Oscar Wilde* (London: T. Werner Laurie, 1917) p. 385.
20 Robert Sherard, *Oscar Wilde Twice Defended* (Chicago: Argus, 1934) p.10.
21 Reginald Turner letter to Robert Sherard, 3 Jan. 1934 (MS Reading).
22 Richard Ellmann, *Oscar Wilde* (London: Hamish Hamilton, 1987) p. 547n. The original MS is in a private collection.
23 Reginald Turner letters to Robert Sherard, 3 Jan. 1934 and 11 Oct. 1934 (MSS Reading).
24 Macdonald Critchley, 'Oscar Wilde's Fatal Illness: The Mystery Unshrouded', in *Encyclopaedia Britannica Medical and Health Annual 1990*, pp. 190–207.
25 Sherard, 'Ultima Verba', pp. 59, 74 (TS Private).
26 Christie's sale, 19 Nov. 1993, lots 312 and 313.
27 Ada Leverson, *Letters to the Sphinx from Oscar Wilde* (London: Duckworth, 1930) p. 44; Hesketh Pearson, *Oscar Wilde* (London: Methuen, 1946) p. 113; Stanley Weintraub, *Reggie: A Portrait of Reginald Turner* (New York: George Braziller, 1965) p. 58; Ellmann, *Wilde* p. 258.
28 The Turner–Symons correspondence is in the Clark Memorial Library at UCLA. See also opening anecdote to this chapter which I confess to fabricating to illustrate the point: the typescript does not in fact exist though the historical elements of the footnote are genuine. Wilde would undoubtedly have approved: see *CW* 1233 and 'The Decay of Lying' *passim*. Other references need not be doubted.
29 *Un mari idéal* opened on 8 Sept. 1995. By demand the run was extended four times. It won two 'Molières', the prestigious French theatre awards, after being nominated for a record-breaking ten. It closed on 31 Dec. 1996.

2

REGENIA GAGNIER

Wilde and the Victorians

Wilde died in 1900, the year before Queen Victoria and the same year as Nietzsche. Dating him in such a way evokes the modernity of the Victorian age, with its values of progress, technology, global markets and individualism. It also evokes the postmodernism of Nietzsche, the philosopher with whom Wilde is most often compared, in their transvaluation of values, in the second half of the twentieth century. The Victorians agonised over values – family values, British values, value as use or exchange – while Nietzsche revealed value as a fraud, a tool of domination of some over others, on the one hand, and promoted a radical perspectivism or scepticism, on the other. Wilde, a figure of paradox and contradiction, participated in both modern value critique and postmodern perspectivism.

Modernism in social theory, as distinguished from modernist aesthetics, refers to processes that began to be theorised during the European Enlightenment. First among these were the democratic revolutions – the abolition of race slavery, the enfranchisement of working men and then women, and the struggle for increasing circles of rights – until today one speaks of the rights of many social groups, children, (non-human) animals, even non-animal life, as in radical ecology. Inseparable from the conditions that gave rise to the democratic revolutions was the growth in scientific knowledge and technology that led to the economic and population explosion that we call the industrial revolution: it was in fact the political economists rather than the moralists who first argued against slavery, as an inefficient use of labour. It is important at the outset to note that for the Enlightenment and for the Victorian modernists described here, progress was a moral and political category as much as a technological or economic one.

The social characteristics of modernity and their postmodern 'crises of legitimation' may be clarified by way of the postmodern theorist Jean-François Lyotard (*The Postmodern Condition*) and the Victorian cabinet-maker, radical publisher and activist William Lovett (*The Pursuit of Bread*,

Knowledge, and Freedom). When Lyotard characterised the West's 'master narratives', or the broad cultural stories that are central to a society's self-understanding, he included the dual pursuits of knowledge and freedom. I shall later describe how these two master narratives are reduced in postmodern thought to the pursuit of individuation and the maximisation of individual choice and preference (something about which Wilde also had much to say). But for the Victorian modernists there were three such master narratives, as Lovett's title indicates: the pursuit of bread or material well-being, or freedom from Nature and scarcity; the pursuit of knowledge or Truth, or freedom from ignorance, superstition and lies; and the pursuit of justice, or freedom from political tyranny and economic exploitation. The Victorians sought control of the physical world through the use of science and technology, with a faith in the objectivity of their knowledge, and they sought political emancipation, with a faith in the liberal tenets of individual freedom, equality and autonomy. Individualism was central to modernity: although the modern 'self' sustained intermittent assault from both psychological and social irrational forces, it was indubitable, rational and progressive, where rational and progressive meant more than economic rationality and progress.

Yet the self-reflexiveness of modernity is such that this orderly world view, which Wilde shared as described below, was suffering even in the nineteenth century what Lyotard called the crises of legitimation that we associate with postmodernism. The worst excesses of market ideology and the industrial revolution showed that technology could be as destructive as beneficial (the so-called dialectic of enlightenment), and mass communication, as Wilde pointed out most notably in 'The Soul of Man Under Socialism', could lead to mass control as easily as to enlightened understanding. Secondly, as Wilde observed throughout his criticism, perhaps most suggestively in 'Pen, Pencil and Poison', our scientific ways of understanding, our 'objectifying', have been complicitous with ways of oppressing. For some this led to the theory of objectivity as value-neutrality, but for others it led to an awareness of the relativity – or at least relationality – of knowledge, and to Nietzschean perspectivism. Finally, it became increasingly clear that liberalism's most cherished terms of 'freedom' and 'individualism' had masked differences and inequalities – so that, again in 'The Soul of Man', Wilde had to make equality the material precondition of freedom, and later Wildeans like Terry Eagleton in *Saint Oscar* (1989) have insisted that Wilde was a socialist *because* he was so deeply an individualist. Far from the late twentieth-century view that freedom and equality are incompatible (see the libertarian notion that 'all taxation is theft'), Wilde and others discussed here believed that individuals were products of societies, not their fundamental social units, and that social inequality would prevent the general flourishing of individualism.

In a final crisis of legitimation of modern values, Wilde saw that the 'self' was not inevitably indubitable, rational and progressive, but was socially constructed. It was constructed through language, which was why he waged a life-long subversion of conventional speech patterns. It was constructed through social institutions, which was why the school, marriage and the family, medicine, the law and the prison – what Althusser called the ideological and repressive state apparatuses – so exercised his critical faculties. And it was constructed irrationally, unconsciously, which was why, although he never capitulated to the moralists on the superiority of heterosexual to homosexual love, he did frequently (in *De Profundis* and after) deplore his materialism and sensuality as a weakness that his better rationality could not control.

With this introduction to the modernity and postmodernity of the Victorians, we turn directly to their pursuit of bread, knowledge and freedom.

BREAD

Born in 1854, Wilde lived through an economic transition from industrial production to high mass consumption that would have global effects. One can see the transition through the development of classical political economy into neoclassical economics after the 1870s. Classical political economy arose in the industrial 'take-off' period, when the economy was incapable of significantly ameliorating poverty. Since the economy then required a high level of production, the science of political economy, like its contemporary cultural form the 'industrial novel', gave priority to production and its interpersonal and objective values: work, action (*'praxis'*), co-operation, abstinence (meaning forgoing personal consumption in favour of investment). The basic categories of political economy were the productive relations between the three great socio-economic classes of their time (landowners, workers and capitalist entrepreneurs) and their commodified objects of exchange (land, labour and capital) resulting in rent, wages and profits in domestic and colonial markets. These were also the basic categories of high Victorian cultural production: of representations of the relations between stable (or lazy) landed aristocrats, energetic (or cruel) entrepreneurs, docile and dependent (or angry and seditious) labourers. High Victorian fiction went even further than political economy in its study of social relations, scrutinising also the gendered division of labour, including the sphere of 'women's' work (from housework and childcare to, notoriously, prostitution) traditionally excluded from economic notions of value. As Ruskin in *Unto This Last* (1862) and Olive Schreiner in *Woman and Labour* (1911), among others, argued at length, the imputation of value to women's labour at home would have changed the entire course of political economy as well as the definition and fate of 'economic man'.

Political economy was a substantive and normative theory of social relations. Adam Smith showed that by acting upon self-interest entrepreneurs could perform the social good, or increase the aggregate wealth of nations, but that the self-interest of capitalists would make it unlikely that that wealth – to use a later phrase – would 'trickle down' to benefit those whom Smith habitually called 'the great body of the people'; Marx predicted that by its own growth capitalism would liberate those it had victimised; and John Stuart Mill hoped that political economy itself and the market relations it represented were merely a primitive stage of human development: that, once humankind was raised out of a condition of scarcity, the happiness of the many would be in a just distribution and no-growth state. As Marx said, 'capital [was] not a thing, but a social relation between persons'.[1] This political dimension of the economy was obscured as the science developed after the 1870s.

As industrialism matured and productive capacity increased, a high level of consumption both in Britain and the Empire became more important, and a corresponding shift took place towards the values of leisure, privacy, subjectivity and choice. Although always present in the Malthusian branch of political economy, scarcity became the dominant feature of economic man's environment only when the economy seemed ostensibly to shift from scarcity to abundance. Only multiple consumer choice made people aware of *relative* scarcity. In the course of discussion of 'economic man', initially defined in relation to production, a new kind of man was created: one who was civilised by virtue of his technology and whose advanced stage of development was signified by the boundlessness of his desires. He must choose from a universe of goods on display, and his status, his level of civilisation (his 'tastes'), were revealed by his choices or preferences. Interpersonal comparisons of utility were deemed unquantifiable, unformalisable, and therefore unscientific, and economists focused their attention on the 'marginal' utility of an addition or subtraction of a good to an individual consumer. The terms are the terms of twentieth-century economics – rational choice, revealed preference – and so are the methods: methodological individualism, subjectivism, behaviourism. The characters are the man and woman of late-Victorian economics *and* aesthetics, from Pater's discriminating consumer of the art object, to the specularity of Arthur Symons's and J. A. Symonds's respectively hetero- and homoerotic poetic objectifications, to the characters who people Wilde's spectacular stages, to Conrad's corporate coloniser Kurtz. They are insatiable. Indeed Wilde captured the essence of modern economic man when he named the cigarette the perfect type of a perfect pleasure: it left one unsatisfied. For this reason the cigarette is the perfect commodity.

Wilde's work exhibits the values of both classical political economy and the neoclassical or 'Marginal' school. On the one hand, his criticism shows a faith in technology and enlightened self-interest to liberate people from drudgery and the mind-forged manacles of property, and it consistently promotes the utopian goal of individual creativity. As he says in 'The Soul of Man', which calls on socialism and science to eradicate poverty and pain, state-planned machinery should make useful things so that individuals will be free to make what is beautiful. Wilde's argument in 'The Soul of Man' is clearly within the mainstream tradition of Victorian socialist thought, which, in rejecting classic definitions of work as 'toil and trouble' (Adam Smith) in favour of 'the fulfilment of species-being' (Marx), did not distinguish between the economic and aesthetic life. This insistence on the possibility of the progress of all humanity's faculties – intellectual, moral and sensuous – once humankind was liberated from necessity went back to the Enlightenment and continued through the Frankfurt School.[2]

On the other hand, if Wilde shared many of the progressive values of the modernists, he was also tempted by the more subjective calculations of pleasure that the new psychologically based economics had introduced. Like the connoisseur Des Esseintes consuming the exotica of the world outside the West, Wilde was sensitive to the revelation of personality through choice and preference. Chapter 11 of *The Picture of Dorian Gray* (1891) is a textbook psychology of *fin-de-siècle* economic man. Chapter 10 concludes with Dorian's discovery of a fascinating book, a story of an insatiable young Parisian 'who spent his life trying to realise ... all the passions and modes of thought that belonged to every century except his own' (*CW* 96). For years, we are told in chapter 11, Dorian could not free himself from its power of suggestion: 'The more he knew, the more he desired to know. He had mad hungers that grew more ravenous as he fed them' (*CW* 98). He cultivates 'a new Hedonism' that, à la Pater, 'was never to accept any theory or system that involved the sacrifice of any mode of passionate experience' (*CW* 99). For years, Dorian 'searches for sensations that would be at once new and delightful' (*CW* 100). His conspicuous consumption, variously referred to as 'collecting' and 'accumulating', like Des Esseintes's, includes the products of 'all parts of the world' (*CW* 102): perfumes, music, embroideries, tapestries, ecclesiastical vestments and finally what late-Victorian economists called the highest order of pleasure, not the crude material goods but rather 'the wonderful stories' of the goods, or the rarefied pleasure of literature itself.

Yet while the desire for escalating orders of goods is itself insatiable, each good reaches its point of diminishing marginal utility: 'Yet, after some time, [Dorian] wearied of them [all]' (CW 102), and he experiences 'that terrible *taedium vitae* that comes on those to whom life denies nothing' (CW 108). In the midst of this cycle of excess and ennui, Dorian finds himself in a society that prefers form to substance. The narrator describes market society as society of the spectacle, style or form over substance: 'Society, civilized society at least, is never very ready to believe anything to the detriment of those who are both rich and fascinating', says the narrator. 'It feels instinctively that manners are of more importance than morals' (CW 107). The very lack of substance, for those who can afford the multi-plication of pleasure, is liberating. 'Form' or 'insincerity'; is 'merely a method by which we can multiply our personalities … man was a being with myriad lives and myriad sensations, a complex multiform creature' (CW 107). The chapter reaches a climax with a fantastic crescendo of insatiables: 'Pietro Riario . . . whose beauty was equalled only by his debauchery . . . who gilded a boy that he might serve at the feast as Ganymede . . . Ezzelin, whose melancholy could be cured only by the spectacle of death, and who had a passion for red blood, as other men have for red wine . . . Giambattista Cibo . . . into whose torpid veins the blood of three lads was infused' (CW 109), and so forth until the famous concluding sentence, 'There were moments when [Dorian] looked on evil simply as a mode through which he could realise his conception of the beautiful.'

The consequence of Dorian's insatiability, escalation of wants and formal equivalencing of all desires is, of course, his portrait, where the shame of his consumption is permanently, absolutely, recorded. At this price, he is given a beauty without limit, the scarcest commodity in a mortal world, that is his sole source of value to others, who commodify and consume him in turn.

Wilde's *Salome* (1894) is perhaps the most dramatic representation we have of the world of neoclassical economics, including the assertion of personal preference over social values and of subjective isolation over social life, and it has been used to illustrate problems with the formal theory of rational choice.[3] In sum, a set of philosophical beliefs that could not see beyond the horizon of necessary scarcity and human struggle in the face of nature came apart towards the end of the nineteenth century, as industrial society saw excess and surplus. It was replaced by a set of beliefs which took for granted abundance and the capacity of human industry to conquer nature. Although economics was called the science of scarcity, scarcity was no longer a social obstacle but a recognition of society's ability to create unlimited new needs and desires as its productive capacity and leisure time increased. 'Bread' no longer dominated the consciousness of individuals. This is why Lyotard let it drop out of his summary of ideology. Economically, he was premature: much of the world still needs bread, and political economy would tell us, rightly, that the rest of the world is interdependent with the West. Ideologically, however, he probably overcomplicated his case. Knowledge and freedom in market society may be reducible to a single dominant narrative about the total actualisation of individual pleasure. Is not freedom in market society merely the capacity to exercise choice in the marketplace? Is not knowledge simply the ability to maximise these choices in the most efficient way? Each of these narratives is but a part of a deeper contemporary narrative of individuation, which is *the* master narrative of postmodern society.

Just as 'bread', or material well-being, is not an end in itself but a means towards a grand conception of individuation, so today knowledge and freedom are also means towards increasing individuation rather than ends in themselves. Wilde certainly had read Herbert Spencer, whose social evolutionism had its *telos* in increasing individuation. In *The Picture of Dorian Gray* and *Salome* Wilde interrogated the modern and Victorian dilemma between personal individuation and social good.

KNOWLEDGE

In the major document of Victorian liberalism in the realm of thought and action, *On Liberty* (1859), John Stuart Mill titled the three central sections 'Of the Liberty of Thought and Discussion', 'Of Individuality, as One of the Elements of Well-Being', and 'Of the Limits to the Authority of Society Over the Individual'. He summarises the necessity of liberty of thought and discussion thus:

> We have now recognized the necessity to the mental well-being of mankind (on which all their other well-being depends) of freedom of opinion, and freedom of expression, on four distinct grounds . . .
>
> First, if any opinion is compelled to silence, that opinion may, for aught we can certainly know, be true. To deny this is to assume our own infallibility.
>
> Secondly, though the silenced opinion be an error, it may, and very commonly does, contain a portion of truth; and since the general or prevailing opinion in any subject is rarely or never the whole truth, it is only by the collision of adverse opinions that the remainder of the truth has any chance of being supplied.
>
> Thirdly, even if the received opinion be not only true, but the whole truth,

unless it is suffered to be, and actually is, vigorously and earnestly contested, it will, by most of those who receive it, be held in the manner of a prejudice, with little comprehension or feeling of its rational grounds. And not only this, but, fourthly, the meaning of the doctrine itself will be in danger of being lost, or enfeebled, and deprived of its vital effect on the character and conduct: the dogma becoming a mere formal profession, inefficacious for good, but cumbering the ground, and preventing the growth of any real and heartfelt conviction, from reason or personal experience.[4]

Perhaps more than any specific content of knowledge, the values of dialogue and debate, of individuality in the face of mass custom and of autonomy infuse Wilde's life and work. This section will consider Wilde as a philosopher engaged with other philosophers, but also as a philosopher whose fate it was to publicise ideas in a mass society composed of audiences with often conflicting interests – what Mill called 'the marketplace of ideas'.

The strongest case for Wilde as philosopher has been made by Philip E. Smith II and Michael S. Helfand, who base their argument on Wilde's Oxford notebooks of the 1870s and the influence of his Oxford education in his later writing.[5] Presenting a consistent Hegelian dialectician, Smith and Helfand argue that at Oxford Wilde reconciled evolutionary science and philosophical idealism. Specifically, he rejected any methodological individualism that saw the individual as the basic sociological unit and identity as analysable apart from society, in favour of Herbert Spencer's and William Kingdon Clifford's theories of cultural evolution, in which individuals inherited their characteristics from their cultures. This theory of cultural evolution took on an organic purposiveness when combined with Hegel's notion of an historico-critical spirit working towards freedom.[6] Thus Smith and Helfand argue that Wilde's rejection of realism in his critical work, especially the essays in *Intentions* ('The Critic as Artist', 'The Decay of Lying' and 'The Truth of Masks'), in favour of utopian art is consistent with the inheritance of progressive characteristics: precisely because life imitates art, art should be progressive. Wilde's famous analogy in 'The Critic as Artist', that 'Aesthetics ... are to Ethics in the sphere of conscious civilisation what, in the sphere of the external world, sexual is to natural selection. Ethics, like natural selection, make existence possible. Aesthetics, like sexual selection, make life lovely and wonderful, fill it with new forms, and give it progress, and variety and change' (*CW* 1154), allied him with the politically progressive Darwinists who saw individuals as naturally social, creative and co-operative and the 'law of the jungle' as an imposition of Britain's particular socio-economic system. Since evolutionary progress was towards differentiation and specialisation of function, individuals would be drawn into voluntary co-operation and mutual aid. The inheritance of culture would ultimately make authority unnecessary.[7]

Recent scholarship has added some new twists on the influence of Mill and the Oxford Hegelians on Wilde's generation. Undergraduates from the 1860s through the 1880s steeped in Millian intellectual principles often had trouble reconciling the intellectual content of, say, the Platonic *Dialogues* that Mill so admired and their dubious – for the Victorians – moral corollaries. That is, they had trouble reconciling the free exchange of ideas that Jowett called 'spiritual procreancy' and the corruption of youth that Jowett himself saw as a threat to the homosocial system epitomised in the Oxford tutorial. Linda Dowling has been the most recent to argue that modern homosexual identity was forged at Oxford within this contradiction between liberal ideals and Victorian moral constraints.[8] Thus John Addington Symonds withdrew from his project of public persuasion regarding homosexuality (as in *Studies of the Greek Poets* (1876)) in favour of medical lobbying of sexologists in the 1890s, and Pater's ahistorical recombination of cultural materials in *The Renaissance* attempted to dodge the religious and moral queries that might be asked of them. Mill's call for curiosity, individuality and diversity as necessary for social and industrial modernity was thus appropriated to ends the pure-minded author had not anticipated in his appeal to Platonic dialectics.

The issue, of course, is where intellectual history, in this case the liberal values of freedom of thought, individuality and diversity, meets the society in which Wilde played his role as a very public intellectual. In fact, 'The Portrait of Mr W. H.' is a classic example of a liberal theory – in effect, a homosexual polemic – whose history was determined by its relation, or anticipated relation, to audience. Much recent work on the *fin de siècle* has focused precisely on the specific markets – audiences – for Wilde as aesthete (puffing Gilbert and Sullivan's *Patience* in the United States or *japonisme* and *chinoiserie* in Britain), his journalism (in *Court and Society Review, Woman's World* and *Queen*, for example, as well as the more 'masculine' *Pall Mall Gazette, Blackwood's* and *Fortnightly Review*), his plays as Society drama, and even his monologues in private places as enticements to libertinage.[9] The commodification of Wilde and his works, of the artist in general and bohemian artists in particular, in consumer society, complicates the pursuit of individuality and freedom of thought and expression.

In his political and aesthetic theory Wilde was both romantic and cynical. In his drama he was both sentimental and satirical. For literary critics he has been both a martyr or a mannequin, a model of depth or a master of poses. In *Idylls of the Marketplace* I argued that such contradictory messages could be understood only by reference to his audiences. Critics of the comedies before *The Importance of Being Earnest* have noticed their divergent tendencies of melodrama and epigrammatic wit or melodrama and satire, and these divergent components may be viewed as Wilde's manipulations of his play-going public. He mercilessly exposed his audiences' superficiality and lack of moral substance while he simultaneously presented to them images of themselves so glamorous and powerful that they could not help but forgive, even lionise, him. Since Brummell this had been the dandy's stratagem: to stylise Society; to so refine that style personally as to put its bearers to shame; and then to be of two minds regarding that style and that Society. Similarly, the British aesthetes' critique of purposiveness, productivity and Nature was related to homosexuality and what amounted to a social revolution in domestic options, which means that the art world was not so divorced from life as it may have appeared. In another example, Wilde's experience of solitary confinement in prison had concrete effects on what is perhaps his greatest work of art, *De Profundis* – at once his own autobiography, a biography of Alfred Douglas and, to adapt his own phrase, a symbolic representation of the art and culture of the age; and the absence of an audience affected the form of that work as significantly as the presence of audiences affected his other works. Like many artists of his generation, Wilde perennially feared the vulgarising influence on his ideas of those absolutely necessary audiences. He explored the relation of art to influence in *The Picture of Dorian Gray*, as well as in his social and aesthetic theory. Situating *The Picture of Dorian Gray* and the scandal it provoked in a crisis of images of dandies, gentlemen and women, and situating Wilde in the context of late-Victorian social institutions of journalism, advertising, public schools, homosexual communities, criminology, etiquette, theatre and prisons, sheds light not only on Wilde's paradoxical style but also on the circulation and consumption of knowledge in market society, in which knowledge is never pure of its packaging, the message never separable from the medium.

FREEDOM

Three of the greatest aesthetic teachers of nineteenth-century Britain were also great social critics: Ruskin, Morris and Wilde. Their critiques of industrial capitalism and mass society, and the influence of their teachings on each other, the British Labour Party, the welfare state, Indian nationalism, modern ecological and gay rights movements and European socialism are well known. Ruskin was not only an authoritative art critic and prose stylist, but throughout his work and especially in *Unto This Last* (1860) he attacked the basic assumptions of the dominant social science of his day –

political economy – including its assumptions concerning wealth, value, the laws of the market and the nature of economic man. He attacked the division of labour, the wage and the arms races as a source of economic growth; and he proposed the foundations of social justice in a paternalistic welfare state. Morris, a poet, novelist, master designer and craftsperson, was also a political propagandist and agitator. And Wilde, the most popular aesthetic figure of the *fin de siècle*, insisted in 'The Soul of Man Under Socialism' (1891) that a healthy material base and equality of opportunity for all were the preconditions of liberal democratic society. He further queried whether the mass media might not be its death. Each of them called himself a socialist (Morris, of course, most consistently), although Ruskin's brand was Tory paternalist, Morris's was Marxist and Wilde's tended towards anarchism, or what might be called an anarcho-cynicalism.[10] More important than such labels, though, was the centrality to each's aesthetic of different kinds of freedom: Ruskin desired a world free from poverty; Morris, a world free from hierarchy, or the fixed hierarchy of the class system; and Wilde, a world free from social intolerance, or the oppression of conventional thought and behaviour. The centrality of such freedoms to each's aesthetic deserves mention here for it suggests how little the spheres of art and life, value and fact, or the Good, True and Beautiful, were differentiated under what Ruskin called 'the political economy of art'.

Consider Ruskin's aesthetic critique of daily life in England in his section contrasting the 'Two Boyhoods' from the fifth volume (1860) of his defence of Turner, *Modern Painters*. In 'Two Boyhoods' Ruskin contrasts the Venice of Giorgione (1477–1510) with the England of Turner (1775–1851). He begins with an idealised description of social order and physical beauty, the romanticised Venice of the quattrocento, whose beauty is premised on its justice.

> A wonderful piece of world. Rather, itself a world. It lay along the face of the waters, no larger, as its captains saw it from their masts at evening, than a bar of sunset that could not pass away; but for its power, it must have seemed to them as if they were sailing in the expanse of heaven, and this a great planet, whose orient edge widened through ether. A world from which all ignoble care and petty thoughts were banished, with all the common and poor elements of life ... Such was Giorgione's school.[11]

He then turns to Turner's school, Covent Garden, and makes the quintessential Ruskinian aesthetic statement, the reduction of aesthetics to material base: 'With such circumstances round him in youth, let us note what necessary effects followed upon the boy['s art].' His impoverished childhood resulted in Turner's 'notable endurance of dirt ... and all the soilings and stains of every common labour'; an 'understanding of and regard for the poor ... and of the poor in direct relations with the rich'; and a discredited religion, 'not to be either obeyed, or combated, by an ignorant, yet clear-sighted youth, only to be scorned'. Turner saw beauty neither in local humanity nor transcendent spirit, but, by contrast only, in the solitude of Nature. In the Yorkshire hills, he found

> Freedom at last. Dead-wall, dark railing, fenced field, gated garden, all passed away like the dream of a prisoner ... Those pale, poverty-struck, or cruel faces; – that multitudinous, marred humanity – are not the only things God has made. Here is something He has made which no one has marred. Pride of purple rocks, and river pools of blue, and tender wilderness of glittering trees, and misty lights of evening on immeasurable hills.

Although affection for the country was an enduring sentiment of the nation that in 1900, the year Ruskin died, boasted the largest city in the world and a quarter of the world's largest cities, Turner is not an escapist nature painter, nor does Ruskin praise him for his representations of the green and pleasant land. The typical Turner painting was a wash of light – the beauty of the physical earth – exposing the piteous failures of human-kind. Ruskin attributes these failures first to the European drive for conquest and domination.

> The European death of the nineteenth century was of another range and power [than that depicted by Salvator or Dürer]; more terrible a thousand-fold in its merely physical grasp and grief; more terrible, incalculably, in its mystery and shame. What were the robber's casual pang, or the range of the flying skirmish, compared to the work of the axe, and the sword, and the famine, which was done during [Turner's] youth on all the hills and plains of the Christian earth, from Moscow to Gibraltar? He was eighteen years old when Napoleon came down on Arcola. Look on the map of Europe and count the blood-stains on it, between Arcola and Waterloo.

In his condemnation of Empire, Ruskin alludes to Turner's projected epic poem on the decline and fall of naval powers, and to Turner's own verses accompanying his *Slavers Throwing Overboard the Dead and Dying – Typhoon Coming On* (1840). In the painting and verses, Turner extends his censure of the slave trade to the global market in general.

After slavery and Empire, Ruskin turns to 'the English practice' of exploitation, as embodied in the domestic casualties of the industrial revolution: 'The life trampled out in the slime of the street, crushed to dust amidst the roaring of the wheel, tossed countlessly away into howling winter wind along five hundred leagues of rock-fanged shore. Or, worst of all, rotted down to forgotten graves through years of ignorant patience, and vain seeking for help from man, for hope in God – infirm, imperfect yearning, as of motherless infants starving at the dawn.' This was what Turner painted: Nature shedding its abundant light on human misery of human making: 'Light over all the world. Full shone now its awful globe, one pallid charnel-house, – a ball strewn bright with human ashes, glaring in poised sway beneath the sun, all blinding-white with death from pole to pole – death, not of myriads of poor bodies only, but of will, and mercy, and conscience; death, not once inflicted on the flesh, but daily fastening on the spirit.'

One can find the same rich sympathy regarding human need, human suffering and human memory in Morris's utopian novel *News from Nowhere* (1890), in which the virtues of an economically just, sexually liberated and ecologically preserved utopia pale, for generation after generation of readers, before the psychological splendour of the one character from the pre-utopian past – a character with memory – William Guest. An old man, one of the few in utopia conscious of the unbearable temporality of the body, Guest's bafflement and pain in the new world order characteristically remain Morris's (and most readers') imaginative centre. If, according to the customary dialectic of utopian fiction, the idyllic nature of the utopia only throws into relief the deficiencies of the present the author is criticising (like Turner's light revealing the failings of humankind), William Guest's complex relationship to memory (the hell that England was) and desire (the vision of what it could be) cannot help but make the callow young utopians look thin.

In his critical writing, Morris differed from Ruskin in that he found the class system – today called 'functionally interdependent juxtapositions' – more detrimental to society than poverty: 'I went to Iceland and I learned one lesson there, thoroughly I hope, that the most grinding poverty is a trifling evil compared with the inequality of classes',[12] a notion that put him fundamentally at odds with the majority of political economists, who, with the notable exception of Mill, equated growth with production rather than distribution of wealth. In 'Art Under Plutocracy', a lecture Morris delivered in 1883 (Ruskin chaired the session), he denied the autonomy of art, claiming first that 'art should be a help and solace to the daily life of all men', and he extended art's arena 'beyond those matters which are consciously works of art ... to the aspect of all the externals of our life'.[13] In 'How We Live and How We Might Live' (1884), Morris says that after competition between nations, classes and firms has ceased (i.e. under socialism), humankind will be free to determine its genuine needs. He anticipates the first demand as for the body: the demand for good health, of which the 'vast proportion of people in civilization scarcely even know what it means'. This good health extends to liberatory sensuous experience: 'To rejoice in satisfying the due bodily appetites of a human animal without fear of degradation or sense of wrong-doing ... I claim it in the teeth of those terrible doctrines of asceticism, which, born of the despair of the oppressed and degraded, have been for so many ages used as instruments for the continuance of that oppression and degradation.' The second demand is for education, which includes skill of hand and craft as well as brainwork: 'Opportunity, that is, to have my share of whatever knowledge there is in the world according to my capacity or bent of mind, historical or scientific; and also to have my share of skill of hand which is about in the world, either in the industrial handicrafts or in the fine arts ... I claim to be taught, if I can be taught, more than one craft to exercise for the benefit of the community.' Morris then claims the right to reject certain kinds of work, those Ruskin had called 'destructive' (e.g. war) and 'nugatory' (e.g. jewel-cutting): 'I won't submit to be dressed up in red and marched off to shoot at my French or German or Arab friend in a quarrel that I don't understand; I will rebel sooner than do that. Nor will I submit to waste my time and energies in making some trifling toy which I know only a fool can desire; I will rebel sooner than do that.' With the advent of useful and freely chosen labour, 'Then would come the time for the new birth of art, so much talked of, so long deferred; people could not help showing their mirth and pleasure in their work, and would be always wishing to express it in a tangible and more or less enduring form, and the workshop would once more be a school of art, whose influence no one could escape from.' Morris concludes with the demand 'That the mutual surroundings of my life should be pleasant, generous, and beautiful',[14] blaming urban squalor, overcrowding, disease and industrial pollution not, as in the Malthusians, on natural scarcity and human overpopulation, but rather on exploitation and the desire for profit.

Wilde's contribution to progressive aesthetics has retained popularity longer than Ruskin's and Morris's, probably because it is more assimilable to market values. It appears most often, though not exclusively, today as toleration of thought and 'lifestyle' in gay/queer circles, but it is often evoked in defences of speech and art against censorship. Just as the artwork under aestheticism was autonomous, had to be true to its own organic development, to the laws of its own form, so Wilde insisted in 'The Portrait of Mr. W. H.', 'The Soul of Man Under Socialism', 'The Critic as Artist' and elsewhere that human individuals had unique temperaments and tastes that should be allowed to flourish according to the laws of their own being; and his fictional work, both novel and short stories, typically consisted of thought experiments on the social limits of this aesthetic autonomy. Yet unlike later proponents of the life-as-art thesis, such as Foucault in his last years, who wanted 'to live life with the freedom of art', Wilde was sufficiently like his teachers Ruskin and Morris to insist upon initial distributive justice as a precondition of genuine individual development and social utility.[15] Some years ago I contrasted Wilde's socially oriented aestheticism with the properly decadent aestheticism of Huysmans's Des Esseintes in *A rebours* (1884). I said that if Des Esseintes was solitary, neurotic, reactive against the bourgeoisie he despises, formally monologic and concerned with perversion, Wilde was public, erotic, active, formally dialogic and concerned with the dialectical inversions of middle-class language and life.[16] Des Esseintes buried himself in a fortress, made a fortress of himself against others, and consumed the exotica of the world outside the West. In 'The Decay of Lying' (1891), Wilde debunked both the connoisseur's practice of accumulation and the ethnographer's of objectification, saying, 'the actual people who live in Japan are not unlike the general run of English people; that is to say, they are extremely commonplace, and have nothing curious or extraordinary about them. In fact the whole of Japan is a pure invention' (*CW* 1088). The goal of the political economists of art was not to objectify others as art, but to provide the conditions that would allow oneself and others to live with the freedom of art.

NOTES

1 Karl Marx, *Capital*, ed. Friedrich Engels (New York: International Publishers, 1967), p. 766.
2 For Wilde's position in the history of socialist aesthetics, see *Critical Essays on Oscar Wilde*, ed. Regenia Gagnier (New York: G. K. Hall, 1991), pp. 7–9.
3 Regenia Gagnier, 'Is Market Society the *Fin* of History?', in *Cultural Politics at the Fin de Siècle*, ed. Sally Ledger and Scott McCracken (Cambridge: Cambridge University Press, 1995), pp. 290–311.
4 John Stuart Mill, *Three Essays* (London: Oxford University Press, 1975), p. 65.
5 But see also the section 'Wildean Critique', in *Critical Essays on Oscar Wilde*, pp. 12–15; J. E. Chamberlin, *Ripe Was the Drowsy Hour: The Age of Oscar Wilde* (New York: Seabury, 1977); and Rodney Shewan, *Oscar Wilde: Art and Egotism* (London: Macmillan, 1977).
6 Smith and Helfand particularly point to Wilde's early essay 'The Rise of Historical Criticism' (1879) for this synthesis. See *Oscar Wilde's Oxford Notebooks: A Portrait of Mind in the Making* (New York: Oxford University Press, 1989), especially pp. 37–46.
7 This view is, of course, strikingly parallel to Smith's answer to Hobbes: the disposition to truck, barter and trade led to the division of labour and ultimately to the equilibrium of the 'Invisible Hand'. This economic evolution solved the problem posed by Hobbes – of how self-interested, autonomous agents could live in harmony – without the need for Hobbes's autocratic state.

8   Linda Dowling, *Hellenism and Homosexuality in Victorian Oxford* (Ithaca: Cornell University Press, 1994). Dowling is building upon the work of Richard Jenkyns in *The Victorians and Ancient Greece* (Cambridge, MA: Harvard University Press, 1980) and Frank M. Turner in *The Greek Heritage in Victorian Britain* (New Haven: Yale University Press, 1988).

9   See Regenia Gagnier, *Idylls of the Marketplace: Oscar Wilde and the Victorian Public* (Stanford: Stanford University Press, 1986); Garry Leonard, 'Women on the Market: Commodity Culture, "Those Lovely Seaside Girls", and "Femininity" in Joyce's *Ulysses*', *Joyce Studies Annual* 2 (Summer 1991) 27–68, and 'Molly Bloom's 'Lifestyle'': The Performative as Normative', in *The Historical Molly Bloom*, ed. Richard Pearce (Madison: University of Wisconsin Press, forthcoming); Thomas Richards, *The Commodity Culture of Victorian England: Advertising and Spectacle 1851–1914* (Stanford: Stanford University Press, 1990); Joel Kaplan and Sheila Stowell, *Theatre and Fashion* (Cambridge: Cambridge University Press, 1994); and Jonathan Freedman, *Professions of Taste: Henry James, British Aestheticism, and Commodity Culture* (Stanford: Stanford University Press, 1990).

10 Whether Morris was a libertarian Marxist or a communist anarchist with strong leanings towards Marxism, or whether Wilde was more influenced by Kropotkin or Chuang-tzu are issues hotly debated. Here, however, I can only refer the reader to such specialist volumes as the collection by Florence Boos and Carole Silver, *Socialism and the Literary Artistry of William Morris* (Columbia: University of Missouri Press, 1990). For Wilde, see *Idylls of the Marketplace*, pp. 29–34, 215 nn. 24–7 and the Introduction to *Critical Essays on Oscar Wilde*, pp. 7–9.

11 John Ruskin, *Unto This Last and Other Writings* (Harmondsworth: Penguin, 1985), pp. 144–53.

12 *Political Writings of William Morris*, ed. A. L. Morton (New York: International Publishers, 1973), p. 17.

13 Ibid., pp. 57–8.

14 Ibid., pp. 148–53.

15 For a comparison of Foucault's and Wilde's aestheticism, see *Critical Essays on Oscar Wilde*, pp. 8–9.

16 Gagnier, *Idylls of the Marketplace*, p. 5.

3

STEPHEN CALLOWAY

Wilde and the Dandyism of the Senses

THE POSE OF INTENSITY AND THE CULT OF AESTHETIC RESPONSE IN THE 1880s AND 1890s[1]

When Oscar Wilde first rediscovered and began to write in 'Pen, Pencil and Poison' of the life and opinions of the Regency painter, belletrist, convicted forger and 'subtle and secret poisoner almost without rival', Thomas Griffiths Wainewright, he found revealed in the character of this artistic and intellectual dandy not only an aspect of his own nature and genius, but also, perhaps, the key to an essential quality of the Aesthetic and Decadent sensibility as it developed in England in the 1880s and 90s.[2] That quality we might define as a Dandyism of the Senses – a self-consciously precious and highly fastidious discrimination brought to bear on both art and life. The dandy-aesthetes of the *fin-de-siècle* period above all honed their senses and cultivated the rarest of sensibilities; they made the perfection of the pose of exquisiteness their greatest aim and they directed all their languid energies towards nurturing a cult of aesthetic response that begins beyond ordinary notions of taste, that lies beyond mere considerations of fashion, and operates quite outside the dictates of all conventional canons of morality.

Wilde was perhaps the first to perceive that this very specific sensibility had been intriguingly foreshadowed by the ideas and opinions enshrined in Wainewright's precociously brilliant art-journalism of the early years of the nineteenth century; in particular in those essays in which the mercurial dandy-critic first adumbrated his own idiosyncratic version of a pose of exquisite sensibility and the notion of a cult of aesthetic response.[3] Wainewright does this first by the, then, original means of sharing with the reader his own reactions to favoured and clearly carefully selected works of art or literature rather than, in the usual way, merely describing the works and apportioning praise or blame according to rigid canons of taste. Secondly, he paints for his public a series of fascinating psychological profiles of himself, in his opulent but, it seems, largely imaginary surroundings. His pose is entirely novel. His prose, like Wilde's, is seldom less than precious; it is highly crafted, even lapidary in style, but saved from being tiresome by the fact that often, too, his phrasing can be delicately expressive and amusingly ironic in its touch.

In his various literary self-portraits, written under the amusingly chosen *noms-de-plume* of 'Janus Weathercock' and, yet more tellingly, 'Egomet Bonmot', Wainewright appears always as the exquisite; in the most celebrated of these passages he chooses to portray himself stretched languidly upon his 'pomona-green morocco *chaise-longue*', by turns idly browsing through choice impressions of rare engravings plucked from a sumptuous portfolio, or toying with his equally indolent cat. The room is, he informs us, bathed in the soft and romantic light that falls from the painted shade of an elegant French lamp. With a delightful and calculated impudence, our connoisseur, in describing the contents of the room in order of importance, begins his list with 'myself'. It is an image which seems, in many ways, more immediately redolent of the 1890s than the 1820s; the opening scene, perhaps, of one of the daringly modern *Keynotes* novels, such as Florence Farr's *The Dancing Faun*.[4]

At a moment in the later eighties, with Oxford and America behind him, when Wilde was consciously redefining his early self-appointed role as the highly conspicuous and, if anything, somewhat robust rather than etiolated 'Apostle of Aestheticism', the example of Wainewright played a crucial part in the creation of his later, more subtle and carefully drawn pose. For Wilde, Wainewright appealingly possessed the 'dangerous and delightful distinction of being different from others' – undoubtedly a vital, if ultimately self-destructive, trait of the character which Wilde would develop for himself in the years to come. Again discovering something of his own persona in Wainewright, Wilde observes that 'as an art critic he concerns himself primarily with the complex impressions produced by a work of art ...'. 'Certainly', Wilde agrees, 'the first step in aesthetic criticism is to realise one's own impressions ... he never lost sight of the great truth that Art's first appeal is neither to the intellect nor the emotions, but purely to the artistic temperament.'

Wilde of course belonged initially to that generation of Oxford Aesthetes who, beginning as disciples of Ruskin, had first espoused his earnest, Christian, medieval and Pre-Raphaelite enthusiasms and his desire for 'Truth to Nature' in art, only to be seduced in due course by the more indulgently neo-pagan, Renaissance-inspired, 'decadent' and, consequently, rather dangerously glamorous teachings of Walter Pater. From the mid-1870s a number of the impressionable students of this reticent and seemingly quite unrevolutionary don were indeed 'misled', as Pater himself would later put it, by the infamous 'Conclusion' to the first edition of his *Studies in the History of the Renaissance* (1873);[5] the book which, twenty years on, Wilde would describe as having had 'such a strange influence over my life'.[6] In its most infamous passage, suppressed by the author himself in the second edition, but rewritten in a less inflammatory style and reinstated in subsequent editions of the work, Pater had proposed that young men should, in the search for aesthetic experience and in pursuit of the all-important heightened sensibility, 'burn always with [a] hard, gem-like flame'. He further exhorted them to seek primarily for sensation and 'great passions' in both art and life, and to 'get as many pulsations as possible into the given time'.

Curiously, this Paterian ideal of the quivering artistic sensibility, as interpreted and embraced by the Wildean cenacle, found a very distinct resonance in attitudes and ideals which they also perceived in the cast of mind of the Regency period. In fact, unlike the majority of more mainstream Aesthetic Movement theorists and designers, men such as the architect Richard Norman Shaw for example, Wilde and his circle were never swept away by the usual unconditional admiration for the solid virtues of the Queen Anne period; they looked instead with a somewhat novel interest at the far more self-consciously chic, elegant and even, at times, flashy world of Regency culture and society, observing with delight its constant obsessions with manners, style and *ton*, the value it placed upon exoticism, on the creation of effect, and, perhaps most relevantly for Wilde himself, the high regard in which the fast, fashionable society of that era held verbal brilliance.

The Aesthetes of the Wilde circle were fascinated, naturally, by what they knew of the Brummell era, not least perhaps because those all-too-earnest mid-Victorians of the generations between the 1830s and 1880s had disapproved so strongly of the Dandies' languid self-centredness and their amoral, hot-house culture. With their insistence upon the importance of 'the pose' ultimately outweighing even their concern for the niceties of dress and deportment, the Dandies had made an art of their lives, and this the Aesthetes found irresistible. But also in equal measure they revered the Romantics, whose lives as much as their art had such great appeal as models for this new generation of aspiring poets and painters. Keats, of course, was worshipped by the Aesthetes for the way in which his immortal verses and early death epitomised their ideals of *Ars longa, Vita brevis*, the sentiment so perfectly expressed in his 'Ode on a Grecian Urn';[7] indeed, John Addington Symonds in a letter of 1881 to Wilde writes of the great desirability of cultivating a 'Keatsian openness at all the pores to Beauty'[8] whilst Wilde, in a similarly reverential vein, refers later, in his Wainewright essay, to 'the tremulously sensitive and poetic Shelley'. Wilde had also pursued this cult ideal of the quivering sensibility in several of his earlier poems, such as 'Hélas!', in which appear these lines where in the voice of the poet he yearns

> To drift with every passion till my soul
> Is a stringed lute upon which all winds can play.

Pater's call to his followers to embrace a notion of 'Art for Art's sake',[9] a new kind of art untrammelled by social rules, by quotidian concepts of good or evil, or indeed by any other concerns extraneous to the central aim of aesthetic experience or the single-minded pursuit of beauty, had a tremendous appeal for these young men seeking an escape from the, at times, stifling confines of Victorian painting and writing; from those arts weighed down by an ever increasing burden of moral, social and sentimental baggage.

In this search for a still high-minded, but essentially amoral theory of art, Wilde yet again found his precursor in Wainewright. Describing Wainewright's 'subtle and artistic temperament', whilst remaining curiously untroubled by any real consideration of his serious crimes, Wilde draws particular attention to the way in which Wainewright effortlessly separates art and morality, quoting the following, highly significant passage:

> I hold that no work of art can be tried otherwise than by laws deduced from itself: whether or not it be consistent with itself is the question.   (CW 1097)

'This is one of his excellent aphorisms', concludes Wilde with clear admiration for a phrase and sentiment which will echo and re-echo through a number of his own works at this time, including the closely contemporary dialogues 'The Critic as Artist' and 'The Decay of Lying', and reappear as one of the central themes of *The Picture of Dorian Gray*.[10]

When he comes to write of Wainewright's specific artistic tastes Wilde makes a startling discovery:

> his essays are prefiguring of much that has since been realised. He seems to have anticipated some of those accidents of modern culture that are regarded by many as true essentials. He writes about la Giaconda, and early French poets, and the Italian Renaissance.   (CW 1095)

These, as Wilde was perhaps the first to notice, are precisely the subjects of key essays in *Studies in the History of the Renaissance*, and the very themes onto which Pater would graft his highly charged plea for intensity and passion in aesthetic response in the notorious 'Conclusion'.

In cataloguing Wainewright's novel and varied artistic predilections,

Wilde also discovers another remarkable aspect of his taste, which sets it apart from the pedantic, stylistic obsessions of the early and high Victorians and links him, rather, with the new aesthetic freedom of the eighties:

> it is clear that he was one of the first to recognise what is, indeed, the very keynote of aesthetic eclecticism, I mean the true harmony of all really beautiful things, irrespective of age or place, of school or manner. He saw that in decorating a room, which is to be not a room for show, but a room to live in, we should never aim at any archaeological reconstruction of the past, nor burden ourselves with any fanciful necessity for historical accuracy. In this artistic perception he was entirely right. All beautiful things belong to the same age. (CW 1096)

Continuing his list of Wainewright's interests, Wilde goes on to cite these further evidences of the proto-aesthete's anticipation of the tastes of the late 1880s and 1890s:

> he loves Greek gems, Persian carpets, Elizabethan translations of *Cupid and Psyche* and the *Hypnerotomachia*, and book-bindings and early editions and wide-margined proofs. He is keenly sensitive to the value of beautiful things, and never wearies of describing to us the rooms in which he lived, or would like to have lived. (CW 1095)

This inventory of rare, precious and pleasingly obscure delights of the connoisseur, together with its concomitant implication of a super-subtle artistic temperament to match, might almost serve as a description of any one of a number of the Aesthetes of the 1890s and of their exquisitely contrived rooms. More especially, it seems now to us, as it must have struck Wilde even more forcefully then, to reflect with an almost uncanny degree of precision the life-style, surroundings and particular artistic passions of his friends, Charles Ricketts and Charles Shannon, artists and collectors who lived, as it was said of them at that time, 'une existence idéale – tout pour l'art'.[11]

By this date Ricketts and Shannon had come to occupy a position that has been aptly described as 'almost official artists to Wilde'; their friendship at this time was certainly both close and stimulating, and for Wilde, at a transitional phase in his career, of great significance for the development of his ideas. Wilde had probably first met the younger artists and visited their house, The Vale, in Chelsea when, in 1889, they sent him a copy of the first number of their sumptuously printed literary and artistic journal, *The Dial*. Wilde was undoubtedly impressed by its cosmopolitan sophistication both in terms of design and contents and its clear symbolist leanings; he jokingly suggested, however, that they print no further editions, 'because all perfect things should be unique'. From that point Ricketts, with the occasional intervention of Shannon, designed almost all Wilde's major books with the single exception of *Salome* (1894), which was 'pictured', as he preferred to phrase it, by their only serious rival among the illustrators of the day, Aubrey Beardsley.

Even at this early date Ricketts's and Shannon's varied collections were already becoming celebrated and their precocious connoisseurship something of a legend. The catholicity of their tastes, which embraced important Old Master drawings, exquisite Japanese prints, early printed books, Renaissance pictures and Greek and Egyptian antiquities as well as simpler treasures such as the rare shells which they displayed in bowls of water, seemed the perfect vindication of Wilde's dictum, derived from Wainewright, that 'all beautiful things belong to the same age'. In addition, their much-vaunted ability as arrangers of their prized objects gave to their flower-filled rooms a visual distinction rare even among the most polished of the Aesthetes. Taken over from Whistler, who had lived there for a short time with his beautiful Irish model and mistress, Jo Heffernan, the old house in The Vale still retained fascinating traces of his idiosyncratic decorative treatments, including walls distempered in 'artistic' sage green and other distinctive colours, such as the strong bright yellow in the entrance hallway which Wilde volubly admired and praised as 'the colour of joy'.

For Wilde, as for many brilliant visitors, The Vale always remained 'the one house in London where you will never be bored';[12] often, in preference to socially smarter but duller invitations, he would spend evenings there amid the congenial company of the Vale coterie, discoursing on beauty in art and poetry in the abstract, listening to Ricketts's immensely knowledgable and detailed discussion of pictures and other art objects, or simply gossiping. To Shannon, always charming, open and straightforwardly sunny by temperament, Wilde gave the name 'Marigold', whilst upon the more rarefied and infinitely more complex of the partners, and thus the more typically nineties aesthete, Ricketts, he bestowed the apt soubriquet of 'Orchid'. He held both their artistic work and their aesthetic opinions in high esteem, and, just as he had once deferred to Whistler's ideals of art and his visual judgement, or to E. W. Godwin's taste in decoration, so now he regarded Ricketts in particular, though ten years his junior, as an infallible arbiter in matters of taste far beyond the choice of the remarkable bindings of his books.

Paradoxically, the question of the precise nature of Oscar Wilde's own visual taste is one that has been very little addressed. His opinions on most aesthetic matters are so well known, that it comes as something of a surprise to realise just how little his actual personal artistic predilections can be documented. In three areas in which his aesthetic discrimination played a part: in his dress, his interiors and in the appearance of his published books, we can fortunately gather just enough information to follow the major developments in his tastes, in particular in that important transitional period between about 1883/4 and 1889, during which his earlier, simpler aestheticism underwent a sea-change into something darker and more 'decadent' as a result, it would appear, of his increasing exposure to the richer veins of European, and in particular French, literary and artistic theory and activity.

But what was the nature of this subtle shift in emphasis in Wilde's aestheticism in these years? Wilde had gone to America as the apostle of an essentially very English Aestheticism; the intellectual, Oxford Aestheticism that was a hybrid of Ruskinian and Paterian ideals. His lecture on 'The English Renaissance of Art', first delivered in New York on 9 January 1882,[13] touched upon the art of the Greeks, on Shakespeare and on Blake, but dwelled at greatest length on the now familiar aesthetic themes of the beauty of Keats and the genius of the Pre-Raphaelite sensibility. His pronouncements upon the theme of the decoration of houses, which formed the subject matter of his second, rather more hurriedly assembled talk, first delivered considerably later on the tour, on 11 May, kept well within the comfortable parameters of Morrisian ideology and good taste.[14] His remarks, in fact, mostly comprised a catalogue of derogatory remarks on the aesthetic poverty of the machine-made furniture he saw everywhere in America, and on the sadly inartistic nature of the decorative schemes of his hosts' houses, when contrasted with the colour, the beauty and idealism, and the spiritual richness of the products of the emergent Arts and Crafts Movement in England.

However, Wilde's appearance – his long hair and velvet suit and fur-trimmed greatcoat, and his superbly judged, highly mannered style of delivery – contrived to ensure that it was essentially his pose in the 'high-aesthetic line', even more than any serious aspect of his message, which struck home to his vast transatlantic audience, fascinating and enraging in about equal measure. This was, in effect, a confirmation of Wilde's key role as the promulgator of the Aesthetic message. But there can be little doubt that this was very much the gospel of Aestheticism as presented in the caricatures of Du Maurier in *Punch*, and parodied with such wicked precision in Gilbert and Sullivan's *Patience*, in telling lines such as

> You must lie upon the daisies
> And discourse in novel phrases
> Of your complicated state of mind.

Wilde returned from America very much more famous, with a greatly

Figure 3   Wilde the Aesthete, dressed for his American tour in 1881

enhanced self-image, but in all probability with his ideas unchanged. It is in the next phase of his life that several more extreme aspects of the Decadent sensibility and other new influences seem to have coalesced in his attitudes towards both art and life. Round about this time, his friendship with Whistler began to become more strained and gradually to fall apart (as indeed all friendships with the author of *The Gentle Art of Making Enemies* tended to do, often very much more quickly than in this case). In his

Figure 4   Charles Ricketts's title-page for *The Sphinx*, 1894

curious, but eloquent and aesthetically rather important, foray into the arena of the public talk, the 'Ten O'Clock Lecture', Whistler opened a still jocular, but nonetheless more overt phase of hostilities. He attacked Wilde, who was present at the performance, as 'the dilettante', lamenting that 'the voice of the aesthete is heard in the land and catastrophe is upon us'.[15]

In fact this cooling of Wilde's never less than bracing relationship with his old artistic mentor coincided with his increasing realisation that some, at least, of 'the Master's' ideas were not entirely as idiosyncratic and original as he liked to suggest, and that much of his preaching, in particular in the 'Ten O'Clock Lecture', had been anticipated by Baudelaire, by Gautier and by others of his French friends. By this period Wilde had French friends of his own. He had met many of the most distinguished Parisian *hommes de lettres*, including literary grandees, such as Catulle Mendes and the mysterious Rosicrucian, Joséphin Péladan; and he was close to and corresponded with many of the rising young writers of his own generation, such as Pierre Louÿs, who helped with the early drafts of the original French version of *Salomé*,[16] and the symbolist Marcel Schwob, to whom he would dedicate his most precious book, *The Sphinx*.[17]

When at the end of the nineties Wilde wrote of himself as 'a man who stood in symbolic relations to the art and culture of my age', he spoke perhaps more truly than he knew. For his grand pose of heightened sensibility, which combined such a passionate championing of art and obsession for beauty with a defiant contempt for the ordinary, was greatly influential – not least for the way in which it represented the quintessential expression of many of the artistic ideals, both French and English, that had been forming throughout the nineteenth century, and were ready to coalesce in the new Decadent spirit of the *fin de siècle*.

In England the example of Dante Gabriel Rossetti, the Pre-Raphaelite poet–painter, was of inestimable importance to the formation of the nineties sensibility. It was not, however, to the young Rossetti and those early, hearty days of Pre-Raphaelitism that the Aesthetes would look; rather it was to his last, decadent years, during which he lived as a virtual recluse, his spirit sunk under the heavy influence of the addictive, opium-derived drug, chloral, working obsessively at the great series of dreamlike, sensual canvases depicting the *femmes fatales* of his own private mythology. W. B. Yeats in 'The Tragic Generation' spoke of Rossetti as 'a subconscious influence, and perhaps the most powerful of all',[18] whilst Richard Le Gallienne, a minor poet and, at first, a protégé of Wilde and his set, recalled many years later in his contribution to the myth-making of the period, *The Romantic Nineties* (1926), that 'of all the great figures ... but recently departed' the most numinous was Rossetti, who 'dwelt in mysterious sacrosanct seclusion like some high priest behind the veil in his old romantic house in Chelsea'.[19]

This notion of the high calling of art had a strong appeal, even for the worldly and sensual such as Wilde. He constantly returns in his writings to the theme of beauty, and to fables which enshrine the basic principle of the Dandyism of Aesthetic Response; to the belief that the ability to recognise beauty, and to respond to it with a rare and refined passion, carries with it the implicit corollary that one possesses therefore, inherently, a particular beauty of temperament and spirit. For Wilde, such true Aesthetes had 'slim gilt souls'. Increasingly, the closely related desires for rarefied experience and the attainment of subtle discrimination, as displayed for example in artistic connoisseurship, became, along with an obsession for form and style, the central ideas of the English Decadent writers, poets and artists. As Arthur Symons would define it, their aim was 'to fix the last fine shade, to fix it fleetingly; to be a disembodied voice and yet the voice of a human soul; that is the ideal of decadence'.[20]

Of course not every poet or artist of the period, even within the fairly broad definition of Aesthetes (as opposed to the tweedy, pipe-smoking 'Hearties' such as W. E. Henley or Rudyard Kipling) aspired to the creation and careful tending of a Wildean slim gilt soul. John Davidson, a Scottish writer who made a hard living by his pen in London, was one of those drawn at first into the Aesthetic and Decadent camp. He became a member of the celebrated Rhymers' Club, where Yeats and Dowson presided over convivial gatherings, until one night in a moment of despair he came to the momentous realisation that all these assembled Aesthetes 'lacked blood and guts'. Later Yeats would recall in sadness how in the end Davidson 'saw in delicate, laborious discriminating taste an effeminate pedantry', and how finally he burst out: 'if a man must be a connoisseur, let him be a connoisseur in women'.[21]

It was, in truth, a not unusual refrain, though normally such attacks had come from the opposition; for example from the university 'bloods' who had sacked Wilde's provocatively decorated college rooms at Oxford, so lovingly and elaborately tricked out with fashionable blue-and-white vases and other oriental gew-gaws and 'artistic' treasures. In print form *Punch* had carried out a relentless sniping campaign in its carefully observed parodies in prose and verse and in the drawings of Du Maurier. Even Kipling had had a go; his little satirical poem hit the mark with characteristic precision. In it a dying Captain of Empire berates his artistic son, educated at 'Harrer an' Trinity', for his depraved tastes:

> The things I knew was proper you wouldn't thank
> me to give

And the things I knew was rotten you said was the
    way to live.
For you muddled with books and pictures an' china
    an' etchings an' fans,
And your rooms at college was beastly – more like a whore's
    than a man's.[22]

That such criticisms and attempts at ridicule were in their time routinely levelled at the social and sartorial Dandies of the Regency of England, at the French intellectual and literary Dandies of the mid-century, and against the Dandy-Aesthetes of the 1880s and 1890s, serves strongly to underline the close connections between these groups and the essential identity of their ideals as well as their forms of expression. It was a connection that gained increasing conviction and currency in the latter decade, as writers such as Wilde, Arthur Symons and, in a more delicately humorous vein, Max Beerbohm traced the origins of their philosophy from Beau Brummell and the Count D'Orsay, through the writings of Jules Barbey d'Aurevilly, on to the central characters of the decadence in France, Baudelaire, Gautier and so, later, to Joris-Karl Huysmans.

Beerbohm's exquisitely crafted prose and seemingly genial irony have tended to cloak the sharp and perceptive modernity of his thought. He is at his very best in the celebrated essay 'Dandies and Dandies', first published in the New York magazine *Vanity* in 1895, and reprinted with a slightly crisper revised text in the slim, facetiously titled volume *The Works of Max Beerbohm* (1896). Here Beerbohm toys with the observations made by Barbey in his study *Du Dandyisme*, a key essay in the identification of the type, first published in a tiny and now extremely rare edition of thirty copies in 1845.[23] He concedes Barbey's importance as the first writer and intellectual truly to understand the dandiacal character, but proceeds suavely to reclaim the Beau from the French interpretation of him as a predominantly social phenomenon.

Beerbohm establishes the Dandy as the role-model *par excellence* for *fin-de-siècle* sensibility; almost, one might say, recreating Brummell in his own image. 'Mr Brummell', writes Beerbohm, 'was, indeed in the utmost sense of the word, an artist.' He goes on, as if describing a portrait by Whistler, or perhaps by William Nicholson: 'In certain congruities of dark cloth, in the rigid perfection of his linen, in the symmetry of his glove with his hand, lay the secret of Mr Brummell's miracles.' In Beerbohm's highly polished periods the intimate connections between the dandyism of dress, a dandyism of thought and one of the senses was irrevocably established.

Although he had died as early as 1867, Baudelaire was, like Barbey d'Aurevilly, destined to remain a key figure for the 1890s, revered by the

Aesthetes for his pose of morbid sensitivity, and by the Decadents for his opium- and hashish-inspired explorations of strange and exquisite sensations. His most celebrated works, the extraordinary cycle of poems *Les fleurs du mal* of 1857 and the later meditation on De Quincey and opium, *Les paradis artificiels*, which followed in 1860, exerted a powerful influence, both thematically and stylistically, over the men of the nineties, who responded to Baudelaire's uncompromising search for a strange, new and often perverse kind of beauty.

In some ways Baudelaire was perceived, by English Aesthetes at least, as resembling a figure from Poe's tales; like Roderick Usher he appeared to have sought (in William Gaunt's memorable phrase) to bring 'the cultivation of the senses to the uttermost limits of perversity'.[24] Similarly, Arthur Symons, who made vivid translations of both books, wrote with characteristic admiration that 'Baudelaire brings every complication of taste, the exasperation of perfumes, the irritant of cruelty, the very odours and colours of corruption to the creation of a sort of religion in which an eternal mass is served before a veiled altar.'[25] That new sort of religion was, of course, to be identified with a new sort of art; an art which, as Wilde succinctly put it in 'The Decay of Lying', had as its object 'not simple truth, but complex beauty'. In another celebrated passage in that dialogue Wilde reveals his very deep admiration for *Les fleurs du mal*:

> and if we grow tired of an antique time, and desire to realise our own age in all its weariness and sin, are there not books that can make us live more in one single hour than life can make us live in a score of shameful years? Close to your hand lies a little volume, bound in some Nile-green skin that has been powdered with gilded nenuphars and smoothed with hard ivory. It is the book that Gautier loved, it is Baudelaire's masterpiece.

The description is revealing, too, of Wilde's sophisticated attitude to book design, a subject to which we shall return. The binding he describes, with its 'Nile-green skin', seems almost his inevitable choice for a decadent masterpiece; its decoration with nenuphars, a type of waterlily (and perhaps more significantly one of the sonorous names from the richly over-elaborate poetic lexicon of Wilde's *Sphinx*), entirely in the manner of Ricketts, and comparable with his elegant and highly mannered covers for Wilde's *Picture of Dorian Gray* or John Gray's *Silverpoints*.[26]

Baudelaire was, too, highly conscious of his own image, and though never himself an exquisite in the true sense, he perceived that the dandy represented an aspect of the quintessential, self-proclaiming artist of contemporary sensibility that he sought. In a key passage of 'The Painter of

Modern Life', much admired in the 1890s and highly evocative of the new temperament, he wrote:

> Dandyism is the last glimmer of heroism amid decadence; like the sunset of a dying star, it is glorious, without heat and full of melancholy.[27]

In such lines we may already discern in a highly developed form something of the *fin-de-siècle* sensibility, of the languid pose and of the symbolic and often theatrically over-stated pessimism that is now identified by the inelegant term 'endism'. John Davidson tried to give this sentiment a more lighthearted twist in the 'Proem' to his strange social satire and sado-masochistic fantasy novel *The Wonderful Mission of Earl Lavender* (1895):

> Though our thoughts turn ever downwards,
> Though our sun is well-nigh set,
> Though our century totters tombwards,
> We may laugh a little yet.[28]

But Le Gallienne, reviewing this odd volume, found it still all too expressive of 'the tired taste and jaded sensibilities of our end of the century';[29] a thought echoed by Wilde in what seems to be a rare moment of amused self-parody in 'The Decay of Lying' where he invents a society called

> the Tired Hedonists ... it is a club to which I belong. We are supposed to wear faded roses in our buttonholes when we meet, and to have a sort of cult for Domitian. I am afraid you are not eligible. You are too fond of simple pleasures.

The very quintessence of this jaded and decadent sensibility is to be found in the fictional character of Duc Jean de Floressas des Esseintes, the febrile and neurotic aristocrat and connoisseur who is the central, or indeed only significant, character in J. K. Huysmans's *A rebours*. Published in 1884 the novel 'fell like a meteorite into the literary fairground', as its author recalled, 'provoking anger and stupefaction'.[30] Bizarre and perverse both in its attitudes and in its obsessive elaboration of obscure detail, it was hailed as the 'Breviary of the Decadence', and enthusiastically taken up as an essential text and would-be crib by Aesthetes on both sides of the English Channel. Many would use its long, meticulously researched, but ultimately over-whelming, lists of rare and curious things and *recherché* ideas as a primer for their own developing tastes in art, in life and in the creation of rooms.

Wilde, an early admirer, refers obliquely to its great influence when, in *The Picture of Dorian Gray*, he describes Basil Hallward's reaction to an unnamed book lent to him by Lord Henry Wotton – a reaction that, consciously or not, oddly recalls Wilde's own admission concerning Pater's *Studies in the History of the Renaissance*:

> It was the strangest book that he had ever read. It seemed to him that in exquisite raiment and to the delicate sound of flutes, the sins of the world were passing in dumb-show before him. Things that he had dimly dreamed of were suddenly made real to him. Things of which he had never dreamed were gradually revealed. (CW 96)

Wilde would later, when cross-examined at his trial, freely identify this seemingly dubious book as *A rebours*. He praised it for its artistic merit, but true to form refused to be drawn on the question of its morality, claiming that for one artist so to judge the work of another would be 'an impertinence and a vulgarity'. But as Wilde's Lord Henry reflected, 'the heavy odour of incense hung about its pages'.

Inevitably, Huysmans's Des Esseintes became the Decadents' role-model *par excellence*, both for his compelling insistence upon the cultivation of the senses, and for his unequivocal assertion of the absolute superiority of artifice over naturalness; of art over nature. Ellmann has noted that perhaps the most significant of the changes in Wilde's attitudes and his distinct move towards this darker and more 'decadent' artistic and moral sensibility that we have examined, coincided curiously with not only his increasing celebrity and growing social status as *the* literary lion of the day, but also more importantly with his marriage and move to a new and very much family-orientated house in Tite Street; both developments which may have made the exploration of illicit pleasures and 'strange sensations' rather more appealing than heretofore (E 237ff.). Ellmann further speculates that the appearance of Huysmans's novel actually during Oscar and Constance's honeymoon, and Wilde's subsequent fascination with its themes of anti-naturalism and the celebration of the perverse at the expense of the comfortable and conventional, could bear an interesting psychological interpretation.

Certainly Wilde's new visual predilections at this date are significant. His rapidly evolving taste in clothes can, of course, be seen and precisely charted in the numerous painted and photographic portraits which survive. What is revealed is that in his dress by the end of the eighties there is almost no trace of the former attention-seeking bohemianism of only a few years earlier. The velvets and furs of his American lecture tour costume are no more, and his appearance is, by contrast, now suave, sophisticated and, as an obvious reflection of his increasing success as an author and playwright, expensive, but without undue showiness or opulence. His hair, after a last short interlude of eccentricity during which he sported 'Neronian curls', becomes shorter, until it is pomaded and entirely conventional by the standards of the day. All hint of anachronism in his costume has been eschewed in favour of the rigid Brummellian ideal of fine cloths and understated, but up-to-the-minute modernity of cut. Only the slightest touches of extravagance in the choice of jewelled tie-pins, and button-holes, and an occasional indulgence in handsome rings relieve the new austerity. Wilde has become the perfect man about town, with perhaps the merest hint of the 'swell' inherent in his character. However, like Brummell in his later years, Wilde's girth also continued to increase, thereby giving him, in images from the final few years at least, a look that was rather more well upholstered than strictly elegant.

Sadly, not one single image appears to be extant of any of the interiors which Wilde created and lived in; further, his collections of pictures, books and other objects, and even his furniture and personal effects, were dispersed by the scandalously hurried sale of the contents of the Tite Street house following the bankruptcy immediately brought about by his trials in 1895. All these possessions remain tantalisingly obscure, other than by the meagre descriptions contained in the very inadequate catalogue prepared in a great rush by the auctioneers who handled, or rather mishandled, the sale.[31]

From the rather patchy evidence of Wilde's decorative schemes, it would seem that in a similar way his sophistication in this area of taste also increased in these years of the eighties, but with the result that, in contrast to the move towards sartorial conformity, his rooms became more avant-garde and perhaps more deliberately intended to gain attention. An interest in oriental objects, common to almost all the Aesthetes, is perhaps the one unifying factor in Wilde's earlier and later arrangements. From his student days in Oxford and later at Keats House, the Tite Street home he shared for a while from July 1880 with the tragic painter Frank Miles, blue-and-white and other ceramics, Japanese prints and paintings, and fans formed a part of his collection, but unlike Ricketts and Shannon for example, Wilde seems never to have developed much of a connoisseur's eye for quality in these, or indeed in any other individual works of art.

A certain amount has been written about the schemes which E. W. Godwin helped to contrive for Wilde's own house in Tite Street. Most accounts concentrate on the daring use of all-white enamelled woodwork and furnishings, none of which now survives, and on the remarkable level of stylisation of the interiors; as a result of these factors, the rooms intrigued visitors and journalists alike. W. B. Yeats, invited by Oscar and Constance to spend Christmas Day of 1888 with them, was both fascinated and not a little intimidated by the rigorously artistic effects, such as the way in which a red lampshade hung over a small terracotta classical figure standing on a matching square of red cloth on the otherwise pristine white table. This impression of an extreme chic is, however, somewhat dispelled by the rather contrary evidence of the sale catalogue. From the admittedly sketchy descriptions of the contents of the house room by room, the objects enumerated suggest that the general visual effect may very well have been, in reality, more that of a conventional family home of the 1880s and 90s, simply overlaid with some of the 'artistic' decorative ideas of the Aesthetic Movement, such as the use of oriental matting as a background to Persian carpets strewn across the floor. Clearly Wilde's taste in *japonisme* when translated into the purchase of actual objects lacked the finesse and sure aesthetic discrimination of either Rossetti or Whistler; and the feeling persists that Godwin's clever touches were in general grounded with, on the one hand, more prosaic or homely touches, and, on the other, a hint of the commonplace, or at least somewhat commercialised, orientalism of Liberty's Bazaar.[32] Wilde's splendour, it seems clear, was a splendour of phrases not of visual effects; a richness of word-pictures rather than of objects.

In one area, however, Wilde's discrimination was extraordinary. In the appearance of his books there can be no doubt that his judgement was remarkably astute. Even the earliest, and rather less distinguished, edition of his *Poems* published by the highly commercial house of Bogue, nonetheless attracted a certain degree of attention. *Punch* in a parodic review (which Walter Hamilton reprinted in his 1882 study of the Aesthetic Movement[33]) actually used the splendour of the design of the volume as a stick with which to beat its contents:

> the cover is consummate, the paper is distinctly precious, the binding is beautiful, and the type is utterly too ... [the book] comes to us arrayed in white vellum and gold. There is a certain amount of originality about the binding, but that is more than can be said about the inside of the volume. Mr Wilde may be Æsthetic but he is not original. This is a volume of echoes, it is Swinburne and water.[34]

In terms of reviews of his work Wilde usually gave as good as he got, but he also vigorously defended the actual appearance of his books. His sparkling riposte to a dull critic who had disparaged the cover of *A House of Pomegranates* is superb. Wilde replied that the fact that the critic did not like the cover was

> no doubt to be regretted, though it is not a matter of much importance, as there are only two people in the world whom it is absolutely necessary the cover should please. One is Mr Ricketts, who designed it, the other is myself, whose book it binds. We both admire it immensely! (*L* 300)

Much has been written of the sequence of beautiful and often unusual designs which give to Wilde's published works such a high level of visual distinction; undoubtedly, from 1891 it was the influence of Ricketts which was paramount in shaping this visual style, but it is equally clear that Wilde as author and Ricketts as 'builder' of the books were in close accord, their ideas often sparking off each other. Wilde's appreciation of the technical aspects of the design, printing and binding of books also shows that he had learned much from Whistler and the other pioneers of this arcane art even before the nineties, the pre-eminent decade of 'the Book Beautiful'. Some of his very specific comments reveal a very highly developed sensibility. For example, discussing with John Lane the cloth used for *Salome*, he writes:

> The cover ... is quite dreadful. Don't spoil a lovely book. Have simply a folded vellum wrapper with the design in scarlet – much better and much cheaper. The texture of the present cover is coarse and common and spoils the real beauty of the interior. Use up this horrid Irish stuff for stories, etc; don't inflict it on a work of art like *Salome*...   (L 348)

whilst Vincent O'Sullivan later recalled another similarly expert dictum of Wilde's to the effect that

> Nothing looks more vulgar and cheap than a book with an ornament on one side of the cover and the other side blank.[35]

Over one aspect of the book Wilde did, however, disagree with Ricketts. On the publication of *The Sphinx*, their rarest and most precious collaboration, Wilde, in his usual manner, sent to Ricketts a copy with a fulsome inscription on the first blank leaf. Ricketts shuddered with horror at this desecration of perfection and, tearing out the offending leaf, damned Wilde as a 'vulgar beast'. Such was the importance of nuance in the battle of aesthetic sensibilities in 1894. As it was once remarked by one of Ricketts's friends on visiting The Vale: 'one false note would be an outrage'.

If Wilde's claim to have been 'a man who stood in symbolic relations to the art and culture of my age' (L 466) was indeed true, then his greatest contribution to those times, beyond even his writings, his wit and his reputation, may well have been his perfecting of the super-subtle pose of heightened sensibility that lies at the heart of our notion of the Dandyism of the Senses. From his early days, when he first elaborated the character of the dandy-aesthete, through to his last, most tragic period when he came to epitomise all the qualities, both good and ill, of the literary *flâneur*, he never ceased to fulfil that most important, if also ultimately most Decadent, aim and requirement of every great Dandy: that of creating oneself afresh each day as a work of art. Or as Oscar Wilde himself would explain the final paradox of the pose of Aesthetic Dandy, he chose, as all great Dandies must, to put only his talent into his work, but his genius into his life.

NOTES

1 This study draws on ideas and uses some material previously included in my essay ' "The Dandyism of the Senses"; Aesthetic Ideals and Decadent Attitudes in the 1890s', in *High Art and Low Life: 'The Studio' and the* Fin-de-Siècle (Studio International Special Centenary Number 201: 1022/1023 London: 1993), 54–63.

2 'Pen, Pencil and Poison; A Study in Green' was first published by Frank Harris in *The Fortnightly Review* in January 1889; Wilde reprinted it in book form in *Intentions*, 1891.

3 Wainewright's essays appeared in a number of periodicals, including *The London Magazine* and *The New Monthly Magazine*. They are collected and reprinted in *T. G. Wainewright: Essays and Criticism*, ed. W. Carew Hazlitt (London: Reeves and Turner, 1880). The standard critical biography of Wainewright is Jonathan Curling, *Janus Weathercock: The Life of Thomas Griffiths Wainewright* (London: Thomas Nelson, 1938).

4 Florence Farr, *The Dancing Faun* (London: E. Mathews and J. Lane, 1894). The eleventh of Mathews and Lane's Keynotes novels, but the author's first book. A well-observed satire of the Aesthetes, it is a clever confection of Wildean aesthetic ideas, with many passages written very much in the voice of his dialogues in *Intentions*.

5 Walter Pater, *Studies in the History of the Renaissance* (London: Macmillan, 1873). Of the 'Conclusion', as printed in the first edition, Pater wrote 'I conceived it might possibly have misled some of those young men into whose hands it might fall.' He omitted the passage from the new edition of 1877, but rewrote it entirely for the third edition of 1888. See Holbrook Jackson, *The Eighteen Nineties: A Review of Art and Ideas at the Close of the Nineteenth Century* (London: Grant Richards, 1913; 2nd rev. edn 1922), p. 39.

6 In a letter to Ernest Radford (n.d., *E* 80, 561n.) Wilde described Pater's *Renaissance* essays as 'the golden book of spirit and sense, the holy writ of beauty'.

7 Many of the Aesthetes attended the unveiling of the Keats memorial bust in Hampstead church in 1894. Sickert's famous sketch of Beardsley recalls the sight of the artist leaving the churchyard. Wilde's reverence for Keats was rewarded by the gift from the poet's niece, Mrs Speed, of a holograph manuscript of a Keats poem, the 'Sonnet on Blue'. This treasure hung framed at Tite Street, but disappeared in the sale of Wilde's goods in 1895 (see note 31 below). It is listed in the catalogue as lot 122, along with an etching by Whistler's disciple, Mortimer Menpes.

8 J. A. Symonds to Wilde, 1881. Quoted from a draft copy of the lost original (*E* 139).

9 Pater's phrase first used in the 'Conclusion' to his *Renaissance*, was to become the rallying call of the Aesthetic Movement.

10 'The Critic as Artist' was first published in two parts in *The Nineteenth Century*,

July and September 1890, as 'The True Function and Value of Criticism'. 'The Decay of Lying' appeared first in *The Nineteenth Century* for January 1889. Both were revised and reprinted in book form in *Intentions*, 1891. *The Picture of Dorian Gray* was first published in *Lippincott's Magazine* for July 1890. The first edition in book form, 1891 was revised and contained six extra chapters.

11 See Charles Ricketts, *Journals*, 7 July 1903 (MS British Library). The phrase comes from an entry recalling a remark made by the French portrait painter Jacques Emil Blanche. I quote it in full in Stephen Calloway, *Charles Ricketts: Subtle and Fantastic Decorator* (London: Thames and Hudson, 1979), p. 10.

12 Wilde's description was remembered by William Rothenstein in his memoirs, *Men and Memories 1872–1900* (London: Faber and Faber, 1931).

13 The lecture was first delivered at Chickering Hall, New York. First published in the *New York Tribune*, 10 Jan. 1882.

14 Subsequently reprinted in the collected editions as *House Decoration*.

15 J. McN. Whistler, *Mr Whistler's 'Ten O'Clock'*, 1888, p. 23. Whistler first delivered the lecture in London on 20 Feb. 1882, but only printed the text as a pamphlet in 1888.

16 The French text was published in 1893, the English translation with illustrations by Beardsley in 1894.

17 *The Sphinx* was printed in green, red and black with illustrations and a sumptuous gold-blocked, vellum binding all designed by Ricketts. Published in 1894 at a high price it sold slowly, and many unsold copies were destroyed in a warehouse fire at the printers, the Ballantyne Press, thereby making the book extremely rare.

18 W. B. Yeats, 'The Tragic Generation', in *The Trembling of the Veil* (London: T. Werner Laurie, 1922), reprinted in *Autobiographies* (London: Macmillan, 1955), p. 302.

19 Richard Le Gallienne, *The Romantic Nineties* (London: G. P. Putnam's Sons, 1926), p. 12.

20 Arthur Symons, 'The Decadent Movement in Literature', in *Harper's New Monthly Magazine*, Nov. 1893. Quoted in Holbrook Jackson, *The Eighteen Nineties* (1913) p. 57.

21 W. B. Yeats, 'The Tragic Generation', p. 317.

22 Rudyard Kipling, 'The Mary Gloster', in *The Seven Seas* (London: Methuen, 1896), p. 148.

23 Jules Barbey d'Aurevilly, *Du Dandyisme, et de George Brummell*, 1845. First issued in an edition of only thirty copies by the Caen printer, Mancel. Almost simultaneously a more conventional Parisian edition was published by Ledoyer, with a reissue in 1861. The best English translation is that by D. B. Wyndham-Lewis, illustrated by Hermine David, and published by Peter Davis, 1928.

24 William Gaunt, *The Aesthetic Adventure* (London: Jonathan Cape, 1945), p. 114.

25 Arthur Symons (trans.), *Charles Baudelaire: Les fleurs du mal, Poèmes en prose, Les paradis artificiels* (Casanova Society edition, 1925), p. ii.

26 *Dorian Gray* was bound in pale grey with a pattern of flowers; Gray's *Silverpoints* (1893), its publication sponsored by Wilde, had a green cloth binding with a formal pattern of tiny flame-like leaves 'powdering' the cover.

27 Charles Baudelaire, 'The Painter of Modern Life', in *The Painter of Modern Life*

and Other Essays, trans. and ed. Jonathan Mayne (New York: Da Capo Press, 1964), p. 29.

28 John Davidson, *The Wonderful Mission of Earl Lavender, which Lasted One Day and One Night* (London: Ward and Downey, 1895).

29 Quoted in R. K. R. Thornton, *Poetry of the Nineties* (Harmondsworth: Penguin, 1970), p. 225.

30 J. K. Huysmans (trans. Robert Baldick), *Against Nature* (Harmondsworth: Penguin, 1959), quoted in Introduction, p. 21.

31 '16, Tite Street, Chelsea. Catalogue of the Library of Valuable Books, Pictures, Portraits of Celebrities ... Household Furniture ... Old Blue-and-White China ... which will be sold by Auction, By Mr Bullock, on the Premises, On Wednesday, April 24th, 1895, at One O'Clock...'.

32 Liberty's Oriental Warehouse and Bazaar had been opened in Regent's Street by Arthur Lazenby Liberty. Early customers included Gabriel Rossetti and other artists; however, by this later period the store had become more populist in its artistic stance.

33 Walter Hamilton, *The Aesthetic Movement in England* (London: Reeves and Turner, 1882). Hamilton in this key early examination of the wider Aesthetic Movement devotes 26 of his 127 pages to Wilde. In a MS draft of the preface to the third (?) edition (Author's Collection) Hamilton states that 'to Lady Wilde I am greatly indebted for the very complete account I am enabled to offer to [*sic*] the career of her son, Mr Oscar Wilde, about whom, at present, considerable curiosity exists, both at home and in the United States'.

34 Hamilton, *The Aesthetic Movement*, p. 99.

35 Quoted by Vincent O'Sullivan in *Aspects of Wilde* (London: Constable and Co., 1936) and see Henry Maas, J. L. Duncan and W. G. Good (eds.), *The Letters of Aubrey Beardsley* (London: Cassell, 1971), p. 377, n. 1.

II
WILDE'S WORKS

4

KARL BECKSON AND BOBBY FONG

Wilde as poet

Though Oscar Wilde has usually been regarded as an Aesthete or Decadent whose devotion to art for art's sake was immutable, in fact he never adhered rigidly to such a doctrine. From the beginning of his career, he wrote poems as a conventional Victorian, expressing moral, political and religious attitudes expected in serious art. His concern with the cultural crises of the time found expression in much of his early verse written during and after his Oxford years (1874–8) – that is, before he turned his attention to the nature of art in advancing the Aesthetic Movement. But even while rejecting the Victorian notion of art as moral edification, Wilde could not sustain his aestheticism, for he was driven by the conviction, drawn from such disparate figures as Baudelaire, Ruskin, Pater and Whistler, that life and art were ultimately shaped by one's moral and spiritual nature. Inevitably, the tension between his avowed aestheticism and his Victorian sensibility resulted in contradictions throughout his work, as summed up in the title of Norbert Kohl's study: *Oscar Wilde: The Works of a Conformist Rebel* (1989). Indeed, Wilde expressed his own position in his essay 'The Truth of Masks' in *Intentions* (1891): 'A Truth in art is that whose contradictory is also true' (*CW* 1173).

A significant early focus of Wilde's poetic impulses occurred when he visited Italy in the summer of 1875. Already attracted to Roman Catholicism, he wrote a number of religious poems, such as 'San Miniato', in which he describes his ascent (physical and spiritual) to the twelfth-century church on one of the hills overlooking Florence. Measuring his own life by that of the pure Virgin and implying a parallel between the crucified Christ and the Romantic image of the martyred artist, he apostrophises:

> O crowned by God with thorns and pain!
> Mother of Christ! O mystic wife!
> My heart is weary of this life ...[1] (*CW* 749)

After this address to the Virgin, the poem closes with the suggestive cry directed to her for help (the 'sun' perhaps an allusion to *her* Son):

> O listen ere the searching sun
> Show to the world my sin and shame.

In another poem, 'Rome Unvisited', Wilde regards his journey to Italy as a 'pilgrimage' (curtailed because of lack of funds), and he envisions Rome as a 'Blessed Lady, who dost hold / Upon the seven hills thy reign!'. His great joy before he dies will be to see the Pope – the 'only God-appointed King' and 'gentle Shepherd of the Fold' – borne in procession, 'A triumph as He passes by!'.

The hope of celebrating Easter Sunday (on 1 April 1877) in the Holy City by seeing the Pope also informs 'Sonnet on Approaching Italy' (*CW* 768), which passionately invokes an image burning in the speaker's soul when he reaches the Alps: 'Italia, my Italia ...'. Before departing for Italy, Wilde had written to an Oxford friend: 'This is an era in my life, a crisis. I wish I could look into the seeds of time and see what is coming' (*L* 34). The knowledge that, in the Vatican, Pope Pius IX, who now regarded himself as 'imprisoned' because of his refusal to recognise the united kingdom of Italy (achieved in 1870), impels Wilde to conclude his sonnet: 'In evil bonds a second Peter lay, / I wept to see the land so very fair', the image of 'The prisoned shepherd of the Church of God' reappearing in 'Urbs Sacra Aeterna'. Already, however, Wilde had decided to accompany his former Trinity College tutor, J. P. Mahaffy, to Greece, a decision that would lead to a gradual waning of interest in Roman Catholicism and a growing enthusiasm for things Greek. Unable to be in the Holy City on Easter Sunday, Wilde wrote 'Sonnet Written in Holy Week at Genoa', which recalls the death of Jesus during Holy Week. But 'those dear Hellenic hours' (looked forward to after his sojourn in Italy) drown 'all memory of Thy bitter pain, / The Cross, the Crown, the Soldiers, and the Spear'.

Ancient Greece – its culture uncontaminated by later medievalism, which for Wilde impeded the full development of personality – is depicted in the sonnet 'The Theatre at Argos' as a lost relic of the past, the site of its dramatic achievements at Argos now overgrown by nettles and poppies (Wilde's choice of the latter flowers implying the forgetfulness in the modern world that such a glorious civilisation had once existed):

> No poet crowned with olive deathlessly
> Chants his glad song, nor clamorous Tragedy
> Startles the air ...   (*CW* 770)

Greece is now a 'shipwreck on the rocks of Time', the present now 'full of plague and sin and crime, / And God Himself is half-dethroned for Gold!'.[2] Such moral edification reveals Wilde still immersed in the conventional view that art should be instructive.

Not generally known as a pastoral poet, throughout his career Wilde wrote a number of poems with Greek mythological and pastoral settings: in 'Theocritus: A Villanelle', he bows to the founder of the pastoral tradition in a French fixed form for light verse, the villanelle derived from the pastoral (*villa* meaning a country house or farm). In 'Theocritus' (*CW* 795), Wilde alludes to such figures as Persephone (the wife of Hades) and Amaryllis (a conventional name for a shepherdess in such poems), to whom the question becomes a thematic refrain: 'Dost thou remember Sicily?' Though the Sicilian-born Theocritus had depicted actual shepherds, as the pastoral tradition developed poets increasingly regarded the earlier pastoral world as a utopia, hence the question asked in Wilde's poem as though he yearned to recapture the irretrievable past.

In the late nineteenth century, pastoral was a means of contrasting the glowing Classical past with the sordid industrial present. In 'The Song of the Happy Shepherd', W. B. Yeats sounds a familiar note: 'The woods of Arcady are dead, / And over is their antique joy', but Elizabeth Barrett Browning sounded a different note in 'The Dead Pan', which celebrated the sacrificial death of Christ, who ended the 'vain false gods of Hellas'. In 'Pan: Double Villanelle', Wilde, like Yeats, laments the passing of the mythic world:

> O Goat-foot God of Arcady!
> This modern world is grey and old,
> Ah what remains to us of Thee?

To redeem the modern world, Wilde calls upon Pan, the pre-Christian god now fallen into decay, but the introduction of the Puritan Milton seems a jarring association:

> This is the land where liberty
> Lit grave-browed Milton on his way,
> This modern world hath need of Thee!   (*CW* 854)

Pastoral elements inform several of the longer poems, such as portions of 'Ravenna' (awarded the Newdigate Prize at Oxford), a poetic evocation of the ancient city where Dante ('O mightiest exile') is entombed ('Long time I watched, and surely hoped to see / Some goat-foot Pan make merry minstrelsy ...'). 'Charmides' (*CW* 797–813) also has passages evoking pastoral scenes ('And soon the shepherd in rough woollen cloak / With his long crook undid the wattled cotes'), and 'The Burden of Itys' (*CW* 786–95) introduces the myth of Philomel, whose 'throbbing throat' the speaker once heard on 'starlit hills of flower-starred Arcady'. In addition to Greek pastoral themes, 'Panthea' (*CW* 830–4) has echoes of Pater ('This hot hard flame with which our bodies burn') and Wordsworth ('How my heart leaps up / To think of that grand living after death / In beast and bird and flower', which inspires Wilde to borrow further: 'New splendour come unto the flower, new glory to the grass'). 'The Garden of Eros' (*CW* 844–51) depicts the speaker's imaginative life in the modern world informed by the myths of the past:

> And I will cut a reed by yonder spring
> And make the wood-gods jealous, and old Pan
> Wonder what young intruder dares to sing
> In these still haunts . . .

While the 'Spirit of Beauty' (Shelley's phrase from 'Ode to Intellectual Beauty') remains, the speaker calls upon it to 'tarry still a-while, / They are not dead, thine ancient votaries . . .'. Thus, Wilde evokes the spirit of Keats, Byron, Swinburne and Morris, whose genius can restore Beauty to the ugliness of the modern world.

Though 'In the Forest' (1889) (*CW* 874) – which captures the flashing vision of a faun, who 'skips through the copses singing' as 'his shadow dances along / And I know not which I should follow, / Shadow or song!' – was believed to be Wilde's final pastoral poem, a recently discovered manuscript titled 'The Faithful Shepherd' (written around 1892) reveals the enduring attractions of artifice and lyricism.[3] Wilde wrote it for a new acquaintance, the composer John Mais Capel, who, he apparently hoped, would set the poem to music, hence the use of a roundelay (a short simple song with recurring refrains) to express the lover's yearning for Phillis, his absent love:

> Phillis, Phillis, come my way,
> And I'll sing a roundelay,
> Roundelay, a roundelay,
> I will sing a roundelay.

At the same time that religious and Classical preoccupations informed his early verse, Wilde was schooling himself in the Pre-Raphaelite painters and poets, as revealed in his earliest poem touched by their influence: 'La Bella Donna della mia Mente' (*CW* 773–4), 'The Beautiful Lady of My Memory', is inspired by the late-medieval phenomenon of courtly love, involving the secret veneration by a knight of a high-born 'Lady'.[4] For models, Wilde had at hand the Pre-Raphaelite verse of Swinburne, Rossetti and William Morris, who had made use of such conventions. Wilde's diction in his poem adopts the archaic language of 'thy' and 'passeth', suitable to the setting.

The courtly lover's suffering in Wilde's lyric – 'My limbs are wasted with a flame' – suggests the speaker's unrequited passion, as suggested in 'Her little lips, more made to kiss / Than to cry bitterly for pain' (borrowed from Morris's 'Praise of My Lady': 'Her full lips being made to kiss'). Swinburnian echoes also appear (as they frequently do in Wilde's other early verse): 'O delicate / White body made for love and pain!'. And, completing the Pre-Raphaelite triumvirate, Rossetti's sonnet sequence in *The House of Life* provides further inspiration to Wilde, who writes: 'O House of love! O desolate / Pale flower beaten by the rain!'.

Another of Wilde's poems touched by Pre-Raphaelite influences is 'The Dole of The King's Daughter' (*CW* 755–6), the title drawn from Swinburne's 'The King's Daughter', the world of the poem again constructed from the triumvirate: the opening, for example, of Wilde's poem echoes the opening lines of Rossetti's 'The Blessed Damozel' ('And the stars in her hair were seven'): 'Seven stars in the still water, / And seven in the sky'. The dole (archaic for *grief*) of the king's daughter results from the death of the 'knight who lieth slain / Amid the rush and reed'. Indeed, she has sent seven knights to their graves ('The sins on her soul are seven'), for, in the convention of courtly love, they have fought bravely to demonstrate their love of the king's daughter.

The thematic variation in Wilde's early verse extended to political concerns dating from 1876, when he was moved by the atrocities against Christians in the Balkans, where the Slavs rebelled against Turkish rule. In the following year, he wrote 'Sonnet on the Massacre of the Christians in Bulgaria' (*CW* 771), modelled after Milton's 'On the Late Massacre in Piedmont'. After calling upon Christ to intervene ('Come down, O Son of God!'), Wilde laments: 'Over thy Cross a Crescent moon I see!' (the triumph of Islam); hence, the sestet concludes with a further plea to Christ 'to show thy might, / Lest Mahomet be crowned instead of Thee!'

Closer to home, 'To Milton' (*CW* 774) expresses a theme that appears in Wilde's poems in the late 1870s: England has lost its moral stature, Wilde's response to the government's reluctance to intervene in the Balkan crisis of 1876–8. Wilde, no doubt, had Wordsworth's 'London, 1802' in mind ('Milton! Thou shouldst be living at this hour'): 'Milton! I think thy spirit hath passed away / From these white cliffs …' 'Quantum Mutata' (*CW* 773–4), 'How Much Changed', echoes 'To Milton' in lamenting England's decline:

> There was a time in Europe long ago
>   When no man died for freedom anywhere,
>   But England's lion leaping from its lair
> Laid hands on the oppressor!

'Such high estate' in the past has been perverted by crass commercialism ('barren merchandise'), presumably an allusion to the British Empire in a land where 'noble thoughts and deeds' should prevail; if they had, Englishmen would 'still be Milton's heritors'.

Despite such poems written during the Balkan crisis, Wilde, by 1880, was writing with praise of England's initiative in its war with Afghanistan (1878–80) to counteract Russian expansionism: 'Ave Imperatrix' (CW 851–4) – 'Hail Empress' alluding to Queen Victoria's official recognition in 1877 as 'Empress of India' – hails England 'Before whose feet the worlds divide' and whom 'The treacherous Russian knows so well'. Later in the poem, Wilde expresses grief over the price that war exacts: 'Down in some treacherous black ravine, / Clutching his flag, the dead boy lies' – to be buried, like other English soldiers, 'not in quiet English fields' but throughout the Empire. Nevertheless, 'Up the steep road must England go' to advance the political ideal of republicanism, which will 'Rise from these crimson seas of war'. Thus, as though assuming the role of poet laureate, Wilde celebrates England's noble mission.

The image and status of the poet in the past, as contrasted with the present, had always absorbed Wilde. Christian martyrs (Jesus, whom Wilde regarded in his prison letter, De Profundis, as 'the close union of personality with perfection', hence 'the true precursor of the romantic movement') progressively became fused with images of the martyred artist, as in 'The Grave of Keats' (CW 770–1), inspired by Wilde's visit to the Protestant Cemetery in Rome. Keats – 'The youngest of the Martyrs' – is paralleled to St Sebastian 'and as early slain' (Sebastian, the favourite saint of late nineteenth-century homosexuals, was the source of Wilde's pseudonym, 'Sebastian Melmoth', adopted after his release from prison). In 'Sonnet. On the Sale by Auction of Keats' Love Letters' (CW 870–1), Wilde criticises the Sotheby sale of letters written by the doomed poet to Fanny Brawne:

> And now the brawlers of the auction mart
> Bargain and bid for each poor blotted note,
> Ay! for each separate pulse of passion quote
> The merchant's price ...

The sestet compares this bartering to an earlier sacrilege:

> Is it not said that many years ago,
> In a far Eastern town, some soldiers ran
> With torches through the midnight, and began
> To wrangle for mean raiment, and to throw
> Dice for the garments of a wretched man,
> Not knowing the God's wonder, or His woe?

In another sonnet, 'The Grave of Shelley' (*CW* 775–6), also inspired by his visit to the Protestant Cemetery, Wilde sought less direct expression than that in 'The Grave of Keats': suggestive images of death associated with the grave and with the sea, which ended Shelley's life, achieve greater effectiveness than the more discursive poem on Keats: thus, 'Gaunt cypress-trees stand round the sun-bleached stone', the image of the 'womb / Of Earth' leading to the fateful sea:

> But sweeter far for thee a restless tomb
> In the blue cavern of an echoing deep,
> Or where the tall ships founder in the gloom
> Against the rocks of some wave-shattered steep.

In the introductory sonnet to *Poems* (1881), in which many of the poems discussed above appear, 'Hélas!' (*CW* 864) expresses his devotion to Keats's view of experience (in a letter, Keats wrote to a friend: 'O for a Life of Sensations rather than of Thoughts') and to the 'Conclusion' to *Studies in the History of the Renaissance* (1873), in which Pater urges readers 'to be for ever curiously testing new opinions and courting new impressions' – which Wilde adapted for Lord Henry Wotton's advice to Dorian Gray in chapter 2: 'Be always searching for new sensations.'

In 'Hélas!', Wilde begins with an anti-Victorian attitude towards any moral purpose in life: 'To drift with every passion till my soul / Is a stringed lute on which all winds can play . . .'. However, surrender to a mere life of sensations, the speaker concludes, may incur the loss of 'ancient wisdom and austere control'. Ambivalence thus informs the sonnet, and eroticism is implied in Wilde's transformation of Jonathan's disobedience in 1 Samuel 14:43, which Pater had quoted (in 2 Samuel 1:26, David refers to his relationship with Jonathan as 'passing the love of women', which Wilde does not mention). Wilde adds the word *romance* to the biblical passage: '. . . lo! with a little rod / I did but touch the honey of romance – / And must I lose a soul's inheritance?'. As Richard Ellmann remarks, though Wilde 'practised self-indulgence, it was never without remorse' (*E* 133).

Wilde's wish to associate himself with the major poets of the nineteenth century not only indicated his aspirations but also determined the theme and structure of many of his poems. When he was asked by the librarian of the Oxford Union Society for a presentation copy of his *Poems* (1881), he sent one signed, but when the Union met, one of its members (Oliver Elton, later a literary historian) wittily condemned it as a pastiche of other poets' works:

> It is not that these poems are thin – and they *are* thin: it is not that they are immoral – and they *are* immoral . . . it is that they are for the most part not by their putative father at all, but by a number of better-known and more

deservedly reputed authors. They are in fact by William Shakespeare, by Philip Sidney, by John Donne, by Lord Byron, by William Morris, by Algernon Swinburne, and by sixty more ...   (E 140)

For many years, the charge of plagiarism haunted the young poet despite the promise of better things to come. In his reliance on those poets whose achievements provided him with models, Wilde had endeavoured unsuccessfully to develop a distinctive personal voice (perhaps, as Harold Bloom has suggested, the anxiety of influence was not sufficiently strong for Wilde to break with some of his predecessors).[5] Nevertheless, *Poems* did, in fact, contain several lyrics that revealed Wilde's response, in the 1870s, to avant-garde French Impressionism as well as Whistler's visionary paintings, both of which had an extensive influence on late nineteenth-century poets. For example, in 'Impression du Matin', which recalls Claude Monet's innovative painting *Impression – Sunrise*, Wilde suggests the transforming effects of light in Impressionistic painting and uses such musical terms as *nocturne* and *harmony* from Whistler's titles to focus on the artifice of art and its colour harmonies rather than on the 'message':

> The Thames nocturne of blue and gold
> Changed to a Harmony in grey:
> A barge with ochre-coloured hay
> Dropt from the wharf: and chill and cold
>
> The yellow fog came creeping down
> The bridges ...   (CW 862)

Despite such avant-garde impulses, Wilde could not sustain them throughout the poem for, in the final stanza, a prostitute appears, loitering beneath a street lamp. The attitude expressed in the final line is precisely what a conventional Victorian reader would expect – indeed, demand – as moral judgement of this streetwalker, a fallen woman devoid of the capacity for love: 'With lips of flame and heart of stone'.

In 'Impressions: I. Les Silhouettes; II. La Fuite de la Lune', Wilde focuses on fleeting impressions, such as the moon 'blown across the stormy bay' like a 'withered leaf'. In the second part, the final stanza depicts only the image of the moon, anticipating early twentieth-century Imagist verse:

> And suddenly the moon withdraws
> Her sickle from the lightening skies,
> And to her sombre cavern flies,
> Wrapped in a veil of yellow gauze.

Borrowing the term *le réveillon* from painting, in which, like the Italian term *chiaroscuro*, a dramatic touch of light in darkness highlights a scene, Wilde's 'Impression: Le Réveillon' (*CW* 864) depicts the effect of dawn on the 'circling mists' and the fleeting shadows, the 'long wave of yellow light' breaking 'silently on tower and hall'. The final line of this three-stanza lyric presents the light's effect on the chestnut trees: 'And all the branches streaked with gold'. These poems draw no conclusions (as do many Romantic poems) on the effect of nature on the speaker's moral or spiritual development; rather, the making of images, not uplifting messages, is presumed to be the poet's art.

In 'Impression de Voyage' (*CW* 869), the French Impressionist term in the title appears misplaced, for, in establishing a mythological setting, Wilde abandons any attempt at depicting 'impressions'; instead, he describes a voyage to Greece, a return to the world of the 'flower-strewn hills of Arcady'. Thus, the title misleads, for a description of the voyage (including the 'ripple of girls' laughter at the stern') supersedes the effect of briefly experienced fleeting images. In the final line – 'I stood upon the soil of Greece at last!' – the speaker experiences an imaginative voyage, as opposed to the physical voyage, into the mythological past.

Though Whistler was an inspiration to Wilde, Théophile Gautier also provided him with models: Wilde's 'Symphony in Yellow' (1889) owes something to Gautier's 'Symphonie en Blanc Majeur', which Wilde called 'that flawless masterpiece of colour and music' (*CW* 1147). Both poems employ the transposition of art – that is, the fusion of the arts to emphasise artifice with suggestions of synaesthesia. Perhaps Wilde's purest poem in this genre, 'Symphony in Yellow' (*CW* 872–3) also focuses on the pervasive colour named in the title associated with various images, including the fog as depicted in 'Impression du Matin'. In the concluding stanza of this brief lyric, Wilde pictures yellow leaves beginning 'to fade / And flutter from the Temple elms'; then, in a striking line again anticipating Imagist verse, he presents a hard, clear image of the 'pale, green Thames', which lies at his feet 'like a rod of rippled jade'.

In 'The Harlot's House' (1885) (*CW* 867), desire lacks the innocence of love, for the setting is urban and lust its domain. The 'loud musicians' within the house are playing 'Treues Liebes Herz' ('Heart of True Love', the composition attributed to 'Strauss' by Wilde but apparently a misattribution). The irony of their music is counterpointed by the imagery drawn from Gautier and Baudelaire:

> Like strange mechanical grotesques,
> Making fantastic arabesques,
> The shadows raced across the blind.

The 'ghostly dancers' are like 'wire-pulled automatons, / Slim silhouetted skeletons' engaging in a 'slow quadrille'. The speaker remarks to his loved one: 'The dead are dancing with the dead ...' French Decadence, with its focus on artifice and on the bizarre, is the principal inspiration here. But the loved one, hearing the lure of the violin, leaves him; at this point, the Victorian propensity to allegory is evident when Wilde departs from the vividness of the scene to the abstract: 'Love passed into the house of Lust.' Suddenly, the tune goes false, and the dancers weary of the waltz, the poem ending with a questionable simile:

> And down the long and silent street,
> The dawn with silver-sandalled feet,
> Crept like a frightened girl.

The obvious morality of the poem again reveals Wilde's difficulty in adhering to *l'art pour l'art*.[6]

Like 'The Harlot's House', *The Sphinx* (CW 874–82) (substantially completed in the 1880s but published in 1894) is also touched by nineteenth-century French literary Decadence in its exoticism; its lavish, arcane diction (borrowing such terms, for example, from Flaubert's *La tentation de Saint-Antoine* as 'tragelaphos', a fabulous beast, and 'oreichalch', gilded copper or brass alloy); and its depiction of a lascivious Sphinx. Begun while Wilde was still a student at Oxford, the poem underwent sporadic rewriting until its publication. Unusual in its structure, the poem consists of 174 iambic lines with eight stresses, each stanza of two lines containing internal rhymes (in an early draft, Wilde had used Tennyson's stanzaic form of *In Memoriam*, then stretched out the lines of the quatrains into couplets).[7]

In the poem, a student, addressing his statue of a Sphinx, fantasises its loves and its triumphs: 'Who were your lovers? who were they who wrestled for you in the dust? / Which was the vessel of your lust? what leman had you, every day?' But growing weary of the Sphinx's history, the student, touched by the fabulous beast's erotic past, arouses himself: 'You make my creed a barren sham, you wake foul dreams of sensual life ... / False Sphinx! False Sphinx! ... leave me to my Crucifix ...' This lengthy poem indulges in such extended sexual fantasies, self-induced by the student, that his rejection of the Sphinx appears to be merely conventional to assure Victorian readers of his moral probity.

In 1892, Wilde's sonnet 'The New Remorse' (CW 871) (previously published under a different title in 1887) appeared in the Oxford *Spirit Lamp*, edited by Lord Alfred Douglas, who proceeded to give the periodical a homosexual orientation. The speaker in the sonnet acknowledges his sin but conceals its nature in the opening line: 'The sin was mine; I did not understand.' The suggestive line 'So now is music prisoned in her cave' reveals the necessity of concealment, which readers of the *Spirit Lamp* would presumably grasp. The sestet shifts to biblical diction – indeed, echoing Isaiah 63:1 – as though to suggest the speaker's reaction to the possibility of salvation, although eroticism undermines the sacred moment:

> But who is this who cometh by the shore?
> (Nay, love, look up and wonder!) Who is this
> Who cometh in dyed garments from the South?
> It is thy new-found Lord, and he shall kiss
> The yet unravished roses of thy mouth ...   (CW 883–9)

It was, of course, the loss of that concealment that brought Wilde, at the height of his fame in 1895, first to trial and then to prison.

Wilde's best-known poem, *The Ballad of Reading Gaol* (1898), inspired by his two-year imprisonment, is his most didactic work, one that emerged from the clash of various styles, as he himself said: 'The poem suffers under the difficulty of a divided aim in style. Some is realistic, some is romantic: some poetry, some propaganda' (*L* 654). Nevertheless, its force remains undisputed, and its skill in telling the story of the last days of a Royal Horse Guards trooper who killed his wife and who was sentenced to hang evokes the central theme of this deeply felt poem, which echoes Wilde's own self-destruction: 'The man had killed the thing he loved, / And so he had to die.' The autobiographical element is made clear in Wilde's pun on his own name and society's exposure of Wilde's own double life – the successful married writer leading the subterranean life of a homosexual:

> And the wild regrets, and the bloody sweats,
> None knew so well as I:
> For he who lives more lives than one
> More deaths than one must die.

His imprisonment was, indeed, a symbolic death, and his resurrection occurred in this final poem, a confessional of which Arthur Symons wrote: 'We see a great spectacular intellect, to which, at last, pity and terror have come in their own person, and no longer as puppets in a play.'[8]

NOTES

1   See *Poems and Poems in Prose*, ed. Bobby Fong and Karl Beckson, vol. IV of *The Complete Works of Oscar Wilde*, general editors Russell Jackson and Ian Small (Oxford: Oxford University Press, forthcoming).

2   For further discussion of this poem, see Bobby Fong, 'Oscar Wilde: Five Fugitive Poems', *English Literature in Transition, 1880–1920* 22:1 (1979), 8–9.

3 For a further discussion of this poem, see Karl Beckson and Bobby Fong, 'A Newly Discovered Lyric by Oscar Wilde', *Times Literary Supplement*, 17 Feb. 1995, p. 9.

4 See, especially, the chapters titled 'The Knights' and 'The Ladies' in Maurice Valency's *In Praise of Love* (1958; rpt. New York: Schocken Books, 1982).

5 In *The Anxiety of Influence: A Theory of Poetry* (London: Oxford University Press, 1973), Harold Bloom contends that Wilde, 'who knew he had failed as a poet because he lacked strength to overcome his anxiety of influence, knew also the darker truths concerning influence. *The Ballad of Reading Gaol* becomes an embarrassment to read, directly one recognizes that every lustre it exhibits is reflected from *The Rime of the Ancient Mariner*; and Wilde's lyrics anthologize the whole of English High Romanticism' (pp. 5–6).

6 For further discussion, see Bobby Fong, 'Wilde's "The Harlot's House"', *Explicator* 48 (Spring 1990), 198–201. See also J. D. Thomas, 'The Composition of Wilde's "The Harlot's House"', *Modern Language Notes* 65 (Nov. 1950), 485–8.

7 For further discussion, see Isobel Murray, 'Some Problems of Editing Wilde's Poem *The Sphinx*', *Durham University Journal* 51 (Jan. 1990), 73–9.

8 Arthur Symons's review of the poem in the *Saturday Review* (12 March 1898) is reprinted in Karl Beckson (ed.), *Oscar Wilde: The Critical Heritage* (London: Routledge and Kegan Paul, 1970), pp. 218–21. See also William Buckler, 'Oscar Wilde's "*chant de cygne*": *The Ballad of Reading Gaol* in Contextual Perspective', *Victorian Poetry* 28 (Autumn/Winter 1990), 33–41.

5

JOHN STOKES

Wilde the journalist

Between March 1885 and May 1890 Oscar Wilde wrote more than seventy unsigned book reviews for W. T. Stead's *Pall Mall Gazette*, between November 1887 and June 1889 he was editor of *The Woman's World*, and throughout the late 1880s he contributed a number of pieces, some signed, some not, to other newspapers and journals.[1]

It may seem surprising that one of the world's great literary stylists should have produced so much anonymous material. Today we would probably assume that anything written by Wilde would be instantly recognisable, but in the 1880s, when he was making his living as a professional journalist, one among many, not only was anonymity the general rule,[2] the famous style had yet to become a badge of personality. That everyone now knows, or thinks they know, what constitutes the 'Wildean' is partly the result of more than a century's familiarity with his writings and with countless imitators. Once a style can be recognised it can also be copied.

There are signs nevertheless that Wilde saw anonymous journalism as a way of mapping out his personal literary territory, even if the hidden pattern can sometimes look like a maze. He certainly did not confine himself to a limited number of favourite topics. Indeed, it was one of the requirements of the kind of reviewer that Wilde aspired to become that he or she should be able to write on a wide range of subjects. From romantic novels to cookbooks, from every kind of translation to musicology: Wilde took pride in attempting the unlikely. His intellectual curiosity was more wide-ranging than has sometimes been assumed.

The journalism reveals, for example, that he had a considerable enthu-siasm for Russian literature. On 2 May 1887 he contributed to the *Pall Mall Gazette* an anonymous review of Dostoevsky's novel *Injury and Insult*, remarking: 'Some time ago we had occasion to draw attention to his marvellous novel *Crime and Punishment*.' The review goes on to recall the moment in *Crime and Punishment* when, 'in the haunt of impurity and vice a harlot and an assassin meet together to read the story of Lazarus and

Dives, and the outcast girl leads the sinner to make atonement for his sin' (*Reviews* 158). An anonymous review of *Crime and Punishment* published on 28 May 1886 again describes how 'in the haunt of impurity and sin, the harlot and the assassin meet together to read the story of Lazarus and Dives'. Yet although this earlier review is obviously by Wilde it is not included by Robert Ross in the *Collected Edition*,[3] perhaps because he simply did not know about it, or perhaps because he felt it too close to the second review, and did not want to bore or cheat the purchaser of the new edition. Or perhaps he wanted to protect Wilde from a charge of self-plagiarism that was certainly deserved.

The distinctiveness of Wilde's admiration for Dostoevsky remains difficult to evaluate since he seems not to have been the only contributor to the *Pall Mall Gazette* with an interest in Russian novels. On 10 February 1887 the paper published another review of *Injury and Insult* that does not sound particularly like Wilde. (We now know what Wilde sounds like when he is writing on Dostoevsky.) Then on 23 February 1888 it carried a piece entitled 'Russian Peasant Life', a review of a French book on Russian novelists, Turgenev in particular, that might well be by Wilde; not least because it contains some sharp remarks about Zola (about whom Wilde was never complimentary), and makes the comparison between Zola and Dostoevsky that is also to be found in the two reviews that we can be certain are by him. 'Russian Peasant Life' is not, though, in the *Collected Edition*.

To take another example of possible self-reference, again not in the *Collected Edition* and attributed quite recently. On 26 July 1888 the *Pall Mall Gazette* carried an anonymous portmanteau review, headed in the usual way 'A Batch of Books', which included a reference to a novel called *The American Marquis* by Wilde's friend Robert Sherard. At the end of the piece there is what is clearly an affectionate in-joke referring to Sherard's earlier book of poems called *Whispers*: 'It is not surprising to recall that Mr Sherard is a great grandson of Wordsworth, and has come safely through "early poems", a three-volume novel, and other complaints not uncommon at his time of life.' If this piece is by Wilde, then it will stand as a good example of his talent for combining private jokes with public advertisement.

But that requires that we also believe him to have been ready to indulge in some 'log-rolling' for the benefit of his own family because, among this 'Batch of Books', there is also one by his mother, Lady Wilde: the 'cheap edition' of *Ancient Legends of Ireland*. This is hailed in uncompromising terms: 'Probably no living writer could produce a better book of its kind', although that shameless puff is, admittedly, preceded by the anonymous mock-confessional: 'It will be as well not to affect impartiality in passing an opinion on Lady Wilde's collection of Irish stories and superstitions, the first edition of which was noticed here when it appeared.' The first edition of Lady Wilde's work was reviewed on 19 February 1887. This is an extended piece devoted entirely to *Ancient Legends of Ireland*, though the scholar who believes that the later review is by Wilde thinks it unlikely that the earlier one in also by him, 'the style being fluid, simple-minded, and full of clichés'.[4] It is certainly true that sentences such as this: 'As we turn over her pages Ireland ceases to be a grim and repulsive battle ground of jarring claims, the rugged outlines of the squalid present melt in the purple of the distant past' offer a version of Irish history that it would be difficult to reconcile with Wilde (despite 'the purple of the distant past'). One could though speculate that he chose to review the later edition of his mother's book in order to correct the vulgar praise it had received on its first appearance.

Then again there are those who believe, on good scholarly grounds, that this particular review is not by Wilde at all, but by Bernard Shaw, who, of course, knew Lady Wilde himself and attended her 'At Homes'. In later life Sherard certainly seems to have assumed that the review of his novel was by Shaw. At the close of the nineteenth century games – familial, political, aesthetic – were frequently played out under the guise of anonymity. It was in any case always a dubious kind of 'anonymity' when the reviewer could confess, in however insinuating a way, to some degree of intimacy with the author under review. There could be no better demonstration of the perils and opportunities offered by anonymity than the difficulty we may now have in distinguishing between Wilde and Shaw.

Habits of self-reference and self-plagiarism reappear when Wilde is writing about women in general. 'The woman writer' (and with her, the 'woman reader') was an increasingly discussed figure in the literary worlds of the late nineteenth century. Wilde was anxious to capitalise on the phenomenon, and, prompted perhaps by the example of his mother, to demonstrate a personal interest. Admiration for women writers could be combined with his own aesthetic and political preferences. As Kate Flint has observed, mid-Victorian complaints that love of literature both threatened manliness and led women astray are 'a reminder that the issue of gendered suitability in reading contributed directly towards the maintenance of a doctrine of separate spheres'.[5] Wilde's contribution was to help in the later erosion of this doctrine by voicing his own enthusiasm for women writers and by helping in the supply of intelligent publications for the female consumer.

On taking over the editorship of *The Ladies' World* in 1887 he promptly changed the title to *The Woman's World* on the grounds that the word 'woman' signalled a more serious and responsible approach to affairs in general. He intended to 'make literary criticism one of the features ... and to give special prominence to books written by women',[6] and he was able to field a formidable array of contributors: Amy Levy (a personal friend who was to die by her own hand in 1889), Olive Schreiner, Matilde Blind, Emily Faithfull, Jane E. Harrison, 'Ouida', his own mother and his own wife. Topics covered in the magazine range from those in which Wilde himself had a strong interest such as French literature (Lamartine, Villiers de l'Isle Adam), current activity in the theatre (including, in the first issue, a piece by Lady Archibald Campbell on the Pastoral Players[7]), and the more scholarly side of fashion (including dress reform), as well as informative pieces on career opportunities for women in medicine and education and news of women's advancement in the universities. In a regular series of 'Literary and other Notes by the Editor' Wilde was free to praise and to protest as he wished.

Yet, as Laurel Brake has pointed out, his approach to the job still shares some of the widespread contradictions of the period:

> Women are constructed as serious readers who want (and need) education and acculturation. It is just these qualities rejected as unsuitable for women – a taste for triviality, dress, gossip and pleasures such as music – which are valorized in Wilde's own writing. In this value structure, men are free to be trivial; women are not; men may be useless, and women must be useful.[8]

A Max Beerbohm cartoon of the early 1890s shows Wilde being led on the one side by a female figure labelled 'Fashion' and on the other by a figure labelled 'Women's Rights' – or perhaps Beerbohm's joke is that he is not being led by women so much as being torn apart by them.[9] In any event Wilde, bored by office life rather than by his contributors, removed himself from the editor's chair after only twenty issues.[10] Had he stayed longer the problem of keeping femininity and feminism in tandem would undoubtedly have remained. It is, after all, a dilemma that faces the editor of a woman's magazine even today.

For his own part Wilde's criticism of women writers is consistently well informed: witty yet quite unpatronising. Two extended treatments of women poets are particularly impressive because they manage to provide a lengthy catalogue of names without reducing the individual writers to a dubious homogeneity. The first is a review of Mrs Sharp's anthology, *Woman's Voices*, which appeared in *The Woman's World* in November 1887 under the title 'Literary and Other Notes' attributed to the editor (*Reviews* 198–202), and the second is a longer piece which appeared under Wilde's own name, with the title 'English Poetesses', in *Queen*, 8 December 1888 (*Miscellanies* 110–20). In the *Woman's World* review Wilde corrects and adds to Mrs Sharp's selection, while in the *Queen* piece he provides his own survey of English poetesses from the fifteenth century to the present day.[11]

In both cases his unacknowledged source is, without any doubt, the

Reverend Alexander Dyce's *Specimens of British Poetesses*, published in 1827. Not only does Wilde refer to poets whom Dyce includes and whom Sharp omits, he adds remarks that come directly from Dyce. Given Wilde's predilection for creative plagiarism there is nothing unusual in this, though one might wonder who guided him to the book and provided a copy. (His mother seems a possibility.) Like any professional journalist in the late nineteenth century, a time when outlets were proliferating, Wilde knew that recycling made sense, though the ease with which he moves between one publication and another, and the aplomb with which he writes about women poets overall, is unusually deft. It may be the case that most of his information comes from Dyce, but it is deployed with a skill, a passion even, that could only assumed by someone who had a serious interest in the field.

Laurel Brake, who has made a special study of *The Woman's World*, describes Wilde's editorial project as 'not only the construction of the cultivated new woman but the introduction of a male homosexual discourse into female space'.[12] In retrospect it may be easier to identify the 'cultivated new woman' than 'homosexual discourse'. We may not be sure that we could recognise it in an anonymous piece, let alone demonstrate the part that it plays in the development of the 'Wildean' style. There were, of course, a number of 'little magazines' that were undoubtedly homosexual, or 'Uranian', in their manner and interests – *The Century Guild Hobby Horse* (1884–92), *The Artist* (1888–94), as well as the more notorious *Spirit Lamp* (1892–3) and *Chameleon* (1894). The kind of popular journalism represented by the *Pall Mall Gazette* was of a very different kind.

Wilde began writing for the paper at the precise moment of the 'Maiden Tribute' campaign organised by its editor W. T. Stead which, though designed to protect young girls from prostitution and abduction, resulted in a famous scandal and the new indecency laws under which Wilde himself was eventually to be prosecuted.[13] We might look for a connection between these events, and expect Wilde's journalism in some way to reflect the circumstances of its production, the public and private spheres that were now for a homosexual man inextricably involved one with the other. As Jonathan Dollimore has written:

> Wilde ... lived in terms of the discrepancy between his 'public' and 'private' selves, and took pleasure from it – from having a sexual identity elsewhere at the same time as being socially 'here'.
>
> The anarchic and the political, the anger and the boredom, are all active in Wilde's transgressive aesthetic, and most specially when the survival strategies of subordination – subterfuge, lying, evasion – are aesthetically transvalued into weapons of attack, but ever working obliquely through irony, ambiguity, miming and impersonation.[14]

It is still not clear whether these transgressive strategies in themselves constitute a 'homosexual discourse'. In the case of anonymous journalism much will depend on the topic under review and there is no doubt that Wilde chose to engage, anonymously, with issues that had long possessed homoerotic, if not necessarily 'homosexual', connotations.

On 1 December 1886 he reviewed *Essays on Poetry and Poets* by the Hon. Roden Noel. Although Noel appears neither in Ellmann's *Oscar Wilde* nor in Hart-Davis's *Letters*, he must surely have been known to Wilde. He is said to have been the first lover of John Addington Symonds, he appears as 'Case XXVII' in Havelock Ellis's *Sexual Inversion* (1897), and he wrote some astonishingly frank confessional poetry. According to one scholar of gay history he 'had a patrician indifference to homosexual self-justification'.

> What he enjoyed most was for young men or women to express admiration for him physically; and if he was bold in pursuing this pleasure he may not have been otherwise sexually aggressive. Walt Whitman's creed of democracy through adhesiveness suited him well, and he was among the earliest of Englishmen to write at any length on *Leaves of Grass*, which he did in *The Dark Blue* in 1871 ... In a large part of his published work there seems to be a consistent ambivalent glow, suggesting that here was a man, happily married and with a family, who throughout adult life was beset strongly by both homosexual and heterosexual feelings.[15]

Wilde's review of Noel's essays is lukewarm (Noel is said to have 'a passion for panegyric'), and the reason is clear. Noel had included studies of two of Wilde's most cherished heroes: Thomas Chatterton and John Keats. Wilde takes issue with the modernisation of Chatterton's spelling ('Chatterton's archaisms are an essential part of his inspiration and method'), and complains that Noel's book 'tells us far more about his own personal feelings than it does about the qualities of the various works of art that are criticised' (*Reviews* 117). Chatterton was very much in Wilde's mind at this time and in its October issue *The Century Guild Hobby Horse* had promised an essay by him on the poet. This never appeared, though Wilde did manage to lecture on Chatterton at Birkbeck College on 24 November, where he stood 'with his hands in his pockets and a lily in his button-hole negligently leaning against a table'.[16] The manuscript notes for this lecture have survived. They begin with the assertion that 'the conditions that precede artistic production are so constantly treated as qualities of a work of art that one is sometimes tempted to wish that all were anonymous', and continue with a comparison between Chatterton and Keats.[17] The manuscript is then made up of long passages from published biographies of Chatterton (including those which Roden Noel made use of). It also includes a sonnet addressed to Chatterton which ends with an apostrophe to 'thy grave unknown / And love-dream of thine unrecorded face', which is quite literally true as there are no known portraits of the poet.

In fact this sonnet is not by Wilde, but by Dante Gabriel Rossetti. Presumably Wilde indicated as much when he gave the lecture and would have done so had he published it as an essay.[18] Rossetti's identification with Chatterton was one that Wilde was happy to share because it depended on a Romantic way of thinking about poets and about poetry – remote, inspirational, strangely beautiful – that had lasted throughout the nineteenth century. Given his deep admiration for Chatterton it is not surprising that Wilde should have been irritated by Roden Noel's treatment. He also disliked Noel's account of Keats, remarking:

> We wonder what Keats would have thought of a critic who gravely suggests that *Endymion* is 'a parable of the development of the individual soul'. There are two ways of misunderstanding a poem. One is to misunderstand it and the other to praise it for qualities that it does not possess. (*Reviews* 117)

The proprietorial attitude to Keats was again evident when Wilde came to review, equally anonymously, two lives of the poet: one by Sidney Colvin, the other by William Rossetti, on 27 September 1887. He was unenthusiastic about both: 'Everybody pays a penalty for peeping through keyholes, and the keyhole and the backstairs are essential parts of the method of the modern biographers' (*Reviews* 182). Faced with a choice Wilde somewhat prefers Colvin, who he thinks has presented a Keats characterised by 'common-sense and gentleness', even though 'we prefer the real Keats, with his passionate wilfulness, his fantastic moods and his fine inconsistence'. William Rossetti, however, has committed 'the great mistake of separating the man from the artist. The facts of Keats's life are interesting only when they are shown in their relation to his creative activity. The moment they are isolated they are either uninteresting or painful.'

Rossetti, Wilde tells us, 'opens with a detailed account of Keats's life, in which he spares us nothing, from what he calls the "sexual misadventure at Oxford" down to the six weeks' dissipation after the appearance of the *Blackwood's* article and the hysterical and morbid ravings of the dying man' (*Reviews* 183).[19] Moreover, 'no doubt, most if not all of the things Mr Rossetti tells us are facts; but there is neither tact shown in the selection that is made of the facts nor sympathy in the use to which they are put'. In any case Wilde believes that Rossetti 'entirely lacks the temper necessary for the interpretation of such poetry as was written by John Keats' (*Reviews* 185).

This review deserves comment for several reasons. It concerns a subject that had always been close to Wilde's heart. His first article, published in

1877, had been on 'The Tomb of Keats', and he had written poems about his own greatest poetic influence. Anonymity cannot cloak this possessiveness. We can also detect glimmerings of Wilde's mature aesthetic theory which presumes a dialectical relation between the man and the work, founded on the double notion that while any life is necessarily composed of facts (and of secrets), this material is only of interest in relation to creativity, to invention.

Finally, Wilde's linking of Chatterton and Keats can be seen as a component in any putative 'homosexual discourse' since the poets are joined through the *topos* of 'the beautiful face', a recurrent motif in Victorian literature that returns most hauntingly in *The Picture of Dorian Gray*. In 'The Tomb of Keats' Wilde complains about a marble medallion of Keats's profile that some well-meaning people had placed near the grave:

> The face is ugly, and rather hatchet-shaped, with thick sensual lips, and is utterly unlike the poet himself, who was very beautiful to look upon. 'His countenance', says a lady who saw him at one of Hazlitt's lectures, 'lives in my mind as one of singular beauty and brightness; it had the expression as if he had been looking on some glorious sight'. (*Miscellanies* 2–3)

The same essay connects Keats with St Sebastian, described as 'a lovely brown boy, with crisp, clustering hair and red lips' (4). The vision of the boy with the beautiful face joins, albeit antithetically, Chatterton (whose face is unknown) with Keats (of whom there are several portraits). Both accrue to the archetype of the doomed yet strangely inscrutable martyr-poet, a type with whom Wilde himself had always striven to be identified, if only in a kind of self-dramatisingly playful, but essentially homoerotic, way.

To give another example of games-playing, again with erotic overtones, again from the columns of the *Pall Mall Gazette*, but this time not emanating directly from Wilde: on 13 October 1888 its 'Literary Notes, News, and Echoes' column included a short feature on Rennell Rodd, who had won the Newdigate Prize in 1880, and then become a diplomat. In 1888 Rodd was about to publish a life of the Emperor Frederick, and the *Pall Mall Gazette* recalled how in 1880 the *Daily Telegraph* had 'gushed to overflowing about the poetical promise equalled only by the personal charms of this youthful poet'. It also quoted from Wilde's Introduction to Rennell Rodd's book of poems *Rose-leaf and Apple Leaf* (1882), with its tributes to Rodd's 'flawless and fervent' love of art, his 'subtle' and 'delicate' 'artistic sense of beauty'. 'The best proof of Mr Rodd's genuine ability', concluded the *Pall Mall Gazette*, 'is that he has long ago lived down this eulogy.'

This is a joke surely, reasonably genial, and clearly well informed. On 10

June 1880 the *Daily Telegraph* had printed an extended account of the Oxford Commemoration ceremony which opened with long quotations from the prize-winning poem and went on to describe its author. The poem was said, on the one hand, to be curiously reminiscent of work by Rossetti, Morris and O'Shaughnessy (in other words, it plagiarises), but nevertheless to be in part worthy of 'any one of Oxford's sweetest singers, Otway or Coleridge, Collins, Shelley, or Swinburne'. Moreover, when Rennell Rodd stepped up to the platform to declaim, the reporter was delighted to discover that unlike some poets, who were merely 'machines' for the delivery of verse, 'Nature has given him a poet's face and a poet's voice, that thrills to the pathos or the passion of his thought.'

It is highly unlikely that Wilde wrote the *Daily Telegraph* report in 1880. He rarely if ever took on that kind of assignment and the piece has some very uncharacteristic detail as well as some uncharacteristic errors of fact (Coleridge studied at Cambridge, not Oxford). Nevertheless, whoever wrote it not only had an appreciative taste for male appearance, but was able to draw on conventions of what a poet should look like, to such an extent that the paean was remembered eight years later. It is precisely because such language was common that one would hesitate to call it 'gay discourse'.

To make the point rather differently: to know that the anonymous reviews were by Wilde would not necessarily disclose the truth about him, assuming that the truth was simply sexual. Alan Sinfield and others have argued that concepts of effeminacy and of aesthetic dandyism 'preceded the category of the homosexual, overlapped with and influenced the period of its development'.[20] It is precisely in the period of 'overlapping', between the Criminal Law Amendment Act (1885) and the developing scandals of the late 1880s, that Wilde was working as a journalist.

Either way, as a champion of the 'feminine' in all its guises or as proto-Uranian, it is a complicated life that Wilde lives in the columns of newsprint, whether writing anonymously in the *Pall Mall Gazette* or under the soubriquet of the 'Editor' in *The Woman's World*, or under his own name in *Queen*. He inserts opinions that are, by and large, progressive – in support of women, of the Irish – though generally acceptable within the liberalism of the time. There is little difference between what he writes for one publication or another, and the words are sometimes the same. He never makes explicit references to his sexuality, but he does return to topics that have a long homoerotic history: Keats and Chatterton, the beautiful face. He is hostile to biography, but interested in the details of other people's lives. He is both oracle and echo: with teasing self-reference, he both reveals and disguises himself. And he can maintain that duality because of the conventions of regular journalism which required that he pronounce anonymously upon a catholic range of topics, yet allowed personal emphasis. The sheets of the daily paper are his seven veils. The chance to change your mind without censure not only suited Wilde's temperament, it matched his developing concept of how criticism should operate: as a play of moods continually responsive to the varied qualities of the work. So, for instance, he writes in *The Woman's World* in 1887 that Emily Brontë's poems 'are instinct with tragic power and quite terrible in their bitter intensity of passion, the fierce fire of feeling seeming almost to consume the raiment of form' (*Reviews* 220), but modifies this a year later to 'are instinct with tragic power, and seem often on the verge of being great' (*Miscellanies* 120). The new sting in the tail is a sign of the mature Wilde who will use wit as a mode of fine discrimination, turning his readers into connoisseurs of his contrariness.

When Wilde was finally in a position to give up journalism he did so quite easily, turning to genres where he could be more forthcoming about deception. By 1890 he had given up editing *The Woman's World*, virtually stopped writing for the *Pall Mall Gazette* (Stead himself left the paper in December of that year), and had completed work on his extended critical essays, 'The Decay of Lying' (1889) and 'The Critic as Artist' (1890). With his life as a working journalist now behind him he could choose titles and adopt attitudes that no professional could possibly permit. In 'The Decay of Lying' he was to pronounce that 'newspapers, even, have degenerated. They may now be absolutely relied upon' (*CW* 1072). That, at any rate, is the Wilde we all think we can recognise.

NOTES

1 A substantial collection of this material was put together by Wilde's friend and literary executor, Robert Ross, as a volume in his *Collected Edition* (London: Methuen, 1908), and given the title *Reviews*. Other fugitive material is collected in the volume entitled *Miscellanies*. Further references to these editions are given after quotation in the text. Wilde's journalism is listed in the *Bibliography of Oscar Wilde* compiled by 'Stuart Mason' (Christopher Millard) in 1914. Though both the collected volumes and the bibliography are now known to be incomplete, the full extent of the omissions remains hard to ascertain. Editing Wilde's journalism for a volume in the new *Oxford English Texts Oscar Wilde* is currently being undertaken by Russell Jackson of Birmingham University and myself.

2 For the history of 'anonymity' see Laurel Brake, *Subjugated Knowledges: Journalism, Gender and Literature in the Nineteenth Century* (Basingstoke and London: Macmillan, 1994), *passim*.

3 See John Stokes, 'Wilde on Dostoevsky', *Notes and Queries* 27, June 1980, 215–16.

4 See Kevin H. F. O'Brien, 'Oscar Wilde: An Unsigned Book Review', *Notes and Queries* 30, Aug. 1983, 312–15. O'Brien bases his identification on Stuart Mason's amended copy of his own Wilde bibliography. Both Dan H. Laurence and Stanley Weintraub attribute this review to Shaw. See Dan H. Laurence, *Bernard Shaw. A Bibliography* (Oxford: Clarendon Press, 1983), vol. I, pp. 550–1 and Stanley Weintraub, '"The Hibernian School": Oscar Wilde and Bernard Shaw', *SHAW: The Annual of Bernard Shaw Studies* 13 (1993), 25–49. *Bernard Shaw's Book Reviews. Originally Published in the 'Pall Mall Gazette' from 1885 to 1888*, ed. with an introduction by Brian Tyson (University Park and London: Pennsylvania State University Press, 1991) includes the review and provides appropriate annotation.

5 *The Woman Reader 1837–1914* (Oxford: Clarendon Press, 1993), p. 143.

6 'Oscar Wilde and *The Woman's World*', in Brake, *Subjugated Knowledges*, pp. 127–47.

7 This fascinating piece is discussed in Lawrence Danson, 'Wilde in Arden, or the Masks of Truth', *Modern Drama* 37 (Spring 1994); 12–33.

8 Brake, *Subjugated Knowledges*, p. 142.

9 *A Catalogue of the Caricatures of Max Beerbohm*, compiled by Rupert Hart-Davis (Cambridge, MA: Harvard University Press) 1972, plate 5, p. 182.

10 See Richard Ellmann, *Oscar Wilde* (London: Hamish Hamilton, 1987), pp. 274–8.

11 Wilde had earlier distinguished *Queen* from *The Woman's World* on the grounds of its total preoccupation with fashion. See Brake, *Subjugated Knowledges*, p. 152. Also see Charlotte C. Wilkins, 'Editing a "Class journal": Four Decades of the *Queen*', *Innovators and Preachers: The Role of the Editor in Victorian England*, ed. Joel H. Weiner (Westport, CT: Greenwood Press, 1985), pp. 185–99.

12 Brake, *Subjugated Knowledges*, p. 127.

13 In fact Stead disapproved of the homosexual indecency clauses in the bill; how he felt about the subject in general is not entirely clear.

14 Jonathan Dollimore, *Sexual Dissidence* (Oxford: Clarendon Press, 1991), p. 309.

15 Brian Reade, *Sexual Heretics* (London: Routledge, 1970), pp. 22–3.

16 Somerville Story, *Twenty Years in Paris* (London: Alston Rivers, 1927), pp. 156–7.

17 See Rodney Shewan, *Oscar Wilde: Art and Egotism* (London and Basingstoke: Macmillan, 1977), p. 72.

18 Roger C. Lewis, 'A Misattribution: Oscar Wilde's "Unpublished Sonnet on Chatterton"', *Victorian Poetry* 28:2 (Summer 1990), 164–9.

19 The 'sexual misadventure at Oxford' refers to the belief, now discounted but taken seriously by William Rossetti, that Keats contracted syphilis from a prostitute while staying with a friend in Oxford. Curiously this is exactly the same claim that Richard Ellmann makes about Wilde: that he too contracted the disease while an undergraduate in Oxford. Ellmann's theory has been hotly contested, but deep and perhaps undecidable levels of identification may be involved. See Merlin Holland's discussion earlier in this volume, pp. 10–12.

20 *The Wilde Century* (London: Cassell, 1994), p. 78. Also see Ed Cohen, *Talk on the Wilde Side* (London and New York: Routledge, 1993).

6

LAWRENCE DANSON

Wilde as critic and theorist

Good critics clarify the meaning of a work of art by helping us see what its maker intended; they provide historical facts; and they sincerely express their unbiased opinions. To which Oscar Wilde responds that the best critic, rather than explaining the work of art, 'may seek rather to deepen its mystery'; that 'The one duty we owe to history is to rewrite it'; and that 'the true critic is unfair, insincere, and not rational'. According to Wilde, 'the highest criticism is that which reveals in the work of Art what the artist had not put there'. Such criticism 'treats the work of art simply as a starting-point for a new creation'; it 'is itself an art', and of all the arts it is 'the purest form of personal expression'. As pure creation and personal expression, criticism's responsibility 'is to see the object as in itself it really is not'. Inaccurate and insincere, yet perfectly expressing the critic's moods, 'Criticism ... makes culture possible.' Therefore, 'It is to criticism that the future belongs': it 'will annihilate race-prejudices' and 'give us the peace that springs from understanding'.

Such, at least, are the opinions of Wilde's spokesman in his dialogue 'The Critic as Artist', published in *Intentions* (1891), the book on which Wilde's claims as a critic chiefly lie. Criticism of a more conventional sort – reasonable, factual and often fair – Wilde had done in reviews by the score, from the mid-1880s, when he left the lecture platform, until 1890, when he looked to the West End stage for his earnings. But with *Intentions* he destabilises the very category 'criticism', obliterating boundaries, for instance between the critic and the thing criticised, which ordinarily define it. *Intentions* contains two dialogues ('The Decay of Lying' and 'The Critic as Artist'), the satirical biography of a forger ('Pen, Pencil and Poison'), and an essay about stage realism which concludes with its own retraction ('The Truth of Masks'). In negotiations with publishers, Wilde contemplated also including in it his fiction about the meaning of Shakespeare's Sonnets ('The Portrait of Mr W. H.') and his essay about socialism which extols individualism and the autonomy of art

('The Soul of Man'). What genre can accommodate the essays associated with *Intentions?*

A professor at what would become the Massachusetts Institute of Technology characterised the book as a work of 'theoretical criticism'.[1] And 'theory' – as embracingly vague a word in 1891 as it is a century later – is a reasonable name for *Intentions'* genre. Wilde's elevation of criticism into a 'creative and independent' activity makes his work the precursor of ideas that reappear, still controversially, in modern and postmodern theory. Like later theorists for whom he prepared the way, Wilde's critic as artist inhabits a realm where words construct the world, and society is a text to be rewritten. He disdains the consistently 'sincere' and 'earnest' in favour of shifting 'impressions' and 'moods' because, like later theorists, he rejects 'the shallow psychology of those who conceive the Ego in man as a thing simple, permanent, reliable, and of one essence. To him [as to the character Dorian Gray, whose thoughts these words echo] 'man was a being with myriad lives and myriad sensations, a complex multiform creature ...' Wilde's transvaluation of criticism into the highest form of creativity – or the most irresponsible self-indulgence, depending on your point of view – follows upon his rejection of a transcendent, objective truth, whether it goes by the name of 'history', 'culture' or 'nature'.[2]

It sounds presciently, even shockingly, modern. But despite his own breezy dismissal of history, the best way to understand Wilde's intentions (whether in the biographical lower case or the titular upper) is to locate them in the context of the times.

The essays in *Intentions* had previously been published in the two great British magazines of liberal opinion, *The Nineteenth Century* and *The Fortnightly Review.* The book was received without much alarm by Victorian readers. One critic did complain of 'Pen, Pencil, and Poison' that 'the joke has gone far enough' when, in an otherwise 'clever' essay, 'the reader is gravely asked to believe that "there is no essential incongruity between crime and culture"'.[3] The censure is premonitory: it suggests how differently the essays could be read after Wilde's trials of 1895, when hindsight revealed the subversive potential of his jokes. But in 1891 the reviewers were disarmed by *Intentions'* joyfully epigrammatic style. (Their geniality is remarkable in light of the outrage which greeted the magazine version of *The Picture of Dorian Gray* one year before.) Wilde's playful style allowed reviewers to trivialise essays that baffled their sense of intellectual decorum. Grudgingly attracted to the glitter of his surface the reviewers wished that Wilde would get on with 'the thought itself', dropping his 'showy paradoxes' in order to 'devote himself to writing something more solid and reasonable'.[4]

The assumption that Wilde's style is the gaudy cover for ordinary thought reveals a difference between the late nineteenth-century reception of Wilde as critic and a still-emerging late twentieth-century reception. The older view, which tames Wilde with laughter, is now more often encountered in the caricatures on T-shirts than in critical journals: this Wilde is too amusing to be taken seriously, but being amusing is what makes him worth taking. Much recent criticism contests this assessment. In an alternative view, Wilde's stylistic excess is a challenge to Victorian sensibilities, and the contemporary reviewers' exasperation records his triumph. In this view, Wilde's refusal to be 'solid and reasonable' is a slap in the face of Victorian earnestness, and his inconsistency an implicit critique of common assumptions about the production of meaning.[5] In the 1970s, Northrop Frye (with Wildean extravagance) called 'The Decay of Lying' 'the beginning of a new kind of criticism' and 'the herald of a new age in literature', because Wilde makes language sovereign rather than servant of a prior, non-linguistic truth.[6] Readers who do not believe that 'common sense' is always the highest intellectual virtue may agree with the Victorian reviewers' generally positive response to *Intentions* but on opposite grounds – that the inversions (verbal, moral, philosophical, sexual) of its paradoxes are their point, and that its epigrams are better for not having a bottom of good sense.

Other modern readers compliment Wilde by finding in his criticism an almost apocalyptic threat. A literary historian dedicated to the professionalism promulgated by the New Critics of the 1950s–60s writes that Wilde's 'creative criticism' would lead to 'the breakdown or even the abolition of all traditional literary scholarship and teaching'.[7] In the 1990s, a political scientist calls Wilde's social ideal 'the most durable, seductive, and insidious' of all the 'secular religions' that have outlived Marxism and tempted people to seek happiness instead of God, and 'selfhood' instead of 'self-denial and self-control'.[8] In this view, Wilde is the premature ally of the 'revolutionary students' of the 1960s.

To his contemporaries, Wilde's criticism could seem less radically new than it does to his later admirers or detractors. In the *fin de siècle*, symptoms of modernity – the New Woman, the New Drama, the New Journalism, the New Hedonism – simultaneously figured as symptoms of decline, of movement backwards. But the redeployed aestheticism of *Intentions* provoked an especially strong sense of *déjà vu*: a contemporary critic was not alone in detecting 'a flavour of the early "eighties" … a faint odour of the aesthetic movement, a movement which is of the old world now, though young a decade ago'.[9] And Wilde's contemporaries might be less surprised than later readers at the scope of the activities he comprehends under the rubric 'criticism'. They could see him standing in a line of equally expansive social critics, like Carlyle, Ruskin, Emerson and Arnold. Our modernist Wilde is a revisionist in that Victorian prophetic tradition. Writing from prison, Wilde recalled, 'I was a man who stood in symbolic relations to the art and culture of my age': his criticism justifies the boast in many ways, including its appropriation of the views and sometimes words of the aesthetes and sages of the previous half-century.

Among the echoes in Wilde's criticism, the voice of Walter Pater is unmistakable. Pater can be heard even in Wilde's enigmatic title: *Intentions* calls to mind Pater's *Appreciations*, which Wilde had reviewed in March 1890. Wilde's title instances in small his essays' ability to gather up fragments, to call and reply, to be simultaneously themselves and others, like the 'stringed lute on which all winds can play' or the 'twice-written scroll' of his early poem 'Hélas!'. Wilde's title recalls the title of Pater's book, but energised from receptive acts of appraising to more vigorous acts of stretching out for, aiming at. And it also carries Pater's keyword 'impressions', both words caught up with the original sense of 'essays': attempts, trials – all purposively in the plural.

Pater's *Studies in the History of the Renaissance* was Wilde's 'golden book', 'that book', he would call it in *De Profundis*, 'which has had such a strange influence over my life' (*CW* 1022). The effect on Wilde of Pater's 'beautiful and suggestive essays' calls to mind the 'influence' of the 'poisonous' yellow book Lord Henry Wotton gives to Dorian Gray. In that fictitious distillate of the decadent, 'Things that [Dorian] had dimly dreamed of were suddenly made real to him. Things of which he had never dreamed were gradually revealed.' In the 'Conclusion' to *The Renaissance* Pater demonstrates the transience and relativity of all things and the need, there-fore, 'to be forever curiously testing new opinions and courting new impressions'. Pater omitted the 'Conclusion' from the second edition because 'it might possibly have misled some of those young men into whose hands it might fall': Wilde was among those eager to be misled. So, in a conversation recorded by William Butler Yeats, Wilde again called *The Renaissance* 'my golden book' but added more explicitly, 'it is the very flower of decadence: the last trumpet should have sounded when it was written'.[10]

In 'The Critic as Artist', especially, Wilde makes no attempt to disguise Pater's formative presence. Whenever Gilbert, Wilde's spokesman, passes into the cool galleries of the Louvre and stands before Leonardo's painting, he murmurs to himself, 'She is older than the rocks among which she sits; like the vampire, she has been dead many times, and learned the secrets of the grave'; and he goes on murmuring Pater's great purple patch until his friend answers him, 'Hers is the head upon which all "the ends of the world are come", and the eyelids are a little weary.' It is one of his cruder demonstrations of the proposition that 'criticism of the highest kind ... treats the work of art simply as a starting-point for a new creation'. Pater was the author, more than any other, whose work Wilde takes for his starting-point.

His review of *Appreciations* in 1890 seems to swerve from the decadent Pater, the subtle corrupter, to another Pater, the austere artist who advised the young Wilde to give up poetry and take on the greater challenge of prose. This Pater, Wilde writes, unites, like Cardinal Newman (or, as he will write in *De Profundis*, like Christ) the two indispensable artistic qualities, 'personality [and] perfection'. The Pater of newly awakened senses is also present, however, in Wilde's use of the rhetoric of English decadence: 'exquisite', 'strangeness, 'passionate suggestion'. And, most importantly for his criticism, he is there in a passage about history which Wilde reused in 'The Critic as Artist'. Some of Pater's essays, Wilde writes, are Greek in purity of outline, some are medieval in strangeness and passion, but

> all of them [are] absolutely modern, in the true meaning of the term modernity. For he to whom the present is the only thing that is present, knows nothing of the age in which he lives. To realise the nineteenth century one must realise every century that has preceded it, and that has contributed to its making. To know anything about oneself, one must know all about others. There must be no mood with which one cannot sympathise, no dead mode of life that one cannot make alive. (CW 1137)

The passage gives a positive spin to the decadent project in Dorian's 'poisonous' book. That plotless novel is 'a psychological study of a certain young Parisian, who spent his life trying to realise in the nineteenth century all the passions and modes of thought that belonged to every century except his own, and to sum up, as it were, in himself the various moods through which the world-spirit had passed ...'. According to *Intentions*, to be modern is to be not of one's age, and to know one's self is to know the 'moods' of otherness. According to *The Picture of Dorian Gray*, to be not of one's age and to be made of moods is to be a flower of decadence. Decadence *is* modernity in this formula.

Wilde's definition of modernity as a turning backwards, away from the sufficiency of the moment, runs counter to the Victorian passion for progress. But he has respectable allies in what could seem a perverse idea. Matthew Arnold (the other voice, beside Pater's, which most boldly infiltrates the dialogue of 'The Critic as Artist') had also urged that 'The Function of Criticism' was to turn away from the activities of the 'Present Time' and to look instead both outwards, to Europe, and backwards to the touchstone art of older times. Such a programme requires for its success not the politician, the man of action, or the professional specialist, but the contemplative person, in Arnold's definition the critic, in Wilde's the critic as artist. It empowers the individual who is credentialised by his own 'personality', burning (as Pater recommended) with a harder, more gem-like flame than others, able by virtue of learning, taste, sensibility to receive the greatest number of 'impressions' and to realise most intensely the moods and modes that create this dissident modernity.

Wilde's new version of the old aestheticism deploys subjectivity, individuality and the autonomy of art against the supposed objectivity and professionalism of nineteenth-century science and its offshoot in literature, realism. At the historical moment when professional specialisation – in criticism as in other fields – was newly regnant, Wilde's critic as artist fights a battle on behalf of the uncredentialised, unenforceable, self-creating individual.[11] That social position is related to the critical position Wilde takes towards literary realism in 'The Decay of Lying'. The scientist studies nature, the realist copies it; Vivian, Wilde's spokesman in 'The Decay of Lying', dismisses it: 'the more we study Art, the less we care for Nature' (*CW* 1071). Nature's crude imperfections and unfinished condition, its failure to fulfil its good intentions, is a cause of art: 'Art is our spirited protest, our gallant attempt to teach Nature her proper place.' Nature's 'infinite variety' is 'pure myth' and 'resides in the imagination, or fancy, or cultivated blindness of the man who looks at her'. The neoclassical critic had advised, in Pope's words, 'First follow Nature ... the source, and end, and test of art' ('An Essay on Criticism'); in 'The Decay of Lying' Wilde reverses the course of wisdom: 'Nature imitates Art', and should be made to obey art's laws.

Contemporary reviewers pointed out that Wilde's instantly famous paradox threatens to collapse into a reasonable proposition. No one denies that culture, society, art – whatever we want to call it – conditions our way of seeing. But Wilde's demotion of nature to a derivative of culture actually goes further than this. What we call 'nature' is not natural; it is not an inescapable given of existence. Society made what society now worships as the thing that made it: Nature 'is no great mother who has borne us. She is our creation' (*CW* 1086). In quest of the natural we spend our lives imitating an imitation, when (like art) we should 'never express anything but [ourselves]'. Vivian's paradox depends less on the reversal of 'art' and 'nature' than on the fulcrum, 'imitates'. It suggests that whatever *is* is wrong (even, perhaps, such a 'natural' fact as normative heterosexuality), because it mindlessly repeats a prior act of imitation. What we take as natural is someone else's lie – the previously thought or the already created – which we unwittingly imitate. Not only 'All bad art' but, by implication, all bad social conditions, come 'from returning to Life and Nature, and elevating them into ideals' (CW 1091).

Truth to nature is a deadening contradiction in terms; therefore we must stem the decay of lying. The 'cultured and fascinating liar' refuses to accept the inevitability of conditions that pose as natural facts. The 'beautiful untrue things' he tells are the things that have not entered our repertoire of repetitive, imitative gestures. With his disdain for the supposedly objective truths of science, economics, sociology, or anything not of his own making, the liar's very existence, a constant act of self-invention, is a protest against the realist's submission to nature and to social conditions that pose as natural.

Spinning his elegant paradoxes for the benefit of his fellow 'Tired Hedonists', Vivian's dismissal of realism (or naturalism, as it was inter-changeably called) can seem a gesture far removed from the world of real consequences. But in 1889, when 'The Decay of Lying' was published in magazine form, realism was a hot topic. Two months before the essay's appearance, the publisher of the English translation of Emile Zola's realist novel *La terre* was indicted for 'obscene libel'. The Solicitor-General, characterising the book as 'filthy from beginning to end', tried to read passages to the jury; the jury begged him to desist: the publisher served three months in prison. It was the culmination of a campaign of righteous indignation against the realism of which Zola was the leading theorist and practitioner. On 8 May 1888, the House of Commons entertained a motion deploring 'the rapid spread of demoralizing literature in this country'. These 'vile and obscene' novels were 'a gigantic national danger'. They were bad enough in French but a calamity now that they were being published in cheap translations, which meant that the young, the poor and the female could acquire them and, by learning about their own lives, be corrupted.[12]

Early in 1889 – shortly after the publication of 'The Decay of Lying' – the National Vigilance Society distributed the record of its campaign against 'Pernicious Literature' in a pamphlet which included this parliamentary debate and the account of the publisher's trial. It urged individuals to bring private prosecutions against obscene literature. When *The Picture of Dorian Gray* appeared the following year, a reviewer, alluding to this pamphlet campaign, suggested that the Vigilance Society might now think it worth-while to prosecute Oscar Wilde. The overwrought language used to attack Wilde's presumably anti-realist novel was strikingly similar to the language of the anti-Zolaists: to many outraged Victorians, there was little difference between the French realist and the English aesthete.

Why, then, does Wilde oppose what would seem to be his natural allies?

To many politically progressive artists of the nineties, including those interested in sexual freedom for women and homosexuals, realism, with its attention to the grim facts of an inequable social system, was the art of the future. Some of Wilde's opposition to realism sounds like aestheticised snobbery: 'In literature we require distinction, charm, beauty, and imaginative power', says Vivian; such qualities cannot be found in 'an account of the doings of the lower orders' (CW 1075). But this apparent disdain for the larger part of humanity – 'Who cares what happens to them?' – transposes the language of social class into a critique of the realists' view of 'human nature' itself. Their 'human nature', like the wider 'nature' Vivian rejects, is produced by conditions beyond individual control; but in Wilde's terms, only the unique individual, or (to use his keyword) the 'personality', who is a creator not a product, is fully human. You have to be artificial to be really yourself. Wilde scornfully applies the language of social superiority to characters created in the realists' reductive image as the determined products of environment and heredity.

The realists' supposedly scientific objectivity produces a simulacrum of humanity which has the same effect on Vivian as so-called nature itself: 'It is a humiliating confession, but we are all of us made out of the same stuff . . . Sooner or later one comes to that dreadful universal thing called human nature' (CW 1075–6). The realistic novel is condemned to be a copy of the worst, not because its morals are bad (as the National Vigilance Society presumes), but simply because it aims to tell the 'truth' instead of making it new. To Wilde, realism is on the wrong side of a divide which separates imitation from creation, nature from form, life from art, realism from romance, and a supposedly 'natural' sexuality from a sexuality which, like art, disdains any attempt to dictate limits.

Realists claim that they refer to a world out there; Wilde claims that 'Art never expresses anything but itself.' The crucial insistence on art's self-referentiality keeps his essay at the centre of later theoretical debates. Creating a separate, privileged zone for art may protect artists – Zola as well as Wilde – from moralising censorship; but aesthetics can be as rigidly policed as ethics. According to The Preface to *The Picture of Dorian Gray*: 'There is no such thing as a moral or an immoral book. Books are well written, or badly written. That is all.' But it isn't: people decide what is well or badly written, and as Wilde's own response to Zola suggests, subject matter easily creeps into the decision. Wilde's anti-mimeticism leads to his anti-historicism. If 'Truth is entirely and absolutely a matter of style' and if 'Art finds her own perfection within', then (according to Vivian) art in no way 'expresses the temper of its age, the spirit of its time, the moral and social conditions that surround it, and under whose influence it is produced'. The Middle Ages, the Japanese people – these are not facts of nature but 'the deliberate self-conscious creation of certain artists'; an artist in another time or place could appropriate a medieval or Japanese style as the 'objective' form with which to express a 'subjective' vision. And demonstrably Vivian is right: many Victorian artists did adopt a 'medieval' style or a version of *japonisme*. But nineteenth-century medievalism and *japonisme* are as rooted in and eloquent of the conditions of their production as is nineteenth-century realism, and so, by the same token, is Wilde's anti-historical anti-realism.

'The Decay of Lying' is the most successful essay in *Intentions*: Wilde keeps his speakers within the intricate folds of its paradox and makes its relative limitation a virtue. 'The Critic as Artist' is longer and more ambitious. Wilde's spokesman, Gilbert, directs the dialogue his straightman, Ernest, obligingly summarizes:

> You have told me that it is more difficult to talk about a thing than to do it, and that to do nothing at all is the most difficult thing in the world; you have told me that all Art is immoral, and all thought dangerous; that criticism is more creative than creation, and that the highest criticism is that which reveals in the work of Art what the artist had not put there; that it is exactly because a man cannot do a thing that he is the proper judge of it; and that the true critic is unfair, insincere, and not rational. My friend, you are a dreamer.
>
> (CW 1154)

But theirs are not the only voices in the dialogue: Wilde's puppets are also ventriloquists, parodists, pasticheurs, or – as the painter Whistler, the owner of one of the ventriloquised voices, had claimed – plagiarists.

The charge of plagiarism had dogged Wilde since the Oxford Union refused admission to his *Poems* in 1881. Whistler revived it in 1890, and 'The Critic as Artist' is, among many other things, Wilde's response to Whistler. In fact, Wilde is no more guilty of unacknowledged verbatim borrowings than many writers who are also omnivorous readers with an ear for a good phrase. But in the zone of greys that descend from absolute originality of thought through influence to derivation to copy, the matter is more complex. Wilde's style has been called 'anthological', and 'The Critic as Artist', which welcomes so many voices into the dialogue – not only Whistler's but Emerson's, Arnold's, Pater's (to mention only a few of the Anglophone contributors) – shows why the adjective is apt.[13] Whistler's word, 'plagiarism', is the accusatory version of 'anthological': which word you choose depends on whether you accept Wilde's arguments in 'The Critic as Artist' – that a work of art is the starting-point for a new work of art, and that any 'objective' form can be put to a new and different 'subjective' use. Also it depends on how highly you value the transformative force of performance. Wilde's originality – that distinctive, unmistakable quality we call Wildean – is an originality founded on the already-made, a newness that flaunts belatedness.

So, for instance, in 'The Critic as Artist', Wilde draws on (and acknowledges) a recently published translation of the ancient Chinese philosopher Chuang-tzu, who preached 'the great creed of Inaction, and ... the uselessness of all useful things'.[14] With the help of this otherwise-improbable source, Wilde transforms the dandy's insolent languor – itself a derivative pose, adopted from French writers who had previously adopted it from English example – into a sublime detachment. Wilde's dandyism, in his life and work, had always been a rebuke to the Victorian ideal of manly productivity. Now, in 'The Critic as Artist', 'to do nothing at all' becomes the most difficult and intellectual thing in the world, and the non-productive dandy becomes the critic who is dedicated to self-culture and loves truth for its own sake. The transformation helps the dandy – that is, Wilde himself – move from the raffish edge of society towards a new centre which Wilde's criticism is in process of defining.

Wilde appropriates an ancient Chinese sage, as he appropriates a half-century's worth of aesthetic tradition, to help him create the conditions for his own social and literary success. Those conditions would be the fulfilment of 'The Critic as Artist's' utopian vision. They would invert the usual nineteenth-century geography of social margin and social centre or, better yet, make that whole geography of exclusion and inclusion irrelevant. They would make the son of an Irish patriot the embodiment of a revised ideal of English culture: the colonial subject would outgo the occupier by rewriting history, and capture the future of culture by doing nothing. Under those new conditions, the sexual dissident would destroy the assumptions that make dissidence a comprehensible category – assumptions about 'nature' and the 'natural', about the sway of the supposedly real over the fantasies of liberated desire.

In its original form as a magazine article, 'The Critic as Artist' was called 'The True Function and Value of Criticism: A Dialogue'. The original title quotes, in order to set straight, Matthew Arnold's 'The Function of Criticism at the Present Time' (1865). For Arnold, the function of criticism is to prepare a current of fresh ideas with which the creative artist can work. Although it is not the equal of creation, criticism under certain historical conditions makes progress possible, by avoiding the practical view and remaining, instead, 'disinterested'. And 'the aim of criticism is to see the object as in itself it really is'. Pater, in the Preface to *The Renaissance*, had quoted Arnold's phrase, and emended it: 'the first step towards seeing one's object as it really is, is to know one's own impression as it really is'. The movement from the object to the subject, from a stable and knowable out-there to an always-changing receiver of impressions, is a most controversial step in the movement from Victorian to modern.[15] (Still in 1995 a reviewer preferred a book by a learned amateur to the work of virtually all 'modern literary scholarship' because 'it is in the great tradition of criticism which attempts to see the object as in itself it really is').[16] Wilde takes the progression from Arnoldian disinterestedness to Paterian impressionism a step further: now the critic must see the object as in itself it really is not, in order to escape the prison of the already-constructed, to be creative instead of imitative. The Wildean critic neither knows nor feels the world, but makes it.

Of the three positions, Arnold's is the most paradoxical: in order not to be affected by or to affect the thing they see, disinterested critics have to lift themselves by the intellectual bootstraps and, from that gravity-defying position, perceive objects unchanged by the angle of perception. By contrast, Wilde's way ('to see the object as in itself it really is not') sounds commonsensical: it preserves the object (which must be in order to be misperceived) and makes a virtue of creative subjectivity. But we have seen that Wilde pushes the matter further, to claim for art a self-referentiality and for the artist an autonomy exempt from history and, by that token, in danger of irrelevance or solipsism.

Wilde practised the inconsistency he preached. It shouldn't be surprising, then, that these claims are in stark contrast to a position he had taken in 1882–3, in his American lecture 'The English Renaissance of Art': 'For the artist ... there is no escape from the bondage of the earth: there is not even the desire to escape ... [T]hat work is most instinct with spiritual life which conforms most clearly to the perfect fact of physical life.' It is also in contrast to almost everything in 'The Truth of Masks', the final essay in *Intentions*, except its conclusion:

> Not that I agree with everything I have said in this essay. There is much with which I entirely disagree. The essay simply represents an artistic standpoint, and in aesthetic criticism attitude is everything. For in art there is no such thing as a universal truth. A Truth in art is that whose contradictory is also true. And just as it is only in art-criticism, and through it, that we can apprehend the Platonic theory of ideas, so it is only in art-criticism, and through it, that we an realize Hegel's system of contraries. The truths of metaphysics are the truths of masks. (*CW* 1173)

The mixture of whim and scholarship is in keeping with the tone of *Intentions* throughout. The repetition of the idea of masks, of the multiplicity of personality, of self-contradiction as a virtue, all make the final paragraph of 'The Truth of Masks' an appropriate final paragraph for *Intentions*. But the retraction is not just a witty gesture: it states a real fact. Between the first publication of the essay in 1885 as 'Shakespeare and Stage Costume' (*Nineteenth Century*) and revision for *Intentions* in 1891, Wilde had changed his mind, or reshuffled his terms. A book that opens with a recently written defence of art's autonomy and a rejection of historicity ends with an older essay in defence of historical accuracy in stage design.

'The Truth of Masks' is the weakest, and most scholarly, essay in *Intentions*. Demonstrating that Shakespeare was interested in the impressive and expressive possibilities of theatrical spectacle, Wilde draws the conclusion that only technological limitations kept Shakespeare from employing the full panoply of stage effects available to the late nineteenth-century theatre. Specifically, Shakespeare was, as far as conditions allowed, a theatrical 'archaeologist': one who believes that stage costume and design should accurately reflect the time and place of the play's fiction, however remote or fantastic.

Wilde posed more interestingly as a Shakespearian when he wrote 'The Portrait of Mr W. H.' (1889), his daring fable ostensibly about 'the onlie begetter' of Shakespeare's Sonnets but also about the subjectivity of reading, the indeterminacy of language, and – to appropriate words he would use in the trials of 1895 – the 'great affection of an elder for a younger man ... [which is] so much misunderstood that it may be described as the "Love that dare not speak its name" ...'.[17] But in 1885 theatrical 'archaeology' was controversial, and Wilde loved controversy as much as he loved Shakespeare. His defence of archaeology was consistent with some of his aesthetic principles: he emphasised the need for 'harmony' and 'unity' of effect, and he called for an individual mind – what eventually would be the director (in America) or producer (in England) – to make the elements of a production cohere. But he also emphasised accuracy, fact, realism: everything he rejects in 'The Decay of Lying'.

In revision he gave the essay its newly paradoxical title, added the disclaimer in the last paragraph, and made one other change: wherever in the original article the word 'realism' or its cognates appeared, he changed the word to 'illusion', so that, for instance, Shakespeare's 'realistic method' became his 'illusionistic method'. The difference between reality and illusion in art might amount to an emendation.

For a conventional critic, such inconsistency could be disastrous. But Wilde, rejecting the idea of a unified and self-possessed subjectivity, claims inconsistency as a virtue – 'We are never more true to ourselves than when we are inconsistent' ('The Critic as Artist') – and takes Emerson's 'Whim' as his motto ('The Decay of Lying'). Wilde's criticism succeeds or fails less as philosophy than as performance, which is its own proof; and his performance makes comic turns out of standards we use to judge conventional criticism – sincerity, originality (which presumes more stability than the Wildean performance allows), consistency. 'Pen, Pencil and Poison', another of the essays in *Intentions*, is an instance. Ostensibly it is a critical biography in praise of Thomas Griffiths Wainewright, who was a poet, painter and art-critic, 'but also a forger of no mean or ordinary capabilities, and as a subtle and secret poisoner almost without rival in this or any age' (*CW* 1093). An aesthete who poisoned his niece because her ankles were fat, Wainewright could be the demonstration of the claim 'that the sphere of Art and the sphere of Ethics are absolutely distinct and separate' ('The Critic as Artist'). His forgery is not a crime if 'insincerity is simply a method by which we can multiply our personalities' ('The Critic as Artist'). As the narrator of 'The Portrait of Mr W. H.' says, 'to censure an artist for a forgery [is] to confuse an ethical with an aesthetic problem' (*CW* 302). Wainewright's crimes, Wilde says, 'gave a strong personality to his style' (*CW* 1106).

The surprise, then, is that Wilde's attitude towards Wainewright is unclear – or, less surprisingly, that it is impossible to say when he is being sincere or insincere. His deadpan style annihilates the opposition between those categories. The narrative pose of scholarly judiciousness allows small touches of incongruity or excess to unsettle obvious ironies. Literary tradition – for instance, the example of Swift's 'Modest Proposal' – suggests that the reader's job is to reject the shocking initial assumption, that there is no difference between art and crime. But the evidence of Wilde's own writing, the statement, for instance, that 'What is termed Sin is an essential element of progress' ('The Critic as Artist'), suggests that we should leave the initial assumption where we found it. One modern critic says that Wilde adopts 'Wainewright as a kindred spirit, a precursor of aestheticism, and a dandy'.[18] Another, conversely, says that 'Pen, Pencil and Poison' satirises aestheticism as 'a limited conception of social life and a dangerously isolated egotism', and only pretends to adopt Wainewright's idea of 'culture'.[19] Wilde's satire is poised two-square for both readings, and more.

Wilde had been trying to have things both, or all, ways at least since the eighties, when he dressed like a clown to preach beauty in America and risked the audience's laughter; the dissonance of his performance, absurdly sublime, was a calculated effect. In *Intentions*, the dissonance is more subtle, but in all Wilde's performances the sublime and the ridiculous, like sincerity and insincerity, or like illusion and reality, are not necessarily opposites. For some readers, *De Profundis* is his greatest work because it is the one in which he realised for the first time in his life the vital importance of being earnest. For other readers, *De Profundis* is 'the artistic essay of an artist ... [in which] he was still playing with ideas, playing with emotions'.[20] Such division of opinion is the expectable fate for a writer who claimed to have realised his personality in multiplicity. The funniest and, with hind-sight, most chilling line in 'Pen, Pencil and Poison' is the one in which Wilde acknowledges the danger of his performance: of Wainewright's imprison-ment for a crime committed thirteen years earlier, Wilde writes, 'The permanence of personality is a very subtle metaphysical problem, and certainly the English law solves the question in an extremely rough-and-ready manner' (*CW* 1104).

A few months before the appearance of *Intentions* but too late to be included in it, Wilde published 'The Soul of Man Under Socialism'. The paradox of the essay's title is amplified by its contents: 'Socialism ... will lead to individualism', and the model individualist is Christ, whose 'message ... to man was simply "Be thyself"' (*CW* 1179). Wilde's decision to write on socialism may have been influenced by the success the previous year of the *Fabian Essays*, to which G. B. Shaw was the most prominent contributor. But Wilde's socialism has little in common with that of the Fabian Society, which was founded on a reverence for the 'facts' Wilde everywhere disdains. And it has little in common with classical Marxism. Wilde does look forward to the abolition of private property, but for an unmarxian reason: property crushes the individualism of its possessors. And for the same unmarxian reason he looks forward to the withering away of the state:

> Individualism ... is what through Socialism we are to attain. As a natural result the State must give up all idea of government. It must give it up because, as a wise man once said many centuries before Christ, there is such a thing as leaving mankind alone; there is no such thing as governing mankind. *All modes of government are failures.*   (*CW* 1181)

The 'wise man' of Wilde's socialism is not Marx but the sage Chuang-tzu. Wilde's 'socialism' is ahistorical, or it exists after history's end, when ideology in no way mediates either individual existence or relationships between individuals. 'The Soul of Man' refuses to recognise any shaping force more powerful than the individual imagination.

'Is this Utopian?', as Wilde himself asks about his imperious demand that machines do all the dirty work in the future. And he answers himself:

> A map of the world that does not include Utopia is not worth even glancing at, for it leaves out the one country at which Humanity is always landing. And when Humanity lands there, it looks out, and, seeing a better country, sets sail. Progress is the realisation of Utopias.   (*CW* 1184)

The individualism of 'The Soul of Man' is, in part, a defensive reaction to the vilification he suffered for *The Picture of Dorian Gray*: in Wilde's anarchic socialist utopia, artists will be responsible only to themselves, unmolested by a badly brought up public or wage-hungry journalists. In light of his imprisonment, however, his plea to leave others alone as we would be left alone reveals its urgently wider applicability, to sexual minorities and to all dissident or marginalised people. 'Art is the most intense form of Individualism that the world has known' writes Wilde (*CW* 1184); and when everyone is realised as an individual, everyone will be an artist.

This conspectus of Wilde as critic and theorist has stressed his performative qualities, acknowledged his inconsistency and allowed him the virtue of insincerity. 'The Soul of Man' is typically Wildean in all these matters, but it is also typical in its generosity and, despite his best efforts, its sheer good sense. Like all Wilde's best prose, its epigrammatic surface repels analysis and tempts one to quotation. 'The only way to get rid of a temptation is to yield to it', as Oscar Wilde said. Therefore, from 'The Soul of Man Under Socialism': 'a community is infinitely more brutalised by the habitual employment of punishment, than it is by the occasional occurrence of crime' (*CW* 1182); 'Selfishness is not living as one wishes to live, it is asking others to live as one wishes to live' (*CW* 1194); 'Pleasure is Nature's test, her sign of approval. When man is happy, he is in harmony with himself and his environment' (*CW* 1197).

NOTES

1 G. R. Carpenter, 'Three Critics: Mr Howells, Mr Moore, and Mr Wilde', *Andover Review* 16 (1891), 568–76; p. 571. Carpenter distinguished Wilde's 'theoretical criticism' from the 'individual criticism' in George Moore's *Impressions and Opinions* (London: D. Nutt, 1891).

2 On Wilde's affiliations with twentieth-century criticism and theory, see Zhang Longxi, 'The Critical Legacy of Oscar Wilde', *Texas Studies in Literature and Language* 30 (1988), 87–103; Guy Willoughby, 'Oscar Wilde and Poststructuralism', *Philosophy and Literature* 13 (1989), 316–24; R. J. Green, 'Oscar Wilde's *Intentions*: An Early Modernist Manifesto', *British Journal of Aesthetics* 13 (1973), 397–404.

3 *Literary Opinion*, July 1891, p. 10.

4 From, respectively, the *Nation* (New York), 6 July 1891, p. 34, and the *Athenaeum*, 6 June 1891, p. 731.

5 Jonathan Dollimore, in *Sexual Dissidence: Augustine to Wilde, Freud to Foucault* (Oxford: Clarendon Press, 1991), p. 14, writes that Wilde's 'transgressive aesthetic' operates in the name of 'insincerity, inauthenticity, and unnaturalness [which] become the liberating attributes of decentred identity and desire'.

See also Joseph Loewenstein, 'Wilde and the Evasion of Principle', *South Atlantic Quarterly* 84 (1985), 392–400.

6 *The Secular Scripture* (1976), p. 46. Cited in Zhang Longxi, 'The Critical Legacy of Oscar Wilde'.

7 René Wellek, 'Destroying Literary Studies', *New Criterion* 2 (1983), 1–8. Cited in Longxi, 'The Critical Legacy of Oscar Wilde'.

8 Christopher Lasch, *The Revolt of the Elites and the Betrayal of Democracy* (New York: W. W. Norton, 1995), p. 232.

9 *The Graphic*, 12 Dec. 1891, p. 706.

10 *The Autobiography of William Butler Yeats* (London: Macmillan, 1938), p.114.

11 On Wilde's relation to the institutional practice of criticism, see Green, 'Oscar Wilde's *Intentions*', Ian Small, *Conditions for Criticism: Authority, Knowledge and Literature in the Late Nineteenth Century* (Oxford: Oxford University Press, 1991).

12 From the National Vigilance Society pamphlet *Pernicious Literature* (1889), reprinted in George J. Becker (ed.), *Documents of Modern Literary Realism* (Princeton, NJ: Princeton University Press, 1963), pp. 350–82.

13 Patricia Clements, *Baudelaire and the English Tradition* (Princeton, NJ: Princeton University Press, 1985), p. 142, echoing Harold Bloom's characterisation of Wilde's poetry in *The Anxiety of Influence*.

14 Wilde, reviewing a translation of Chuang-tzu, in *Speaker* 8 Feb. 1890 (Ross, *Reviews*, p. 529).

15 See Wendell V. Harris, 'Arnold, Pater, Wilde, and the Object as in Themselves They See It', *Studies in English Literature 1500–1900* (1971), 733–47. On Pater's and Wilde's relationship to modernism, see John McGowan, 'From Pater to Wilde to Joyce: Modernist Epiphany and the Soulful Self', *Texas Studies in Literature and Language* 32 (1990), 417–45.

16 Stephen Logan, 'Shakespeare is Not Just for Dons', *The Times* (London), 9 Feb. 1995, p. 38.

17 H. Montgomery Hyde, *The Trials of Oscar Wilde* (London: Hodge, 1948), p. 236.

18 Norbert Kohl, *Oscar Wilde: The Works of a Conformist Rebel*, trans. David Henry Wilson (Cambridge: Cambridge University Press, 1989), p. 118.

19 Regenia Gagnier, *Idylls of the Marketplace: Oscar Wilde and the Victorian Public* (Aldershot: Scolar Press, 1986), p. 39.

20 Max Beerbohm, 'A Lord of Language' (1905), in *A Peep into the Past and Other Prose Pieces*, collected and introduced by Rupert Hart-Davis (London: Hart-Davis, 1972), pp. 38–9.

7

JERUSHA MCCORMACK

Wilde's fiction(s)

To talk about Wilde's fiction, is to talk about everything, for Oscar Wilde was his own best work of art.

Born and educated in Ireland, Wilde came from a country which gives a privileged status to fiction. In the words of his predecessor, William Carleton, meditating on 'Paddy's' skill at the alibi: 'Fiction is the basis of society, the bond of commercial prosperity, the channel of communication between nation and nation, and not unfrequently the interpreter between a man and his own conscience.'[1] It follows that, if fiction is the very stuff by which society is made, Wilde could only become a writer – and an Irishman – in England. Only there could he create himself through the fictions which formed 'the channel of communication between nation and nation', the stereotypes by which one understood the other.

A member of the leading class known as Anglo-Irish, Wilde created himself by living on both sides of the hyphen. If in Ireland, his family had been a queer kind of English people – at once upholders of the embattled British regime and, at the same time, more Irish than the Irish themselves – in England, Wilde became a queer kind of Irishman.

Arriving in Oxford from Dublin, Wilde beat the scholars at their own game, scooping a Double First. Although born of the 'gentry' in Ireland, Wilde assumed the status of an English aristocrat, leisured, extravagant, charming and mannered. If these virtues were exaggerated, it was only to give a double edge to the performance, parodying as well the stereotype of the Irish: lazy, improvident, charming and witty. As Matthew Arnold trenchantly observed, the Irish had, by their very nature, more in common with the English upper class than either of them held with the hard-working, thrifty and dour English middle class.[2]

Setting the stamp on that collusion, Wilde made himself over as a dandy, one who, as a leisured outsider, sought to establish (in the words of Baudelaire) 'a new kind of aristocracy'.[3] Despising the very society into which he seeks initiation, the dandy takes his revenge by creating himself in its image, miming its clothes, its manners and mannerisms. ('Imitation', as Wilde observed, 'can be made the sincerest form of insult' (*CW* 1086). Inherently exaggerated, such mimicry exposes the fissures of its own performance: the double standards on which it rests. What the dandy performs is a kind of psychic jujitsu – he 'throws people' by using the force of their attitude to defeat them. In effect, by means of his performance the dandy gets his audience to share his contempt for itself.

By these methods, the dandy fashions himself literally at the expense of his audience, thus coming to represent the transactions by which the powerless, the nobodies, assume power and importance. As was said of the great Beau Brummell: 'He was a nobody, who made himself a somebody, and gave the law to everybody.'[4] His pursuit is of power; his style not a mere act of homage to fashion but, in fact, a passionate revolt against convention itself. Revolt is not repudiation. Its potency relies on the force of what it repudiates. As another exponent of dandyism, Barbey d'Aurevilly, observed: 'Dandyism, while still respecting the conventionalities, plays with them. While admitting their power, it suffers from and revenges itself upon them, and pleads them as an excuse against themselves; dominates and is dominated by them in turn.'[5]

It is this reciprocity of turn and counterturn, the implicit structure of an act of provocation and revenge, upon which I wish to focus in the performance of Wilde's dandyism.

COUNTERSPEECH

Having come to the centre from the periphery, Wilde arrived as an outsider, attuned to the doublespeak of the Empire at home. Empirespeak mirrored its master. Just as the Englishman prided himself on his integrity, Empire-speak presented itself as single, insistent and sincere. It was spoken in one tone, without nuance or irony; and it was the voice of passion, commitment and command – the voice of what passes as truth. It speaks the big words that men die for – God, King, Country. And it presumes unanimous consent. To this single, passionate voice, Wilde thus proposes another: one that speaks double, in the ironical and self-cancelling wit of the dandy.

In creating himself through this voice, Wilde drew on the resonances of his own cultural heritage. Growing up in a British colony, he had (inevitably) become conscious of its methods of linguistic control: those directed, through the colonial regime, to indoctrinating the tenets of Empirespeak. Wilde's Irish background made him forever suspicious of official cant. In his one sustained political critique of British society, 'The Soul of Man under Socialism', Wilde comments that 'one of the results of the extraordinary tyranny of authority is that words are absolutely distorted from their proper and simple meaning, and are used to express the obverse of their right signification' (CW 1194).

Such an insight could only be won from a radical estrangement – not merely from the father country, but from the father-tongue. Wilde came to manhood in a colony where the peasants (as he later recalled) were bilingual (L 483). During his lifetime, when they lived under the compulsion of adopting a foreign tongue, he had witnessed a policy of what can only be called linguistic terrorism. Wilde himself had learned a little Irish during the long holidays with his family in County Mayo (his own son, Vyvyan, recalls him singing him a lullaby in Gaelic.)[6] He was also, in his own style, aware of 'Celtic' deviations in occasional turns of phrase (L 289). As a writer, it was the issue of language which sealed Wilde's sense of displacement; as he wrote to Edmond de Goncourt: 'Français de sympathie, je suis Irlandais de race, et les Anglais m'ont condamné à parler le langage de Shakespeare' (L 303).

Wilde escaped that fate by writing Salomé in French. When he returned from Paris to London to make himself as a writer, it was as a double agent, one who, under cover of wit, turned the doublespeak of Empire back on itself. To plot Wilde's career in counterspeech, one must begin with his subversion of the sentence.

APHORISMS GONE WILDE

Wilde made himself through the quip: the quotable one-liner. Examination of the ways he composed (such as the drafts of his plays) suggests that he began with a series of witty phrases, jokes or puns and shuffled them around between characters – and even between other texts. Once he had coined a phrase, it was likely to reappear anywhere.[7] Thus Wilde became his own best plagiarist, improvising on a series of lines he kept in his head, a worker in an oral tradition of his own creation.

It is important to note that Wilde came from a culture which, on both sides of the Anglo-Irish divide, prided itself (and to some extent, still does) on being able to turn a phrase. Arriving at Oxford, Wilde entered a culture which was literate, and distrusted the oral; which was solemn, and distrusted wit; which was threatened, and policed the borderlines of such contentious issues as gender by a regime of reflex platitudes: those 'formulas' which, as Matthew Arnold observed, the Englishman 'has always at hand in order to save himself the trouble of thinking'.[8]

Those 'formulas' were sentences in all denotations of the word: a grammatical unit which expressed an opinion as if it were an axiom – a judgement which, posing as a kind of eternal truth, condemned all opposing opinion as untruth. Enforcing social consensus, such aphorisms were deployed as a kind of border patrol to keep distinct such areas as 'good' and 'bad', 'manly' and 'womanly', 'trivial' and 'important'. In the society of the late Empire, it is along these fronts that the linguistic battles were being fought.

Despising safety, Wilde turned the linguistic front into a kind of no man's land.[9] He did not fight by the rules – what he was fighting *were* the rules. His methods were strictly those of guerrilla warfare. Camouflaging his own attack in the language of the enemy, he blew it up. Take, for instance, this instance from 'Phrases and Philosophies for the Use of the Young': 'Wickedness is a myth invented by good people to account for the curious attractiveness of others' (*CW* 1244). In other words, 'good' people often try to discredit attractive people – presumably for the threat they pose to their goodness – by calling them 'wicked'. In doing so, 'good' people of course also discredited themselves as being 'good': precisely the kind of self-cancelling oxymoron by which the dandy detonates the self-satisfied platitudes of his audience.

They are, in effect, hoist on their own cliché: amused at their own expense. Wilde is able to do this precisely because he uses the language of his audience – a language already faithless, the language of common double-talk. In Wilde, Thomas Mann discovered much of the essential Nietzsche, his 'furious war on morality', and his transvaluation of moral into aesthetic values.[10] But Wilde did not have Nietzsche; nor did he need him. Victorian hypocrisy was in itself a transvaluation of values. What Wilde did was to expose the sleight of hand whereby one set of values counterfeited another; whereby the control of art, and certainly of Wilde, became an agenda – as it did in his trials – of social and political control:

EDWARD CARSON: Listen, sir. Here is one of the 'Phrases and Philosophies' which you contributed to this magazine: 'Wickedness is a myth invented by good people to account for the curious attractiveness of others.' You think that true?

OSCAR WILDE: I rarely think that anything I write is true.

Wilde was sent to prison for a breach of the Criminal Law Amendment Act of 1885 which made indecencies between men, even in private, a criminal offence. But (it may be argued) Wilde condemned himself by his performance in the dock. One might even say, he sentenced himself by challenging the very status of truth itself.

THE GOSPEL ACCORDING TO WILDE

Truth for the British culture of the day was a matter of authority: of the moral fundamentalism of a middle-class consensus as to what was right and wrong, true and false. Its self-righteousness was characterised by Arnold as deriving from its 'Hebraic' roots. Culturally, its source *par excellence* was the 'Authorised Version' of the Bible – commissioned by King James I in 1604 to consolidate the new Established Church, named, significantly, the Anglican.

To advance oneself as the author of an alternative Bible was – nakedly – to put under question the very basis of British authority, both of church and state. (As Wilde quipped: 'Beer, the Bible and the seven deadly virtues have made our England what it is' (*CW* 140).) The authority of the Bible itself had been challenged by biblical scholars since the early decades of the century. Their scrutiny had been taken into account in the production of a new Revised Text which had appeared of the New Testament in 1881 and the Old Testament in 1885. Oscar Wilde decided to rewrite it completely.

Perhaps it is (as one scholar claims) the most neglected biographical item in Oscar Wilde's life that he was the nephew of three clergymen. Wilde had been a brilliant student of Classical literature; while at Oxford he had also engaged in close textual study of the New Testament. Work in either field would have alerted him to the oral nature of the written text: its original, variable, improvised form now fossilised by almost two millennia of controversy and diktat. As an Irishman, Wilde came from one of the most oral cultures in Europe. He made himself through his talk, and it was to talk that he returned the most literal of texts in his versions of the sayings of Jesus.

To return these stories to their oral form was a radical act, a strike against the axiom of the Bible's origin in a single, inscribed text, and a strike against the very ground of sacred authorship, authorised by centuries of official *imprimatur*. It is precisely that institutionalisation of the Word to which Wilde objected as a sin against the Spirit, observing bitterly to Coulson Kernahan, 'It is cant and officialdom ... which is keeping the men and women who think out of the churches today. It is cant', he continued,

which more than anything else stands between them and Christ. Shall I tell you what is my greatest ambition – more even than an ambition – the dream of my life? Not to be remembered hereafter as an artist, poet, thinker, or playwright, but as the man who reclothed the sublimest conception which the world has ever known – the Salvation of Humanity, the Sacrifice of Himself upon the Cross by Christ – with new and burning words, with new and illuminating symbols, with new and divine vision, free from the accretions of cant which the centuries have gathered around it. I should thereby be giving the world back again the greatest gift ever given to mankind since Christ Himself gave it, peerless and pure two thousand years ago – the pure gift of Christianity as taught by Christ.

'Yes,' he went on, 'I hope before I die to write the Epic of the Cross, the Iliad of Christianity, which shall live for all time'.[11]

In 'the Iliad of Christianity', Wilde would have chanted the reconciliation of Hellenism and Hebraism, of Socrates and Christ: the kind of amalgamation of the pagan and authorised religious practice which was in his time a commonplace in rural Ireland. Then frowned upon officially, the rituals of the 'pattern day', of visiting holy wells and climbing sacred mountains, persist to this day in Ireland in the name of Christianity. These opposing cultures, mingling in his native Ireland, offered the fruitful conflict of many of Wilde's prose poems. Or, as André Gide observed, Wilde's 'most ingenious apologues, his most disturbing ironies were designed to bring the two ethics face to face with one another, I mean pagan naturalism and Christian idealism, and to put the latter out of countenance'.[12]

As Wilde intended, his prose poems have the status of parables. They aim to overturn; they proceed as precise, almost mechanical, inversions of the audience's expectations. Their form is oral, with a cadencing of perfect music. Often they exist in several versions, adjusted according to different audiences and different contexts; a full collection is still to be made. Their value, however, is evident. These are the kernels from which the larger fictions grow: such as *The Picture of Dorian Gray*, which is little more than a literary elaboration of such a slight, but pregnant, tale.

Also, more significantly, these fables allow us to understand the source of much of Wilde's power: his use of an authorised language in such a way that it subverts itself. 'The Doer of Good' has effectively destroyed a man by saving his life – but not teaching him how to live. *Salome* explores how desire, both erotic and religious, is perverted within a rotting colonial regime. Its plot, characters and language are derived (in the English translation) from the Authorised Version; it was banned by the Lord Chancellor from the British stage on the grounds of blasphemy. These grounds are exact; it was not so much the contempt for the Bible that Wilde was demonstrating, but a claim to the same attributes of authority which offered the grounds of offence. Wilde did not only attack sacred texts; he aspired to rewrite them as well, saying of the Bible: 'When I think of all the harm that book has done, I despair of ever writing anything to equal it.'[13]

TELLING TALES

Wilde's first official expeditions into literary fiction are misleadingly slight. From 1887 onwards, he published a series of stories designed as light entertainment; most are grouped under the rubric of 'fairy tales'. Like his famous one-liners and his parables, Wilde's shorter fictions are oral in origin and are written as performances which explore fissures in Wilde's own complex fate: as Irishman turned English; dandy become father; husband converted to illicit lover.

To some extent, the rubric 'fairy story' does, in all its resonances, respond to each of these categories: as tales from Irish folklore; as fables for children; as encoded narratives of homoerotic desire. All, while posing as innocent, were dangerous; all drew their inspiration from a degraded culture, driven underground – whether that of the 'little people', fairies or children, or of the emerging gay subculture of the 1880s. It is from the margins of society, from the perspective of the poor, the colonised, the disreputable and dispossessed, that these stories must be read.

In composing his stories, Wilde drew on the collection of folk-tales made by his father, Sir William Wilde, and published after his death by Lady Wilde. As one critic observes, when folk-tale collectors such as Sir William Wilde or Douglas Hyde took down the tales of pre-literate peasants in the west, they were 'engaging in something more than an anthropological or literary exercise; they were making a statement of cultural and political Nationalism'.[14] Oscar Wilde was thus, in publishing his tales, associating himself with such Protestant nationalists as his parents, Lady Gregory, William Butler Yeats and John Synge. By linking themselves with a despised, indigenous and pre-literate culture, these writers identified Ireland with (in Yeats's words) 'the unwritten tradition which binds the unlettered ... to the beginning of time and the foundation of the world'.[15]

Wilde found the form of his tales as he talked them. Writing an introduction to *The Happy Prince and Other Fairy Tales* in 1923, Yeats observed of Wilde that 'when I remember him with pleasure it is always the talker I remember .... The further Wilde goes in his writings from the method of speech, from improvisation, from sympathy with some especial audience, the less original he is, the less accomplished.'[16] Yeats considered that Wilde had, in writing down what he himself considered 'the best story in the world' ('The Doer of Good'), 'spoiled it with the verbal decoration of his epoch, and I have to repeat it to myself as I first heard it, before I can see its terrible beauty'.[17]

What the reader has today in Wilde's shorter fictions is, then, a hybrid: a literary fairy tale. As such, it reflects accurately the situation of *diglossia* in his native culture. Wilde was writing at a turning-point for Ireland when, of two divergent cultures – the rural and oral, the urban and literate – the balance was beginning to be tipped towards the latter. But insofar as Wilde drew on a tradition considered primitive and degraded, his tales – as a first major literary venture – are also the means by which he invented himself as an Irish writer for an English audience.

In comparison with Yeats's *Fairy and Folk Tales of the Irish Peasantry* – published in the same year as Wilde's *The Happy Prince and Other Tales* – Wilde's construction of his Irishness is circumspect and oblique, refracted through the literary tradition of the Anglo-Irish gentry, rather than drawn from the pure springs of native folklore. What marks Wilde as a writer of his class is his preference for fantasy over realism; for a narrative line that operates on several levels and is itself suspended and complicated by a series of digressions; for a fracture between plot and discourse, in which action is suspended indefinitely for a kind of logorrhea, to the extent that the only interest of the tale is an engagement of language with itself as a kind of pure verbal decoration.

Such disengagement of language from 'reality' or plot is in fact the subject of 'The Remarkable Rocket'. The Rocket is remarkable literally because of his remarks on himself: his declaration of success in spite of the evident fact of spluttering failure. The Rocket thus represents an extreme case of counterspeak, in which speech itself is granted the power to counter, if not transform, reality. In itself, Wilde's tale might have been written as an exemplar of what Matthew Arnold called the Celtic revolt against 'the despotism of fact'.[18]

Elsewhere, speech literally enjoins an alternate reality. In 'Lord Arthur Savile's Crime', the dire prediction of the chiromantist, Mr Podgers, prescribes the plot: Lord Arthur Savile only seeks to fulfil his fate as if it were a duty (and, in so doing, satirises the whole notion of moral choice). Other tales abide by the logic of folklore, demonstrating the power of the spoken wish. Thus, the swallow responds to the pleas of the Happy Prince, even unto death. The devoted friend interprets his exploitation within the terms of his exploiter's self-justifying logic. The spontaneous outburst of Dorian Gray seals his fate long before he comes upon the 'fatal book'. In each tale, the spoken is primary; it dictates what is to be inscribed as plot.

'The Fisherman and his Soul' best exemplifies the terrible power of words. There, the wish of the fisherman that his soul be exiled so that he may love his merman-wife, is countered by the words of the soul, who seeks to win back the fisherman – to his mortal destruction. The style by which the soul seduces the fisherman may be only described as Asiatic: jewelled, ornamented, heavily allusive to the exotic allure of the East. By its means,

Wilde defines the 'other' of the fairy tale in a mode which might be called
Celtic orientalism. As England lies to the east of Ireland, and is to the Irish a
symbol of corruption (commonly referred to as 'Babylon'), so the oriental
defines for Wilde the life of luxury, the life of the senses, indulged by the
spoils of Empire, exemplified by those esoteric collections consolidated in
his century by the Kensington (later Victoria and Albert) and British
Museums.[19] Yeats employed the same metaphor when he commented that,
to the young Wilde fresh from Dublin, the English aristocracy 'were as the
nobles of Baghdad'.[20]

In other stories, the depredations of Empire, the stark contrast between
obscene luxury and appalling poverty, form the hidden subtext of two of
Wilde's strongest tales, 'The Happy Prince' and 'The Young King'. 'The
Happy Prince' is a statue of lead covered with gold leaf: an apt representation of the gilded dross of Empire. Appalled by the poverty about him, the
Prince insists that a sparrow carry his jewelled embellishments – the last of
which are his eyes – to the poor to alleviate their suffering. In the end,
stripped of his superficial glory, the statue of the Prince, now declared ugly,
is torn down by the Town Councillors.

The Young King, disowned by his father, had been brought up in the
provinces by a poor goatherd. Dying, his father sends for him and reinstates
him to his rightful place, the palace, a place rich with the spoils of his
Empire, an inventory of which (as one early critic commented) 'reads for all
the world like an extract from a catalogue at Christie's'.[21] There the Young
King indulges his love of beauty, ordering for his coronation a robe of gold
tissue, a ruby-studded crown and a sceptre with rings of pearls. That night,
three dreams come to him, each a harrowing tableau of the 'slaves' who
sicken and die to weave the robe, mine the rubies, dive for the pearls.
Awaking, the Young King refuses to invest himself: 'For on the loom of
sorrow, and by the white hands of Pain, has this my robe been woven.
There is Blood in the heart of the ruby, and Death in the heart of the pearl'
(CW 219). Thus speaking, he dresses himself in his leathern tunic and rough
sheepskin coat and, taking his rude shepherd's staff, walks to the Cathedral.
Mocked by his people, rebuked by the Bishop, the Young King prays and,
praying, is transformed into an image of a transfigured Christ.

Too often this tale, which has the predictability of its well-worn plot, is
passed over as an anodyne Sunday-school fantasy. What modern readers
miss is the 'bitter satire' identified by a friend of Wilde's, one who appeared
to read the story from Wilde's own perspective as an Irishman.[22] Coming
from the modest wealth of Dublin, London's obscene luxury, its conspicuous waste, could only provide a corrosive contrast to the extreme poverty
Wilde had seen in post-Famine Ireland, particularly on his visits as a child to

the west. His parents, having lived through the Famine, were critical of an imperial regime which had, through commercial greed and political indifference, allowed large numbers of the people of its nearest colony to starve, while food was openly exported abroad. 'In peace', his people tell the Young King, 'the rich make slaves of the poor.'

> We tread out the grapes, and another drinks the wine. We sow the corn, and our own board is empty. We have chains, though no eye beholds them; and we are slaves, though men call us free. (CW 216)

The first critics of 'The Young King' identified it as 'Socialist'[23] and indeed the kernel of Wilde's essay is here, in the image of Christ as revolutionary, an adversary of personal property and prophet of personal freedom. Masked as a child's story. 'The Young King' did not cause the offence of 'The Soul of Man under Socialism' (published earlier in the same year). In the opinion of one of Wilde's earliest biographers, that essay 'aroused the secret enmity of the rich and powerful classes' and, in the end, did Wilde 'a greater disservice with the governing classes than anything else he could have said or done and at a time when they might have lent him a helping hand they turned a cold shoulder'.[24]

Reviewing *Lord Arthur Savile's Crime and Other Stories* for the paper, *United Ireland*, Yeats was more specific. A part of the Nemesis which has fallen on Wilde's (English) readers, Yeats comments, 'is a complete inability to understand anything he says. We [the Irish] should not find him so unintelligible – for much about him is Irish of the Irish. I see in his life and works an extravagant Celtic crusade against Anglo-Saxon stupidity.'[25]

The stupefied reading of Wilde's tales would also relegate them to nursery literature. 'It is the duty of every father to write fairy tales for his children', Wilde declared, and many of these tales, composed after the birth of his two boys, were recited to them – as Vyvyan recalls – in one form or another.[26]

What one fails to take into account is that the stories were not so much composed for children – as for Wilde himself. No one (to my knowledge) has considered what it meant for Wilde to become a father. I believe what it meant for Wilde is inscribed in 'The Selfish Giant'. A kind of giant himself, Wilde might be taken as recording his initial response to the arrival of his first son, Cyril, as one of rejection: ' "My own garden is my own garden," said the Giant; "any one can understand that, and I will allow nobody to play in it but myself." So he built a high wall all round it, and put up a notice-board. TRESPASSERS WILL BE PROSECUTED. He was a very selfish Giant' [283].

By the time Cyril was born, the house on Tite Street which Wilde shared with Constance had been redecorated by Edward Godwin. With the

Figure 5   Wilde as story-teller, etching by the American artist James Edward Kelly, 1882

principal rooms painted in white, Wilde's 'house beautiful' was hardly suited to young children. Now Wilde had to share that space, as well as his privacy and, perhaps more shocking, the body – as well as the love – of his wife, with successive intruders. Reviewing a handbook of marriage shortly after Cyril was born, Wilde remarked ruefully that 'men must give up the tyranny in married life which was once so dear to them, and which, we are afraid, lingers still, here and there'.[27] Closing off his own space to the child, the Giant doomed the garden to winter; relenting, he brought spring. For Wilde, fatherhood was also to bring emotional rebirth and a flowering of his genius; in the following years, he was to produce his best work.

Vyvyan recalls that when Wilde recited the story of 'The Selfish Giant', his father had tears in his eyes. When asked why, Wilde replied that really beautiful things always made him cry.[28] At the heart of such beauty there is pain: the death of the Giant's old selfish ego; his own death; and the image of the wounded child, at once the Giant's saviour – and his sacrifice.

In that image Wilde embodied his final discovery of himself: not as Irishman, not as father, but as a lover of other men. In 1886, just before the birth of his second son, Vyvyan, Wilde had been seduced by Robbie Ross, himself only a boyish sixteen. In loving Ross, Wilde discovered an illicit world, an exotic world, a world of fantasy which, in popular slang, had already become identified with that of the fairies, those preternatural folk colonised by Christianity and driven underground, to live a degraded and taboo life denied official recognition.[29] It is appropriate that Wilde should employ the 'fairy tale' to explore the conflicts of such a seduction.

The Giant gives up his garden, only to find the child he most loves is wounded with the wounds of Christ: ultimately, Wilde's homosexuality meant the sacrifice of his children. After he went to prison he never saw them again, although, as he wrote, he loved them to idolatry. But that sacrifice began long before, in the divided loyalties of father and lover. Wilde was no longer husband. The love of women, as the fairy tales explicitly show, is shallow and cruel. The Infanta only tolerates the Dwarf because he amuses her; when the Dwarf, seeing himself for the first time in a mirror, sees how ugly he is and, with that revelation, the impossibility of the Infanta's love, he kills himself. (Could the ugliness here be a reflection of Wilde's own confrontation with himself in the mirror of homosexual love?) The seduction of the Fisherman by his Soul ends in the suicide of his wife, a death in which her husband chooses to join her. As poignantly, the love of the Swallow for the Happy Prince means his own death, in doing the bidding of his friend. If, as one critic argues, 'The Happy Prince' announces the beauty and value of homosexual – in contrast to heterosexual – love, then it also discloses its price, in suffering and sacrifice.[30]

Nothing is as poignant to Wilde as the death of a young boy. This image lies at the heart of his fairy stories: in the radiant child of 'The Selfish Giant', the Young King miraculously transfigured, the glittering statue of the Happy Prince. These figures are incandescent because they focus the light of different sources: of the young Apollo, transmuted into the Christ-child and refracted through the Romantic tradition of the 'marvelous boy' – Keats, Chatterton, Mr W. H., Dorian Gray. To love simultaneously Robbie Ross and his own two boys, Wilde must have extended the boundaries of love itself to embrace not only the Greek ideal of *paideia* – which depends on the love of an older for a younger man, a spiritual as well as an erotic love – but also the Judeo-Christian ideal of the loving father, willing to sacrifice his own son for the love of his sinning people. In the end, it is the endorsement of sacrifice by which Wilde resolves his two loves of comfort and despair: a sacrifice which inscribes these loves as central and sacred.

FRAMING SHAKESPEARE

As is usual with Wilde's fictions, 'The Portrait of Mr W. H.' began as a recital. In his accustomed manner, one biographer remarked, Wilde 'turned an idea into an anecdote, the anecdote into a story, embroidering as he went along, and the freer play he gave to his imagination the deeper conviction he imparted to others and the more inclined was he to believe the story itself'.[31] What one believes in this story relies on the impact of its performance, forged in the heat of inspiration, and carrying conviction only within the context of its utterance. Its oral nature dictates the fiction's contingent and arbitrary nature and offers the premise of its own erasure: here lies a fiction writ in hot water.

By returning his own text to talk, Wilde subverts every notion of authority. The story is narrated by a person unknown, reporting a conversation about (significantly) literary forgeries. (Who is the author of this tale? What are his credentials? We never know.) It proceeds to have a character named Erskine report a theory about Shakespeare's Sonnets advanced in turn by his friend Cyril Graham. (Hearsay: wouldn't stand up in court. We also know little about Cyril, other than the fact that he is 'effeminate' and was 'always cast for the girl's parts' in Shakespeare's plays.) The report is prefaced by saying that Cyril, believing his theory, had a portrait forged to authenticate it. (Theory discredited even before it is argued.)

Erskine then proceeds to tell how Cyril confided in him the 'secret' of Shakespeare's Sonnets. Released from any obligation to believe the theory by Cyril's early admission of its forged authenticity, the reader is free to enjoy its speculative thesis: that the Mr W. H. of the Sonnets is in reality a boy-actor, Willie Hughes, whose beauty is their 'onlie begetter'. Nearly convinced of the theory, Erskine insists that there is still not enough proof; at this point, Cyril has a painter forge the portrait. When Erskine inadvertently discovers the forgery, it destroys his faith in the theory. The two men quarrel, and Cyril commits suicide, 'to offer his life as a sacrifice to the secret of the Sonnets' as he writes in his suicide note (CW 311). (Do we believe this? Does it not sound like another forgery? Surely the 'secret' of the friendship between Erskine and Cyril, rent by their quarrel, had more to do with the suicide than a literary theory.)

In his letter, Cyril entrusts the Willie Hughes theory to his friend, but Erskine declines to propagate such a 'perfectly unsound' idea. Protesting that his friend will so 'wrong the memory of ... the youngest and most splendid of all the martyrs of literature', the narrator returns home to become possessed by the idea (CW 312). But, despite his very convincing exploration of the theory's ramifications, all collapses when the narrator writes his final version of the theory down in a letter to Erskine. 'No sooner ... had I sent it off than a curious reaction came over me. It seemed to me that I had given away my capacity for belief in the Willie Hughes theory of the Sonnets' (CW 345).

Erskine, on the other hand, is reconverted. In a replay of the first narrative sequence, the two men quarrel and part. Two years later, the narrator receives a letter, claiming that 'by the time you receive this I shall have died by my own hand, for Willie Hughes' sake ... and for the sake of Cyril Graham' (348). It was (as its written form implies) a forged demise: Cyril had actually died from consumption. Ironically, this final act of invalidation lures the narrator back to the theory, about which, he concludes, there is still 'a great deal to be said' (*CW* 350).

What is 'said' in the story inspires a kind of infectious confidence; what is written is inevitably 'forged', artificial and not to be trusted. (In the dock, Wilde himself denied the import of his own 'written' article.[32]) If what is 'said' begets the written, what is written only validates the primacy of what is said. Locating the impulse of Shakespeare's own creation in the performance of an actor, Wilde returns the literary text of the Sonnets to their source in his own performance of their interpretation. At every level, that performance subverts the authority of the text, and the 'forged' reputation of its author, William Shakespeare.

Middle-class England held its Shakespeare next in authority to the sacred text of the Bible. 'But Shakespeare one gets acquainted with without knowing how', Austen wrote in *Mansfield Park*. 'It is part of an Englishman's constitution.' Shakespeare's status as a poet of Empire, as part of the ideological apparatus of the state machinery, has been explored under the rubric of Bardolatry. But Wilde's target was not so much the public Shakespeare as the insidious Shakespeare of Austen's lines: the 'forged' author of the Family Shakespeare (reputed to have been edited by Thomas Bowdler) or the Shakespeare edited into respectability and interpreted as a moral guide for British maidens, such as Rosa Baughan's editions of 1863–9, 'Abridged and Revised for the use of Girls'.[33]

To those readers, Wilde advances an equally insidious version of Shakespeare: the Bard as lover of boys, and not only of boys, but of lower-class boys who were, strictly speaking, not English at all. Wilde is (dis)credited with the (dis)honour of being the first to impute homoerotic love as both subject and source of a Shakespeare text. Wilde goes further: in his story he describes how Shakespeare's text itself provides a literally fatal source of homoerotic infection, providing not only code but authority for what was, at the time of its writing, a criminal activity.[34] Up to Wilde's time, it may have been rumoured – but not written – that the Sonnets centred on homoerotic love. Hitherto, interpreters explained the dubious passages in terms of esoteric Elizabethan convention.[35] In any case, the language that was being devised during the closing decades for 'the love that dare not speak its name' was largely a gentlemanly and encoded discourse, confined to allusions about crushes between boys at prestigious public schools: a kind of initiation into sexual activity common to the élite – who could justify it by citing their Plato in the original.

Willie Hughes is an insult to such a discourse. In Wilde's text, he is described as low-born and of a class near the bottom of the Elizabethan social strata. Advancing such a theory went against every earnest effort to make Shakespeare safe. Wilde's theory was dangerous; moreover, Wilde knew how dangerous it was: 'Our English homes will totter to their base when my book appears', he predicted.[36] As it happened, although a preliminary version of his story was printed in 1889, the definitive version did not appear in his own lifetime.[37] But the English home did totter when Wilde took its text for his own script. After his affair with Lord Alfred Douglas cooled, Wilde sought sexual gratification from 'rent-boys', lower-class boy prostitutes. It is their testimony against Wilde that, more than anything else, sent him to prison.

These lovers were not gentlemen. Nor, in Wilde's fantasy, were they English. Willie Hughes in all his glory is described in Wilde's tale as incorrigibly Celtic: having the chameleon-like personality which Arnold found the hallmark of its temperament.[38] That wonderful boy-actor, whom Shakespeare, in one of the punning sonnets, hailed as 'A man in hew, all *Hews* in his controwling', could also exasperate him: ' "How is it", Wilde has Shakespeare saying to Willie Hughes, "that you have so many person-alities?" ' (*CW* 314). In 'The Portrait of Mr. W. H.', Wilde – ironically known to his own circle of disciples as 'Shakespeare'[39] – forged a picture which was to haunt him: that of his other, Celtic self: that of his shadow and fate, Dorian Gray.

THE MIRROR OF DORIAN GRAY

It is hard to say anything original about *The Picture of Dorian Gray*, largely because there is so little that is original in it. As if in two facing mirrors, the novel and its analogues seem to multiply towards a possible infinity, in a kind of self-perpetuating critical machine. Contemporary reviewers spotted Stevenson's *Dr Jekyll and Mr Hyde* as a model, but they also found sources in Poe, Balzac, Bulwer-Lytton, Disraeli and 'the leprous literature of the French Decadents'. Modern critics have argued for derivations from Suetonius, Walpole, Gibbons, Goethe, Radcliffe, Maturin, Tennyson, Arnold, Pater, D. G. Rossetti, Symonds, Hawthorne, Louisa May Alcott and the journalist George Augustus Sala. Similarly, a myriad predecessors have been listed for Dorian's portrait in the 'magic portrait' genre.[40] One thing is clear: careers can still be made in the hunt for originals of *The Picture of Dorian Gray*.

But they would be careers in futility. As Wilde well knew, originality is simply not a value in the oral tradition. The teller of tales does not aim for the novel; he counts on the audience's recognition of 'annexed' lines; their praise is to be reserved for the skill with which he turns them to his purpose. For Wilde's purpose, the intention is not, strictly speaking, literary, but mythic: to retell a story whose end is known; a story as old as that of the dying gods, Dionysos and Christ, or of those who sought themselves to appropriate their power, Adam and Faust. To reconcile the myths of Greek and Jew, Wilde might also have turned to a legend from his own culture, which he cites at the time of his writing of *The Picture of Dorian Gray*: that of the bard Ossian who, wandering away on a white horse, entered the mythic country of the young, Tir-nán-Og, 'lived there three hundred years, and then returned in search of his comrades. The moment his foot touched the earth his three hundred years fell on him, and he was bowed double, and his beard swept the ground.'[41]

As every new 'source' confirms, it is the book's very lack of originality that is the secret of its power. In *The Picture of Dorian Gray*, Wilde has tapped a root of Western folklore so deep and ubiquitous that the story itself has escaped the literary and returned to its origins in the oral tradition. Almost everyone knows the plot of *The Picture of Dorian Gray*; very few have read it. The tale flourishes as a modern myth while the book itself lies rotting in the attic.

Split between the oral and the literary, the story explores the faultline that, in itself, defines the modern. To move from an oral to a written culture, as Ireland was moving in the later part of the nineteenth century, is to move from the age-old to a precise moment in history. The oral depends on a performance in a kind of eternal present: it never ages, although its performers may grow old and die. The written is published at a certain date, frozen in history, outmoded as soon as it is inscribed and tied to a dying animal, the author, whose creation it is and who becomes its creature.

Among other things, modernity – like writing – entails the blurring of the boundary between the human and the artefact. While the oral depends on presence, writing occurs in absence, by means of the assimilation of author into object. Having read the novel when it came out, Mallarmé wrote to Wilde: 'This disturbing, full-length portrait of a Dorian Gray will haunt me, as writing, having become the book itself.'[42] The portrait haunts because it contains all that is written: the portrait of the first chapter is the portrait of the last. But, between these two effigies, lies the history of Dorian Gray, composing, or rather decomposing, the portrait during its course. Thus Wilde draws on the deep structure of a kind of tale which 'pretends to order sequentially, in a narrative, what is actually the destruction of all sequence'.[43]

Sequence, or history, is destroyed by myth, which Wilde understood to be more enduring than history – just as the myths surrounding Wilde will outlast all the informative biographies ever written about him. An Irishman transplanted to England, Wilde fashioned himself through his talk; but he made his reputation as a writer. His writing, as I have tried to show, began as an inscription of his talk. In its most successful form, it took the very shape of talk: of epigram, fable and dialogue. But, in the end, it was written – and once written, inscribed its text with a kind of fatality. He had written the script for his own life even while, in writing it, he precipitated the events which were to lead to his downfall.

Wilde exemplified in *The Picture of Dorian Gray* the strategies by which he made, and unmade, himself. As he famously said: Lord Wotton was what the world thought him: one of the new aristocracy, a dandy who lives by his wits, mocked as 'Prince Paradox' (*CW* 140). Lord Wotton engages in the counterspeak that was to make Wilde notorious as 'a corrupter of youth' and a thorn in the side of Authority. A 'lord of language' (as Wilde once called himself), Lord Henry Wotton challenges the British hierarchies of truth by systematically sabotaging Empirespeak.

Dorian Gray is 'what I would like to be', an eternal youth, one who, at any price, connives to escape moral responsibility. He is the very image of the feckless Irish lad – the 'Great Irresponsible', as William Archer called Wilde – who, living only for the pleasures of the moment, will pay heavily for his fecklessness in the end. As such he plays into John Bull's stereotype of the 'wild Irish boy' (Wilde as the 'Fad [fat] Boy' depicted in *Punch*, handing a copy of *Dorian Gray* to Mrs Grundy). The 'fat boy' has a child's greed; he feeds on the spoils of Empire with the insatiability of displaced desire. The Asiatic style by which Dorian is inscribed is that of the Soul detached from the Fisherman, the Soul without humanity or heart. It speaks in the bardic tones, the mesmerising repetitions of his own native sagas, which suspend the tale's history indefinitely for the timeless chant of the song, ageless, unending, enduring. Thus does the speech of Dorian's soul authorise the eternal child in Wilde, for whom he wrote the fairy stories; the Peter Pan who never grew up; the youth who, with all the adolescent convictions of his own invulnerability, wishes to attain immortality – and then to die.

'Basil Hallward is what I think I am': the key to the Trinity, playing to the Father and Son, the Holy Ghost. Absorbed into the silence of the portrait, Basil exemplifies the unutterable longing which saturates the book – the longing for beauty, for youth, for immortality. It is the quality of that desire which lends the book greatness; but it is the strategy by which that desire is accomplished that makes it modern. What Basil precipitates is a drama of

Figure 6 Wilde as the Fad Boy, presenting a copy of *Dorian Gray* to a scandalised Mrs Grundy, in *Punch* (19 July, 1890)

appropriation, as Dorian is 'made his own' by being painted. Seeing himself there, Dorian speaks the fatal wish, underwritten by the preternatural powers of Lord Henry Wotton and, finally, inscribed in a 'poisonous' book.

From the moment he speaks his desire, Dorian himself becomes an artefact, neither alive nor dead: one of the fabulous undead, such as Dracula, who must draw life from others. To keep the secret of the picture, he kills Basil Hallward. The man who disposes of his body, Alan Campbell, commits suicide. Seeking to numb his guilt, Dorian anaesthesises himself with things, inventing himself by means of his own collections. His relationship with himself, as with others, is dictated by an object; but which Dorian is now the artefact? Neither can live outside the world of the fabricated, nor tolerate the 'life' which threatens it with destruction. Detesting Sibyl Vane as not sufficiently artificial, Dorian drives her to suicide. He struggles to retain the numbness of an object; but in a rare moment of unconscious grace, Dorian rediscovers the power to feel – for others as for himself. That moment is his undoing; for, seeking to erase the record of his guilt and thus liberate himself for ever from the nightmare of history, Dorian, slashing the portrait, kills himself.

The Picture of Dorian Gray is thus the record of a 'long and lovely suicide', which it mimes. In it Wilde makes and unmakes himself in the image of three aesthetes who are themselves incorporated into a picture. Itself decomposing, this icon successively destroys all who come into contact with it (except Lord Henry Wotton, who, as the devil himself, is merely the agent of destruction). In deconstructing itself, the text is released back into the indeterminacy of an oral tradition.[44] There, among its public, *Dorian Gray* became notorious as a 'poisonous', a 'fatal' book: a book which was literally to prove 'fatal' to Wilde himself, when it was used as evidence of his 'immorality' in the three trials which ended in his imprisonment. Had it stayed safely between its covers, as a novel which could be comfortably read, *The Picture of Dorian Gray* would have quietly mouldered away. But by undermining any conventional reading, the book infected the public mind, and, escaping its covers, shaped for posterity its image of Wilde.

More insidiously, Wilde took *The Picture of Dorian Gray* as a script for his own life, quoting its very lines in the dock and, by so doing, inscribed himself for ever in the fiction which he had already written.

NOTES

1 'An Essay on Irish Swearing', in *Traits and Stories of the Irish Peasantry*, ed. D. J. O'Donoghue (London: J. M. Dent, 1896), p. 205.

2 'The Incompatibles', *English Literature and Irish Politics*, ed. R. H. Super, in *The Complete Prose Works of Matthew Arnold*, vol. IX (Ann Arbor: University of Michigan Press), p. 272. Wilde excused his extravagance on the basis that 'the virtues of prudence and thrift were not in my own nature or my own race'. In the same letter, he cited his 'own proverbial good nature and Celtic laziness' (*L* 427, 429).

3 Charles Baudelaire, 'The Painter of Modern Life: The Dandy', in *Baudelaire: Selected Writings on Art and Artists*, trans. P. E. Charles (Harmondsworth: Penguin, 1972), p. 421.

4 Catherine Gore on Brummell, cited in Regenia Gagnier, *Idylls of the Marketplace: Oscar Wilde and the Victorian Public* (Aldershot: Scolar Press, 1987), p. 76.

5 *Dandyism*, p. 23, cited in Gagnier, *Idylls of the Marketplace*, p. 221.

6 Vyvyan Holland, *Son of Oscar Wilde* (New York: Oxford University Press), p. 54.

7 For a commentary on Wilde's 'borrowing', see *Oscar Wilde Revalued: An Essay on New Materials and Methods of Research*, ed. Ian Small, 1890–1920 British Authors Series, no. XIII (Greensboro, NC: ELT Press, 1993), pp. 99–100.

8 'The Incompatibles', p. 267.

9 The following analysis is indebted to Sandra Siegal, 'Wilde's Use and Abuse of Aphorisms', *Victorian Studies Association of Western Canada* 12 (1986) 1, 16–26.

10 'Wilde and Nietzsche', from 'Nietzsche's Philosophy in the Light of Recent History', *Last Essays*; reprinted in *Oscar Wilde: A Collection of Critical Essays*, ed. Richard Ellmann (Englewood Cliffs, NJ: Prentice Hall, 1969), p. 169.

11 'Oscar Wilde', in *Oscar Wilde: Interviews and Recollections*, ed. E. H. Mikhail, vol. II (London: Macmillan, 1979), p. 316.

12 'Oscar Wilde: In Memoriam', ibid., p. 293.

13 Hesketh Pearson, *Oscar Wilde: His Life and Wit* (New York: Harper and Brothers, 1946), p. 165.

14 Deirdre Toomey, 'The Story-Teller at Fault', in *Rediscovering Oscar Wilde*, ed. C. George Sandulescu, The Princess Grace Irish Library: vol. VIII (Gerrards Cross: Colin Smythe, 1994). The following sentence, as well as the general thrust of the argument of this section, is indebted to Toomey's essay.

15 W. B. Yeats, 'What is "Popular Poetry?"', in *Essays and Introductions* (London: Macmillan, 1961), p. 6. For Wilde's knowledge of fairy lore, see his review of Yeats's *Fairy and Folk Tales* in *The Artist as Critic: Critical Writings of Oscar Wilde* ed. Richard Ellmann (New York: Vintage, 1970), pp. 130–5.

16 W. B. Yeats, 'Introduction' to vol. III, *The Complete Works of Oscar Wilde*, reprinted in *Oscar Wilde: The Critical Heritage*, ed. Karl Beckson (London: Routledge and Kegan Paul, 1970), pp. 396–7.

17 W. B. Yeats, *Autobiographies* (London: Macmillan, 1955), p. 286.

18 'On the Study of Celtic Literature', *Lectures and Essays in Criticism*, ed. R. H. Super, in *Complete Prose*, vol. III, p. 344. This became a catch-phrase for Arnold, who repeated it in 'The Incompatibles', p. 245.

19 For Wilde's use of catalogues to the collections of the South Kensington Museum, see *The Picture of Dorian Gray*, ed. Isobel Murray, in *The Oxford Authors: Oscar Wilde* (Oxford: Oxford University Press, 1989), p. 283, notes 147 and 148.

20 Richard Ellmann, *Eminent Domain: Yeats among Wilde, Joyce, Pound, Eliot and Auden* (London: Oxford University Press, 1970), p. 10.

21 Unsigned notice in the *Athenaeum*, 6 Feb. 1892, p. 177, reprinted in *Oscar Wilde: The Critical Heritage*, p. 117.

22 Alexander Galt Ross, review in the *Saturday Review*, 20 Oct. 1888, reprinted in *Oscar Wilde: The Critical Heritage*, p. 61. Alexander was the older brother of Robert Ross, Wilde's close friend and confidant during this period.

23 Cf. the remarks on the 'socialist' tendencies of the stories published in *A House of Pomegranates* (1891), in the reviews cited as items 36 and 37 in *Oscar Wilde: The Critical Heritage*, pp. 114, 115.

24 Pearson, *Oscar Wilde*, pp. 121, 143.

25 'Oscar Wilde's Last Book', *United Ireland*, 26 Sept. 1891, p. 5. Reprinted in *Oscar Wilde: The Critical Heritage*, p. 111.

26 Pearson, *Oscar Wilde*, p. 164.

27 'A Handbook to Marriage', *Pall Mall Gazette*, 18 Nov. 1885, quoted in Richard Ellmann, *Oscar Wilde* (New York: Alfred A. Knopf, 1988), p. 258.

28 Holland, *Son of Oscar Wilde*, pp. 53–4.

29 The most thorough semantic enquiry into the word 'fairy' is to be found in Noel Williams, 'The Semantics of the Word "Fairy" in English between 1320 and

1829', Ph.D. dissertation, Sheffield University, 1983. Williams believes that 'fairy' meaning male homosexual may have been a usage as early as the sixteenth century. *Wicked Words* (New York: Crown, 1989) cites a publication from 1896 and argues that the homosexual meaning of the term 'seems to be an American contribution to the language' (p. 141).

It would seem that Wilde had this meaning in mind when he inscribed a copy of *The Happy Prince* to 'Clyde Fitch from his friend Oscar Wilde. Faery-stories for one who lives in Faery-Land. Sept. '90.' Fitch, an American eleven years younger than Wilde, was an actor who went on to become a successful playwright; he wrote several effusive letters to Wilde during the period 1889–90.

30 Robert K. Martin, 'Oscar Wilde and the Fairy Tale: "The Happy Prince" as Self-Dramatization', *Studies in Short Fiction* 16 (1979), 74–7. For a more extensive exploration of the homoerotic subtext of Wilde's fairy tales, see 'Tales of a Prodigal Baby', in Gary Schmidgall, *The Stranger Wilde: Interpreting Oscar* (London: Abacus, 1994), pp. 145–68.

31 Pearson, *Oscar Wilde*, p. 127.

32 Montgomery Hyde, *The Trials of Oscar Wilde* (London: William Hodge, 1948), p. 130. 'I believe you have written an article to show that Shakespeare's Sonnets were suggestive of unnatural vice?' – 'On the contrary, I have written an article to show that they are not: I objected to such a perversion being put onto Shakespeare.'

33 Louis Marder, *His Exits and Entrances: The Story of Shakespeare's Reputation* (London: John Murray, 1963), p. 114.

34 Ibid., p. 162. But cf. Alan Sinfield, *The Wilde Century: Effeminacy, Oscar Wilde and the Queer Movement* (New York: Columbia University Press, 1994), pp. 18–21, for a more subtle analysis.

35 Marder, *His Exits and Entrances*, p. 162.

36 Pearson, *Oscar Wilde*, p. 127.

37 The enlarged, 1893 version of 'Mr W. H.' was first published in 1958; it is reprinted in *The Complete Works of Oscar Wilde*, ed. Merlin Holland. The 1889 edition is reprinted in *The Works of Oscar Wilde*, edited by G. F. Maine (London: Collins, 1948).

38 'On the Study of Celtic Literature', pp. 343–8.

39 Cf. Jerusha Hull McCormack, *John Gray: Poet, Dandy, and Priest* (Hanover, NH: University Press of New England, 1991), pp. 89–90.

40 The preceding list of sources is drawn mainly from Kerry Powell, 'Tom, Dick, and Dorian Gray: Magic-Picture Mania in Late Victorian Fiction', *Philological Quarterly* 62 (1983), 147–70, in particular, notes 3 and 4, 166–7. For the most recent account of sources, cf. Small (ed.), *Oscar Wilde Revalued*, pp. 186–90.

41 Wilde, review of W. B. Yeats's *Fairy and Folk Tales* (Feb. 1889), reprinted in *The Artist as Critic*, p. 133. See also a pioneering if rather rudimentary study: David A. Upchurch, *Wilde's Use of Irish Celtic Elements in 'The Picture of Dorian Gray'*, American University Studies, Series IV, England: Language and Literature vol. 140 (New York: Peter Lang, 1992).

42 '"It was the portrait that had done everything." Ce portrait en pied, inquiétant, d'un Dorian Gray, hantera, mais écrit, étant devenu livre lui-même.' L 298, n. 1.

43 Paul de Man, 'Pascal's Allegory of Persuasion', quoted in Donald L. Lawler,

'Allegorical Performance in *Dorian Gray*', in *The Picture of Dorian Gray*, Norton Critical Edition, ed. Donald L. Lawler (New York: Norton, 1988), p. 453.

44 The argument has been made by Angus Fletcher, in *Allegory: The Theory of a Symbolic Mode* (Ithaca: Cornell University Press, 1964), that Wilde did much in his revisions of *The Picture of Dorian Gray* to contest and modify the original moral allegory that directed the reader to an 'authoritative, thematic, "correct" reading of his text'.

8

JOSEPH DONOHUE

Distance, death and desire in *Salome*

I

'I have one instrument that I know I can command, and that is the English language', Wilde said in an interview published in 1892. 'There was another instrument to which I had listened all my life', he explained, 'and I wanted once to touch this new instrument to see whether I could make any beautiful thing out of it.'[1]

The beautiful thing he had made was a one-act play, *Salome*, written in French in Paris in late 1891 and offered to Sarah Bernhardt for a London production, in French, in 1892. 'Sarah va jouer *Salomé*!!', Wilde wrote excitedly to the novelist Pierre Louÿs, perhaps in June of that year (*L* 316).[2] By late June, the celebrated French actress was in rehearsal at the Palace Theatre, London, when the Lord Chamberlain's Examiner of Plays, E. F. S. Pigott, denied a licence for performance on the grounds of a prohibition against biblical characters on the stage. William Archer, champion of Ibsen and other avant-garde dramatists, condemned the Examiner's decision in bitter terms: 'A serious work of art, accepted, studied, and rehearsed by the greatest actress of our time, is peremptorily suppressed.'[3] On reflection, what is puzzling is not the denial of a licence but the blithe assumption (attributed by Wilde's friend and literary executor Robert Ross to Bernhardt's ignorance of English stage censorship[4]) that a licence would be forthcoming. For beneath Pigott's official reliance on Henry VIII's interdiction of mystery plays lay a condescending disdain for serious poetic drama and, some might have added, a covert preoccupation with sexuality that he shared with the public he served. Describing England's 'loathsome pruriency' in their 1913 study of English censorship, Frank Fowell and Frank Palmer observed that sex had been degraded 'into a national obscenity, a thing of dark places, of shame and disease'.[5] Pigott illustrated the alleged national bias in a letter to his colleague Spencer Ponsonby. Characterising *Salome* as 'half Biblical, half pornographic', he proposed to send the play on to him for his '*private* edification & amusement'.[6]

Pruriency aside, Wilde's enthusiastic acceptance by this same English public just a few months before *Salome* went into rehearsal would seem ironically to have precluded his presenting himself to them as a serious poetic dramatist. Earlier that year, Wilde had become the toast of the London theatre audience as a result of the stunning success of his first West End comedy-drama, *Lady Windermere's Fan*, which had opened at the St James's Theatre on 20 February 1892 and was still playing to packed houses before beginning a provincial tour at the end of July. The reputation this play garnered for its author, augmented over the next three years by the appearance of *A Woman of No Importance, An Ideal Husband* and *The Importance of Being Earnest*, has lasted down to the present day, surviving Wilde's catastrophic series of trials in the spring of 1895 and his incarceration, subsequent self-exile and early death in 1900. For decades after, that reputation entirely overshadowed Wilde's own persistent attempts over nearly the whole of his career to write producible poetic drama, a mode of dramatic art unaffected (he may have thought) by the constraints exerted by West End actor–managers' uncurbable impulse towards stardom and their audiences' well-known taste for an amalgam of the acceptably risky and the tried and true. *Salome* appeared on stage for the first time only in early 1896, in Paris, for just a single performance by Aurélien Lugné-Poe's Théâtre de l'Œuvre, even as its author was serving a two-year sentence with hard labour for acts of 'gross indecency' committed in violation of the vague but broadly repressive terms of the Criminal Law Amendment Act of 1885.[7]

Moreover, in the years after Wilde's death, intermittent efforts to produce *Salome* on the English-speaking stage had little impact on the posthumous profile of this misunderstood and, for a long period, badly neglected writer. Subsequent to its Paris production the play itself came to be much better known on the Continent, becoming, as Ross bitterly noted, 'a household word wherever the English language is not spoken'.[8] Its great popularity in Europe, indicated by Walter Ledger's 1909 bibliography of translations into German, Czech, Greek, Italian, Hungarian, Polish, Russian, Spanish, Catalan, Swedish and Yiddish,[9] was challenged but not eclipsed in 1905 by the remarkable success of an opulent operatic treatment under the same title, based on a German translation of Wilde's French original, by Richard Strauss.[10] Meanwhile, English literary and dramatic criticism ignored the work even more thoroughly than it did the rest of Wilde's writings, leaving his reputation dependent on occasional revivals of the West End successes and on early biographers notable for their bias. Comments such as Alfred Schattmann's sympathetic appraisal of *Salome*, published as early as 1907, as a play 'full of character and effective contrast' from which grows 'organically and convincingly, casting its spell over one, a mood of anxiety', are rare.[11] As late as mid-century James Agate would engage in a wholesale debunking of Wilde and his work, condemning his lack of 'any kind of artistic conscience' and his dependence on 'all the stalest devices of the theatre'.[12] In time, intelligent treatments by such critics as Edouard Roditi (1947) and Epifanio San Juan, Jun. (1967) began to appear, but as late as 1977 Rodney Shewan could observe that *Salome* was 'seldom at present taken seriously'.[13] Twenty-five years ago, in an essay grounding *Salome* in the dense context of Wilde's formative influences, Richard Ellmann extended 'overtures' to a play that still seemed to inhabit unknown territory.[14]

Today, something over a century beyond the date of its original composition, a wealth of criticism representing a variety of approaches has brought the play decisively into a new sphere of understanding. The present essay offers a partial summary of these approaches and a contribution to the far-reaching revaluation of *Salome* now under way.

II

The mixed tone of wistfulness and bitterness in Wilde's 1892 interview on *Salome* seems only appropriate in view of its subsequent fortunes. *Salome* is the one play of Wilde's maturity of which he himself never saw a production during his lifetime. As the earliest surviving manuscript conclusively demonstrates, it is also the only play he ever wrote in a language other than English, despite Lord Alfred Douglas's groundless assertions that Wilde composed it in English and then translated it into French.[15] Wilde's friend the poet Stuart Merrill described the play as having been written 'très rapidement, de premier jet, en français'.[16] This partial draft, written in a bound, lined composition book, documents Wilde's astonishing facility, evident in part in the widespread absence of headings for speeches that nonetheless reflect clearly differentiated characters.

Comparison of this first, holograph manuscript with later manuscripts and the first edition indicates that Wilde had formulated his essential dramaturgical concept even at this early point. In simple outline, this was to be a play about a young woman, hardly more than a girl, who falls precipitously in love with a man who rigidly spurns her advances; in perverse retribution she claims his severed head as the price of a sensuous dance before the Tetrarch – only to be killed herself by the humiliated and outraged ruler. Thematically, *Salome* was to be a play about a subject Wilde had claimed for his own as early as 1883. In a letter to the actress Mary Anderson he identified 'the two great speculations and problems' of *The Duchess of Padua*: 'the relations of Sin and Love' (*L* 136). In the particular configuration taken on by these relations in *Salome*, the play is about illicit but overwhelming desire and its fateful clash with ultimate authority. Ellmann identifies Wilde's first indication of interest in writing a play on the subject in his discovery of the image of a dancer: an engraving of Herodias dancing on her hands (just as Flaubert pictures her in *Hérodias*). Wilde, approaching the picture, commented, '*La bella donna della mia mente*' (*E* 322). He began, Ellmann observes, by thinking of the play 'as posing a perverse passion, the desire of vice for virtue, pagan for Christian, living for dead', and 'the abhorrence of vice by virtue, the extremity of renunciation' (*E* 322). These polarities are implied in Frank Kermode's earlier description of the Romantic context of the play: 'Salome is the Dancer in the special role of the Image that costs the artist personal happiness, indeed life itself.' What struck Richard Strauss, Kermode points out, in considering Elisabeth Schumann for the role of Salome in his projected opera was 'precisely the transparent, even girlish, clarity of her tone'; Strauss heard in her voice 'some vocal equivalent for that unemotional, disengaged quality'. Kermode concludes: 'There should be an innocent, totally destructive malice; beauty inhumanly immature and careless cruelty. This is the type.'[17] In *A Vision* Yeats later captured a similar idea of aesthetic and moral distance in describing his mental image of Salome, 'dancing before Herod and receiving the Prophet's head in her indifferent hands'.[18]

Salome as dancer, and Salome's dance, together set the keynote for understanding the play. Salome's remarkable psychic distance, her evident preoccupation and her unflinching remorselessness as she negotiates terms with Herod and, later, speaks to the severed head of Iokanaan itself, are crucial factors in Wilde's creation of his play and its central character. The dancer's ambiguous image, its clear, 'objective' form a contrast to the self-absorbed, self-delighting performer, would seem to have held a special meaning for him as he proceeded to impose his own compelling authorial and personal interests on a well-known biblical story – or concatenation of biblical stories – that had engaged writers, poets, painters and musical composers from a very early time, many of whose treatments of the subject Wilde must have known.

Reviewing relevant evidence, Norbert Kohl ascribes the period of composition of *Salome* to November–December 1891, citing a letter of Wilde's to Pierre Louÿs sending him an uncorrected manuscript whose 'idée de la *construction*', the author explained, should be nonetheless clear.[19] To judge by the earliest surviving manuscript, Wilde wrote until he came to a sticking point, then skipped ahead to another scene or sequence, presumably intending to return later to fill in gaps and assign character names to speeches. A second manuscript, much more complete and containing the speech headings found in published texts of the play, suggests something of the complexities of the composition process.[20] Still a third manuscript, a fair copy of the previous manuscript made by Wilde himself, shows evidence of a number of revisions in more than one hand. Evidence exists to indicate that four friends or associates of Wilde – Pierre Louÿs, Marcel Schwob, Stuart Merrill and Adolphe Retté – were asked by him to review the work and make suggestions (which in some cases Wilde rejected, as the manuscript itself indicates).[21]

A full year elapsed before the first edition appeared, published in Paris in February 1893 and simultaneously in London.[22] Wilde's French colleagues were enthusiastic, especially Mallarmé, who especially praised the character of Salome, 'cette jeune princesse, que définitivement vous évoquâtes'.[23] Maeterlinck called the play 'mystérieux, étrange et admirable' (E 354). An English translation was published in London by Elkin Mathews and John Lane the following year, 'pictured', as the title-page curiously puts it, by Aubrey Beardsley.

The Mathews and Lane English edition indicated no translator on the title-page, but bore Wilde's dedication 'To My Friend Lord Alfred Bruce Douglas the Translator of My Play'.[24] Wilde had asked Douglas to make the translation, but was evidently not satisfied with the results and so became a reluctant collaborator, introducing some changes into Douglas's version, the exact nature and extent of which are unknown but which were evidently sufficient to preclude crediting Douglas in more than an informal way. Peter Raby concludes that Wilde revised Douglas's draft 'to the point where it became his own once more'.[25] Nor was Wilde happy with Beardsley's illustrations; Charles Ricketts reported Wilde's saying that Beardsley's designs were 'like the naughty scribbles a precocious schoolboy makes on the margins of his copybooks'.[26] Their highly individualistic style and perverse, anachronistic substance quickly became controversial. Beardsley himself said the drawings 'aroused great excitement and plenty of abuse'.[27] In 1938 Holbrook Jackson could still find 'something sinister' about them and argue that their 'solemn naughtiness', their use of 'obstetrical and phallic "properties"', and their 'essential seriousness' generated opposition and prejudiced the play's reception from the beginning.[28] They have remained notorious, and irresistibly attractive, ever since.[29]

Wilde's discontent with Beardsley's work is not surprising, given the obvious caricaturing of the author himself in four of the renderings, in which Wilde appears as, among other figures, a woman in the moon and a jester in cap and bells, holding in the crook of his arm a book whose partially visible title reads 'SALOM ...' – Beardsley's flippant suggestion that the book of which this image is itself an illustration is not to be taken seriously.[30] All the same, in an autographed copy of the first French edition Wilde attributed to Beardsley an insider's private knowledge, identifying him as 'the only artist who, besides myself, knows what the dance of the seven veils is, and can see that invisible dance' (*L* 348n.). The importance of the dancer and the dance emerges again in this comment. Elaine Showalter has argued that the dance Beardsley has seen 'is the dance of gender, the delicacy and permeability of the veil separating masculine from feminine, licit from illicit desire'.[31] In an important essay on Beardsley's drawings for *Salome* that ranges well beyond its precise subject, Elliot Gilbert has persuasively argued that the pictures and text are closely related and complementary, and that they illuminate one another in many ways, finally achieving 'a single strong focus', not least because of the concern they share with the 'demonic and perverse sexuality' figured pervasively in the play itself.[32]

The responses of English reviewers were diametrically opposed to the positive French reception. *Salome* must have seemed to them almost a betrayal; the idiom was too unfamiliar, too threatening, and Wilde's models, dramaturgical and characterological, were too far afield from the West End repertoire of dramas and comedies of modern life and romantic costume plays, peopled by upper-class Londoners or their surrogates. *The Times* described the play as 'an arrangement in blood and ferocity, morbid, *bizarre*, repulsive, and very offensive in its adaptation of scriptural phraseology to situations the reverse of sacred'.[33] The *Pall Mall Gazette* perceived it as a mosaic produced by many masters; the reader 'seems to stand in the Island of Voices, and to hear around him and about the utterances of friends, the whisperings of demigods' – among them Gautier, Maeterlinck and, above all, Flaubert, whose *Hérodias*, the reviewer asserted, oppressively overshadows Wilde's play.[34] In a way, these hostile accusations of derivativeness and even plagiarism published in mainstream London journals seem supererogatory; for many later and much more sympathetic accounts of Wilde's dependence on previous treatments of the subject emphasise the same almost embarrassing indebtedness. Kohl's assessment is typical: 'Wilde combined Maeterlinck's symbolism with the rich imagery of the Song of Solomon, the exoticism of Flaubert, and the sensuality of Moreau as interpreted by Huysmans, and out of all these elements he created a *fin-de-siècle femme fatale*.'[35] Largely passing over Wilde's own ideas about art and aesthetics as expressed in his *Intentions* and other critical essays,[36] scholarship and criticism on *Salome* have thus remained preoccupied with the plethora of external sources and 'influences' exerted on the author's thinking and writing by previously existing materials, as recent as Mallarmé's *Hérodiade* and as old as the New Testament.

Considering the enormous literature they have spawned, the biblical sources for the story of Salome are surprisingly brief sketches, found in Matthew 14:1–12 and Mark 6:14–29.[37] Nor is Salome mentioned by name in either of them. In a full discussion of Wilde's use of biblical and other early sources, Shewan traces the development of the legend of Salome, including the first appearance of her name in Josephus's first-century AD *Antiquities of the Jews*, and notes that, early on, there was continuing confusion of Salome with her mother Herodias, along with a tendency to confuse the three Herods mentioned in the Gospels and elsewhere. Shewan shows that Wilde had read Josephus, but concludes that the dramatist, usually sensitive to issues of historical accuracy, abandoned such concerns once he had decided to focus his play on the relationship between Salome and John the Baptist and to have Salome quite unhistorically killed at the end.

Of a similar character is the much discussed impact on Wilde's ideas about his subject allegedly exerted by contemporary or earlier nineteenth-century treatments, such as Heine's *Atta Troll*, Laforgue's *Moralités légendaires* and, most strikingly, Flaubert's *Hérodias*. Shewan emphasizes the relevance of Ernest Renan's poetic interpretation of Christ in his *Vie de Jésus* (1863) and goes so far as to state that 'virtually all the Biblical materials' needed for the play 'could have been suggested' by Wilde's readings in Renan. All the same, Shewan concludes, Wilde's *Salome* belongs, not to an historical or quasi-historical tradition, but to a mythical one in which ethical and religious emphases make way for an aesthetic and symbolic orientation.[38] Evidently, the extensive literature on the subject acted suggestively, not peremptorily, on Wilde's imagination. He could have turned almost anywhere, from late Classical myth and ecclesiastical architecture[39] to contemporary opera, fiction and painting, and encountered some version or some mention of Salome and her dance before the Tetrarch and Salome's insistent claim of the head of the Prophet. J.-K. Huysmans's notorious and widely read novel *A rebours* and its description of two powerfully evocative paintings by Gustave Moreau, of Salome dancing and Salome with the head of John, are only two, albeit chief, items in a long list of likely sources and relevant possibilities adduced by Ellmann, Shewan, Kohl, Daffner, Zagona, Kuryluk, Meltzer, Seidel, Ellis and other commentators, including the hostile but astute reviewers of the first English-language edition of the play.[40]

What still remains insufficiently assessed, after exhaustive review of sources, parallels, analogies and affinities, is the real extent of Wilde's originality. In availing himself of the multifarious materials of the legends and later treatments and basing on them a symbolist play for performance, Wilde employed the drama, the 'most objective' form of art, as he characterised it in his long letter to Douglas from prison, as a way of exploring some essentially private ideas and values that were as 'personal ... as the lyric or the sonnet' (L 466) and were evidently, at the time of writing, paramount.

III

The most immediate indication of Wilde's originality lies in his evident departure from the biblical accounts of the sequence in which the unnamed daughter of Herodias agrees to dance, dances and then exacts a reward from Herod. In Wilde's hands, the character of Salome becomes the instigator of the demand for the head of John instead of relying, as in earlier treatments, on her mother Herodias's prompting. This is only one, easily noticed, instance of Wilde's concerted attempt at a deep, even radical, originality of treatment within the ostensible boundaries of conventional and traditional approaches to his subject.[41] Further indications of originality appear in the process of his blending the biblical texts of the various accounts of Herod, and of the three biblical Herods themselves, into a single character operating in a unified situation. Wilde uses historical and biblical sources with much freedom, as Peter Raby has observed. Wilde's Herod incorporates elements of Herod Antipas, Herod Agrippa and Herod the Tetrarch; as a result, Iokanaan seems identified with the John familiar from the synoptic Gospels but alternatively serves as a vehicle for a much less specific prophetic tradition. This, Raby points out, allows Wilde to 'construct his own apocryphal text, with quotation, semi-quotation and echo ranging from Isaiah to the Book of Revelation'.[42]

An additional aspect of Wilde's fresh approach was his making Herod's court comprehensively representative of the ancient world at the time of Christ. Shewan discerns two groups, cynics and dreamers, representing two contrasting attitudes, 'worldly cynicism and symbolist fantasy', represented in their extremes by Herodias and her Page.[43] Present here are representatives of virtually the entire Mediterranean world: there are a Syrian, a Cappadocian, a Nubian; Tigellinus has spent time in Rome; Caesar has recently sent emissaries from Rome to Herod's palace; there are Jews, engaged in impassioned disputation; there are allusions to Jesus and his extensive travels through parts of the Mediterranean world; and, for good measure, there are two Nazarenes.

The resulting impression is of a microcosm of the known world –

depraved, unredeemed and seemingly irredeemable, despite the reputed healing and saving work of Jesus Christ and despite the presence at Herod's court of John the Baptist – Iokanaan, as Wilde calls him, in a notable instance of distancing – the harbinger of the Saviour, but long imprisoned by Herod in the filthy cistern that lies below the palace courtyard. A striking impression thus emerges of a world in flux, yet held in check by mysterious forces, a world suspended in a kind of Spenglerian – or, perhaps, Yeatsian – moment of transition towards something at least as fearful as what has so far prevailed.[44] In this way Wilde establishes a clear orientation, an effective contextualisation, and an increasing sense of foreboding for the dramatic action that ensues, presenting, as San Juan phrases it, a 'crisis in which extremes, paradoxes, and contraries revolve in a continuum of widespread disorder'.[45]

This disorder is effectively dramatised from the outset: in character, language and action, Wilde depicts perverse, inordinate, illicit and impulsive desire and its clash with ultimate authority. Herod's incestuous lust for his stepdaughter Salome is evident from the moment he follows her on stage, concerned that she has disobeyed his command to return to the banquet inside. Salome's initial, wilful impulse to disobey and thwart Herod has drawn the central action from his banqueting hall onto his private terrace. Herod's evident desire for his wife's daughter has a touch of the comic about it – and Herodias's objections to his interest in her daughter have more than a touch – but the foreboding tension of the sequence is nonetheless clearly felt. And then Salome goes one better than Herod in her unbridled curiosity and insatiable thirst for new experience beyond her years, as well as in her rapidly developing sexual instincts, which culminate in her falling in love with the filthy and disgusting yet perversely attractive figure of the prophet Iokanaan the moment he is brought forth. Mingling desire and disgust, and proving ultimately fatal for the man who is its object, Salome's love becomes, in the major peripety of the dramatic action, all too destructive – and self-destructive for her as well. Like much else in the play, that turn-about contributes to a sustained and conclusive disorder that is deeply ironic as well: condemning Herodias for her incestuous marriage to the brother of her slain husband, Iokanaan calls for her destruction beneath the shields of Herod's soldiers; but at the end it is Salome herself whom Herod, in this fashion, mercilessly destroys.

In the early sequence of the action, before Herod and Herodias and their entourage make their way on stage, the Young Syrian, Narraboth, who has recently been made captain of the guard, serves as a pivotal figure. Clearly, he is infatuated with Salome, and when she insists that he give the order to bring Iokanaan out of the cistern, Narraboth, at first resisting but then wilting before her powerful determination, issues the command that brings Iokanaan out of the hellish depths onto the stage. Then, having gone against the express order of Herod, and witnessing Salome's erotically charged confrontation with Iokanaan, he impulsively kills himself, falling between Salome and the prophet and leaving a pool of blood on the floor that Herod will slip in and find ominous. Narraboth is thus both visually and actually a sacrifice to the opposing forces of Herod's authority and Salome's will and, as such, a sign of the crisis yet to come.

Part of Salome's persuasive effect on Narraboth derives from her promise that the next day as she passes in her litter she will drop 'une petite fleur verte' (25) / 'a little green flower' (CW 588)[46] for him to retrieve as the sign of her special interest. By common critical consent the reference is to a green carnation. Wilde claimed he had invented the flower,[47] but in fact it was, as H. Montgomery Hyde explains, the covert sign of homosexuality in Paris.[48] Wilde presumably counted on his London audience's naïvety when he called for a character in *Lady Windermere's Fan* to wear such a flower and arranged for friends in the audience to be wearing duplicates of it. A reviewer for *Lady's Pictorial* (Mar. 1892, p. 50) nevertheless denounced the flowers worn by Wilde's supporters as 'unmanly'. In Regenia Gagnier's view, Wilde's scheme made them unwitting bearers of 'the emblem of homosexuality', and she argues that the same significance of a veiled homosexuality emerges in Salome's offer of the 'little green flower' to the young captain.[49] Although Wilde maintained to Graham Robertson that the oddly coloured flower meant nothing at all,[50] in retrospect one may speculate that it possessed a coded significance identifying Salome's sexuality as perversely and clandestinely male, suggesting that the Syrian thus kills himself out of homosexual jealousy over Salome's infatuation with Iokanaan.

Much commentary has focused on *Salome* as a covert homosexual work.[51] As early as 1970 Kate Millett characterised the play as a 'drama of homosexual guilt and rejection',[52] a view condemned as too one-sided by Kohl, who nonetheless seems sympathetic to Edmund Bergler's earlier, and simplistic, psychoanalytic view of Wilde as consoling himself and justifying his homosexuality by concluding that women are cruel.[53] In Kohl's view, accepting 'the connection between demonic female sensuality and the author's homosexuality' leads to an identification of the character of Iokanaan with Wilde himself.[54] Yet it is unnecessary to read Iokanaan as a covert image of the author – or, as Ellmann would have it, Herod as a covert representation of him[55] – in order to appreciate the complex dynamic of sexual elements in *Salome*. In his biography of Wilde, Frank Harris recollected a conversation in which his subject explained his attitude towards passionate sexual relations:

A woman's passion is degrading. She is continually tempting you. She wants your desire as a satisfaction for her vanity more than anything else, and her vanity is insatiable if her desire is weak, and so she continually tempts you to excess, and then blames you for the physical satiety and disgust which she herself has created. With a boy there is no vanity in the matter, no jealousy, and therefore none of the tempting, not a tenth part of the coarseness; and consequently desire is always fresh and keen. Oh, Frank, believe me, you don't know what a great romantic passion is.[56]

Taken for its attitude towards heterosexual relations, the passage offers by implication an oddly pejorative view of Salome herself, tempting Herod to an excess of sexual arousal that precipitates a disgust whose ultimate issue is Herod's condemnation of her to death. The complexity of characterisation in the play nonetheless allows for a more covert homosexual aura for Salome, as Gagnier and others have observed. One may even construe Salome's own attraction to Iokanaan as a virtual homosexual seduction, unconscious on his part, that robs Salome of her innocence: 'J'étais une vierge,' she says to Iokanaan's severed head, 'tu m'as déflorée. J'étais chaste, tu as rempli mes veines de feu' (82) / 'I was a virgin, and thou didst take my virginity from me. I was chaste, and thou didst fill my veins with fire' (CW 604).

We may thus see embodied in the play two separate aspects of perversion, heterosexual and homosexual, linked ambiguously together. The clearest example of heterosexual perversity in the play concerns Salome and her insistent desire to kiss the mouth of the prophet – not, one infers, for the wisdom she may derive, but for the sheer sensuality and erotic thrill of the act – and, when he refuses, her desire to kill him, to punish him for his own sexual innocence and, paradoxically, to appropriate the power of that innocence to attract and compromise its perceiver. The threat posed by Salome's aggressiveness reflects an age-old fear of heterosexual relations as dangerous and destructive for men. The idea is evocatively captured, as Robert C. Schweik points out, in the iconography of Gustave Moreau's painting Salome Dancing Before Herod, in which 'Salome's waist is girdled with the trophy-like heads of men'. In his notebooks Moreau described Salome as an 'emblem of sensuality, of unhealthy curiosity, and of that terrible fate reserved for searchers after a nameless ideal'.[57] The idea of the fatally destructive woman, traditionally epitomised in the Medusa, carries an image Beardsley deftly allows to infiltrate his own representations, featuring the 'peculiarly defiant irrationality', as Schweik puts it, of Salome.[58] In what may be the earliest appreciation of Beardsley's first representation of Salome, J'ai baisé ta bouche, Iokanaan (figure 7, p. 132), Theodore Wratislaw published in 1893 a graphic description of the character's morbid attractiveness:

In this drawing, Salome, arrayed in a strange headdress in which the locks and ball of hair take the vague form of a hideous spider, on her knees, holds before her wizened face the severed head of the Baptist; a head with snaky locks like those of Medusa, from which fall a stream of blood which, as it touches the ground springs up again as a marvellous lily. It is like a spider's web, this drawing, with fantastic lines and spirals wandering about at hazard. But the horror lies in the headdress of Salome: the hair falls before her as she kneels, runs over her back and springs from her head like the legs and body of a gigantic spider or scorpion.[59]

There is, then, no clear line between heterosexual and homosexual concerns in *Salome*. Beardsley's perverse celebration of Iokanaan as a Medusa-like seducer of Salome, who is herself depicted as a treacherous threat, effectively captures the pervasive ambiguity of sexuality and sexual attraction in this dense, paradoxical play. To Edward Carpenter, author of *The Intermediate Sex* and a student of 'transitional types of men and women', such ambiguity was explainable as representing persons 'in the middle region' between two poles, who differ biologically but are 'by emotion and temperament very near to each other', displaying 'a union or balance of the feminine and masculine qualities' that allows them to 'interpret men and women to one another'.[60] Showalter argues for the aptness of Beardsley's drawings, in particular the one called 'The Woman in the Moon', insofar as they deliberately blur 'the line between art and reality, sexuality and gender', and so comprise a reflection of the homosexual subtext of an ostensibly heterosexual play.[61]

The play is thus invested, by the middle of the action if not earlier, with an intense and complex erotic charge that lingers to the very end, even where the forces of *thanatos* have seemingly overwhelmed the forces of *eros*. Gagnier argues that Wilde makes sexual desire the 'ruling divinity', an emphasis evident even in Wilde's perversion of scripture for his purpose. In Luke 3:22, God the Father's word on the descent of the Dove – 'Thou art my beloved Son; in thee I am well pleased' – becomes Herodias's 'I am well pleased with my daughter', accomplishing a blasphemous fulfilment of prophecy in Wilde's play. In this way, Gagnier says, a 'Pentecostal vision of fire and doves, spoken in the new tongue of sexual love, celebrates the triumph of Salome and her mother', and so 'Wilde's *Salome* posits the castration of the forces of law and order by the forces of illicit sexual desire.'[62]

It is nevertheless for a brief moment only that the play may be seen to celebrate an alternative sexuality, for ultimately it enacts the destruction of that sexuality at the hands of an official, philistine power. In the later context of Wilde's trials in 1895 for actions prohibited under the Criminal

Law Amendment Act of 1885, the play is powerfully and ironically prescient.

IV

And yet, as Jonathan Dollimore has shown in a masterly discussion of Wilde's transgressive behaviour,[63] even more fundamental matters are at stake in the play than sexual orientation. What is ultimately central in *Salome* is the representation of unquenchably strong desire itself, aside from its specific manifestations in gender and gender relations.

Moreover, it is crucial to perceive how deep-rooted desire is persistently articulated in the idea of seeing things. As many commentators have noted, the play is rife with words and images related to vision, to gazing or looking upon some object of attraction. Foremost among reiterated images of this kind is that of the moon. As the action progresses, we are told the moon is like 'une femme qui sort d'un tombeau' – 'une femme morte' (9) / 'a woman rising from a tomb' – 'a dead woman' (*CW* 583), according to the Page of Herodias. To the Young Syrian, preoccupied with Salome, it is like 'une petite princesse qui porte un voile jaune, et a des pieds d'argent', / 'a little princess who wears a yellow veil, and whose feet are of silver', like 'une princesse qui a des pieds comme des petites colombes blanches' (9–10) / 'a princess who has little white doves for feet' (*CW* 583). To Salome, much preoccupied with herself and her still virginal state, the moon is like 'une petite pièce de monnaie ... une toute petite fleur d'argent ... froide et chaste vierge ... Elle ne s'est jamais souillée. Elle ne s'est jamais donnée aux hommes' (20) / 'a little piece of money, a little silver flower ... cold and chaste ... a virgin. She has never defiled herself. She has never abandoned herself to men' (*CW* 586). The Page and the Young Syrian continue describing the moon in their respective views: like 'la main d'une morte qui cherche à se couvrir avec un linceul' / 'the hand of a dead woman who is seeking to cover herself with a shroud', says the Page; like 'une petite princesse qui a des yeux d'ambres' (26) / 'a little princess, whose eyes are eyes of amber' (*CW* 588), replies the Syrian. Later, in appreciating the physical qualities of Iokanaan, Salome asserts that 'le sein de la lune quand elle couche sur le sein de la mer' (32) / 'the breast of the moon when she lies on the breast of the sea' (*CW* 589) is not so white as Iokanaan's body. The Page's preoccupation with images of death has had an ominous quality that proves all too appropriate when the Young Syrian kills himself: 'Je savais bien que la lune cherchait un mort, mais je ne savais pas que c'était lui qu'elle cherchait' (35) / 'I knew that the moon was seeking a dead thing, but I knew not that it was he whom she sought' (*CW* 591), the Page remarks in sorrow. Herod himself sees the moon as a troubling presence. 'La lune a l'air très étrange ce soir' / 'The moon has a strange look to-night', he observes, like 'une femme hystérique, une femme hystérique qui va cherchant des amants partout' / 'a mad woman, a mad woman who is seeking everywhere for lovers'; it 'chancelle à travers les nuages comme une femme ivre' (38–9) / 'reels through the sky like a drunken woman' (*CW* 592). In this broad context of almost compulsive association, Herodias's disclaimer – 'Non. La lune ressemble à la lune, c'est tout' (39) / 'No; the moon is like the moon, that is all' (*CW* 592) – is positively comic.

Even aside from the moon, there is much to look at in this play, and much to understand in symbolic ways, while at the same time the perils of gazing at things are continually stressed. Salome is a beautiful young woman but dangerous to be looked at, whether by the Young Syrian or by Herod himself. A greater danger arises in the middle of the play in Herod's licentious feasting of his eyes on the body of his stepdaughter as she performs the dance of the seven veils. Wilde's stage direction – '*Salomé danse la danse des sept voiles*' (70) / '*Salome dances the dance of the seven veils*' (*CW* 600) – is surely one of the most laconic directions in all of modern drama. Slaves have brought the seven veils, and Salome has veiled herself only to unveil herself again. The unavoidable conclusion is that what she does is, however tasteful and however much within the limits of theatrical and social decorum, a strip-tease. No matter how ethereal its style, there must be something directly sensual and erotic on view in the dance in order to capture what is surely Wilde's idea of presenting to the gaze – ostensibly the male gaze of Herod himself – something that is strongly desired and equally forcibly forbidden.

Desire does indeed lie at the very centre of the play, multivalent, chaotic and ungovernable. *Salome* presents a protagonist with a critical lack of self-knowledge, but one whose yearnings are too strong to overmaster. However perverse Salome's desire for Iokanaan's head may be, the immutable strength of that desire itself – so great that it overcomes all the world and life itself – is, fundamentally, what the play is about. Almost at the end, Salome utters an exceedingly long speech before the decapitated head of the Baptist. She acknowledges having at last got what she has asked for: the fulfilment of her desire to kiss the mouth of the prophet: 'Ah! tu n'as pas voulu me laisser baiser ta bouche, Iokanaan. Eh, bien! je la baiserai maintenant' (80) / 'Ah! Thou wouldst not suffer me to kiss thy mouth, Iokanaan. Well! I will kiss it now' (*CW* 604). She has triumphed over both Iokanaan's scandalised refusal and Herod's pusillanimity. The speech ends, true to her preoccupation, with Salome's declaration that the mystery of love is greater than the mystery of death: 'Il ne faut regarder que l'amour'

Figure 7   Aubrey Beardsley's first Salome illustration; the original drawing was published in the first number of *The Studio*, April, 1893, prompting John Lane to commission Beardsley to illustrate the English edition of *Salome*

(83) / 'Love only should one consider' (*CW* 604). Only love is what matters; nothing else. Herod's reaction is one of deep revulsion and fear, and he condemns Salome as a monstrous person who has committed a crime against an unknown god. Herodias defiantly declares her approval of what her daughter has done, but Herod's fears persist; he calls for the torches to be extinguished and for even the moon and stars to be hidden

from view. Ever more fearful of looking at things, he commands Herodias to retreat with him into the palace.

At this point the stage directions call for a great cloud to obscure the moon, momentarily throwing the scene into darkness and gloom. Salome continues to kneel before the head of Iokanaan, oblivious to all except that one object and remaining, for the moment, silent. Then, as Herod begins to climb the staircase, the voice of Salome is heard once more, emanating from the obscurity, speaking a much briefer speech that ends '... J'ai baisé ta bouche, Iokaanan, j'ai baisé ta bouche.' Aubrey Beardsley demonstrated his understanding of how important this climactic moment is when he used the speech as a caption for his very first illustration of the play.[64] While Herod slowly mounts the staircase, Salome again takes up her chanted speech addressing the head of Iokanaan, protracting the reverie-like state into which she has fallen and luxuriating in her situation. Katharine Worth sees a tragic quality in the moment, capturing the presence still of the 'little lost girl' of the beginning of the play.[65] The longer the moment lasts, the higher the dramatic tension rises. Herod's protracted mounting of the staircase through the persistent darkness suggests that he feels defeated and has abandoned Salome to her perverse morbidity. Every indication now is that she will be allowed to retain her gruesome prize undisturbed, unmolested. And then, in a sudden, unprepared reversal that brings full the resolution of the drama, a ray of moonlight falls on the figure of Salome and illuminates her; at the same instant Herod turns and, seeing her captured in the pool of light, cries out in vengeful fury: 'Tuez cette femme!' (84) / 'Kill that woman!' (*CW* 605). The terrible end is swift and sure. Herod's soldiers advance out of the darkness into the circle of light and crush beneath their shields '*Salomé, fille d'Hérodias, Princesse de Judée*'.

Curiously, in these concluding stage directions Wilde identifies the dying Salome in quite formal, and specifically matrilineal, terms. What has happened is that, notwithstanding her sudden and violent death, Salome has had the ineffable pleasure of being granted her fondest desire, and her unshakeable will has brought her at last to the point of enjoying the intimate kiss denied her by the prophet while he lived. As Ellmann explains,

> Like Huysmans's Des Esseintes, she is a *jusqu'au-boutiste*, willing her passion beyond human limits, beyond the grave even. Those who do this become exemplary; their value as illustrations mitigates their monstrousness. When death comes to Salome, it takes the measure of her boundless desire. She dies into a parable of self-consuming passion. (*E* 326)

Salome has acted with such single-mindedness of purpose and has remained so implacable in her desire that she has overmastered the weaker will of the patriarch, compromising his supreme power and stature in the kingdom and forcing him into the most extreme of actions: first, the killing of the prophet despite deep misgivings about the advisability of such a deed, and then the cowardly, vindictive murder of Salome herself. Far from having been defeated, it is she who has defeated the patriarch; it is she who will live in myth and legend, and in the imaginations of all who have seen her dance.

Some of the best criticism on *Salome* focuses on the complex character of its central figure and its achievement of a larger, transcendent status. Gilbert finds Salome's kissing of the lips of the severed head, in itself a repellent act, 'unaccountably touching': Wilde half convinces us that 'in experiencing the dark obsessions of Salome we are experiencing our own'. About this play, Gilbert adds, Wilde might have proclaimed, 'Salome, *c'est moi.*' 'A conventionally monstrous act', Gilbert explains, 'can be made to appear recognizably human through association with ourselves'; by analogy, one may discover a more general process in which objective reality yields to 'the dissolving influences of individual perception'.[66] San Juan, in a convincing reading, sees in Salome's long metaphoric flights the release of libidinal impulses. Hers are lawless motivations reflecting a 'poisonous malice' and a 'careless cruel passion' lying at the centre of Wilde's conception. Salome gains 'a quality of heroic firmness', San Juan argues, in executing 'the law of Eros ... within her'. At the same time, she transcends bodily desire, and in her death annihilates guilt and 'the discords of existence'.[67] Taking a similar view, Peter Raby describes the death of Salome as 'a symbolic reenactment of the Fall, and a highly charged, ritualistic attempt at synthesis, as Salome assumes a prophetic role in her own search for fulfilment'.[68]

This remarkable enlargement of a character who begins as an ostensibly weak, waif-like pubescent girl occurs partly through Wilde's brilliant use of the potential of the physical theatre.[69] In the concluding moments of the play, at a point somewhere near the centre of the stage, Salome seizes from the Executioner the head of Iokanaan, placed on '*un bouclier d'argent*' (80) / '*a silver shield*' (*CW* 603). Salome resolutely makes this central point her own resting place, delineating a space that mentally excludes all traces of the exterior setting and so achieving 'a subjectivity and an interiority', as Gilbert explains, notably absent from Wilde's sources.[70] Salome has been instinctively intent on establishing this interiority almost from her entrance. Her strong will to gain what she wants – initially, the presence of the prophet on Herod's private terrace and, later, the head of the prophet himself – makes her singularly able to ignore whatever might distract from her purpose. She seems to be walking in a kind of dream. This developing correspondence of Salome's outer and inner reality, fully articulated at the moment when the head of Iokanaan is set before her, identifies the play of which she is the eponymous and central character as an authentic symbolist drama. In his essay on Huysmans, Arthur Symons defined symbolism as an aesthetic force working to establish 'the links which hold the world together, the affirmation of an eternal, minute, intricate, almost invisible life, which runs through the whole universe'.[71] A true measure of the keen sense of theatre attributed to him by Robert Ross emerges in Wilde's remarkable dramaturgical ability, evident here, to impose onto the objective, alien ground of Herod's terrace an entirely subjective and transformative vision of Salome. In this vision, she becomes the effective centre of a spiritual world enveloping what is a frankly and perversely sensual sphere of action and reifying it as a world instinct with love. When the moonlight falls upon Salome, it illuminates her as the ultimate interpreter of what the moon means: it means no less than herself, and all that her self comprehends. As Gilbert argues, Salome draws her strength from 'a wholly apolitical self-indulgence', and when Herod accuses her of being merely her mother's agent she replies: 'It is not my mother's voice that I heed. *It is for my own pleasure* that I ask the head of Iokanaan on a silver charger.'[72] *Salome*, Gagnier observes, is Wilde's 'personal fantasy of the triumph of sexual love over the repressive forces of society'.[73] In this final moment, Salome has now become a fully articulated icon of desire and love, even while, in a more tragic mode of understanding, she has become the victim of an embattled patriarchal society's remorseless revenge.

V

In a letter to Douglas from Berneval-sur-Mer shortly after his release from prison, Wilde discussed his prospects as a writer and summed up his accomplishment to date. Adapting a crucial statement from the earlier, much longer letter to Douglas written from Reading prison (*L* 466), he reasserted what he believed was his singular contribution to dramatic art: 'If I were asked of myself as a dramatist, I would say that my unique position was that I had taken the Drama, the most objective form known to art, and made it as personal a mode of expression as the Lyric or the Sonnet, while enriching the characterisation of the stage, and enlarging – at any rate in the case of *Salome* – its artistic horizon' (*L* 589). This rendering of his art from the vantage point of a mask-like objectivity was, Wilde argues, what paradoxically liberates the artist and affords him scope to tell the truth. In this case, as he himself points out, Wilde has not only told the personal truth about himself; he has enriched dramatic characterisation and, just as important, enlarged the artistic horizon of the stage. That is, in creating Salome he has broadened and deepened the generic basis of character, and he has moved beyond the realistic stage to a more modern *mise-en-scène* of symbolic dimensions.

Edouard Roditi, quoting Wilde's Berneval letter, points out that this notion of an artful articulation of inherent authorial subjectivity should be understood as a development or refinement of genre. In *Salome*, his most essentially lyrical drama, Wilde had reduced the traditional components of effective dramaturgy – plot, structure, characterisation and the like – which had unnecessarily complicated such earlier plays as *Vera* and *The Duchess of Padua*, to 'basic elements of genre'. As Wilde 'sorted his varied gifts', Roditi argues, he discovered through a persistent and original study of genre 'the aspects of his personality which could be cultivated there most fruitfully ...'.[74] Those aspects combine into a limpid subjectivity that, for Wilde, expresses the very nature of modernity. As early as 1883, in the letter to Mary Anderson quoted earlier, he explained that audiences will be surprised to find modern life in an Italian tragedy (*The Duchess of Padua*), but '*the essence of art is to produce the modern idea under an antique form*' (*L* 137). Later, writing to Douglas, he asserted that 'the egoistic note' had always been to him 'the primal and ultimate note of modern art' (*L* 590).

Roditi's explanation of Wilde's mastery of genre as a process of effective self-expression makes much sense as a gloss of the principal features of Wilde's dramatic art. Worth concurs; Salome's unveiling, she explains, is 'an appropriate image' for what Wilde considered the artist's primary task: 'self-expression and self-revelation'.[75] If anything at all is clear about Wilde's way of writing plays, it is that he did not begin with a notion of coherent genre into which he fitted what he had to say; rather, he began with a sense of his own subjective self and personal situation, a self impelled irresistibly towards some kind of formal expression that his own architectonic imagination would then enable him to control and manipulate. Every such attempt was different from every other. In the long letter from Reading prison, Wilde explained that he could not rest content with repetition of the familiar, but had to 'pass on' to the 'other side of the garden', which also 'had its secrets'. At this time, there was a constancy in the effort that held promise of a larger coherence. 'At every single moment of one's life', he explained, 'one is what one is going to be no less than what one has been. Art is symbol, because man is a symbol' (*L* 475–6). Elsewhere, in 'The Soul of Man Under Socialism', Wilde said that 'Art is the most intense mood of Individualism that the world has known', in a passage Shewan has identified as the germ of the character of Salome.[76]

In responding to such visionary pronouncements, criticism has often floundered. Philip Cohen's view that Wilde's oeuvre reflects a continuing spiritual and moral crisis – Salome and Iokanaan, he asserts, 'function largely as symbolic projections of Herod's – and Wilde's – divided mind' – reflects a simplistic notion of Wilde's generic objectivity as no more than 'camouflage' for 'his confession'.[77] G. Wilson Knight's comment that Wilde's plays can be read in part as 'oblique expressions of his inner torments'[78] runs in the same vein, as does Worth's endorsement of Ellmann's view that Herod is a Wildean self-portrait, a clandestine expression of Wilde's alleged ambivalence over the extremes represented by Salome and Iokanaan.[79] Herod's striking self-consciousness, noted by Showalter, Worth and others, and Beardsley's representation of Wilde as Herod in one instance, may have encouraged such interpretation. Holbrook Jackson's earlier notion of *Salome* as a modern morality play, 'a tragedy of spiritual disharmony' in which each character 'founders through lack of balance between body and soul',[80] offers a more clear-sighted view. Yet none of these approaches fully accounts for the extraordinarily inward-turning, self-sufficing, self-revealing character of Salome herself, and for the author who stands ambiguously – or perhaps triumphantly – behind her.

For Wilde such subjectivity is a prime generative force for art. To miss this basic characteristic of Wilde's writing for the theatre is to misunderstand the experiential and dramaturgical foundation of his plays. Wilde's *Salome*, far from being an anomalous work in the oeuvre of a popular master of comedy-drama and farcical comedy, stands exemplarily at the very centre of his dramatic writing. As Shewan observes, 'the opposing forces of self-expression and self-repression are present in all of Wilde's plays, though they reach their Romantic climax' in *Salome*.[81] Far from obscuring or distorting his efforts in a variety of dramatic genres, the play sheds a clarifying and orienting light on every one of his efforts in that form. Roditi observes that Wilde developed 'a paradoxical ethics of good and evil whose Manichean identity of contraries is typical of many heresies that once flourished among the more Oriental sects of Gnosticism and Early Christianity'.[82] However true this is, the more essential point about Wilde's heretical dramaturgy is that it is not only based on a paradoxical ethic of good and evil, but on one ultimately expressive of the man himself.

And so *Salome* deserves renewed consideration as a master work of dramatic authorial self-expression and, simultaneously, a powerful and exemplary piece for the modern theatre: these are the polarities, subjective and objective, of its nature as a work of symbolist art. Although it will never unseat *The Importance of Being Earnest* as Wilde's most perennially popular play, *Salome* nevertheless challenges the Wildean audience to a fresh engagement with the generative forces of his dramaturgy, even as it leads the serious student of Wilde and his plays towards a broader reassessment of his accomplishment.

NOTES

1 Unidentified interview, in 'Stuart Mason', *Bibliography of Oscar Wilde* (1914, rpt. New York: Haskell House, 1972), pp. 372–3.
2 Although some contemporaries and later commentators insisted that Wilde wrote the play for Bernhardt, Wilde himself steadfastly denied he had ever written a play for a specific actor (*L* 336). Wilde's spelling of his title character's name often omits the final accent; I have followed Hart-Davis's practice of omitting it in editing the *Letters* as the norm except in quotations from original sources.
3 *Pall Mall Gazette*, 1 July 1892.
4 *Salomé, La Sainte Courtisane, A Florentine Tragedy*, new edn (London: Methuen, 1909), p. ix.
5 Frank Fowell and Frank Palmer, *Censorship in England* (London: Frank Palmer, 1913), p. 236.
6 Letter, 27 June 1893, quoted in John Russell Stephens, *The Censorship of English Drama 1824–1901* (Cambridge: Cambridge University Press, 1980), p. 112.
7 48 & 49 Vic. cap. 69. See F. B. Smith, 'Labouchere's Amendment to the Criminal Law Amendment Bill', *Historical Studies* 17 (Oct. 1976), 165–75.
8 'A Note on "Salome"', *Salome A Tragedy in One Act Translated from the French of Oscar Wilde* (London: John Lane, 1907), p. xiii.
9 *Salomé, La Sainte Courtisane, A Florentine Tragedy*, pp. 93–109. The British Library holds over thirty editions of the play; the Ross-Ledger Collection in the Bodleian has some forty-nine (*Salome*, trans. R. A. Walker (London: William Heinemann, 1957), p. 13).
10 See the extensive coverage of Strauss's opera in *Richard Strauss: Salome*, ed. Derrick Puffett, Cambridge Opera Handbooks (Cambridge: Cambridge University Press, 1989).
11 Alfred Schattmann, *Richard Strauss: Salome: A Music-Drama in One Act after Oscar Wilde's Work of the Same Name* (London: Breitkopf and Härtel, 1907?), p. 7.
12 James Agate, 'Oscar Wilde and the Theatre', *The Masque* 3 (1947), 7.
13 Rodney Shewan, *Oscar Wilde: Art and Egotism* (London: Macmillan, 1977), p.147. See Edouard Roditi, *Oscar Wilde* (Norfolk, CT: New Directions, 1947), and Epifanio San Juan, Jun., *The Art of Oscar Wilde* (Princeton: Princeton University Press, 1967).
14 Ellmann's 'Overtures to *Salome*' originally appeared in the *Yearbook of Comparative and General Literature* 17 (1968) 17–28, rpt. *Oscar Wilde: A Collection of Critical Essays*, ed. Richard Ellmann (Englewood Cliffs, NJ: Prentice Hall, 1969), pp. 73–91.
15 *The Autobiography of Lord Alfred Douglas* (1929, rpt. Freeport, NY: Books for Libraries, 1970) p. 160n. Clyde de L. Ryals disposes of this legend and two others in examining the evidence of the three surviving manuscripts, which, he concludes, yield the clear indication that the first French edition constituted the play 'almost entirely as Wilde wrote it' ('Oscar Wilde's *Salome*', *Notes and Queries* 204 (1959), 57). The earliest manuscript is in the Bibliotheca Bodmeriana in Cologny, Geneva; two later manuscripts are in the Harry Ransom Humanities Research Center, University of Texas, Austin, and the Rosenbach

Collection in Philadelphia. Proofs of the first French edition are in the Clark Memorial Library, Los Angeles.

16 Stuart Merrill, 'Souvenirs sur le Symbolisme', *Prose et vers, œuvres posthumes* (1925), quoted in *L* 305n.

17 Frank Kermode, *Romantic Image* (New York: Macmillan, 1957), pp. 73–4.

18 W. B. Yeats, *A Vision*, 2nd edn (1937, rpt. London: Macmillan, 1962), p. 273.

19 *L* 305, quoted in Norbert Kohl, *Oscar Wilde: The Works of a Conformist Rebel* (Cambridge: Cambridge University Press, 1989), p. 178.

20 Now in the Harry Ransom Humanities Research Center, University of Texas, Austin.

21 Now in the Rosenbach Collection, Philadelphia. Retté recalled Wilde's request to remove 'les anglicismes trop formels', adding that Merrill proposed some slight alterations and Louÿs likewise altered a few phrases. This, Retté explains, was the manuscript that then was printed (Retté, *Le Symbolisme, anecdotes et souvenirs* (1903), quoted in *L* 305n). Proofs of the first French edition are now in the Clark Memorial Library. Shewan's account of the composition and publication is the fullest and most accurate; see 'Oscar Wilde's *Salomé*: A Critical Variorum Edition', Ph.D. diss., University of Reading, 1982, vol. 1.

22 Oscar Wilde, *Salomé: drame en un acte* (Paris: Librairie de l'Art Indépendant; London: Elkin Mathews and John Lane, 1893).

23 Unpublished letter to Wilde from Mallarmé, March 1893, quoted in Ellmann, 'Overtures to Salome' 73–4 & n.

24 *Salome A Tragedy in One Act: Translated from the French of Oscar Wilde: Pictured by Aubrey Beardsley* (London: Elkin Mathews and John Lane, 1894), p. [viii].

25 Peter Raby, *Oscar Wilde* (Cambridge: Cambridge University Press, 1988) p. 102. Ellmann (*Oscar Wilde*, pp. 379–81) describes the running quarrel Wilde and Douglas had over the translation, ultimately involving the publisher John Lane and the illustrator Aubrey Beardsley as well, who in November told Ross that he had withdrawn three of the illustrations and supplied three new ones 'simply beautiful and quite irrelevant' (*The Letters of Aubrey Beardsley*, ed. Henry Maas, J. L. Duncan and W. G. Good (Rutherford, NJ: Fairleigh Dickinson University Press, 1970, p. 58).

26 *Oscar Wilde: Recollections by Jean Paul Raymond and Charles Ricketts* (London: Nonesuch, 1932), p. 52.

27 Maas, Duncan and Good (eds.), *The Letters of Aubrey Beardsley*, p. 55.

28 Oscar Wilde, *Salome*, intro. Holbrook Jackson (London: Limited Editions Club, 1938), p. 13.

29 Neil Bartlett, in *Who Was That Man? A Present for Mr Oscar Wilde* (London: Serpent's Tail, 1988) p. 39, observes that Beardsley's illustrations 'dragged the Princess screaming from Paris to London sw3, picturing her as a modern society woman on whose bookshelf festered unread copies of Apuleius, Baudelaire and de Sade'.

30 See Elliot L. Gilbert, '"Tumult of Images": Wilde, Beardsley, and *Salome*', *Victorian Studies* 26 (Winter 1983), 133–59, and Maureen T. Kravec, 'Wilde's *Salome*', *Explicator* 42 (Fall 1983), 30–2. A full portfolio of the Beardsley drawings, not all of which were published in the Elkin-Mathews first edition, is in the British Library.

31 Elaine Showalter, *Sexual Anarchy: Gender and Culture at the* Fin de Siècle (London: Bloomsbury, 1991), p. 152.

32 Gilbert, ' "Tumult of Images" ', pp. 133, 138.

33 23 Feb. 1893, p. 8, in Karl Beckson, *Oscar Wilde: The Critical Heritage* (New York: Barnes and Noble, 1970), p. 133.

34 Review of 27 Feb. 1893, quoted in Beckson, *Critical Heritage*, pp. 135–6.

35 Kohl, *Oscar Wilde*, p. 192. In his essay 'The Artist and the Dancer' Rodney Shewan emphasises the priority of the influence on *Salome* of the *Song of Solomon*, alongside which Maeterlinck's influence is, he argues, relatively superficial; he cites the instance of Salome's speech to the head of Iokanaan ('The Artist and the Dancer in Three Symbolist *Salomés*', *Bucknell Review* 30 (1986), 123, 126).

36 John Styan is one of a small number of critics who call attention to this obvious relationship; see J. L. Styan, *Modern Drama in Theory and Practice*, vol. II: *Symbolism, Surrealism and the Absurd* (Cambridge: Cambridge University Press, 1981), p. 35.

37 Among numerous modern reviews of the biblical accounts, see especially Françoise Meltzer's in *Salome and the Dance of Writing: Portraits of Mimesis in Literature* (Chicago: University of Chicago Press, 1987), pp. 29–41.

38 Shewan, 'Oscar Wilde's *Salomé*', I: 61, 19–73; I: 73–9; I: 122.

39 See Meltzer, *Salome and the Dance of Writing*, p. 16, for a discussion of representations of the Salome story on church doors.

40 Hugo Daffner, *Salome. Ihre Gestalt in Geschichte und Kunst: Dichtung – Bildende Kunst – Musik* (Munich: Hugo Schmidt, 1912); Sylvia C. Ellis, *The Plays of W. B. Yeats: Yeats and the Dancer* (New York: St Martin's, 1995); Ewa Kuryluk, *Salome and Judas in the Cave of Sex: The Grotesque: Origins, Iconography, Techniques* (Evanston, IL: Northwestern University Press, 1987); Linda Seidel, 'Salome and the Canons', *Women's Studies* 2 (1984), 29–66. For the others see the citations in the Select bibliography; see also Beckson, *Critical Heritage*, for excerpts from the reviews and other contemporary criticism.

41 I have explored this characteristic feature of Wilde's writing at greater length in '*Salome* and the Wildean Art of Symbolist Theatre', *Modern Drama* 37 (Spring 1994): 84–103.

42 Peter Raby, *Oscar Wilde* (Cambridge: Cambridge University Press, 1988), p. 108.

43 Shewan, *Oscar Wilde: Art and Egotism*, p. 137.

44 In *A Vision* Yeats said that when he thought of the moment before revelation he thought of Salome, anointing her bare limbs with lion's fat that she might 'gain the favour of a king'; from the same impulse, Yeats said, will come 'the Galilean revelation' (273). In *The Art of Oscar Wilde*, p. 123, Epifanio San Juan, Jun. points out that Yeats saw the figure of Salome as symbolising 'precisely that moment of cultural equilibrium that precedes the Christian dispensation and follows the full heroic life of Hellenism, the exaltation of the muscular flesh and civilized perfection. One can make a persuasive argument that *Salome* is an allegory of a Spenglerian moment in European history.'

45 San Juan, *The Art of Oscar Wilde*, p. 126.

46 Quotations from *Salome* (page references in parentheses) are from the first French edition, followed by the English translation as reprinted in *Complete Works of Oscar Wilde* (London: HarperCollins, 1994).

47 'I invented that magnificent flower', he wrote to the *Pall Mall Gazette* (2 Oct. 1894, p. 3), denying in the same letter that he had anything to do with a 'middle-class and mediocre book' of that title, obviously a reference to Robert Hichens's *The Green Carnation* (1894).

48 Hyde (ed.), *The Three Trials of Oscar Wilde* (New York: University Books, 1956), p. 370.

49 Regenia Gagnier, *Idylls of the Marketplace: Oscar Wilde and the Victorian Public* (Stanford: Stanford University Press, 1986), pp. 163–4.

50 *Time Was: The Reminiscences of W. Graham Robertson* (London: Hamish Hamilton, 1931), p. 135.

51 See, in particular, Jonathan Dollimore, *Sexual Dissidence: Augustine to Wilde, Freud to Foucault* (Oxford: Clarendon Press, 1991), and Showalter, *Sexual Anarchy*.

52 Kate Millett, *Sexual Politics* (Garden City, NY: Doubleday, 1970), p. 153.

53 Edmund Bergler, M.D., '*Salome*, the Turning Point in the Life of Oscar Wilde', *Psychoanalytic Review* 40 (Jan. 1956), 100.

54 Kohl, *Oscar Wilde*, p. 193.

55 'Overtures to *Salome*', p. 165. A photograph identified by Ellmann as Wilde, dressed as Salome and dancing before the severed head of Iokanaan, appears in Ellmann's biography (*Oscar Wilde* ill. 49) but see Merlin Holland's discussion in this volume, pp. 10–12.

56 *Oscar Wilde: His Life and Confessions* (1918, rpt. New York: Horizon, 1974), pp. 465–6.

57 'Oscar Wilde's *Salome*, the Salome Theme in Later European Art, and a Problem of Method in Cultural History', in *Twilight of Dawn: Studies in English Literature in Transition*, ed. O. M. Brack, Jun. (Tucson: University of Arizona Press, 1987), pp. 126, 224n.

58 Schweik, 'Oscar Wilde's *Salome*', p. 129. Freud's explanation of the significance of the image and its relationship to the castration complex may be found in 'Medusa's Head', *Complete Psychological Works* (London: Hogarth Press, 1953–), XVIII, 273–4.

59 [Theodore Wratislaw,] 'Some Drawings of Aubrey Beardsley', *The Artist and Journal of Home Culture* 14 (Sep. 1893), 259.

60 Edward Carpenter, *The Intermediate Sex: A Study of Some Transitional Types of Men and Women* (London: Swan Sonnenschein, 1908), pp. 17–18.

61 Showalter, *Sexual Anarchy*, pp. 152, 150. See also Gail Finney's correlative view of Salome as a man 'on a disguised, symbolic level', in *Women in Modern Drama: Freud, Feminism, and European Theater at the Turn of the Century* (Ithaca: Cornell University Press, 1989), pp. 62–3, 65.

62 Gagnier, *Idylls of the Marketplace*, pp. 168–9.

63 See *Sexual Dissidence*, ch. 1 and *passim*.

64 The illustration was first published in *The Studio*, accompanied by a short appreciation of Beardsley by Joseph Pennell ('A New Illustrator: Aubrey Beardsley', *The Studio* 1 [Apr. 1893] 11, 14–19). Shewan points out that this drawing, an uncommissioned first attempt, reinterprets Holman Hunt's engraving (1859) for Tennyson's 'The Lady of Shalott'; see *Wilde: Art and Egotism*, p.139 and plates 11–12.

65 *The Irish Drama of Europe from Yeats to Beckett* (Atlantic Highlands, NJ: Humanities Press, 1978), p. 101.
66 Gilbert, ' "Tumult of Images" ', 144.
67 San Juan, *The Art of Oscar Wilde*, pp. 121–2.
68 Raby, *Oscar Wilde*, p. 109.
69 See Richard Allen Cave, 'Power Structuring: The Presentation of Outsider Figures in Wilde's Plays', *Rediscovering Oscar Wilde*, ed. C. George Sandulescu, Princess Grace Irish Library Series 8 (Gerrards Cross: Colin Smythe, 1994), pp. 37–51; and Worth, *Irish Drama of Europe*, pp. 102–11.
70 Gilbert's italics. Gilbert, ' "Tumult of Images" ', 142.
71 Symons, *The Symbolist Movement in Literature* (London: W. Heinemann, 1899), p. 146.
72 Gilbert, ' "Tumult of Images" ', 152.
73 Gagnier, *Idylls of the Marketplace*, p. 169.
74 Roditi, *Oscar Wilde*, p. 65.
75 *Oscar Wilde* (New York: Grove, 1983), p. 66.
76 Shewan, *Oscar Wilde: Art and Egotism*, p. 134.
77 Philip K. Cohen, *The Moral Vision of Oscar Wilde* (London: Associated University Presses, 1976), p. 158.
78 G. Wilson Knight, *The Golden Labyrinth: A Study of British Drama* (London: Phoenix House, 1962), p. 307.
79 Worth, *Oscar Wilde*, p. 61.
80 Oscar Wilde, *Salome*, intro. Jackson, p. 16.
81 Shewan, *Oscar Wilde: Art and Egotism*, p. 145.
82 Roditi, *Oscar Wilde*, pp. 65–6.

9

PETER RABY

Wilde's comedies of Society

Wilde's three Society comedies were produced by different managers: *Lady Windermere's Fan* by George Alexander at the St James's Theatre (20 February 1892), *A Woman of No Importance* by Herbert Beerbohm Tree (19 April 1893) and *An Ideal Husband* (3 January 1895) by Lewis Waller, both at the Theatre Royal, Haymarket. Had Henry James's *Guy Domville* not been a failure and left Alexander with a gap in his season, Wilde would have added Charles Wyndham and the Criterion Theatre to his list with *The Importance of Being Earnest*. In the months before his career collapsed in the witness box of the Queensberry libel trial, he was sketching out a new play of modern life for Alexander, the Gerald Lancing scenario which Frank Harris later fleshed out as *Mr and Mrs Daventry*; and negotiating with American producers such as Albert Palmer about a play ' "with no real serious interest" – just a comedy', and with Charles Frohman for a 'modern "School for Scandal" ' style of play. This flurry of activity indicates both Wilde's perceived marketability on both sides of the Atlantic and his own growing confidence in a genre he had only taken up in 1891, in fact at Alexander's invitation. 'I wonder can I do it in a week, or will it take three?' he reportedly commented to Frank Harris. 'It ought not to take long to beat the Pineros and the Joneses.'

Writing to Alexander in February 1891, Wilde offered a rather different attitude towards his progress on *Lady Windermere's Fan*: 'I am not satisfied with myself or my work. I can't get a grip of the play yet: I can't get my people real ... I am very sorry, but artistic work can't be done unless one is in the mood; certainly my work can't. Sometimes I spend months over a thing, and don't do any good; at other times I write a thing in a fortnight' (*L* 282). Even allowing for a writer's defensiveness to explain his delays in delivering a commissioned piece, Wilde makes clear the artistic seriousness with which he approached his plays; an attitude to which the numerous drafts and rewritings of all his comedies also testify. In the case of *Lady Windermere's Fan*, it was a process which, famously, continued after the opening night, with changes made at Alexander's strongly urged suggestion to reveal Mrs Erlynne's relationship to her daughter Lady Windermere by gradual degrees, instead of reserving it for the fourth act. Following the first run of each play, Wilde would then make alterations and additions to the post-production printed text. No playwright before him writing in English had paid such minute attention to the text of both his performed and published work.

What did Wilde mean by 'I can't get my people real'? In the London theatrical context of 1891, one might assume that he was responding to Ibsen. Janet Achurch had appeared as Nora Helmer in the 1889 production of *A Doll's House* which Harley Granville-Barker described as 'the most important dramatic event of the decade': Lady Windermere prepares to leave her child, like Nora, even if she changes her mind as she waits in Lord Darlington's rooms. In March 1891 came the singular, explosive English presentation of *Ghosts*; in April, Wilde returned a second time to see Elizabeth Robins as Hedda Gabler. He was well aware both of the revolutionary kind of dramatic writing Ibsen was practising, and the different kind of acting that Ibsen's roles demanded, especially those of the women.

Wilde, like Ibsen initially, worked within the dramatic conventions of his time. This was particularly evident in terms of plot. When *Lady Windermere's Fan* was produced in February 1892, some of the critics leaped eagerly to proclaim its ancestry: Victorien Sardou was the name frequently thrown at Wilde, but other suspects included Haddon Chambers's *The Idler*, recently performed at Alexander's St James's Theatre, while Sydney Grundy complained that he could not revive his own deservedly forgotten 1883 piece *The Glass of Fashion* because Wilde had already done so, 'under the title of *Lady Windermere's Fan*'. Some of the situations, motifs and devices which Wilde employed – the woman concealed in the room of a man who is not her husband, the mislaid fan, the misdirected letter – are decidedly, even deliberately, familiar: in an early draft of the play, Wilde has Lady Windermere hide behind a screen, rather than a curtain, an obvious echo of Sheridan's *School for Scandal* (a 'quote' which might today be applauded as sophisticated intertextuality, the kind of theatrical echo which Stoppard deploys so skilfully). Wilde was a master of conventions, and particularly the conventions of popular form: he did not hesitate to exploit any medium within which he chose to work.

Wilde, with one eye on the dramatic genius of Ibsen and the other on the commercial competition in London's West End, targeted his audience with adroit precision. Alexander's audiences at the St James's Theatre were well connected, well dressed, wealthy and influential; and Wilde set *Lady*

Windermere's Fan explicitly within their world. The Windermeres' town house is located in Carlton House Terrace, a few hundred yards from the theatre in King Street, and close to the Foreign Office and the London Clubs. Wilde maps out the restricted geography of English upper-middle-class society: Grosvenor Square, Curzon Street, the Park and, beyond this little parish of St James's, the rose gardens of country houses like Selby. The names of the principal characters root the action in the English landscape: Windermere, Darlington, Berwick. Beyond England lies a Europe which provides temporary refuge for erring husbands in the ambivalent spas of Wiesbaden, Homburg and Aix, or a more permanent exile in capitals such as Vienna or Rome to be reached in the luxury of the Club Train.

This world of 'Society', circumscribed by conventions, monitored by formidable dowagers such as the Duchess of Berwick, measured by the rituals of the English version of the tea ceremony, or the endless round of 'small and early' dances and luncheons, is created brilliantly by Wilde. (Like Henry James in *The Portrait of a Lady*, or T. S. Eliot in 'The Love Song of J. Alfred Prufrock', he suggests both the comforting security and the terrible emptiness of the routines.) This was a world Wilde was already confident about, and one he would become even more familiar with after the success of this play; and he strove to get the details right. During the rehearsal period, he bombarded Alexander with comments, writing him long letters when he was not able to have 'a formal quiet interview at the end of each day's rehearsal', as he had requested. He learned that Alexander planned to use the Act I setting – originally specified as Lord Windermere's library – for Act IV, which Wilde had intended to be Lady Windermere's boudoir, an arrangement which would have shifted the context from male to female territory. 'If through pressure of time, or for reasons of economy, you are unable to give the play its full scenic mounting, the scene that has to be repeated should be the second, not the first. Lady Windermere may be in her drawing-room in the fourth act. She should not be in her husband's library.' A compromise, the morning-room, was reached, a setting which could accommodate both Lady Windermere's area, the table with the bowl of roses and the fan and the site of afternoon tea, and, in male opposition, Lord Windermere's bureau, with books and papers and the locked bank-book. Wilde's comments revealed a sharp understanding of stage dynamics in creative tension with his social awareness. He demanded a central position for Mrs Erlynne in the last act. 'Windermere, being in his own house, can pace up and down – does, in fact, do so; Mrs Erlynne, of course, cannot do anything of the kind. She rises from the sofa, as marked in the play, and sits down, but with the possibility of Lady Windermere entering at any moment, for her to walk about, or cross, or the like, would be melodramatic, but not dramatic or artistic.'[1] Wilde's comments must have been extremely irritating to Alexander, as he claimed superior knowledge both of high Society and stage-craft, whilst implying that Alexander's movement patterns tended to the broad and obvious. Wilde's art was not an exercise in naturalism. As he wrote in a subsequent letter to Alexander, 'Details in life are of no importance, but in art details are vital.'[2] His reproduction of wit, the polish and balance of the phrasing, the rhythm of the exchanges, suggest for much of the play a certain mocking detachment. The habits and rituals of the tribe have been adjusted, subtly exaggerated and heightened, until they are made transparent and so exposed to ironic scrutiny.

Wilde opens the play with a deliberately light sequence, as the young Society hostess arranges roses while deflecting the charming compliments of the witty Lord Darlington, a Lord Henry Wotton with feelings. Significantly, she instructs the manservant that she is at home 'to anyone who calls', thus marking the visit as entirely innocent, though the effect of the instruction is to alert the audience to the subtext. As Darlington handles the fan which is Lord Windermere's twenty-first-birthday present to his wife, and talks about covering the street with flowers for her to walk on, the tone is one of admiring and trivial flirtation, until the offer of friendship – 'you may want a friend some day' – disturbs the innocent ritual momentarily, and reveals the unquiet reality beneath the smooth social patina. Wilde then introduces the Duchess of Berwick, a prototype for Lady Bracknell, to conduct a more formidable and broadly comic assault on the conventions of conduct and alliance. Her scorn for the new money of commerce is matched by her ruthless pursuit of the rich young Australian, Hopper, as a suitable husband for her monosyllabic daughter. She has kindly called to warn Lady Windermere about her husband's supposed affair with Mrs Erlynne, and, with the additional confidence of her own experience, passes on to her the received wisdom – 'Just take him abroad.' 'Yes, dear, these wicked women get our husbands away from us, but they always come back, slightly damaged, of course' (CW 427). What makes Lord Windermere's conduct so particularly scandalous is that he has given away large sums of money – Berwick was 'far too principled for that!'. Marriage is here seen as an economic transaction: the woman acquires security, and the wealth to maintain a conspicuous social position; in return, the man's sexual infidelities are condoned, or at least overlooked. After the Duchess's bombshell, Wilde shifts the tone to focus on the serious. Lady Windermere is given a soliloquy, its artificiality modified by her shocking action, as she cuts open her husband's bank-book and discovers the 'truth' of the Duchess's allegations. By the end of the night, she will have moved traumatically from idealised innocence to experience, a series of shifts highlighted by the ostrich-feather fan as it passes from hand to hand in this glittering comedy of masks and manners.

The juxtaposition of the comic and the serious is one of Wilde's most successful dramatic techniques; once the absurd and the patently false have been established, the serious emotions and ideals which are explored have been given a context which prevents them from ever seeming too solemn. Inevitably, in what was his first attempt within the genre, Wilde has some awkward passages, perhaps most evident in Lady Windermere's long soliloquy at the beginning of Act III, when she has fled to Lord Darlington's rooms. In terms of achieving the right balance and tone, Alexander gave Wilde good advice. It was at his suggestion that Wilde wrote an additional speech for Lord Augustus, 'Well, really, I might be her husband already. Positively I might', ensuring that Act II closed on a comic downbeat, rather than on Mrs Erlynne's strong and serious instruction. Alexander also persuaded Wilde to reveal Mrs Erlynne's identity as Lady Windermere's mother gradually through the course of the play, rather than holding it back for a fourth-act revelation. Wilde resisted this suggestion fiercely: 'I have built my house on a certain foundation, and this foundation cannot be altered' (L 309). However, after the first night, he agreed to the alteration, claiming that all his friends, 'without exception', thought that the psycho-logical interest would be greatly increased by the disclosure of the actual relationship (L 313). In ways like these, Wilde achieved a subtle variation on what appeared to be a traditional plot, with a hidden secret which would be explained in the last act, accompanied by repentance and reconciliation. Wilde's handling of the narrative elevates the art of concealment, if not of outright lying. Lady Windermere never discovers the identity of Mrs Erlynne. Lord Windermere never knows that his wife had been prepared to throw herself into Lord Darlington's arms. (In much the same way, Harabin in Jones's *The Case of Rebellious Susan* never learned what happened, or did not happen, in Cairo, during that suspiciously long sermon.) Lord Darlington and Lord Augustus Loring are both left in ignorance. Lady Windermere's final comment to Lord Augustus, in contradiction to her husband's po-faced put-down, 'Well, you're certainly marrying a very clever woman!' is: 'Ah, you're marrying a very good woman!' (CW 464). The speech picks up the play's subtitle (and original working-title). This conven-tional ending works effectively as an expression of Lady Windermere's coming-of-age, and her exposure to a new morality; it is also wonderfully ironic, a joke shared only between the audience and Mrs Erlynne. (Philip Prowse's 1995 production added a fresh dimension, as Lady Windermere slapped her husband's face in response to his sneering delivery of 'clever'.)

Figure 8 *Lady Windermere's Fan* at the St James's Theatre, 1892; outfits by Savage and Purdue for Mrs Erlynne (Act IV, centre) and Lady Windermere (Acts II and III, left; Act IV, right) (*The Lady*, 10 March 1892)

Wilde's playing with the audience, who, in contrast with the somewhat mixed reception from the critics, were amused and enthusiastic, did not close with the play's final lines. He gave a curtain speech. The contents have been variously reported. According to Alexander, it concluded by praising the audience for their most intelligent appreciation: 'I congratulate you on the *great* success of your performance, which persuades me that you think *almost* as highly of the play as I do myself' (*E* 346). But it was Wilde's manner which attracted attention, and, from some quarters, censure, as he walked onto the stage smoking a cigarette, in mauve gloves and with a green carnation in his button-hole. Graham Robertson had been despatched to buy green carnations from Goodyear's in the Royal Arcade, and Wilde's young friends wore them to the first night, so creating an echo with the on-stage costume of the young dandy in the play, Cecil Graham: life imitating art.

Wilde paid what was, for the English stage, unprecedented attention to dress and accessories. Joel Kaplan and Sheila Stowell, in *Theatre and Fashion: Oscar Wilde to the Suffragettes*, have illuminated the relationship between the London stage and fashion, peeling off the translucent layers of meaning which surrounded the social event of Wilde's play of modern life at a smart theatre, attendance at which itself formed part of the Social Season. They quote Florence Alexander, in charge of the women's costumes, who commented that 'in those days people went to see the St James's plays *before* ordering a new gown';[3] and the key costumes for Marion Terry as Mrs Erlynne and Lily Hanbury as Lady Windermere were made by the couturières Mesdames Savage and Purdue. These ensembles were minutely reviewed and illustrated in the press, ensuring that significant details were given close attention. Wilde, as instanced by the notorious button-hole, which reached its apotheosis in Lord Goring's lapel in *An Ideal Husband*, operated through male as well as through female costume detail: one of his notes to Alexander concerned Lord Augustus's coat in Act III – 'too horsy: also he should take it off. He wants to make a night of it.'[4] (Wilde would reserve his most brilliant *coup de théâtre*, achieved by costume alone, for Jack's entrance in *The Importance of Being Earnest* in full Victorian mourning.) Kaplan and Stowell have drawn attention to the visual contrast between Lady Windermere and Mrs Erlynne in Act III: Lady Windermere, the Puritan, standing in Lord Darlington's rooms with bare arms and low-cut gown, having thrown off her cloak and flung it on the sofa, while Mrs Erlynne, the woman with a dozen pasts, remains cloaked throughout 'in a garment of sound English manufacture'.[5] The cloak itself conveys complex associations. The mother covers up her daughter; the sexually promiscuous protects the innocent; the action signifies Lady Windermere's decision to return to her child, a decision which will be immediately challenged by the arrival of her husband. But the cloak has already been emphasised in Act I, when Lady Windermere orders it to be taken out to the terrace, where she has walked and talked with Lord Darlington. On her return, she places it on the sofa, as he asks her to leave the house with him. It thus becomes a reminder of the declaration of love, and an image of the false life Darlington says that she will have to contend with if she remains with her husband: 'You would have to be to him the mask of his real life, the cloak to hide his secret' (CW 438). The cloak remains, while Mrs Erlynne seats Lord Windermere on the sofa and bargains with him about the extent of her settlement, with Lady Windermere a silent witness in the background. Finally, Lady Windermere puts on the cloak, to leave ball, house, husband and child, an action potentially as shocking as Nora's in *A Doll's House*. Wilde orchestrates and emphasises Lady Windermere's feelings through the cloak, which forms part of the pattern of parallels and contrasts between daughter and mother, as well as furnishing their one moment of physical intimacy. It is one of a sequence of motifs which binds them, the most obvious being the fan with 'Margaret' (in diamonds) on it; the last is Mrs Erlynne's Act IV bonnet, decorated with real roses, a natural touch which echoes both Lady Windermere's reference to the garden at Selby, and the play's opening image. In the words given to Mrs Erlynne, 'manners before morals': this is a play where surface is triumphantly dominant, a surface which throughout hints at what lies beneath, and which repeatedly causes an audience to question what is seen and heard.

Established firmly in the ranks of the smart and fashionable by the success of *Lady Windermere's Fan*, Wilde was courted to write a second social comedy by Herbert Beerbohm Tree, half-brother of Max. Initially, he refused, with a characteristic put-down. 'As Herod in my Salome you would be admirable. As a peer of the realm in my latest dramatic device, pray forgive me if I do not see you.'[6] Tree's argument, that he had been admired as the Duke of Guisebury in Jones's *The Dancing Girl*, was hardly phrased to convince Wilde; but Tree persisted, and Wilde retired to the Norfolk coast in the late summer of 1892 to write, accompanied by Lord Alfred Douglas. Norfolk place-names – Hunstanton, Brancaster – survive in the play's text; the setting, indeed, seems to be one of the great East Anglian country houses, and the almost silent figure of Lord Alfred Rufford, whose only occupations are his debts and the gold-tipped cigarettes he cannot afford, provides an echo of Lord Alfred Douglas. But the most disturbing portrait within the play is that of Lord Illingworth, a 'witty aristocrat' whom Wilde described to Tree in these terms: 'He is certainly not natural. He is a figure of art. Indeed, if you can bear the truth, he is MYSELF.'[7] Tree, quite carried away with the role, took to playing it off-stage, which Wilde described as a wonderful case of nature imitating art: he himself did his best to make Tree less theatrical, attending rehearsals, and cutting and rewriting. Tree's retrospective comment that he had produced the play with 'the interference' of Wilde is likely to be less than the truth. The two men were much closer in temperament than, for example, Wilde and Alexander, and theirs was a fruitful collaboration.

Where *Lady Windermere's Fan* centred on a woman who left her husband and so lost her daughter, *A Woman of No Importance* features a father, Lord Illingworth, who seduced and abandoned a young girl, and now tries to win back his son Gerald; a story taken, so Wilde claimed, from *The Family Herald*: he professed not to be interested in plot. The orphan is a recurrent motif in Wilde's plays, and this one has two of them, Gerald Arbuthnot and the beautiful American Puritan, Hester Worsley. Challenging the stereotype, Rachel 'Arbuthnot', Wilde's woman of no importance, is both a woman with a past, an innocent victim, and the centre of goodness and moral truth within the play; she is also extremely beautiful, appearing after dinner at Hunstanton Chase in her black velvet gown, whose colour was appropriate for a penitent, but whose close-fitting bodice and low neckline conveyed a disturbingly ambivalent image, and stood out strongly 'in grim, sombre majesty against the brilliant dresses of the butterfly women of the play'.[8] Her name, Rachel, conveys her condition of grief. Her young American counterpart's first name, Hester, was deliberately chosen for its New England Puritan ring, echoing Hester Prynne in Hawthorne's *The Scarlet Letter*. Hester Worsley, too, created ambivalence in performance, her moral condemnation of English society issuing from the mouth of the extremely pretty Julia Neilson dressed in white, the fabric 'glistening and shimmering with every movement', 'a superb Juno dressed by Worth'.[9]

The social and moral values of this play are as complex as the dress codes. Wilde places his social world with great precision. The first act – a perfect act, he claimed, because nothing happens in it – is set on the lawn in front of the terrace of a great English country house, with guests sitting under a large yew tree – an image of tranquillity, stability, wealth. There is little truly rural about this evocation of 'English country life'. Footmen move in and out with shawls and cushions and letters, converting the lawn into an extension of the house. (In Philip Prowse's design for his 1990 production, he brilliantly suggested this colonising of the outdoors by a kind of upholstered lily pond which was transformed into a sofa for Act II.) As the act proceeds, the sense of unruffled calm becomes increasingly disturbed. The make-up of the house party is immediately brought under question: Lord Illingworth is a man of 'high distinction' – but Mrs Allonby is 'hardly a very suitable person', declares Lady Caroline Pontefract, though she immediately defends her as 'very well born' when Hester Worsley expresses her dislike. Wilde introduces a number of value systems in the first two acts, and invites the audience to place Lord Illingworth and Mrs Allonby at the apex, dandies who dominate by wit and assurance, who match each other in their manipulation of words, and who define the fashionable and the modern. Yet they are also associated with a sense of decadence: Mrs Allonby leaves the lawn for the conservatory, where, she has been told by Lord Illingworth, 'there is an orchid as beautiful as the seven deadly sins'. 'Yes, let us stay here', suggests Lord Illingworth to Mrs Allonby, as an alternative to taking tea in the Yellow Drawing-room; 'The Book of Life begins with a man and a woman in a garden.' Mrs Allonby replies, 'It ends with Revelations' (CW 477). The flippant joke is also prophetic. Mrs Allonby's challenge to Lord Illingworth to kiss the pretty Puritan is the action which cracks open the fragile shell of this flawed masquerade of civilisation. The barbed shafts directed at America, and Hester's youthful idealism, seem increasingly harmless, and the portrait of aristocratic and political society edges towards caricature and satire. There is only one married couple on stage, Lady Caroline Pontefract and her fourth husband, the quiescent Sir John. Mrs Allonby mocks her absent husband, ominously named Ernest; Mr Kelvil, the ludicrous Member of Parliament who expands on the subject of English home life, is only too happy to be absent from his wife and eight children. When Mrs Allonby and Lady Hunstanton visit the 'happy English home' of Mrs Arbuthnot, in Act IV – 'fresh natural flowers, books that don't shock one, pictures that one can look at without blushing' – the contrast with the luxury of Hunstanton Chase is complete. Their visit is refused: Mrs Arbuthnot pleads a convenient headache. The falseness of this happy English home is then laid bare: an unmarried mother with an assumed name; a bastard son; and an unrepentant seducer, who offers marriage as the price for his son. When his bid is rejected, Lord Illingworth is given a speech of unrivalled condescension: 'It's been an amusing experience to have met amongst people of one's own rank, and treated quite seriously too, one's mistress, and one's — ' Mrs Arbuthnot snatches up one of Illingworth's gloves (he has been pulling on the other during his speech, with the fastidiousness of the dandy) and strikes him across the face with it, to prevent his uttering the word 'bastard'. This private action echoes Lady Windermere's threat to strike Mrs Erlynne with her fan should she appear at her ball.

The conclusion works on a number of levels. The blow has been postponed from the end of Act III, when Mrs Arbuthnot halts Gerald with the notoriously melodramatic 'Stop, Gerald, stop! He is your own father!' Coming from a woman, and unsignalled, hers is a far more telling action; it is the traditional insult of one man to another, an invitation to a challenge, but here wholly unanswerable: a spontaneous subversion of a male code which is absurdly theatrical. Tree was praised by the *Pall Mall Gazette* for his acting in this sequence, suggesting 'a sudden uncomfortable feeling of

Figure 9   Mrs Arbuthnot insults Lord Illingworth, *A Woman of No Importance*, Act IV
(*The Graphic*, 29 April 1893)

old age coming over the brilliant sinner – an old age that betrayed itself in
mere hints of speech and gait, and that contrasted grimly with the elaborate
youthfulness of dress'.[10] Illingworth has been defeated by youth, by that 'fin
de siècle person', the pretty Puritan. His is the defeat of age, of aristocracy,
of the old England; of everything that is suggested by the manicured lawns
and terraces of Hunstanton Chase. Wilde gives the conventional word-

playing last phrase to Mrs Arbuthnot, 'A man of no importance', so lightening the sentiment of the last sequence, which closes on Gerald holding the single glove, an ironic last legacy from his father.

There is a tension in this play, which arises from the language Wilde gives from time to time to Mrs Arbuthnot, and to Hester. Their expression of the new morality is conveyed in terms and rhythms which seem too heavily reminiscent of melodrama and the Bible to be aesthetically convincing; 'What welcome would you get from the girl whose lips you tried to soil, from the boy whose life you have shamed, from the mother whose dishonour comes from you?' (CW 512). The wit, and so the play's dynamic focus, seems to belong by natural right to Lord Illingworth, or to his counterpart, Mrs Allonby. Yet even without the impetus of language this last scene can be made to work with great effect on stage. It is, perhaps, the counterpart, in more serious mode, of the outrageously contrived trivial ending of The Importance of Being Earnest. There is something Chekhovian in this study of England, which exposes the immorality and hypocrisy, and the immense self-satisfaction, of the English ruling classes, and which yet contrives to show glimpses of the charm and elegance, the allure, of a way of life which has no future. The play has an autumnal feel, with its leitmotifs of Shetland shawls and mufflers; and the single white glove of the ageing aristocratic dandy provides an appropriate final image.

Wilde injected a political and social agenda into the text and texture of A Woman of No Importance; the subject of class, and related matters of wealth and morality, forms a recurrent topic of conversation, a parallel to the analysis of relationships between men and women. Even Lord Illingworth, arbiter of the idle classes, professes high ambitions, and announces his intention to travel to India, presumably on some imperial purpose. In Wilde's next play, An Ideal Husband, he transposes the context in which morality, in the broadest sense, is scrutinised overtly to the political arena. The central issue concerns the Under-Secretary for Foreign Affairs, and the way he acquired the wealth which allowed him to succeed by 'selling a state secret'. This was by passing on privileged information about the Suez Canal to a European financier. The backdrop to the play is the imposing London house where the Chilterns entertain people who have powerful political connections; the reference points are to the Houses of Parliament, to Downing Street, attachés at Embassies, and seats in the Cabinet. (Wilde's fictional Argentine Canal scheme echoes the current Panama Canal scandal which was threatening the stability of the French Government as he drafted the play; Sir Edward Grey was Under-Secretary in the English Cabinet at the time, speaking on foreign affairs in the House of Commons since the Foreign Secretary was Lord Rosebery, who took his seat in the Lords.)

Figure 10   Four sketches by Fred Pegram of *An Ideal Husband*: clockwise, Lewis Waller as Sir Robert Chiltern with Florence West as Mrs Cheveley in her unsuitable dress, Act I; Charles Hawtrey as Lord Goring with Maude Millet as Mabel Chiltern; Julia Neilson as Lady Chiltern and Fanny Brough as Lady Markby; and Mrs Cheveley's triumphant exit in Act III, in the presence of Charles Brookfield's Ideal Butler, Phipps (*Lady's Pictorial*, 12 January, 1895)

While Wilde's handling of these references may have the lurid simplicity of melodrama and Fleet Street scandals, this does not invalidate them as reflections of reality. The way such events are discussed and reported has not materially changed in the last century, and audiences in the 1990s simply transpose the general area of reference to some more recent comparable issue. Sir Peter Hall's production of 1992 and 1996 frequently evoked the laughter of recognition.

Wilde did not complete this play with the same fluency as its predecessors; managers raised a number of objections – John Hare declined it, thinking the last act unsatisfactory – and it was not put into rehearsal at the Haymarket, this time under Lewis Waller and H. H. Morell, until the end of 1894. Julia Neilson, who had acted Hester Worsley, was apprehensive about the part of Lady Chiltern, and Wilde wrote to her husband: 'Let me assure you that it is what I believe is called the part of the "leading lady"; it is the important part, and the only sympathetic part. Indeed the other woman does not appear in the last act at all.'[11] Wilde's letter helped to convince Julia Neilson; but the last act's focus on the 'serious' Chilterns, modified only by the 'trivial' engagement between Lord Goring and Mabel Chiltern, suffers from the absence of the 'other woman', Mrs Cheveley.

Wilde seems a little inconsistent in his construction of the 'brilliant Mrs Cheveley'. She is witty, wealthy, moves in European rather than English circles, and has an interesting past which includes an engagement to Lord Goring: for three acts, she plays the game of life with pleasure and aplomb. But her dress codes indicate an adventuress of a rather more blatant kind: she wore, in Lord Goring's words, 'far too much rouge last night, and not quite enough clothes'. Yet she and Goring were once in love; and she is also marked as the companion of Baron Arnheim, the off-stage mentor whom Sir Robert Chiltern describes as 'a man of a most subtle and refined intellect. A man of culture, charm, and distinction' (CW 537). Wilde gives Mrs Cheveley all the best scenes: her arrival at the Chilterns' languorous, decorous reception, where she springs her outrageous request on Sir Robert and ruffles his smooth complacency; her unwelcome afternoon call on Lady Chiltern, which concludes with her denunciation of Sir Robert to his wife; and her late-night visit to Lord Goring, a wonderful exercise on Wilde's part of high comedy and melodrama. Revising the play for publication, in 1899, Wilde expanded some of the stage directions, and the commentary on Mrs Cheveley as she struggles with the snake-brooch/bracelet (itself a very late arrival to the plot) suggests a villainness such as Dumas père might have lifted from stock under pressure of a deadline: 'Her face is distorted. Her mouth awry. A mask has fallen from her. She is, for the moment, dreadful to look at' (CW 567). The role, and the third act, do not work like that in the theatre. The melodrama is held in check and pointed up by the brilliance of the comic structure, as the fast-moving series of visits – Lord Caversham, Mrs Cheveley, Sir Robert Chiltern – and the accumulation of misunder-standings is coolly orchestrated by the Sphinx-like Ideal Butler, Phipps. Chairs fall, bells ring, letters are presented on salvers, burned, stolen: the act is visually framed by two deftly chosen stage emblems, male and female: Lord Goring's fresh button-hole and Lady Chiltern's letter on pink paper. The effect was well described by Shaw when he wrote of the play's 'subtle and pervading levity'. Wilde's imitation of the English ruling class is sufficiently well informed and accurate to anchor it to reality; yet he is also engaged in an exercise in pastiche, lightly mocking the social structures and moral postures both from within, in the manipulations of Mrs Cheveley and Lord Goring, and from without, by his overall control of the physical pattern and verbal tone.

An example of this mockery comes in Lord Goring's argument in Act IV when he solemnly informs Lady Chiltern: 'A man's life is of more value than a woman's. It has larger issues, wider scope, greater ambitions. A woman's life revolves in curves of emotions. It is upon lines of intellect that a man's life progresses.' Could anyone seriously believe that in 1895, let alone a champion of the Higher Education of Woman, as Lady Chiltern purports to be? Yet she allows herself to be persuaded that the decent thing is for her husband to stay in office; and, if any doubt lingers for the audience, Wilde points up the absurdity by having Lady Chiltern repeat this specious argument word for word, to be answered by Sir Robert's breathless 'Gertrude! Gertrude!'. Sir Robert's willingness to conceal his own discredit-able past is then placed in ironic perspective by his moral indignation over Lord Goring's supposed indiscretion with Mrs Cheveley. The cumulative impact of the resolution of Act IV is to reveal the gap between high moral posturing and the reality of political control. Normal service can resume again, with luncheon, and a visit to Downing Street to secure the future. The English system is triumphantly back in place. The play concludes, the spirit of comedy prevails and the audience applauds: Wilde has returned this segment of English society to the people who act it out in real life, slightly but significantly damaged.

From one perspective, these three plays might seem to be concerned with a ridiculously circumscribed and skewed cross-section of English life. Wilde worked within the theatre conventions of his time, and with the world he knew, even if he did not belong to it. He saw it as a fantastic masquerade, highlighting aspects of English public life which themselves inhabited the dimension of theatre: the smart dance, the country house party, the Chilterns' reception. At all of these there is a strong element of performance, and of audience, accentuated by the presence of almost silent 'extras', and a background of servants. In *An Ideal Husband*, the idea of 'real' life as theatre is especially powerful, with Chiltern's off-stage 'performance' in the House of Commons glowingly reviewed in *The Times* the following day. This imitation of Englishness is at once parodic and unnervingly accurate, a subtle form of insult. Wilde uncovers the relentless evasiveness of English speech, the attempts to make resounding definitions and statements of ideals within a world that is clearly no longer static and solid, attempts Wilde described as 'the vice of sincerity'. Morality, private and public, is brought into question in these plays, and found wanting quite as radically as in the 'stronger' dramas of Ibsen.

It is interesting to note what Wilde leaves out. Art and literature, for example, are scarcely mentioned, except as jokes, or as possessions, in the case of Chiltern's Corots. The middle classes, and the working classes, on the other hand, receive a surprising amount of coverage. In *A Woman of No Importance* the earnest Kelvil's defence of the House of Commons for having always shown great sympathy with the sufferings of the poor is dismissed by Lord Illingworth as its special vice, a philosophical point of view which coincided with Wilde's; but the truer responses of the ruling class come from Lady Hunstanton's benignly inane assurance: 'Dear Dr Daubeny, our rector here, provides with the assistance of his curates, really admirable recreations for the poor during the winter. And much good may be done by means of a magic lantern, or a missionary, or some popular amusement of that kind'; while the authentic voice of Empirespeak rings out in Lady Caroline Pontefract's retort: 'I am not at all in favour of amusements for the poor, Jane. Blankets and coals are sufficient. There is too much love of pleasure amongst the upper classes as it is' (*CW* 471). No one, apart from the servants, works, or wishes to work, in these plays: Gerald longs to escape the horrors of a bank in a provincial town. It is a world claiming to live exclusively on inherited wealth, though in reality needing to top up family money by marrying heirs to Australian canned-goods fortunes like Hopper's, or selling a state secret to a European financier. Perhaps the most ironic line in these three plays is Lady Chiltern's solemn valedictory statement: 'For both of us a new life is beginning.'

The interpretation of these plays as essentially ironic exposures of English society, a society still ostensibly ruling a large part of the world, forms part of the meanings which they convey: it is an interpretation which is only intermittently made explicit. Wilde pursued pleasure, and he enjoyed the pleasures which were available at the tables of the English leisured classes: 'I filled my life to the very brim with pleasure, as one might fill a cup to the very brim with wine' (*CW* 1022). But he also saw through them, with the detached, or semi-detached, perspective of his Celtic mind and imagination. Like Maria Edgworth, he moved between Ireland and England, and his position as part-time outsider sharpened his analysis. Moreover, he created a particular form of comedy in which to display his mocking imitation of England, a form which satisfied his audience, and which seemed, by its adroit resolutions, to suggest that all was well with Society. In *The Importance of Being Earnest*, by pushing neatness and coincidence to its outer limits, he came closer to revealing his method. In his short but intense burst of play-writing, he first made his people 'real', and then took his audiences through the looking-glass into a world which seemed to reflect modern life, but which was a surreal improvisation upon it. It seems appropriate that his professional career as a fashionable writer drew to a close with two plays in West End London theatres running simultaneously, *An Ideal Husband* with its echoes of contemporary politics, and *The Importance of Being Earnest*, an ostensible farce. You could look from one to the other, and back again, and wonder which represented English society more acutely. Wilde's claim to have made the drama, 'the most objective form known to art', 'as personal a mode of expression as the lyric or the sonnet', has validity; it was a claim which Society found it hard to accept, or to forgive.

NOTES

1 Rupert Hart-Davis (ed.), *More Letters of Oscar Wilde* (London: John Murray, 1985), pp. 109–12.

2 Ibid., p. 112.

3 Joel Kaplan and Sheila Stowell, *Theatre and Fashion: Oscar Wilde to the Suffragettes* (Cambridge: Cambridge University Press, 1994), chapter 1, 'The Glass of Fashion'. For other discussions of the Society comedies, see: the Introductions by Ian Small and Russell Jackson in their editions of the plays; Katharine Worth, *Oscar Wilde*; Kerry Powell, *Oscar Wilde and the Theatre of the 1890s*; the following essays in *Modern Drama* 37:1 (Spring 1994): Alan Sinfield, ' "Effeminacy" and "Femininity": Sexual Politics in Wilde's Comedies'; Joseph Bristow, 'Dowdies and Dandies: Oscar Wilde's Refashioning of Society Comedy'; Richard Allen Cave, 'Wilde Designs: Some Thoughts about Recent British Productions of his Plays'; and Joel Kaplan, 'Staging Wilde's Society Plays: A Conversation with Philip Prowse'; and the following essays in *Rediscovering Oscar Wilde*, ed. C. George Sandulescu: Richard Allen Cave, 'Power Structuring: The Presentation of Outsider Figures in Wilde's Plays'; Robert Gordon, 'Wilde's "Plays of Modern Life" on the Contemporary British Stage'; Joel Kaplan, 'Wilde in the Gorbals: Society Drama and the Citizens Theatre'; and Peter Raby, 'Wilde and European Theatre'.

4 Hart-Davis (ed.), *More Letters*, p. 114.

5 Kaplan and Stowell, *Theatre and Fashion*, p. 17.

6 Hesketh Pearson, *Beerbohm Tree: His Life and Laughter* (Methuen: London, 1956), p. 65.
7 Ibid., p. 65.
8 Kaplan and Stowell, *Theatre and Fashion*, p. 21 (*Sketch*, 26 Apr. 1893).
9 Ibid., p. 25 (*Echo*, 20 Apr. 1893).
10 *Pall Mall Gazette*, 20 Apr. 1893.
11 Hart-Davis (ed.), *More Letters*, p. 127.

10

RUSSELL JACKSON

The Importance of Being Earnest

The Importance of Being Earnest, Oscar Wilde's most famous and – posthumously – most successful play, was first produced by George Alexander at the St James's Theatre on 14 February 1895. London was enduring a prolonged and severe spell of cold weather: several theatres advertised their steam-heating among the attractions of their programme, and the first night of Wilde's comedy had been put off from 12 February because several of the women in the cast had bad colds.[1] In addition to the habitual glamour of a first night at a fashionable theatre, the occasion was especially interesting because Wilde was in vogue. *An Ideal Husband* had been playing at the Haymarket Theatre since 3 January, and at the same theatre *A Woman of No Importance* had completed a successful run, having opened on 19 April 1893. On 20 February 1892 *Lady Windermere's Fan* had been the second play staged by Alexander's new management at the St James's Theatre, running until 26 July of that year.

Wilde's spectacular début in the early 1880s had been followed by a period of less glamorous work as a reviewer, editor and jobbing author for journals and magazines. In 1888 he published *The Happy Prince and Other Tales*. In 1891 he had published four books, including *The Picture of Dorian Gray* and *Intentions*. Now, a decade after his appearance on the London literary scene, he was a successful West End dramatist and was beginning to seem a more substantial figure. A book-length lampoon, *The Green Carnation*, by imitating (perhaps reporting) his style of conversation, contributed to his renewed prominence in the literary and social gossip columns.[2] To some readers it may also have suggested – or confirmed – the impression that there was a less positive side to Wilde's notoriety.

For his part, George Alexander was a rising theatrical star. He had gone into management in 1889 after establishing himself during a stint with Henry Irving's company at the Lyceum. In 1891 he had taken the St James's Theatre, where he remained until his death in 1915. He was knighted in 1911. Alexander's theatre was run meticulously. His biographer, the playwright and novelist A. E. W. Mason, described Alexander's work on one of his own plays. The manager went through the script line by line and move by move, interrogating him rigorously on every sentence, and planning moves with a toy theatre stage. Then a ground cloth was marked with the lines of walls and exits and for three weeks there were daily rehearsals, beginning each day punctually at eleven and finishing at two, until for the last four days there were morning and afternoon sessions, culminating in two dress-rehearsals. The management's attention to detail in staging and performance was thorough: Lady Alexander described how on a first night she would sit in her box 'sick with anxiety' and then between the acts 'I used to put on an apron and go behind the scenes to place all the little things on the stage myself until the men got used to it. I arranged the flowers; in those days we had so much detail, and I loved to make things look real. I ordered the gowns to suit the decorations of the scene so that nothing clashed or was ugly. Alec gave me the large sum of £5 a week for my work, and I think I was very cheap at the price.'[3]

This was a theatre as well ordered as a drawing-room, with acting and staging whose quality was achieved with the expenditure of immense craft and care but which never drew attention to the effort it required. Its first nights seemed (wrote Lady Alexander) 'like brilliant parties', although they were not so exclusive as to be without the gallery audience, who guarded jealously their privilege of expressing immediate and vocal judgement on what was put on stage. The atmosphere of a fashionable occasion combined with the reminder of a wider public's existence was always there. 'Everybody knew everybody,' wrote Lady Alexander, 'everybody put on their best clothes, everybody wished us success. When I entered my box on a first night I always had a reception from the gallery. They were always so pleased and so kind to me.'[4] They were also quite capable of booing Henry James's *Guy Domville*: the West End theatres were never completely insulated from society with a small 's', and it is a mistake to think of them as playing to a homogeneous middle- and upper-class audience. The masses and the classes were not wholly separated, even though theatre architects did their best by providing separate entrances and box-offices.

It might never have appeared so in public, but Wilde resembled Alexander in his approach to work. Their temperaments were dissimilar in other respects, but both were scrupulous, laborious artists. Wilde liked to give the impression that words flowed easily from his pen, but this was part of a strategy for undermining assumptions about the seriousness of art. In fact, his new 'Trivial Comedy for Serious People' (or, in earlier drafts, 'serious comedy for trivial people') was proposed in outline to George Alexander in July 1894, drafted in August and assiduously revised and polished during the autumn. Alexander had not taken it up at first, and Wilde placed it with Charles Wyndham, who had not so far staged any of his plays. In the event *The Importance of Being Earnest* came to the St James's when the failure of Henry James's *Guy Domville* made a replacement necessary. (Unable to face his own first night, James had tried to distract himself by going to see *An Ideal Husband* at the Haymarket.) In the course of rehearsal, among other adjustments to the text, Alexander insisted that the play be reduced from four to three acts. This is the best-known and most radical alteration made between the first draft and the first night, but Wilde had revised every sequence, most speeches and almost every sentence over the past six months.

Some of the changes might seem trivial in themselves, but in a play so economical in its language and effects, they had a serious consequence. Thus, Wilde considered several variations of the title of Dr Chasuble's sermon, which was given for benefit of a charity described at one time or another as the Society for the Prevention of 'Cruelty to Children' (a real organisation, and therefore not really suitable), 'Discontent among the Higher Orders' and, in the page-proofs of the 1899 edition, 'Discontent among the Lower Orders'. Wilde finally altered this to 'Discontent among the Upper Orders', restoring a topsy-turvy joke of a kind familiar in the play (II, 249–50).[5]

Sometimes in an early manuscript draft one finds the bare bones of a speech later developed and made specific to its speaker and the situation. Thus Wilde produced the following (I, 130–2):

> O! it is absurd to have a hard-and-fast rule about what one should read and one shouldn't. More than half of modern culture depends on what one shouldn't read.

from this (manuscript draft):

> One should read everything. That is the true basis of modern culture. More than half of modern culture depends on the unreadable.

In the first edition (1899) Jack declares to Gwendolen:

> Miss Fairfax, ever since I met you I have admired you more than any girl – I have ever met since – I met you.   (I, 385–6)

The faltering is carefully indicated by Wilde with inserted dashes. The earliest draft of the speech makes it a self-consciously clever and confident sentence, with a play on words that depends on emphasis:

> Miss Fairfax, ever since I *met* you I have admired you more than any girl I have ever met since I met *you.*

Among the multitude of similar tinkerings is one which seems puzzling. When Lady Bracknell is told that Jack has lost both his parents, the earliest manuscript draft of the complete act has her react as follows:

> Both? ... To lose one parent may be considered a misfortune. To lose both
> seems like carelessness.   (I, 539–40)

It seems likely that in 1895 the line was spoken thus:

> Both? To lose one parent may be regarded as a misfortune, to lose *both* seems
> like carelessness.

This was the version of the line printed in the page-proofs for the first edition: Wilde changed it to

> Both? – that seems like carelessness.

As if this were not puzzling enough, Robert Ross, in the first collected edition of Wilde's works, printed yet another variation:

> Both? To lose one parent, Mr Worthing, may be regarded as a misfortune; to
> lose both looks like carelessness.

Wilde's alteration and Ross's emendation have yet to be explained.

This fine tuning is part of a process that Wilde was careful to conceal beneath the image of an artist who worked by inspiration and *sprezzatura*, composing almost in spite of himself. He was a master of what would now be called media opportunities. His epigrammatic, paradoxical utterances made for effective publicity, *fin-de-siècle* sound-bites. The vigorous world of the expanding and increasingly illustrated popular press gave scope for interviews, paragraphs in gossip columns, glimpses of celebrities 'at home', cartoons, parodies, reports of speeches (especially first-night speeches) and lectures. Wilde made great play with the boundary between public and private personality, affecting a kind of lofty intimacy which tantalised journalists and their public. He was always good copy, never at a loss for words and frequently trod a narrow path between effrontery and reserve. In an interview with Robert Ross, published on 18 January 1895, Wilde answers the tentative enquiry, 'I dare not ask, I suppose, whether [the play] will please the public?' with a splendidly definitive statement:

> When a play that is a work of art is produced on the stage, what is being
> tested is not the play, but the stage; when a play that is *not* a work of art is
> produced on the stage what is being tested is not the play, but the public.[6]

Such a 'personality', effortlessly generating publicity, was in one sense a godsend to Alexander, but there was another side to Wilde's presentation of himself. It is clear from some reviews of the plays that Wilde was thought to have intruded himself, to be passing off 'false' wit as 'true' (by Victorian definitions).[7] Some critics used the word 'impertinence' ominously and equivocally to describe both the style and the author. In February 1895 more than one critic wondered whether the fashion for Wilde's paradoxical, epigrammatic wit would survive. However pleasing *The Importance of Being Earnest* might be (and even the sourest reviewers could not ignore its success with audiences), would the new style continue to appeal to the public?

The Importance of Being Earnest has, of course, prevailed. It is one of the few plays from its period to remain in theatrical repertoires, outlasting most of the trivial and almost all the serious works of Wilde's contemporaries. W. S. Gilbert has barely survived without Sullivan's support, Arthur Wing Pinero's farces from the 1880s are far more commonly seen than the later work he set most store by, plays by Henry Arthur Jones have received only a few revivals, and such erstwhile celebrities as Haddon Chambers and Sydney Grundy have sunk without trace. From the theatres of the nineties, only the plays of Wilde and Shaw have consistently held the stage, together with Brandon Thomas's farce *Charley's Aunt* (1892). Of Wilde's own plays, it is *The Importance of Being Earnest* which has enjoyed most revivals.

If Wilde were here now he might well express surprise at posterity's behaviour. As far as he was concerned, *The Importance of Being Earnest* was not the culmination, and of course not at all the conclusion, of a dramatic career. He was anxious to write a more serious play, also sketched in the summer of 1894, and when he first broached the subject of the new comedy to Alexander (asking for an advance of £150) he referred to it as his response to an American impresario's request for a play 'with no real serious interest'. This attitude to *The Importance of Being Earnest* persisted in his letters to Alexander during the autumn, Wilde declaring that it would probably be unsuitable for the more serious repertoire the manager was establishing for the St James's company and wished to take with him on a projected American tour.[8] Wilde's Society plays before *The Importance of Being Earnest* can be seen as a series of experiments, determinedly distorting familiar dramatic situations. This new play seems an excursion – a day-trip into a less demanding, less adventurous kind of theatre. Certainly it appeared so to a number of reviewers, especially those who regarded the unevenness of the earlier plays as signs of Wilde's inadequate grasp of the essentials of construction and character. *The Importance of Being Earnest* lacks not only the 'serious' plot devices of the other Society plays, but also the grandiloquent speeches with which the characters rise to serious subjects in moments of crisis. When we approach *The Importance of Being Earnest* as his first audiences did, from experience of Wilde's previous West End plays and his perceived characteristics as a writer, it seems remarkable for a number of omissions and deviations from what might be expected.

Three figures prominent in Wilde's previous dramatic work are absent. The new comedy lacks a 'woman with a past' like the active and defiant Mrs Erlynne or Mrs Cheveley, or the wronged and repentant Mrs Arbuthnot. (Miss Prism does not emerge as a comic variation on this theme until the final scenes.) In fact, the past in this play has become a benign rather than a menacing secret, with the handbag concealing not a 'social indiscretion' but an absurd mistake. Female culpability (a mainspring even of the 'advanced' serious drama of the time) is limited to absent-mindedness. An audience in February 1895 might also have expected a dandyish aristocrat of Wilde's particular kind – either dubiously charming like Darlington in *Lady Windermere's Fan*, villainous like Illingworth in *A Woman of No Importance* or nonchalantly virtuous like Goring in *An Ideal Husband*. Both Algernon and Jack (in his London mode) lead lives of cultivated pointlessness, and both are given to making authoritative statements on all aspects of modern life and culture (so, for that matter are Gwendolen, Cecily and Lady Bracknell) but neither of the men is a villain or a *raisonneur*. Like the stories of the plays in which Wilde had so far used them, the woman with a past and the dandy were Wildean revisions of the stock devices, and a playgoer might expect that a new play by him would continue to exploit this vein. The third stock figure that *The Importance of Being Earnest* lacks is the innocently idealistic young woman, forced to confront the sordid realities of political and social life – Hester Worsley in *A Woman of No Importance*, or Lady Windermere and Lady Chiltern, all of them gifted with a kind of rhetoric that it is hard to believe the author took seriously. Again, the new play transforms a type, in this instance by making idealism consist in wanting to marry a man called Ernest, and self-righteous indignation is briefly mocked when the two girls declare that they have been deceived by Jack and Algernon.

Another quality associated with Wilde in the early 1890s is also notably absent: self-conscious 'decadence'. *Salomé* (published but refused a performance licence) combined oriental exoticism with perverse passions. *The Picture of Dorian Gray* had confirmed the association of his name with the luxuriant description of unusual and refined artistic tastes, and the theme of a younger man seduced intellectually and aesthetically (and perhaps implicitly, sexually) by an older mentor. In his critical dialogues, 'The Critic as Artist' and 'The Decay of Lying', aesthetic discrimination is associated with luxurious surroundings and the idea of persuasive talk among men. Persuasion and conviction are central to the fictional 'Portrait of Mr W. H.'. One of the real dangers of *The Green Carnation* – given Wilde's personal situation in 1894 – was its suggestion of such a relationship between the Wilde figure and a young man. In the first two West End plays there is relatively little of this element – at least on the surface, although Gerald Arbuthnot is clearly under the spell of the man who is revealed to be his father. In *An Ideal Husband* the theme is handled explicitly. Sir Robert Chiltern's wealth and career have been based on a dishonest act committed at the instance of a sinister international financier, Baron Arnheim. Chiltern describes Arnheim's influence in terms redolent of the corruption of Dorian Gray by Lord Henry Wotton:

> I remember so well how, with a strange smile on his pale, curved lips, he led me through his wonderful picture gallery, showed me his tapestries, his enamels, his jewels, his carved ivories, made me wonder at all the strange loveliness of the luxury in which he lived; and then told me that luxury was nothing but a background, a painted scene in a play, and that power, power over other men, power over the world, was the one thing worth having, the one supreme pleasure worth knowing, the joy one never tired of, and that in our century only the rich possessed it.[9]　　　　　　(CW 537)

This overtly 'decadent' vein (toned down in the revision of *An Ideal Husband*) is entirely absent from the farce. As if to draw attention to the missing element, a contemporary parody in *Punch* by a friend of Wilde makes a joke of infusing the new play with decadence. Ada Leverson's 'The Advisability of not Being Brought Up in a Hand-Bag' features 'Dorian', described in the cast-list as 'a button-hole':

> ALGY: (*eating cucumber-sandwiches*).　Do you know, Aunt Augusta, I am afraid I shall not be able to come to your dinner to-night, after all. My friend Bunbury has had a relapse, and my place is by his side.
>
> AUNT AUGUSTA: (*drinking tea*).　Really, Algy! it will put my table out dreadfully. And who will arrange my music?
>
> DORIAN:　*I* will arrange your music, Aunt Augusta. I know all about music. I have an extraordinary collection of musical instruments. I give curious concerts every Wednesday in a long latticed room, where wild gipsies tear mad music from little zithers, and I have brown algerians who beat monotonously upon copper drums. Besides, I have set myself to music. And it has not marred me. I am still the same. More so, if anything.
>
> > (*Punch*, 2 March 1895, p. 107)

Although it is arguable that there are coded references to the homosexual double life of its author in the play, nothing of the overtly *Dorian* mode is to be found in the finished work or its drafts.[10] Algernon's rooms may be 'luxuriously and artistically furnished', but he never speaks anything remotely resembling the language of decadence. His debts are the conventional attribute of the stage man about town. The manuscript draft of the first act seems to suggest that Wilde thought of making the need for a fortune into a motivation for Algernon's pursuit of Jack's young ward – although this was not followed up and the hint was soon removed.[11] (Interestingly, this would have made the play more like Gilbert's cynical comedy *Engaged*, with its principal characters avidly pursuing money while spouting the rhetoric of love.)

The opening scene of the four-act version has Algernon besieged in Half-Moon Street by creditors (represented eventually simply by the letters Lane hands him in the first scene), and in a sequence subsequently cut from the second act a solicitor pursues him to the country to arrest him for a debt of £762.14s.2d. for dinners at the Savoy Hotel. ('There can be little good in any young man who eats so much, and so often', says Miss Prism). In the light of what became public knowledge a few weeks later, Wilde's reference to the Savoy seems like sailing perilously close to the wind, and the author's own imprisonment lent a sad irony to Algernon's protest against being taken to Holloway: 'Well I really am not going to be imprisoned in the suburbs for having dined in the West End.'[12] Elsewhere in the play as performed and published, only the defiantly unconventional use of the words 'immoral' and 'moral' echoes the deliberate flouting of conventional rules that marks Dorian and his mentor in Wilde's novel.

It can be argued that Wilde had already transposed apprehension about his own situation into the safer, specifically political misdemeanour of Chiltern in *An Ideal Husband*, written a year before *The Importance of Being Earnest* in the autumn of 1893 but not produced on stage until 1895. Like Dorian Gray, Sir Robert Chiltern has a history that is concealed – in this case, specifically from his wife, who has an inflated sense of his character as a sort of chivalric ideal. (She even quotes Tennyson: 'We needs must love the highest when we see it.') The ideal husband is threatened with a non-sexual version of the kind of blackmail that Wilde had already encountered, when Mrs Cheveley tries to secure his ministerial backing for a fraudulent share issue and reminded him of the gutter press: 'Think of the hypocrite with his greasy smile penning his leading article, and arranging the foulness of the public placard' (*CW* 529).

The Importance of Being Earnest effects an altogether less ominous transformation of guilt, secrecy and the double life: it enables two young men to 'get into scrapes'. Confession and absolution are sublimely easy. When Algernon arrives in the country as Ernest he tells Cecily that he is not really wicked at all.

If you are not, then you have certainly been deceiving us all in a very inexcusable manner. I hope you have not been leading a double life, pretending to be wicked and being really good all the time. That would be hypocrisy. (II, 122–4)

In the final scene Jack has to ask Gwendolen if she can forgive him for not having been deceitful after all:

JACK: Gwendolen, it is a terrible thing for a man to find out suddenly that all his life he has been speaking nothing but the truth. Can you forgive me?
GWENDOLEN: I can, for I feel that you are sure to change. (III, 478–80)

However, any biographical interpretation one might wish to put on these passages should be qualified by the consideration that they parody a familiar feature of the approach to marriage: when a man proposed he was expected to confess the peccadilloes of his bachelor life, for which he would be forgiven by his intended. Like Lady Bracknell's memorable interrogation of Jack in Act I, the dialogue between Jack and Gwendolen is part of the play's systematic guying of the conventional etiquette of love and marriage.

This points to one of the play's great attractions, and one of the principal reasons for its continuing appeal. Wilde simultaneously engaged with and mocked the forms and rules of Society. His stance as a dandy, a performer and (as an Irishman) an outsider gave him a particular use for the machinery and conventions both of the social world and of the Society drama of the theatre, which gave fictional expression to its values by dwelling on stories of fallen and falling women, reinforcing social and sexual discriminations, showing the righteous but hard consequences of maintaining ideals, and endorsing the cruel and absolute exclusion of those who erred. This is a subject matter *The Importance of Being Earnest* shares with the earlier plays, but now the spirit of Society's authoritative exclusiveness is analysed in the most satisfying way Wilde had yet devised, in its most absolute and at the same time funniest embodiment: Lady Bracknell.

Lady Bracknell's unwavering dogmatism was reinforced as the play's dialogue was worked on. It is in fact impossible to discuss the play's treatment of authority – its politics, in fact – without considering the style of the speakers. Style in this (as in all serious matters) is of the utmost importance. A tiny example is the immediacy with which, gravely shaking her head, Lady Bracknell pronounces 149 Belgrave Square to be on the unfashionable side (I, 529). In earlier versions she had first consulted a red book, but the omission of this detail makes it clear that even her knowledge of street and house numbers is encyclopedic, definitive and (most important) immediately accessible. She is easily – as well as loftily – magisterial.

In this scene, as throughout the play, all the details of Lady Bracknell's draconian social discriminations are underpinned by her frankly mercenary approach to life and – in particular – marriage. Performers of the role have sometimes intimated that Lady Bracknell has herself clambered to the social position she enjoys, especially when she has been cast younger than is commonly the case. Judi Dench, in Peter Hall's 1982 production for the National Theatre, made it clear that she had a lively interest in young men: she patted the seat invitingly for Jack to sit near her as she took notes of his social and financial qualifications, but drew back (and tore up the notes) as she learned of his obscure parentage. Edith Evans's performance in Anthony Asquith's 1952 film has coloured public perception of this scene to the extent that, like *Hamlet*, *The Importance of Being Earnest* now includes a speech – in fact, two words – which audiences are likely to utter before the performer can speak. However, the 'build' of the sequence is really towards Jack's desperately specific 'The Brighton Line' and Lady Bracknell's amazed retort, 'The line is immaterial', followed by her homily on the possible significance of such a situation:

> Mr Worthing, I confess I feel somewhat bewildered by what you have just told me. To be born, or at any rate bred, in a hand-bag, whether it had handles or not, seems to me to display a contempt for the ordinary decencies of family life that reminds one of the worst excesses of the French Revolution. And I presume you know what that unfortunate movement led to? As for the particular locality in which the hand-bag was found, a cloak-room at a railway station might serve to conceal a social indiscretion – has probably, indeed, been used for that purpose before now – but it could hardly be regarded as an assured basis for a recognized position in good society.
>
> (I, 568–80)

Wilde packed into this speech Lady Bracknell's basic social assumptions ('the ordinary decencies of family life ... social indiscretion ... a recognized position in good society'), an absurd political and historical reference ('the worst excesses of the French Revolution'), and a breathtakingly magisterial manner (in calling the Revolution 'that unfortunate movement'). Stylistically, the sense of authority in the speech is supported by the movement of the last sentence from comic particulars, through a brief parenthetical reflection ('has probably, indeed ...') towards the resounding invocation of an unanswerable principle. Like the elaborate patterns of Elizabethan dramatic writing, this passage moves forward from thesis to antithesis, giving a sense of absorbing and containing all possible considerations along the way. It is assertive by restraint, which is the key to Lady Bracknell's manner, and the ease of utterance she shares with other characters echoes a characteristic of Wilde's own social talk which struck W. B. Yeats: he seemed to speak in complete sentences.

It appears that the first production achieved the assurance and poise – and lack of self-conscious comic effect – that the play requires. Interestingly, none of the reviews imply that Lady Bracknell was a 'star' part. Alexander himself was demure, Allan Aynesworth debonair and stylish. Although some of the stage-business that Alexander attached to the play was more farcical than is indicated in the published text of 1899, the play's relative lack of strenuous physical action must have been apparent. Although the presence (and violent consumption) of food is typical of farce, there is no knockabout. The finest visual effect is achieved by Jack's slow entrance in full mourning, upstage – a moment at which (according to one actor) the first-night audience's laughter told Wilde that the plot point had been achieved. At the end Jack rummages upstairs for the handbag and ransacks bookshelves to find the army lists that will disclose his father's name, but the vehement heaping of sugar lumps into tea-cups and aggressive slicing of cake are the most violent action of the play's second act. In places, notably the opening of the third act, comic repetitions make the dialogue resemble a comic opera libretto. 'The story', said the *Times* reviewer of the first production, was 'almost too preposterous to go without music.' W. H. Auden commented on the 'pure verbal opera' of the dialogue, and other critics have compared the play's formality to that of dance.[13]

In approaching the condition of opera – transforming late-Victorian farce into something resembling *Così fan tutte* – Wilde was on dangerous ground. The self-conscious artificiality of the play, which has reminded some critics of De Musset and Marivaux, was a quality not readily associated with seriousness of purpose in the Victorian theatre. There sincerity, not style, was held to be the guarantor of purposeful laughter. Acknowledging the audience's presence, and allowing the characters of a play to refer to the drama in which they appear, were commonplace in the burlesque and the comic opera, but not admissible in the 'new' modern comedy. Self-consciously patterned dialogue and situations, and the references throughout the play to fictions (from Cecily's diary to the observation that coincidences do not occur in the best families), make *The Importance of Being Earnest* defiantly artificial. It is Miss Prism, the unwitting vehicle of a benevolent Fate, who insists on the rules of conventional story-telling. In her 'abandoned' novel, she tells Cecily, who finds happy endings depressing, 'The good ended happily, and the bad unhappily. That is what Fiction means' (II, 54–5).

In the March 1895 issue of *The Theatre* an anonymous reviewer (probably the editor Clement Scott, who was no great admirer of Wilde) remarked on the author's evident contempt for his own characters – an interesting expression of the idea that a conscientious author should always appear to believe his own fictions. Like the accusations of impertinently 'false' wit from critics who thought anyone could write Wildean epigrams, this reads like a determined effort to exclude Wilde from the society of the serious dramatic craftsmen. With the new play, Wilde was refusing even to play the game which his opponents declared him to have lost in his earlier work. The passionate statement of ideals, which dramatists like Henry Arthur Jones considered the prerogative (and glory) of their more serious-minded characters, is thoroughly mocked.

Wilde's attack on earnestness undermines not only the well-established 'high moral tone' of Victorian plain living and high thinking (invoked by Chasuble in the omitted scene of Algernon's imminent arrest for debt). It is not simply a contest between Wilde and the sages or the 'serious' religious and social missionaries of his time. Implicitly, he also refuses to join in the earnest struggle for intellectual respectability that marked many of our theatres in the nineties.

'We live, as I hope you know Mr Worthing, in an age of ideals', Gwendolen announces, and proceeds to enunciate the reduction to absurdity of all such notions: that marriage with a man called Ernest can be a goal in life. (Lady Bracknell, of course, later characterises the age as one of surfaces.) Among all the play's other systematic inversions of common values (moral/immoral, serious/trivial, town vice/country virtue and so on) this has a direct bearing on the business of the 'New Drama'. It is more radical than the habitually far-fetched motivations that generate stage farces: positing for example that a young man needs to arrange the impersonation of an aunt from Brazil to chaperone a luncheon-party. Wilde is proposing an absurdly irreverent version of that indispensable item in the moral equipment of the earnest character in a serious play, a 'higher' aspiration. He has had the effrontery to write a farce with young women who are idealists, and to make their ideals appropriately farcical. Hovering over the result are both the eponymous heroine of Pinero's *The Notorious Mrs Ebbsmith* (torn apart by high principles at the St James's the previous year) and Brandon Thomas's *Charley's Aunt* (from Brazil, where the nuts come from).

Wilde's characters both embody and mock dramatic stereotypes: his formidable dowager, sweet *ingénue*, fussy clergyman and scapegrace man about town lead double lives as parodies of themselves. Because the dialogue is comparatively free from puns and racy slang, it has an oddly decorous effect: the toughness and urbanity of Jane Austen, the slyness of George Meredith, but none of the flaunting affectation of Ronald Firbank or even E. F. Benson. Wilde's tactics are also quite different from those of Shaw: his paradoxes are not as confrontational and openly argumentative.

His characters are ruthless in the pursuit of selfish goals and absurd ideals, not combative in the furtherance of the Life-force or social justice. Would Shaw ever allow himself a diminuendo like the end of Wilde's first act?

> ALGERNON: I love scrapes. They are the only things that are never serious.
> JACK: Oh, that's nonsense, Algy. You never talk anything but nonsense.
> ALGERNON: Nobody ever does. (I, 751–5)

Shaw's oddly unamused *Saturday Review* notice, in which he reacted against what he saw as the heartlessness of the play, and insisted it was merely an assemblage of old-fashioned farcical devices, seems to express his apprehension for a style that threatened to supplant his own and would not serve the aims he wished the theatre to adopt. *The Philanderer* (written in 1893) and *Arms and the Man* (staged in April 1894) have something of Wilde's talent for talk, but Shaw's paradoxes and parodies never let the audience lose sight of a purpose.[14] Wilde's seem constantly to undermine the very idea of seriousness.

By adopting farce, with what Kerry Powell characterises as 'aggressive pranks, quick-paced action and evasion of moral responsibility', Wilde was abdicating what many – both conservative and 'advanced' – saw as the responsibility of a dramatist.[15] The proposition that nobody ever does talk anything but nonsense was anathema to Shaw. Wilde announced in an interview before the opening that the play was 'exquisitely trivial, a delicate bubble of fancy', but that it had a philosophy, that 'we should treat all the trivial things of life very seriously, and all the serious things of life with sincere and studied triviality'.[16] It is this quality which makes Wilde's play less than tractable to attempts to attach to it various kinds of biographical meaning (that is, being construed as showing an intentional element of self-discovery) while it remains hospitable to all kinds of significance commentators may identify in it. As Alan Sinfield has pointed out, naïvely co-opting Wilde as an ally of gay men a century later is anachronistic.[17] As a conscious contribution to the establishment of a distinctively homosexual literary and theatrical tradition, it seems unconvincing, but seen as a play written by an author whose status as a sexual and social being was precarious, it has a peculiar pathos and dignity. Even if in some quarters 'earnest' was indeed a code-word for homosexual, via 'uraniste', the message hardly seems worth the bottle; but because in general parlance 'earnest' had (and still has) all its deadly Victorian connotations of probity and high-mindedness, then the play's irreverence lives. The claims that Wilde was writing out his Irishness in the double selves of his protagonists are more convincing than the argument for *The Importance of Being Earnest* as a specifically gay play.[18]

Some of the topics spoken of lightly in the play were indeed the subject of earnest debate in the 1890s: the daily papers were full of the Irish Home-Rule question (which underlies the joke of Jack's claim to be a Liberal Unionist). Marriage, education, theology, the fall of the rupee and agricultural depression all get an airing. The gravest social concern invoked is the fear of insurrection. Told that Bunbury was quite exploded, Lady Bracknell exclaims:

> Exploded! Was he the victim of a revolutionary outrage? I was not aware that Mr Bunbury was interested in social legislation. If so, he is well punished for his morbidity.   (III, 101–4)

If education had any effect in England it might lead to acts of violence in Grosvenor Square, and there is the spectre of the French Revolution. In the wake of events during the 1880s (particularly the Trafalgar Square riot in 1885) and current fears about anarchists and revolutionary socialism – the masses and the classes – these jokes are the 1890s equivalent of references to 'The Bomb' in British plays of the 1950s and 1960s.

In this great farce Wilde distanced himself not only from earnest philistinism, or even earnest high culture, but from the earnest theatre. Those dramatists who were heeding Mathew Arnold's call, 'The theatre is irresistible: organise it!', could find little to support them in this trivial comedy. Wilde was uncomfortably unlike the image of the serious playwright as Jones or Pinero or (in his *outré* way) Shaw promulgated it. His position as an outsider who proclaimed his apartness – the dandy's stance as a leader and mocker of fashion – was dangerously close to that of the theatre itself. Alexander – the son of a tradesman – had risen, like his old chief Henry Irving, to be a leading participant in the fashionable world. He excelled at playing gentlemen, his theatre welcomed gentlemen and ladies and gave the public an image of stylish life; his first nights might (like those of fellow actor–managers) resemble fashionable parties; but he was still a member of a profession whose social standing was only now evolving to the condition of deserving respect by right rather than contract – and not altogether so in some social and, especially, 'earnest' religious circles. Nor were all actors on the same social level as Alexander. Like Markby the solicitor (occasionally seen at dinner parties) or the Liberal Unionists who dine with the Bracknells or at any rate come in the evening, the acting profession did not have an assured place in Society.

In the 1890s dramatists had to choose between working within an 'established' theatre, whose social standing and claim to participate in intellectual life were glamorous but fragile, and a radical theatre of symbolism and 'Ibsenite' (or Zolaesque) realism. The choice was between fashionable first nights, or earnest matinées – duchesses or dowdies.

Some endeavoured, like Shaw, to practise a form of what in radical politics could be called entryism: working for the Ibsenites among the disadvantaged of St James's. Wilde's participation in the fashionable, 'established' theatre was symptomatic of his refusal to be marginalised and his insistence – at the same time – on keeping his distance from 'Society'. One of the paradoxes of culture is the absorption of rebels into the canon, so that the work of irony becomes a 'classic', fixing and epitomising a style and a whole period. Wilde treated such notions with a mixture of eagerness and scepticism. He would have relished the irony of his most trivial of comedies being a text for examination in schools. 'Fortunately, in England, at any rate, education produces no effect whatsoever . . .'

NOTES

1 The fullest account of the circumstances of the first production is given in *Oscar Wilde's 'The Importance of Being Earnest'. A Reconstructive Critical Edition of the Text of the First Production*, ed. Joseph Donohue and Ruth Berggren (Gerrards Cross: Colin Smythe, 1995).

2 *The Green Carnation* was in fact written by Robert Hichens: at one point in the composition of his play Wilde added a reference to it (in the final scene Lady Bracknell is given it by mistake instead of a volume of the Army List). This was later removed.

3 A. E. W. Mason, *Sir George Alexander and the St James's Theatre* (London: Macmillan, 1935), pp. 227–8.

4 Ibid., p. 228.

5 On the play's composition and subsequent textual history see Donohue and Berggren, *Oscar Wilde's 'The Importance of Being Earnest'*. See also the Introduction and notes to my edition of the play (London: Benn, 1980; fourth impression, revised, 1992). The act and line references in the text relate to this edition of the play. A partial facsimile and full transcript of the earliest manuscript drafts of the four-act version will be found in Sarah Augusta Dickson (ed.), *The Importance of Being Earnest. A Trivial Comedy for Serious People as Originally Written by Oscar Wilde*, 2 vols., (New York: New York Public Library, 1956). In the present chapter references to the early MS drafts are to Dickson's transcription. The various manuscripts and typescripts of the four-act version are examined in Ruth Berggren's edition, *The Definitive Four-Act Version of 'The Importance of Being Earnest'* (New York: Vanguard, 1987).

6 Quoted from William Tydeman's collection, *Wilde, Comedies. A Casebook* (London: Macmillan, 1982), p. 41. The interview, with Robert Ross, appeared in the *St James's Gazette* on 18 January 1895.

7 On Victorian definitions of wit and humour, see Robert Bernard Martin, *The Triumph of Wit* (Oxford: Clarendon Press, 1974). The social dimension of Wilde's comedy is considered in Roger B. Henkle's study, *Comedy and Culture,*

England 1820–1900 (Princeton: Princeton University Press, 1980) and – with a more complex model of cultural process – by Regenia Gagnier in her *Idylls of the Marketplace. Oscar Wilde and the Victorian Public* (Aldershot: Scolar Press, 1987).

8 In addition to the various letters from the period of composition included in Hart-Davis's editions (a selection is in Tydeman's *Casebook*), see also the first scenario of the play, reprinted in Peter Raby's edition, *'The Importance of Being Earnest' and Other Plays* (Oxford: Oxford University Press, 1995), pp. 308–10.

9 Details of the revisions to this passage are given in my edition of the play (second edition, revised, London 1993) in the longer note to I, 91–109.

10 On the homosexual interpretation of 'earnest', see Karl Beckson, *London in the 1890s. A Cultural History* (New York: Norton, 1992), ch. 8. The commoner usages of the word in the period are described in Walter E. Houghton, *The Victorian Frame of Mind* (New Haven, CT: Wellesley College, 1957), ch. 10, 'Earnestness'.

11 In the manuscript draft of Act I, Algernon's debts are a far more pressing problem than in later versions. 'Wish to goodness some ass would leave me a large fortune. Can't go on as I am going on now. It is ridiculous' (Dickson, vol. I, p. 4). This mercenary motive was displaced onto Lady Bracknell, whose view of Cecily's eligibility is affected by her fortune. (See, *The Importance of Being Earnest*, III, 160 etc.).

12 W. H. Auden, 'An Improbable Life' (*New Yorker*, Mar. 1963), cited from Richard Ellmann (ed.), *Oscar Wilde, A Collection of Critical Essays* (Twentieth Century Views series; Englewood Cliffs, NJ: Prentice Hall, 1969), p. 136. On the formal pattern, see Otto Reinert, 'The Courtship Dance in *The Importance of Being Earnest*', *Modern Drama* I (1958–9), 256–7.

13 Wilde's use of this effect was noted by at least one reviewer: 'A remarkable feature of the piece is the entire absence of anything like a tableau at the end of an act, the curtain dropping in each case upon a comparatively unimportant remark' (*Daily News*, 15 Feb. 1895).

14 Kerry Powell, *Oscar Wilde and the Theatre of the 1890s* (Cambridge: Cambridge University Press, 1990), p. 110. Powell explores the relationship between Wilde's work and contemporary plays, both as direct and indirect sources, and as examples of the modes of writing with which he was engaged.

15 Shaw's review (*Saturday Review*, 23 Feb. 1895) is reprinted in *Our Theatres in the Nineties by Bernard Shaw* (London, 3 vols., 1932), I, 41–8. See also 'My Memories of Oscar Wilde', written as an appendix to Frank Harris's *Oscar Wilde: His Life and Confessions* (2nd edn, 2 vols., New York: Frank Harris, 1918) and reprinted in Ellmann's collection and in Shaw's *Pen Portraits and Reviews* (London, 1932).

16 H. Montgomery Hyde, *Oscar Wilde* (New York: Farrar, Straus and Giroux, 1975), p. 177.

17 Alan Sinfield insists that the effeminacy of Jack and Algernon is part of a dandyism that at the time of writing (before Wilde's trial) did not suggest same-sex love (*The Wilde Century. Effeminacy, Oscar Wilde and the Queer Moment*, London: Cassell, 1994, pp. 69–70). For a determined enlisting of Wilde and his works in a gay canon, see Gary Schmidgall, *The Stranger Wilde. Interpreting Oscar* (London: Abacus, 1994). See also Joseph Bristow's introduction to his

edition, *'The Importance of Being Earnest and Related Writings* (London: Routledge, 1992).

18 The specifically Irish dimension of Bunburying, and the 'double life' in Wilde's writing, is proposed by Declan Kiberd, 'Wilde and the English Question', *Times Literary Supplement*, 16 Dec. 1994, pp. 13–15.

III
THEMES AND INFLUENCES

I I

KERRY POWELL

A verdict of death: Oscar Wilde, actresses and Victorian women

A poem labelled dubiously as having been 'translated' by Oscar Wilde – from Polish, which he did not speak – is buried deep in an obscure anthology edited by Clement Scott, drama critic of the London *Daily Telegraph*. The poem, 'Sen Artysty', supposedly written by actress Helena Modjeska and translated by Wilde near the time of her London début, is as conflicted as many other stories and poems in *The Green Room* (1880), the anthology of theatre-writing in which it appears. The actress, or rather the persona of the poem that Wilde associated with Helena Modjeska, regrets her choice of an artistic life, is left with 'a restless pain' in her heart, and receives the stigmata of 'red wounds of thorns' on her brow when he tries to take off the laurel-crown.[1] 'Sen Artysty' not only harmonises with other writings in Clement Scott's anthology – all of them stories, essays or poems about the theatre – but asserts the same themes as many other Victorian assessments of women performers. Actresses were commonly thought to pay a terrible price for the public lives they led, including even the fortunate minority, like Modjeska, whose genius or hard work opened the way to riches and international fame. That price was figured in the rhetoric of suffering, illness and death, in lives wrecked by maladies both physical and mental. Victorian praise and even adulation of actresses was thus mingled with representations of them as suffering or wounded, like the speaker in the Helena Modjeska poem, or as monstrous, sick, or dying – victims of their own success in transcending the usual limits of a respectable Victorian woman's life.

With their powers of speech and gesture, actresses could hold audiences spellbound instead of merely 'suffer and be still', as Victorian women were typically advised to do.[2] Yet performing women were thought to look with regret to what Wilde calls in 'Sen Artysty' the 'sweet confines' of the garden-close that was sacrificed for a public career. Their lives were believed to be incompatible with the domestic satisfactions of other women whose identity seemed single rather than complex, their lives contained by marriage and motherhood. What could actresses, exiled from the domestic 'garden', have in common with them? Indeed could actresses be said to possess an authentic self of their own amid the whirl of identities that they assumed on stage? Could they be thought of as women at all? Such questions, even when not formally asked, lie just below the surface of a Victorian rhetoric which could glorify or even spiritualise the actress in one breath, and in the next define her in terms of suffering, disease, madness, estrangement from humanity, and death itself.

Wilde's recorded attitudes towards actresses are more often than not characteristically Victorian in their ambivalence. He threw lilies at the feet of Sarah Bernhardt when she first arrived in England and held her in awe for the rest of his life, but his sonnet on Bernhardt represents the actress of his dreams as a monstrous Phèdre – a vampire from hell, the recipient of kisses from 'the loveless lips' of dead men (CW 835). This note of dread in Wilde's 'To Sarah Bernhardt' is evident in many other enthusiastic assessments of Bernhardt's harrowing style as an actress. To the critic Arthur Symons, who sensed an obscure peril and felt an 'electrical shock' on his spinal cord when he saw Bernhardt perform, the actress seemed as inhuman as she did to Wilde. Bernhardt 'tears the words with her teeth', writes Symons, 'and spits them out of her mouth, like a wild beast ravening its prey'.[3] George Bernard Shaw characterises Bernhardt's art as 'entirely inhuman', and the actress herself a kind of diseased vampire, jolting the sensibilities of her audience with gleaming teeth and 'paroxysms of phthisis'.[4] Other actresses of great power were treated similarly by critics, their power neutralised, in effect, by relocating it from the realm of the feminine to that of the altogether inhuman and even unreal. Thus Charlotte Cushman's bloodthirsty portrayal of Lady Macbeth in London struck one reviewer as 'horribly fascinating', but somehow 'inhuman, incredible'.[5] Rachel, whose Phèdre electrified London audiences, was characterised by G. H. Lewes as 'the panther of the stage', moving with an animal's grace and always betraying 'something not human about her'. Her 'irresistible power' as an actress could be explained, Lewes felt, by an absence of femininity in her stage performances – 'no womanly caressing softness, no gaiety, no heartiness'.[6]

A modified rhetoric had to be employed to cancel the womanhood or humanity of a less dominating, more sentimental actress than Rachel or Cushman. For example, Wilde's poetic tribute to Ellen Terry is devoted to her exquisite suffering as the queen in W. G. Wills's *Charles I* (1879), her eyes 'marred by the mists of pain, / Like some wan lily overdrenched with rain' (CW 835). Terry herself understood very well the prejudices of her audience, to which she appealed by playing one suffering victim after another with thrilling pathos, attempting always to 'make them all cry' by crying first herself.[7] Of Wilde's sonnet on her, Terry remarked appreciatively that 'that phrase "wan lily" represented perfectly what I had tried to convey'.[8] Clement Scott himself venerated Terry as the greatest actress of the day because of the 'ideal' and 'mystical' qualities in her pathos-laden enactments, whether as the suicidal Ophelia or the betrayed and maddened women of contemporary plays such as *The Amber Heart* (1887) and *Ravenswood* (1890).[9] Like Bernhardt's, only in a different way, Terry's performances and their reception situated the actress on the margins of humanity – she became a delicate flower or a 'mystical' force, or, in the words of another of her admirers, a 'spiritual essence' more than a woman.[10] Reviewing Terry's performance as the victimised Olivia in W. G. Wills's adaptation of *The Vicar of Wakefield* (1878), Wilde recognises that Ellen Terry's 'power', as he calls it, arises from her genius for thrilling an audience with tender emotions.[11] But even this quiet 'power', so much milder than Bernhardt's or Cushman's, was difficult to reconcile with the private and passive roles that Victorian women were usually asked to play in life. Audiences could be reassured by the reflection that Ellen Terry was not so much a woman as a non-human, vaguely spiritualised essence – a 'wan lily', in Wilde's phrase which so appealed to Terry herself. With safeguards like these, actresses were allowed to upset the usual distribution of power by gender, vocalising powerfully and publicly while men sat passively beyond the footlights – 'spellbound, white and wordless', as one man expressed it, their thoughts and feelings at the command of women.[12]

Shaw, more than Wilde, perceived the disadvantages under which late-Victorian actresses worked, claiming that 'the higher artistic career is practically closed to the leading lady'. In independent productions of Ibsen organised by Elizabeth Robins and other women who disdained merely to 'support' an actor–manager, Shaw discerned the stirrings of an apocalypse – 'something like a struggle between the sexes for the dominion of the London theatres'.[13] One of the professed revolutionaries was a transplanted American actress named Eleanor Calhoun, who imagined a theatre which would rise above the 'vulgar and common plays' that were ordinarily staged in the West End by managers 'acting on self-evident economic principles'. In due time, she believed, the theatre could eliminate 'that type of exploiter', and with progressive leadership rise to 'a standard of perfection and form'.[14] Calhoun put into practice her faith in a new kind of theatre with her production of *As You Like It* in the open air of Coombe Wood in 1885. Wilde, in his notice for the *Dramatic Review*, said the woodland setting increased the value of the play 'as a picture', but took no notice of the really revolutionary aspects of this performance – namely, that two women,

Eleanor Calhoun and her protégée Lady Archibald Campbell, were in charge of the production; that the two of them played both leading roles, Orlando as well as Rosalind; and that in moving the production outdoors they were introducing a drama beyond the reach of male actor–managers and the theatres under their control.[15]

A few years later Eleanor Calhoun tried to give Elizabeth Robins, fresh from Boston, a start in the London theatre by surrendering to her the title role in *A Fair Bigamist*, a play written by a woman. Wilde, who befriended Robins at the time, discouraged her from taking the part, pointing out that the cast was 'unknown' and the Royalty Theatre where it would be performed 'unpopular'.[16] He urged her instead to cultivate the influential manager of the Haymarket, Beerbohm Tree, and provided an introduction which led Robins from one disappointment to another. By the time of her own epoch-making production of *Hedda Gabler* a few years later, at another unpopular theatre, Robins tried to enlist Wilde's support for a visionary 'theatre of the future' which would rise above the commercialism and egotism of theatres in the hands of actor–managers. Wilde seemed excited by the idea, and agreed to 'speak for it' and write an essay in support of it, Robins recalls in a manuscript memoir about Wilde.[17] In the end, however, he did nothing of the kind, and went on to make a successful career for himself in the theatres of leading actor–managers – including Tree. It is not clear whether Robins's final judgement of Wilde's work for the theatre would have been as harsh as that of her friend William Archer, the Ibsen critic and translator who viewed Wilde as a representative of what an advanced theatre would react against. His plays, Archer wrote, were 'in reality mere drawing-room melodramas, and conventional ones at that ... there was no real substance in his work'.[18]

Robins confesses in her memoir of Wilde that she 'disliked' his novel *The Picture of Dorian Gray*, and in her diary speaks of it more frankly as 'vile & revolting'.[19] But in *The Picture of Dorian Gray* Wilde considers in more detail than he does anywhere else, through the character of Sibyl Vane, an actress in particular and acting generally. Like many other Victorians, he contrasts actresses with the majority of women, whose lives seem by comparison predictable and superficial:

> Ordinary women never appeal to one's imagination. They are limited to their century. No glamour ever transfigures them. One knows their minds as easily as one knows their bonnets. One can always find them. There is no mystery in any of them. They ride in the Park in the morning, and chatter at tea-parties in the afternoon. They have their stereotyped smile, and their fashionable manner. But an actress! How different an actress is! (CW 49)

This effusion of Dorian Gray places emphasis on the 'glamour' and 'mystery' of an actress, her ability to transport an audience out of its own place and time. What the actress can do for the male spectator – the qualities which make her 'the one thing worth loving' – are for Dorian Gray the distinguishing and indeed the only worthwhile features of the performing woman, whether Sibyl Vane or any other. Lost in this male-centred analysis is what made acting seem particularly attractive to Victorian *women*, less impressed by the 'mystery' and 'glamour' that seduce a masculine observer such as Dorian Gray than by the independence, professionalism and hard work required of actresses. 'The way in which they have had to grapple with real, hard facts, to think and work and depend upon themselves, and the constant use of the higher faculties of taste and imagination', explains an anonymous author in the *Englishwoman's Journal*, 'raise them far above those women who are absorbed by the petty vanities and trifles and anxieties of a woman's ordinary life.'[20]

Dorian Gray, by contrast, asks of actresses: Can they interest or enrapture *me*, the spectator? Can they appeal to my imagination? Can they make me love them? Even from this vantage point, however, actresses rise above the superficial chatter, shallow thought and empty days of what the novel regards as conventional women. As Dorian's mentor Lord Henry Wotton expresses it, most women 'never have anything to say' even when they are conversing 'charmingly'. They are merely 'decorative', representing the triumph of matter over mind and accounting for the fact that in London no more than five women can be found who are 'worth talking to' (*CW* 47). In denying women a voice, or rather a voice that communicates with meaning and depth, Lord Henry reiterates in his own distinctive and, as Dorian Gray says, unforgettable voice one of the organising ideas of Victorian culture as a whole. This almost universal lack of a voice in women – or the sound of a voice without significance, without effect – is a rule whose exception is the actress, or at least an actress such as Sibyl Vane. She is beautiful, of course, 'the loveliest thing I had ever seen in my life', but Dorian, as he explains to Lord Henry Wotton, is moved as much by the sound of Sibyl Vane as the look of her in the role of Shakespeare's Juliet:

> ... her voice – I never heard such a voice. It was very low at first, with deep, mellow notes, that seemed to fall singly upon one's ear. Then it became a little louder, and sounded like a flute or a distant hautbois. In the garden scene it had all the tremulous ecstasy that one hears just before dawn when night-ingales are singing. There were moments, later on, when it had the wild passion of violets. You know how a voice can stir one. Your voice and the voice of Sibyl Vane are two things that I shall never forget. When I close my eyes, I hear them, and each of them says something different. I don't know

which to follow. Why should I not love her? Harry, I do love her. She is
everything to me in life.   (*CW* 49)

In being stirred by a woman's voice, hearing in it something 'different'
from Lord Henry Wotton's misogynistic comments, Dorian Gray resembles
many other Victorian observers who experienced the difference and power
of an actress in her vocalising. He also resembles other personae in
Victorian novels of the theatre. In *The Life and Love of an Actress* (1888),
for example, the voice of a young performer enacting the role of Juliet is as
transfigurative as Sibyl Vane's in the same role – 'as to her voice, it was
electric', writes the anonymous novelist; 'the dingy, tawdry stage trappings
faded away as if by magic, when she spoke'.[21] Actual critics, too, often
expressed fascination for the *voices* of women performers – an unnoticed
but significant fact which may be explained in part by the reversal of
Victorian standards in the theatre, a place where women could speak
powerfully while men sat mute in the darkness. Within the charmed space
of a theatre the speech of actresses beguiled men into a passivity that seemed
akin to the effects of witchcraft or narcotics. The voice of Sarah Bernhardt,
according to the trade newspaper the *Era*, was 'so exquisitely toned and
modulated that it realised the fable of the Sirens. It acted on the hearer like
some soothing, intoxicating Indian drug.'[22] The 'clear, pitiless voice' of
Genevieve Ward contributed to her own powerful effect on reviewers. 'The
actress last Saturday seemed to cast a spell over her audience', wrote a critic
of her signature role in *Forget-Me-Not* (1879), adding that the profound
'silence' of the audience 'denoted awe as well as interest, and gave an
unmistakable proof of the actress's power'.[23] Ellen Terry, as Imogen in
Cymbeline, was said to have spoken 'in a voice that melted your bosom'.[24]

    Eloquence such as this in an age which doomed women to silence or
empty speech could only intensify the powerful impact of some actresses
upon male spectators, who respond to their genius with a medley of
intimidation and admiration. Dorian Gray is 'filled with awe' when he so
much as thinks of Sibyl Vane, and 'hectic spots of red', like the marks of a
fever, burn on his cheeks when he talks of her. As befits one who is
'absolutely and entirely divine' rather than human, Sibyl compels him in
strange ways; for example, he visits the theatre 'every night of my life' to see
her perform, and does it involuntarily – 'I can't help going to see Sibyl play',
he explains, 'even if it is only for a single act' (*CW* 51). Dorian belongs in
the catalogue of Victorians, real and fictional, who finds themselves placed
under compulsion of women performers, overwhelmed physically or mentally by their remarkable powers. Arthur Symons, for example, manifests
symptoms like Dorian's when describing how the pulse 'beat feverishly'

under the stimulus of Sarah Bernhardt, whose acting Shaw describes in terms of a disease running its violent course. Hector Berlioz haunted the Parisian theatre where Harriet Smithson in the role of Juliet left him 'hardly able to breathe – as though an iron hand gripped me by the heart'.[25] Similarly the hero of William Black's long-forgotten novel of the theatre, *Macleod of Dare* (1878), mechanically follows actress Gertrude White from theatre to theatre, under her 'spell', hopelessly 'bewitched', unable to 'breathe freely' as he watches, in spite of himself, performance after performance.[26]

The 'power' of the actress, as Dorian Gray calls it, makes her 'the one thing worth loving', yet a source of contagion and loss of control experienced in different degrees by Victorian men in both fact and fiction. Her power, furthermore, is measured in Wilde's novel and elsewhere by the extent to which the actress swerves from 'ordinary' womanhood, taking on a self of her own creation – or selves, more accurately. What makes Dorian Gray unusual is the equanimity, indeed the exhilaration, with which he regards this flexible, changing identity of the actress, an identity too complex to be contained within the one-dimensional lives of 'ordinary women' with their predictable minds and inaccessibility to meaningful speech and action:

> Night after night I go to see her play. One evening she is Rosalind, and the next evening she is Imogen. I have seen her die in the gloom of an Italian tomb, sucking the poison from her lover's lips. I have watched her wandering through the forest of Arden, disguised as a pretty boy in hose and doublet and dainty cap. She has been mad, and has come into the presence of a guilty king, and given him rue to wear, and bitter herbs to taste of. She has been innocent, and the black hands of jealousy have crushed her reed-like throat. I have seen her in every age and in every costume. (CW 49)

The genius of Sibyl Vane, as Dorian tells Lord Henry, is precisely that she is 'more than an individual' - indeed, she is 'all the great heroines of the world in one' (CW 51). Dorian can locate no single, fixed identity behind this revolving wheel of selves; the actress is 'never' simply Sibyl Vane, never one of the ordinary women whose minds are as easily known as their hats. The actress is 'different' because she is more than a commodity in a masculine economy – not an ordinary woman, but rather many extraordinary ones.

By contrast, the hero of William Black's novel *Macleod of Dare* experiences a 'strange nervousness' as he waits for the actress he loves to make her entrance on stage, uncertain in what character she will appear. Inwardly Macleod reviews the varied incarnations of Gertrude White as he has seen them in private and in performance – a shy maiden, first of all, then a wronged and weeping woman, an artful coquette, a spoiled child. On another occasion, made up as a duchess, the actress causes Macleod to stammer, 'I – I did not recognize her', and to begin thinking of her as a kind of witch or sorceress. 'Which of them all was she?' he wonders anxiously, certain that there must be, or should be, a core of true and stable identity in the actress. 'Which should he see in the morning? Or would she appear as some still more elusive vision, retreating before him as he advanced?' Macleod's dilemma is given away in the word 'elusive', for the actress slips out of his grasp with her perpetual shape-shifting, resists being fully known and controlled by him, and thus escapes the narrow confines of what Dorian Gray calls 'ordinary women'.[27] The very idea of a woman's having a free and flexible selfhood, as Nina Auerbach shows, contradicted Victorian thought about the self in general and woman's self in particular.[28] Performance, furthermore, endangered by its very nature the Victorian belief in a stable identity, the true or 'buried' self that lies for Matthew Arnold at the core of our being. Actors and actresses, with their multiplication of personalities, suggest that character is unreadable, volatile and subject to transformation. The character of women in particular was supposed to be unmysterious and knowable, circumscribed by the functions of wifehood and motherhood.

Dorian Gray, with his *fin-de-siècle* enthusiasm for the pose and mask, is much less troubled by the self-transformations of actresses than were most Victorians who considered the matter, including some actresses. Mary Anderson, for example, came to think of her popular stage roles as fundamentally unreal, mere 'dramatic effects' hopelessly at odds with the 'great realities' of a woman's domestic life – of her own life after she married and left the stage. As an actress, writes Anderson in her memoirs, 'I was perpetually longing for the *real*, and wishing to abandon the make-believe, and I have found the real, more rich, more beautiful and more engrossing than its counterfeit.'[29] This idea that a woman's core identity is endangered by her adoption of many selves on stage is frequently expressed in novels of the theatre. In *Mimic Life* (1856) actress and novelist Anna Cora Mowatt describes a scene in which a performer is disconcerted by her own reflection when practising a new role before a mirror: 'It seemed to her as if she were scanning the face of another. She was indeed "losing her identity".'[30] And Gertrude White, the actress in William Black's *Macleod of Dare*, worries that her having to sympathise with so many characters – 'be so many different people' – makes it difficult for her to 'know what my own character is, or if I have any at all'.[31] Every woman is supposed to be, in essence, like every other, 'supposed to have the same set of motives, or else be a monster', observes the former actress Alcharisi in George Eliot's novel

Daniel Deronda (1876). What makes Alcharisi unusual is her satisfaction with having lived 'myriad lives in one' as an actress, and her refusal to be written out of humanity, as a kind of 'monster', because she refused of her own choice to be a wife and mother. 'I am not a monster', explains Alcharisi, embracing the possibility of a complex and various femininity, 'but I have not felt exactly what other women feel – or say they feel, for fear of being thought unlike others.'[32]

But such expressions – like Dorian Gray's celebration of Sibyl Vane as 'more than an individual' – really enforce from another, unexpected direction the tendency of the Victorians to isolate the actress in a ghetto of the imagination, unassimilable with other women and what Mary Anderson, having quit the stage herself, calls the 'great realities' of their domestic lives. Deep-seated in Victorian thought, even within the theatre itself, was the idea of an unbridgeable gap between women performers on one hand and wives and mothers on the other. Even the *Stage Directory*, a trade publication, observed in an article of 1880 that actresses were 'hopeless' at the skills of household management which 'tend to make a home happy'.[33] Producer and set designer Gordon Craig argues in a memoir that great actresses and singers rarely marry with success. They are 'impossible people', he says, naming as examples Bernhardt, Duse, Rachel, Siddons, Jordan and above all his own mother Ellen Terry. 'One can't be possible *every* way', Craig elaborates; 'I don't see how you can rock the cradle, rule the world, and play Ophelia perfectly, all in the day's work.' Actresses, especially those of the highest order like Ellen Terry, were sadly belated in their attempts to be wives and mothers, for they were already happily married – 'married to the stage', as Craig says.[34]

Against this background the remark of Lord Henry Wotton to Dorian Gray – 'I don't suppose you will want your wife to act' (*CW* 70) – would have seemed a casual but obvious inference from a rule which set actresses apart from other women. Many working actresses were married, of course, and some happily; but one of the most famous of these, Madge Kendal, felt compelled to devote many pages in her memoirs to a laborious argument that an actor and actress could have a successful marriage despite widespread prejudice to the contrary.[35] Reginald Turner concludes his theatrical novel *Cynthia's Damages* (1901) with the marriage of an actress that will be 'blessed with issue' and happy – 'a proof', says Turner, who realises that sceptical readers would need one, 'that actors and actresses have a family life'.[36] No such 'proof' was known to George Parkes, a Boston actor who jumped to his death in the Charles River in 1887 when his bride Elizabeth Robins declined to give up her acting career and devote herself to making a home for him.[37] In fiction, too, death was imagined as a last desperate measure to avoid contaminating the 'real' life of domesticity with the counterfeit and fragmented experience of actresses. Thus the title character of Robert Buchanan's little-known novel *The Martyrdom of Madeline* (1882) responds impetuously when her husband suggests that she might like to return to acting, her profession before she married him and went to live in the country. 'It is impossible', the former actress exclaims. 'I hate the stage. Rather than return to it I would die.'[38]

Those same words – 'I hate the stage' – are uttered in *The Picture of Dorian Gray* by Sibyl Vane, whom Wilde leaves, just as Madeline is left in Buchanan's novel, choosing death over a life on stage. Sibyl had lived 'only in the theatre' – lived as Juliet and Rosalind, Cordelia and Beatrice, believing the 'painted scenes' and 'shadows' of the stage were real – before falling in love with Dorian and learning 'what reality really is'. Her discovery of love and the prospect of marriage, what Mary Anderson calls the 'great realities', causes Sibyl to turn from the stage in disgust and denounce as a 'sham' her revolving identities as an actress (*CW* 71–2). In her last performance of all Sibyl plays Juliet without emotion or conviction, her power as an actress having been consumed by her love for Dorian Gray. Where Wilde departs from the usual script of Victorian thought on this matter is in expressing through Lord Henry Wotton the view that acting 'is so much more real than life', and in making Dorian prefer Sibyl the actress to the 'real' Sibyl who loves him. Instead of allowing the actress to marry and retire to a domestic life in the country, like the heroine of *The Martyrdom of Madeline*, Wilde turns the tables when he has Dorian break off his engagement to Sibyl immediately after, and because of, her failed enactment of Juliet:

> You have killed my love. You used to stir my imagination. Now you don't even stir my curiosity. You simply produce no effect. I loved you because you were marvellous, because you had genius and intellect, because you realised the dreams of great poets and gave shape and substance to the shadows of art. You have thrown it all away ... I will never see you again. (*CW* 72)

Wilde puts his own stamp on this narrative of an actress in love by giving her a lover, Dorian Gray, who is more exhilarated than worried and puzzled by her transformation of self on stage. Dorian, under the tutelage of Lord Henry, learns to think of the actual person Sibyl Vane as nothing but a 'dream', one who 'never really lived', and thus to accept as reasonable that 'the moment she touched actual life, she marred it, and it marred her' (*CW* 82). Despite these ingenious reversals of customary thinking about actresses, however, Sibyl is left in a familiar dilemma, the usual dilemma of the Victorian actress as conceived by others and often by herself – helpless, that is, to combine a career on stage with a happy domestic life. The two, as usual, are made to seem incompatible.

Looking and feeling ill during her incompetent last performance as Juliet, dying soon thereafter, Sibyl is defined at last with the rhetoric of sickness and death that came so easily to Victorians who wrote about actresses and their difference from so-called 'ordinary women'. Lord Henry, from the look of her in the role of Juliet, imagines Sibyl to be 'ill', and after the show Dorian approaches her, likewise under the impression that 'you are ill, I suppose'. Sibyl herself feels sick – 'sick of shadows', of the 'sham' and 'empty pageant' of the theatre, of the 'profanation' of playing at love once she understands 'what love really is' (CW 70–2). This sickness of mind is fatal; for when the actress learns that her longing for a life with Dorian can never be realised, she swallows, as Lord Henry reports, something containing prussic acid or white lead and dies instantly. Like so many actresses in so many Victorian texts, Sibyl Vane is written out of love and marriage, and, again like other actresses in other texts, written out of humanity too – 'The girl never really lived', as Lord Henry explains, and even in taking her own life 'she never really died' (CW 82).

But Sibyl's death is real enough that an inquest is performed on her body and written up in the St James's Gazette. Her death, in a sense, was written even before Wilde wrote his novel, for Sibyl's fate re-enacts that of many other actresses who sicken or die in Victorian stories of the theatre, including some in the Green Room anthology edited by Clement Scott in which Wilde's early poem associated with Helena Modjeska appeared. In that volume, for example, a story by actress Marie Litton is concerned with a performer whose lover sees her act, and then, 'disgusted', breaks off their engagement. Having lost any chance of life with the man she loves, the actress of the story wills her own death, the 'best chance' remaining to her.[39] Another contribution to The Green Room, written by actress Fanny Bernard Beere, also links the actress's success in the public sphere to pain or failure in the private one. 'The Tale of a Peacock' concerns an actress who receives a note from her fiancé breaking off their engagement just before she goes on stage to play Ophelia. Bereft of love, her marriage plans in ruin, she gives the performance of her life. 'I was mad and desperate as Ophelia herself', she explains. The actress thus blends into the persona of the mad role she performs, fainting on stage before the show ends and being carried off with the symptoms of 'brain fever'.[40] She is Ophelia, just as Sibyl Vane is the Shakespearian characters she performs – at least until her last disastrous performance in Romeo and Juliet when she has begun to wish for a life of her own.

In her sickness and death Sibyl Vane thus performs the doom of actresses generally, as the Victorian imagination tended to conceive it. They suffer from brain fever, as in 'The Tale of a Peacock' and Anna Cora Mowatt's *Mimic Life*, or have collapsed, like the heroine of William Suter's play *The Life of an Actress* (1853), into a physical 'wreck' – casualties, they learn, of the 'feverish profession that would destroy you'.[41] They kill themselves, off-stage like Sibyl Vane, or in the middle of a show, like the heroine of *The Life and Love of an Actress*, who stabs herself under the gaze of the man who just broke off her engagement. They are desperate cases, mentally and physically, although in principle they could be restored to health easily enough. 'A quiet home shared with the man of her heart', as the audience of *The Life of an Actress* was informed, would bring colour back to the cheeks of the ailing actress Violette le Grande. And when Sibyl Vane has come to 'hate the stage', she calls for the same remedy with a plaintive cry: 'Take me away, Dorian – take me away with you, where we can be quite alone' (*CW* 72). Like Sibyl and the speaker of Wilde's poem 'Sen Artysty', the actress gives up everything – her happiness, her hope of love, even her womanhood and humanity – in exchange for a public life. As Francis Gribble describes this dilemma in his novel *Sunlight and Limelight: A Story of the Stage Life and the Real Life* (1898), the actress is perceived to exist in a shadowland of gender – not like other women at all:

> Other women lived by sunlight, lived without the excitement and the music and the applause, and never wanted it, and were happier than she was. They had not the world about their feet, as she had. They had not her power of exacting homage or of breaking hearts. But they could love as she could not. They could win one man's heart, and cleave to it, and grow old tranquilly, knowing that they had not loved in vain.[42]

Despite its enthusiasm for a great actress, *The Picture of Dorian Gray* is held captive by this deeply ingrained Victorian habit of conceiving the performing woman as being outside the boundaries of gender, health and even human life itself. Whether consciously or not, it followed the Victorian strategy of neutralising power when a woman held it, of rationalising a strong voice when it happened to be female and compelled men to silence. There was another, less defensive view of actresses, one usually expressed by women. The notable feature of an actress's life, as Florence Nightingale wrote, was her opportunity to undertake 'studies' within a professional discipline; for actress Madge Kendal it was 'the blessedness of independence'; and from the perspective of novelist Geraldine Jewsbury it was a 'clear, definite channel' through which her energies could flow.[43] These alternative views of the actress equip her for the full, rich and complete life that in Wilde's novel and elsewhere in the literature of Victorian theatre she is denied.

NOTES

1 Oscar Wilde, 'Sen Artysty; or, The Artist's Dream', appeared in *The Green Room: Stories by Those Who Frequent It*, ed. Clement Scott (London: Routledge, [1880]), pp. 66–8. A currently accessible version is included in *Complete Works of Oscar Wilde* (London: Collins, 1994), pp. 856–7.

2 The phrase was coined by Sarah Stickney Ellis, author of *The Women of England: Their Social Duties and Domestic Habits* (London: Fisher, 1838) and *The Daughters of England: Their Position in Society, Character, and Responsibilities* (London: Fisher, 1842), and other popular works on femininity.

3 Arthur Symons, *Plays, Acting, and Music* (New York: Dutton, 1903), pp. 27–30.

4 George Bernard Shaw, 'Duse and Bernhardt', in *Our Theatres in the Nineties* (London: Constable, 1931), XXIII, 158–60.

5 Quoted by Mary M. Turner, *Forgotten Leading Ladies* (Jefferson, NC: McFarland, 1990), p. 64.

6 G. H. Lewes, *On Actors and the Art of Acting* (1875; rpt. New York: Grove, [1957]), p. 32.

7 Edward Gordon Craig, *Ellen Terry and Her Secret Self* (London: Reinhardt, n.d.), p. 155.

8 Ellen Terry, *Story of My Life: Ellen Terry's Memoirs* (1932; rpt. Westport, CT: Greenwood, [1970]), p. 198.

9 Clement Scott, *Ellen Terry* (New York: Stokes, 1900).

10 Shaw Desmond, *London Nights of Long Ago* (London: Duckworth, 1927), p. 183.

11 Oscar Wilde, 'Olivia at the Lyceum', *Dramatic Review*, 30 May 1885; rpt. *The First Collected Edition of the Works of Oscar Wilde* (London: Methuen, 1908–22), ed. Robert Ross, XIII, 29–32, CW 955–6.

12 The words belong to a character in a play by Louis N. Parker, *A Buried Talent* (1890), p. 44, quoted from the licensing text in the Lord Chamberlain's Collection of the British Library.

13 Shaw, preface to *The Theatrical 'World' of 1894*, by William Archer (London: Scott, 1895), p. xiv–xxx.

14 Princess Lazarovich-Hrebelianovich [Eleanor Calhoun], *Pleasures and Palaces: The Memoirs of Princess Lazarovich-Hrebelianovich* (London: Nash, 1916), pp. 193–4.

15 Oscar Wilde, '*As You Like It* at Coombe House', in *Dramatic Review*, 6 June 1885; rpt. *First Collected Edition of the Works of Oscar Wilde*, XIII, 32–6.

16 Elizabeth Robins, *Both Sides of the Curtain* (London: Heinemann, [1940]), p. 16.

17 Elizabeth Robins, 'Oscar Wilde: An Appreciation', MS Fales Library, New York University, p. 9. This previously unpublished typescript has recently appeared in print for the first time: '"Oscar Wilde: An Appreciation": An Unpublished Memoir by Elizabeth Robins, edited with commentary by Kerry Powell', *Nineteenth Century Theatre*, Winter 1993, 101–13.

18 William Archer, *The Old Drama and the New: An Essay in Re-Valuation* (Boston: Small, Maynard, 1923), pp. 303–4.

19 Robins, 'Oscar Wilde: An Appreciation', p. 5, and Robins's diary for 8 July to 4 Dec. 1890, MS Fales Library, New York University.

20 'A Few Words about Actresses and the Profession of the Stage', *Englishwoman's Journal*, Feb. 1859, pp. 385–98.

21 *The Life and Love of an Actress*, 'By an Actress' (New York: Judge, 1888), pp.26–7.

22 *Era*, 17 June 1889, p. 17.

23 Zadel Barnes Gustafson, *Genevieve Ward: A Biographical Sketch from Material Derived from her Family and Friends* (Boston: Osgood, 1882), pp. 248, 250, quoting reviews in *Vanity Fair* and the *Era*.

24 Mrs Patrick Campbell, *My Life and Some Letters* (New York: Dodd, Mead, 1922), p. 436.

25 Quoted by Peter Raby, *Fair Ophelia: A Life of Harriet Smithson Berlioz* (Cambridge: Cambridge University Press, 1982), p. 77.

26 William Black, *Macleod of Dare: A Novel* (London: Harper, [1878]), pp. 39, 68, 178.

27 William Black, *Macleod of Dare*, pp. 39, 48, 67, 76.

28 Nina Auerbach, *Private Theatricals: The Lives of the Victorians* (Cambridge, MA: Harvard University Press, 1990), pp. 4, 18.

29 Mary Anderson, *A Few More Memories* (London: Osgood, McIlvaine, 1896), pp. 2, 17–18.

30 Anna Cora Mowatt, *Mimic Life; or, Before and Behind the Curtain* (Boston: Ticknor and Fields, 1856), p. 27.

31 William Black, *Macleod of Dare*, p. 135.

32 George Eliot, *Daniel Deronda* (Oxford: Clarendon Press, 1984), pp. 583–6.

33 'Actors' Marriages' *Stage Directory*, 1 Mar. 1880, p. 8.

34 Edward Gordon Craig, *Ellen Terry and Her Secret Self*, pp. 52, 57, 63–6.

35 Madge Kendal, *Dame Madge Kendal by Herself* (London: Murray, 1953), pp. 62, 187.

36 Reginald Turner, *Cynthia's Damages: A Story of the Stage* (London: Greening, 1901), p. 311.

37 For accounts of Parkes's suicide, see Angela John, *Elizabeth Robins: Staging a Life, 1862–1952* (London: Routledge, 1995), and Joanne Gates, *Elizabeth Robins, 1862–1952: Actress, Novelist, Feminist* (Tuscaloosa: University of Alabama Press, 1994).

38 Robert Buchanan, *The Martyrdom of Madeline* (London: Chatto and Windus, 1907), p. 209.

39 Marie Litton, 'Chances! Story of a Young Actress', in *The Green Room*, ed. Clement Scott, p. 60.

40 Fanny Bernard Beere, 'The Tale of a Peacock', in *The Green Room*, ed. Clement Scott, p. 20.

41 William Suter, *Violette le Grande, or the Life of an Actress, a Drama in Three Acts*, staged at the Grecian Theatre and apparently never published, is quoted from the MS in the Lord Chamberlain's Collection of the British Library.

42 Francis Gribble, *Sunlight and Limelight: A Story of the Stage Life and the Real Life* (London: Innes, 1898), pp. 146–7.

43 Florence Nightingale, *Cassandra: An Essay* (Old Westbury, NY: Feminist Press, 1979), pp. 40–1; Madge Kendal, *Dramatic Opinions* (London: Murray, 1890), p. 47; Geraldine Jewsbury, *The Half Sisters: A Tale* (London: Chapman and Hall, 1848), II, 73.

12

JOSEPH BRISTOW

'A complex multiform creature': Wilde's sexual identities

I

If Oscar Wilde is remembered for anything since his turn-of-the-century demise, it is his meteoric rise as a raconteur, playwright and cultural critic, and his startlingly rapid fall into disrepute as a homosexual committed to two years in solitary confinement with hard labour in Reading Gaol. Since this memorable story has been told so many times and in so many versions – not least in his own work of life writing, posthumously named *De Profundis*, and in biographies as notable and substantial as Richard Ellmann's – one would reasonably imagine that we must now know all there is to discover about Wilde's scandalous sexual behaviour, not to say the imprint of transgressive desire across the gamut of his works. Indeed, the enduring interest in his life and writings – from Peter Ackroyd's fictional *The Last Will and Testament of Oscar Wilde* (1983) to Philip Prowse's visually arresting productions of the Society comedies[1] – suggests that Wilde addresses issues that still vibrantly preoccupy our own *fin de siècle*, particularly where questions of sexual identity are concerned. This is especially the case in the world of scholarly research where the upsurge of critical attention paid to Wilde's oeuvre has risen sharply in the light of a burgeoning lesbian and gay studies since the mid-1980s. Such developments have meant that academic readers are now altogether freer in articulating the homoerotic patternings that would seem to inflect his writings from beginning to end. It was, after all, not so uncommon in the past for Wilde's personal life to be treated as a source of some embarrassment, if not prurience, in university seminars where students were at times under pressure to interpret *The Importance of Being Earnest* (1895) as an exemplary farce, rather than a carefully coded dramatisation of subversive homosexual intent. Given the impressive amount of recent criticism that has focused on the sexually provocative allusions made in works as generically distinct as *The Picture of Dorian Gray* (1890, 1891) and *The Ballad of*

Reading Gaol (1898), it would not be misleading to think that Wilde – the married lover of young men, the propagator of a Platonic philosophy of homophile friendship – had been finally welcomed out of the academic closet. In the fulsome spirit of emancipation, it would indeed appear that Wilde can at last be applauded for what he assuredly was: a gay man who paid a terribly high price in being publicly shamed for his physical intimacy enjoyed in private with other males.

But just at the point when it seemed that Wilde's distinctive personal style and pre-eminent literary talent could be openly analysed for all their dissident sexual pleasures, a significant conflict emerged that focused on how critics might accurately discuss the erotic identity that has, for the best part of a century, been labelled 'homosexuality'. If Wilde's gay-affirmative readers have devoted a great deal of energy to unearthing the homosexual subtext that may be plausibly brought to light in those works of Wilde's that are rich in telltale codes, puns, gestures and allusions, then it would seem that we can once and for all celebrate what was referred to during the trials of 1895 as 'the "Love that dare not speak its name"' (the renowned phrase from one of Alfred Douglas's poems).[2] In other words, a desire that was formerly silenced is no longer subject to either embarrassment or censorship. Yet sound objections have been raised against critical methods that would reduce each and every moment of suggestive obliquity in Wilde's writings to an undeniable instance of homophile intensity, and such charges – it must be emphasised – have been made, not by conservative scholars who might find such an approach politically motivated, but by readers with a wholehearted commitment to the painstaking discussion of how a category such as 'homosexuality' came into being in the first place, and why it might not readily apply to the life and works of Wilde. The conflict opened up by this debate is crucial because it begs significant questions about how we can apply ourselves to the historical specificity, not only of Wilde's sexual being, but our own.

Let me, then, provide a handful of examples that highlight the points on which critics diverge when it comes to apprising readers of the 'homosexual' Wilde. If, for instance, we look at the distinguished work of Christopher Craft, whose fine essay entitled 'Alias Bunbury' reverberates with the resonant punning we find throughout *The Importance of Being Earnest*, what is surely set before us is an eloquent form of anti-homophobic criticism that examines the 'flickering presence-absence of the play's homosexual desire'. Recognising only too well that throughout the 1890s homoerotic representation remained 'technically unspeakable' (in terms of religious doctrine, *non nominandum inter Christianos*), Craft takes pains to accentuate how the absent friend named Bunbury, who serves as Algernon

Moncrieff's alibi whenever the young bachelor wishes to escape the throes of his family, implies at least seven overlayered meanings – from 'an actual person of no importance, Henry Shirley Bunbury, a hypochondriachal acquaintance of Wilde's Dublin youth' to 'a pseudonym or alias for the erotic oscillation within the male subject, his fundamental waffling [i.e. interweaving] between Jack and Ernest'.[3] So ingenious is Craft's enquiry into the teasing provocations of the 'Bunbury' and related puns – many of which, as he himself admits, have been identified by earlier readers – that his work takes a truly Wildean turn when he declares that there is nothing less than 'pun-burying' in 'Bunburying'. And Craft does so to demonstrate how these connotative possibilities escalate throughout a drama where 'oppositional meanings' (namely, ones that contest the respectable social order of the day) 'are not synthesized or sublated so much as they are exchanged, accelerated, derailed, terminated, cross-switched'. (In deploying these verbs, Craft is clearly exploiting to good effect the metaphors implied by the uproarious disclosure that Jack Worthing was a foundling discovered in a handbag mislaid on the Brighton railway line.) One highly suggestive word testifies more than any other to the electrifying power of Wilde's wit: the titular pun on 'E(a)rnest' which stands – among other things – as Jack's proper name, a patronym, an alias, an imaginary lover, and a code-word for homosexual desire itself: since 'Love in Earnest' titled a volume of Uranian poetry by John Gambril Nicholson, whose boy-loving sentiments had a growing appeal for a marginal group of men with pederastic interests.[4]

Such an approach to *The Importance of Being Earnest* has a persuasive elegance. This style of reading – as Gwendolen Fairfax would say – 'produces vibrations'. To be sure, the great virtue of Craft's analysis is that it patently refuses to construe *The Importance of Being Earnest* in terms of reductive equivalences between the punning textual surface and the sexual truth that might be glimpsed beneath it. Instead – as my résumé of this critique should indicate – 'Alias Bunbury' respects the polyvalence of those exquisite moments in the drama where we can readily detect that an item as seemingly innocent as a cucumber sandwich might, at some undisclosed level, point to rather different and disruptive fields of meaning. But interpretative labour of this kind has been put under careful scrutiny by anti-homophobic researchers who suggest that the critical desire to amplify the 'pun-buries' of 'Bunbury' may well be mistaken. What, then, might be amiss about this dazzling analysis?

The answer lies in the ways in which such an interpretation could be accused of moulding Wilde's drama into a play with a fully developed homosexual undercurrent, one that would comply with our post-Stonewall comprehension of not only what it might mean to be *homosexual*, but also what it means to be *gay*.[5] I make these emphases because, even though the course of the twentieth century has witnessed a decisive shift from the often punitive clinical understanding of the 'homosexual' to the political empowerment signalled by 'Gay Liberation', both terms rely on perceptions shaped by what might be fairly called modernist identity. These are, according to Michel Foucault, decisively modern forms of labelling that assume that sexual identity is dictated by object-choice. In the introductory volume to his *History of Sexuality*, Foucault concentrates on how in the late nineteenth century sexual behaviours were gradually interpreted as constituting specific sexual subjects. One of his main examples concerns how sodomy was until the closing decades of the Victorian period viewed as a manifestation of sexual behaviour: it was a sexual act, not a style of sexual being. The hundreds of men hanged for committing sodomy, up to and including 1836, were not known as homosexual or by any earlier equivalent label. Bearing in mind the power-laden medical and scientific discourses that would undertake to taxonomise differing types of sexual persons, Foucault insists that the 'nineteenth-century homosexual became a personage, a past, a case history, and a childhood, in addition to being a type of life, a life form, and a morphology, with an indiscreet anatomy and possibly a mysterious physiology'.[6] Only by the *fin de siècle*, in the years roughly contemporaneous with the three trials that Wilde underwent in the spring of 1895, were researchers of psychology, medicine and social science making for the first time cardinal distinctions between homosexuals and heterosexuals.

But the growing concentration on the supposed antitheses between homosexuals and heterosexuals did not touch directly on Wilde's own sense of his sexual self before he was imprisoned. Before the débâcle of 1895, there is little evidence to suggest that Wilde had much or any interest in the ways in which sexual behaviour had become a focus of fascination for those thinkers – such as Karl Heinrich Ulrichs, Richard von Krafft-Ebing and Havelock Ellis – who were by that time compendiously classifying types of human sexuality. Special attention was paid by these writers to the physiological and psychological make-up of the sexual 'invert': a figure that, to their minds, showed that a female soul could inhabit a male body, just as a male soul could lie at the heart of a woman's physique. Although the idea of the invert looks absurd today, it provided for several decades – until the 1930s at least – an authoritative conceptualisation of what constituted homosexuality. Explained purely in terms of sexual difference, the invert's characteristic mismatched internal and external features proved relatively easy to apprehend, thus laying the ground for two of the persistent stereotypes of homosexuality that have been highly visible in modern culture: the mannish lesbian and the effeminate gay man. The latter image is the one that, in the course of the trials, made Wilde appear an indisputably deviant being in the eyes of the public. But the very idea that he was in any respect 'inverted' came as something of a shock to him. Several months after his release from Reading Gaol, the dispirited Wilde wrote to his publisher, Leonard Smithers: 'My life cannot be patched up. Neither to myself, nor others, am I any longer a joy. I am now simply a pauper of a rather low order: the fact that I am also a pathological problem in the eyes of German scientists: and even in their works I am tabulated, and come under the law of *averages*! *Quantum mutatus*!'[7] That his sexual crimes might in all their pathological distinctiveness be placed within a statistical table of some kind is wholly alien to a man whose outlook on the world, as the extract from this letter shows, is in many ways shaped by Classical learning, not medical discourse.

Such evidence, then, encourages us to believe that Wilde, until the time of his prison sentence, had no perception of himself as either a 'homosexual' or an 'invert', even though these almost interchangeable labels were gaining credibility within scientific circles in the mid-1890s. In this light, it is wise to follow David M. Halperin's counsel when it comes to deploying the term 'homosexuality' in contemporary cultural criticism:

> Although a blandly descriptive, rigorously clinical term like 'homosexuality' would appear to be unobjectionable as a taxonomic device, it carries with it a heavy complement of ideological baggage and has, in fact, proved a significant obstacle to understanding the distinctive features of sexual life in non-Western and pre-modern cultures. It may well be that homosexuality properly speaking has no history of its own outside the West or much before the beginning of our century.[8]

Halperin's point, however, has proved especially hard to take in relation to Wilde because the author has for the best part of a century served as the ultimate icon of the modern homosexual: the figure who embodied a form of sexual pathology that Wilde himself found bewilderingly strange.

In the preface to his engaging study of Wilde's sexual styles, Alan Sinfield insists that we must be wary of assuming this defiantly effeminate man can be readily understood as homosexual or gay. The same goes for how we set about reading the homophile interests of his works. 'Many commentators', writes Sinfield, 'assume that queerness, like murder, *will out*, so there must be a gay scenario lurking somewhere in the depths of *The Importance of Being Earnest*. But it doesn't really work. It might be nice to think of Algernon and Jack as a gay couple, but most of their dialogue is bickering about property and women; or of Bunburying as cruising for rough trade, but it is an upper-class young heiress that we see Algernon visiting, and they want to marry.' The problem for modern critics, as Sinfield sees it, lies in the fact that 'Wilde and his writings look queer because our stereotypical notion of male homosexuality derives from Wilde, and our ideas about him'.[9] Sinfield, therefore, accentuates how and why Wilde was not intelligibly a specific type of deviant sexual being when he embarked on his disastrous libel suit against the Marquess of Queensberry who had left a calumnious visiting-card that – in a moment of notorious illiteracy – accused the writer of 'posing Somdomite' (sometimes read, given the poor quality of the Marquess's handwriting, as 'Poseur and Somdomite'). Only during the trial proceedings did a hostile press manage to produce, in often contradictory ways, an image of Wilde as someone whose sexual preference styled him as a definitionally different, morally degenerate and thus utterly contemptible kind of man.

This view emerges from Ed Cohen's detailed analysis of the journalistic reports of the court proceedings. Cohen shows how 'the newspapers (re)produced the possibility for designating Wilde as a kind of sexual actor without explicitly referring to the specificity of his sexual acts, and thereby crystallized a new constellation of sexual meanings predicated upon "personality" and not practices'.[10] Although the newspapers found themselves unable to identify the particular nature of the sexual crimes that Wilde had committed, they did everything within their power – both in sensationalising prose and with vivid illustrations – to represent Wilde as a figure who necessarily embodied the traits, mannerisms and styles of bodily comportment that made him into what shortly would become known as the 'homosexual'. If Cohen brings one issue more forcefully to our attention than any other, it is how a newspaper such as the *Morning Leader* (4 April 1895) spuriously contrasts Wilde and Queensberry. On the one hand, Wilde figures as the renowned artist whose mission has since the late 1870s been to 'startle the world, whether it be with sunflowers or sonnets, plush or paradox'. Such tendencies hardly make Wilde, in the journalist's view, an 'ordinary person'. Queensberry, on the other, appears as a respectably 'public person', and no comment whatsoever is made on the peer's own outlandish behaviour that included infamous verbal attacks on Queen Victoria and the prime minister, Lord Rosebery. Piecing together much evidence of this kind, Cohen convincingly demonstrates how the press assembled an image of Wilde as wholly antithetical to the redoubtable manliness of Queensberry – who, after all, invented the rules of modern boxing. Time and again, in these press reports, Wilde is depicted in a variety of unflattering poses. Sometimes portrayed in grotesque profile, where his thickened lips and protuberant nose serve as signs of ugly debauchery, he is elsewhere depicted in an affected manner, his wrist limp, with gloves wilting from a loosely clenched left hand.

It has to be said that this latter kind of iconography had been attached to Wilde's name long before he indignantly went to defend his reputation against the hot-headed father of his lover, Alfred Douglas. But the immediate connection made at that time was with the popular image of Aestheticism in the 1880s, not sodomy. Wilde, after all, had gained notoriety for presenting himself at fashionable public gatherings as the doyen of the so-called Aesthetic Movement. Soon he became celebrated for his unmanly mode of self-presentation. Vivid silks and velvets characterised his attire, as shown in the fine set of photographic portraits taken by Napoleon Sarony in January 1882.[11] Rarely did Wilde attend notable gatherings in the sober accoutrements of any gentleman. Not only did his unorthodox dress sense catch the public's attention, his powers of conversation usually managed to make their mark. Countless illustrations by George du Maurier in *Punch* from 1880 onwards portray Wilde in a variety of satirical guises, and often his facial features are accentuated in the bloated figure of Maudle: a middle-aged man with flowing locks who adopts a languid pose upon a chaise-longue as he declares to Mrs Brown (styled as 'Philistine from the country') that her son is 'consummately lovely' (see figure 11). Undoubtedly, this illustration has a homoerotic content. But it is presented to the public as a teasing joke, not in the tone of scandalised disgust that intensified during the trials some fifteen years later. In fact, the cartoons that feature Wildean types in the pages of *Punch* form part of a much larger debate that largely arises in the late 1860s about the opposition between aesthetic and athletic kinds of masculinity. In the *Saturday Review*, for example, there is a long-running argument about the ways in which a virilising manliness is needed to counteract the effeminising influences of scholarly learning, which makes men too bookish, introverted and un-worldly.[12] So when we read all the fun-poking made of effeminate aesthetes by *Punch* in one issue after another it is important not to assume, as Gary Schmidgall does, that this is an explicitly homophobic campaign. 'Considered altogether, as a kind of continuing saga', writes Schmidgall, 'the modes and details of this satirical campaign against Oscar now seem strikingly forthright, occasionally even blatant, in typecasting him not merely as a social subversive but also as an insidious effeminizer of youth'. It remains hard for Schmidgall 'to believe that any regular and careful reader of *Punch* over the years could have been much shocked at the activities exposed in the trials'.[13] Such a claim grants considerable authority to *Punch*'s powers of prophecy. It is as if the public always knew, at some level or other, that Wilde was always heading for a fall – and all because he was at base a 'homosexual'.

This picture of Wilde is mistaken, if understandable. Indeed, this type of

MAUDLE ON THE CHOICE OF A PROFESSION.

Maudle. " How *consummately* lovely your Son is, Mrs. Brown ! "
Mrs. Brown (a Philistine from the country). " *What ?* He's a *nice, manly* Boy, if you mean *that*, Mr. Maudle. He has just left School, you know, and wishes to be an Artist."
Maudle. " *Why* should he be an Artist ? "
Mrs. Brown. "Well, he must be *something !* "
Maudle. " Why should he *Be* anything ? Why not let him remain for ever content to *Exist Beautifully ?* "
[*Mrs. Brown determines that at all events her Son shall not study Art under Maudle.*

Figure 11   Wilde as the poet Maudle, one of a series of caricatures by George du Maurier
(*Punch*, 12 February 1881)

critical viewpoint – which claims that the trials exposed what his peers had always already assumed about his sexual predilections – has been so powerfully absorbed into modern culture that even Ellmann, in his remarkable biography, included a photograph of an apparently cross-dressed Wilde in the role of his highly sexualised 'daughter of Sodom' – the *femme fatale*, Salome.[14] For several years after the biography appeared in 1987, no one disputed that this scene from Wilde's play featured anyone other than himself. But Merlin Holland disclosed in 1994 that this is nothing other than a snapshot of an opera singer, Alice Guszalewicz.[15] Ellmann's unhesitating use of this memorable picture – which, admittedly, bears plausible physical similarities to Wilde – betokens how willing critics have been to accept that the author was in every respect drawn to perversity, as if there were some clear 'homosexual' continuity from his earliest days dressed as Prince Rupert at a fancy-dress ball in May 1878 to his time in male brothels in the 1890s where drag weddings were parodically staged. It is not that one would want to defend Wilde in any respect against the charge of unconventional dress as a despicable feature of his life and works. Instead, the objection lies against those who take it for granted that the spectacle of cross-dressing is necessarily a component of Wilde's effeminate identity, for to do so rests on a misleading image of the 'invert' whose internal gender is supposedly at odds with his physical disposition.

No one has resisted this unquestioning acceptance of the 'inverted' Wilde with subtler strength that Eve Kosofsky Sedgwick. Fully admiring the power of anti-homophobic readings of *The Importance of Being Earnest*, such as Craft's 'Alias Bunbury', Sedgwick admits that we can readily see how 'Wilde's work was certainly marked by a grappling with the implications of the new homo/hetero terms.' But she urges us at the same time to consider a different paradigm for the patterns of male–male desire that can be glimpsed everywhere through Wilde's works. 'Wilde's own eros', argues Sedgwick, 'was most closely tuned to the note of the [Classical, Dorian, philhellenic] pederastic love in process of being superseded ... by the homo/hetero imposition.'[16] Structured around key markers of difference – principally ones of generation – the pederastic eros or *paiderastia* cannot be construed in anything like the terms which underwrite the modern perception of the 'homosexual' or 'invert'. Plato's *Symposium* stages a dynamic debate about the proper moral codes that should regulate love between a male citizen and a statutory minor. There, for example, Pausanias argues that a boy may gratify his adult lover only if both parties respect 'a set of guidelines – the lover appreciating that any service he performs for a boyfriend who gratifies him would be morally acceptable, and the boy appreciating that any favours he does for a man who is teaching him things and making him good would be morally acceptable' (184d).[17] Socrates, by contrast, emphasises how initial sexual contact should lead to higher forms of love. He recalls how Diotima described 'the right kind of love for a boy' – one that begins with physical attraction only to proceed to altogether more elevated ideals: 'You should use the things of this world as rungs in a ladder. You start by loving one attractive body and step up to two; from there you move on to physical beauty in general, from there to the beauty of intellectual endeavours, and from there you ascend to that final intellectual endeavour, which is no more and no less the study of *that* beauty' (211c). These extracts should make it clear that the *Symposium* analyses a quite conflicted range of views about proper conduct between a male citizen and the boy who will learn about adult responsibilities from him.

Now that I have outlined the main areas of disagreement between those, on the one hand, who wish to identify the 'homosexual' – if not 'gay' – Wilde and those, on the other, who seek to orientate his writings to an earlier cultural model for comprehending sexual love between males, the remainder of this essay will be devoted to examining a handful of significant episodes that force us to reassess Wilde's representation of dissident desires. Given that there has been so much dispute about appropriate methods for reading the homoerotic content of his works, I want to turn first of all to one of his most intractable fictions, 'The Portrait of Mr W. H.' (1889, expanded 1893), since this thought-provoking story cleverly tantalises us with how to verify the desire of one man for another. This novella provides an exemplary starting-point for reflecting on same-sex eroticism in Wilde's works because it is precisely the whole question of whether one should undertake such interpretative labour – to establish the *truth* or *fabrication* of homophile desire – that preoccupies its haunting narrative. Since 'Mr W. H.' focuses our attention on the difficulties Wilde himself explored in reading passion between men, it provides a helpful introduction to the complex interest in *male friendship* detailed in many of his major writings. Each of these works suggests that the ideal of male–male intimacy is especially hard to realise in late-Victorian England. Once we have ascertained why the reading of 'homosexuality' is by necessity thwarted by 'Mr W. H.', then it will become easier to comprehend two further issues: first, the notorious invisibility – and yet unwavering implication – of same-sex desire in *The Picture of Dorian Gray* (1890, revised 1891); and second, the unbearable pressures on friendship exerted by the conventional marriages depicted in his Society comedies.

II

There is no doubt that 'The Portrait of Mr W. H.' is responding to a quite broad canon of literary writing that in the closing decades of the nineteenth century sought to exploit cultural models that would permit at least some public legitimation of sexual desire between men. Brian Reade's fine anthology, *Sexual Heretics* – first published in 1970 and regrettably long out of print – provides ample evidence of how far such eroticism reached into the intellectual and emotional worlds of middle-class intellectuals, and often not without controversy.[18] Notable figures such as Walter Pater and John Addington Symonds – both of whom wrote courageously on the homophilia in Classical Greek and Renaissance art – were perpetually regarded with suspicion by their Oxonian peers, and in 1877 both quickly resigned from an election to Professorship of Poetry when it was clear that the 'Greek spirit' with which their work was imbued was causing offence in certain puritanical quarters.[19] But the hostility these writers aroused was hardly on the scale that Wilde had to bear in 1895. Neither Pater nor Symonds, of course, enjoyed Wilde's redoubtable public celebrity. They were scholars whose works appealed to much smaller audiences, mainly in the universities. Yet it was exactly the thrust of their scholarly research that inspired 'The Portrait of Mr W. H.' in its teasing pursuit of the homoeroticism that seemingly lay at the heart of the work by Shakespeare that had for decades caused Victorian readers great unease. Shakespeare's Sonnets, after all, had prompted the historian Henry Hallam to remark in 1839 that 'it was impossible not to wish that Shakespeare had never written them'. 'There is', added Hallam, 'a weakness and folly in all excessive and misplaced affection, which is not redeemed by touches of nobler sentiments that abound in this long series of sonnets.'[20] Ever since Hallam made this influential statement – one that is recalled in 'The Portrait of Mr W. H.' (CW 326) – there have been numerous explorations of the nature of the 'excessive' affection enshrined in the sonnets, and Wilde's 'The Portrait of Mr W. H.' offers one of the most ingenious repudiations of the view that such affection was in any respect 'mis-placed'.[21]

Shortly before Hallam's condemnatory remarks on the Sonnets are recounted by Wilde's narrator, 'Mr W. H.' seeks to locate the homoerotic intimacy of the Sonnets in the context of Renaissance understandings of love. Following Pater's *Studies in the History of the Renaissance* (1873) almost to the letter, the narrator observes that 'the spirit of the Renaissance' had by the turn of the sixteenth century 'already touched Hellenism at so many points', and the connection between the Classical Greek and the early modern sensibility was most clearly defined in the respect both showed towards male friendship. Especially significant, he argues, was the publication of Marsilio Ficino's translation of Plato's *Symposium* in 1492. This 'wonderful dialogue, of all the Platonic dialogues, began to exercise a strange influence over men, and to colour their words and thoughts, and manner of living'. Indeed, works such as this one encouraged Renaissance men to 'elevate friendship to the high dignity of the antique ideal, to make it a vital factor in the new culture, and a mode of self-conscious intellectual development' (CW 324). Exactly the same ideal, we are told, is embodied in Michel Eyquem de Montaigne's celebrated essay on 'Friendship', available to Shakespeare through John Florio's translation (CW 326). Friendship – that which transcends 'gross bodily appetite' (CW 325) – is upheld as the highest, because most spiritual, form of love, and in its Platonic formulation it is intensified by its movement across a generational divide, where an older man devotes his attentions to a younger lover. Such is the framework in which 'The Portrait of Mr W. H.' asks us to construe the passion of Shakespeare's sonneteer for the unnamed figure encrypted in the twentieth poem as a 'man in hew, all *Hews* in his controwling'. But rather than use this historical context to stabilise our understanding of Shakespeare's passion for a younger man, 'The Portrait of Mr W. H.' presents a story that confounds every scrap of evidence that might be rallied to specify the 'friendship' it is clearly championing. Since Wilde's novella is quite intricate in the story it tells, I am obliged to recapitulate the main details of the teasing plot, where – much in the manner of a Victorian sensation novel – what promises to be the dénouement turns out to be yet another piece of narrative trickery.

Not insignificantly, the narrator opens with his recollections of spending an evening with his dear friend Erskine discussing James Macpherson and Thomas Chatterton, both infamous in the eighteenth century for their literary forgeries. The topic prompts Erskine to recount the fatal story of Cyril Graham who devises a theory – as many people have done over the years – about the true identity of the young man to whom the majority of Shakespeare's Sonnets are addressed. Having forced himself to believe that the 'man in hew, all *Hews* in his controwling' in Sonnet X was, by way of two puns, a boy-actor named 'Willie Hughes', Cyril discovered a 'full-length portrait of a young man in late sixteenth-century costume, standing by a table, with his right hand resting on an open book' (CW 302). But it was a while before Erskine recognised the lengths to which Cyril was willing to go to convince everyone, including himself, that his theory was true. No sooner has the narrator discovered that the portrait of Willie Hughes was a forgery than Cyril commits suicide. Yet rather than prove the insubstantial nature of Cyril's fantastic theory, the impact of the young man's sudden death so moves the narrator that he is completely entranced by the idea of Mr W. H. 'Every day', he observes, 'I seemed to be discovering something new, and Willie Hughes became to me a kind of spiritual presence, an ever-dominant personality' (CW 319). In other words, the theory – even if it cannot be credited with empirical evidence – becomes an absorbing act of faith. In fact, it develops into something more than that. The theory turns out to be a complete obsession, one that makes Erskine aghast because there is something 'fatal' about it.

In a sense, the narrator takes up the place formerly occupied by the late

Cyril Graham. 'It seemed to me', the obsessed narrator remarks, 'that I was always on the brink of absolute verification, but that I could never really attain to it' (*CW* 328). No amount of research will once and for all settle the matter that Willie Hughes ever existed. But that, it appears, is no loss. For what emerges, in the very process of learning about the Renaissance, is that the narrator is 'initiated into the secret of that passionate friendship, that love of beauty and beauty of love, of which Marsilio Ficino tells us, and of which the Sonnets in their noblest and purest significance, may be held to be the purest expression' (*CW* 343). His wide reading enables him to under-stand how the Elizabethan stage, on which only boys and men could perform, disengaged the 'mere accident of sex' from the actor, thus enabling greater 'imaginative insight and creative energy' from the playwright, the cast and the audience. Nothing could contrast more starkly with the 'over-realistic identification of the actor with his *rôle*, which is one of the weak points of modern theatrical criticism' (*CW* 330). So one can see how this all-male ethos keenly fostered ideals of friendship in which the transformative possibilities of art were applauded, and in which gender had great mobility, insofar as its accidental nature was revealed by the fact that boys could and did play the woman's part. No wonder the story of Willie Hughes held such attractions for the 'wonderfully handsome' and repeatedly 'effeminate' Cyril who 'was always cast for the girls' parts' in college productions of Shakespeare's plays (*CW* 305). It is only too clear that Cyril projected his own identity into that of the fictional Willie Hughes, supposedly the object of Shakespeare's adoration. But such projections carried with them no uncertain risks, as Cyril's fate attests.

Once the narrator appeals to Erskine by letter to unleash Cyril's theory upon the world, two unexpected reversals occur. First of all, the very act of writing to Erskine erases the faith in the theory that it enshrines. Although it proves impossible to know why the narrator has become 'perfectly indif-ferent to the whole subject of Willie Hughes', he knows for sure that this figure has become 'mere myth, an idle dream, the boyish fancy of a young man who, like most ardent spirits, was more anxious to convince others than to be himself convinced' (*CW* 345). It is as if the very process of experiencing the idea of Mr W. H. is ultimately more significant than verifying his actual being. The second reversal, however, is somewhat stranger than the first. On receiving the letter, Erskine immediately converts to the theory, and it is he who now becomes obsessively involved in finding further proof for the legend Cyril had devised – to the point of sacrificing his life for it. Unable to prove the true identity of Mr W. H., Erskine informs the narrator that he shall die by his own hand 'for Willie Hughes' sake ... and for the sake of Cyril Graham', whom he 'drove to his death by shallow scepticism and ignorant lack of faith' (*CW* 348). Only a week later does the narrator discover that Erskine has not committed suicide but has in fact died from the consumption that had been wasting him for several months. Such were the lengths to which Erskine was driven to reconvert the narrator to the theory of Mr W. H. What, then, should we make of this intriguing tale of belief and disbelief? What is the driving force behind this story that contrasts authenticity and forgery, death and desire, life and art?

If we were to follow Lawrence Danson – in a noteworthy essay that has been subject to quite sharp criticism – then it would appear that 'The Portrait of Mr W. H.' revealed Wilde's political resistance to the hetero-normative imperatives that increasingly demanded that all men should conform to the needs of the nuclear family. So determined was the clause that Henry Labouchere included in the Criminal Law Amendment Act of 1885 to eradicate sexual acts between men that it even prohibited them *in private*. Since, according to Danson, the literal assertion of the same-sex desire in 'The Portrait of Mr W. H.' would have immediately incriminated Wilde, the 'deferral of naming was a necessary act of resistance'.[22] Yet to Sinfield it is exactly this kind of approach that misrepresents Wilde's writings because it insists that there was a fully developed modern concep-tion of homosexuality waiting to come out of the narrative and be named. More apposite, Sinfield implies, would be a reading that accepted that 'Wilde, whatever his wishes, could not simply discover a queer precursor in Willie Hughes because "Mr W. H.", the plays, the trials, and the whole package we call "Oscar Wilde", were key sites upon which a modern queer identity has been constituted.'[23] Once again, the critical problem lies in interpreting Wilde's writings on the premise that he was without doubt a 'homosexual' – since the very thought of such 'naming' in 'The Portrait of Mr W. H.' is preposterous. Unquestionably, the model of reading advanced in 'The Portrait of Mr W. H.' should provide an object-lesson in how we should not jump to anachronistic conclusions of this kind. The novella, after all, demonstrates how the non-existent Willie Hughes can only be produced out of imaginary projections into the past, thus suggesting that our desire to figure Wilde as 'homosexual' speaks more to our fantasies about his sexual identity than his own. But no matter how much we might read against the grain of Danson's belief in the political 'resistance' displayed by 'The Portrait of Mr W. H.' in its 'deferral of naming', it remains the case that the narrative is fascinated with the power and significance of what it calls male friendship in an earlier period that paid respect to the highest achievements of the Socratic ethos. Even if it is impossible in 'The Portrait of Mr W. H.' to substantiate, name and thus fix the nature of the loving relationship recorded in Shakespeare's Sonnets, it would not be unreasonable to think that the Renaissance fostered forms of intimacy between males – across a generational divide no less – that could only be censured in Victorian England.

One notable critic dissents from this view. The fierce legal prohibition on sexual relations between men does not deter Linda Dowling, in her erudite study of Oxonian Hellenism, from asserting that Wilde's commitment to the Platonic *paiderastia* is not in any shape or form apologetic, let alone a legitimating gesture in the face of a hostile public. Such an argument, declares Dowling, misguidedly enmeshes Wilde's highly developed appreciation of the Socratic ethos in an 'ideological economy of repression, displacement, and resistance' that has become common in cultural criticism taking its cue from Foucault's enquiries into nineteenth-century attitudes towards sexuality. The very idea that 'The Portrait of Mr W. H.' constitutes a 'necessary act of resistance' – *pace* Danson – strikes Dowling as 'the mistake of reductionism'. She argues instead for a reading of the novella and its similarly themed companion-piece, *The Picture of Dorian Gray*, as 'perfectly expressive, in their unspecific amplitude of implication, of precisely that imaginative richness, that many-sidedness and "variety" so central to the sociocultural agenda of Victorian Hellenism'.[24] It is her belief that such works mark the culmination of the broadening and liberalising Platonism of Oxford that in the mid-1870s opened Wilde's eyes to exemplary forms of intellectual, spiritual and emotional companionship between men. There is, she insists, no reason to doubt that Wilde was being entirely sincere when he made the following rousing defence of 'the love that dare not speak its name' in the course of the second trial:

> 'The love that dare not speak its name' in this century is such a great affection of an elder for a younger man as there was between David and Jonathan, such as Plato made the very basis of his philosophy, and such as you find in the sonnets of Michelangelo and Shakespeare. It is that deep, spiritual affection that is as pure as it is perfect. It dictates and pervades great works of art like those of Shakespeare and Michaelangelo, and those two letters of mine, such as they are [held before the court as incriminating evidence]. It is in this century misunderstood, so much misunderstood that it may be described as the 'Love that dare not speak its name', and on account of it I am placed where I am now. There is nothing unnatural about it. It is intellectual, and it repeatedly exists between an elder and a younger man, when the elder has the intellect, and the younger has all the joy, hope, and glamour of life before him. That it should be so, the world does not understand. The world mocks at it and sometimes puts one in the pillory for it.[25]

No sooner had these carefully rehearsed words been spoken than there was – apart from some hissing – a spontaneous outburst of applause from the public gallery. Dowling claims that this show of support marks the emergence of Oxonian Hellenism into an altogether larger sphere than it had hitherto enjoyed. While it is the case that this famous speech – which Wilde had delivered at the Crabbet Club four years before, and which gleans some of its finer insights from Pater's *Renaissance* – puts forward a view that many Victorian intellectuals would wholeheartedly support, the fact that such words passed little muster with the equally well-educated members of the judiciary attests to the precarious position such philhellenic sentiments held at a time when a man could only be pilloried for making them. It goes without saying that the speech was delivered by Wilde in his *defence*, one certainly that sought to *resist* what were indeed *repressive* measures meted out against men-loving men by the state, even though no specific modern homosexual identity was waiting to be thus spoken and named. So maybe it is not altogether inappropriate to read 'The Portrait of Mr W. H.' as an act of resistance, arguing – as it does – that *paiderastia* is not in any respect 'gross'. In showing how such loving relationships are unrepresentable, fantastic and 'fatal', the narrative is hardly assuring us that the Socratic ethos survives admirably intact in the late-Victorian period. If anything, male friendship appears unfulfillable, dystopic, not to say tragic, no matter how richly 'many-sided' in its ideality.

III

Similar difficulties in articulating 'the "Love that dare not speak its name"' have often beset critics of *The Picture of Dorian Gray*. Since the modern notion of 'homosexuality' is nowhere proved and yet everywhere suspected in the world that Dorian Gray inhabits, there has been an understandable tendency to claim that the gothic transmogrification of the picture that aims to preserve the protagonist's youthful beauty occurs because he cannot express his true desires in public. I have previously assumed that the narrative has thus disclosed a remarkable resistance to the wholesale ban on 'gross indecency'.[26] But even if it may now seem inapposite to assume that *The Picture of Dorian Gray* is also one that enacts a strategic 'deferral of naming' same-sex desire, it is somewhat harder to gauge its attitude towards the Hellenism that drives the Greek-named Dorian to his death. Readers will recall that the picture painted by Basil Hallward is hidden in Dorian Gray's home once it troublingly begins to change from an exquisite portrait into a grotesque image of deformity, testifying to the young aristocrat's endless wrongdoing. The betrayal of the actress Sibyl Vane; the brutal murder of Basil Hallward; the blackmailing of the chemist Alan Campbell; and the accidental shooting of James Vane – each desperate fate is associated with Dorian's outwardly unblemished identity. Time and again, one is led to infer that truly 'gross' acts are at the bottom of all these other crimes. Just before he is crushed beneath Dorian's repeated blows with a knife, Hallward implores him: 'Why is your friendship so fatal to young men?' (CW 112). Such friendship leads to suicide, shame and sorrow. Yet, to reiterate, the cause of such disgrace remains nowhere – and yet everywhere – to be seen. Like the picture of Dorian Gray itself, the narrative that enshrines him both conceals and reveals the nature of the 'friendship' that has such 'fatal' effects. How, then, might we interpret Dorian's desires? Are they doomed by a homophobic culture? Or is their homophilia itself an instrument of murder?

Answers are not easily forthcoming, since the narrative – like 'The Portrait of Mr W. H.' – refuses to substantiate the 'fatal' influence that Dorian has on increasing numbers of men. Even though *The Picture of Dorian Gray* is littered with well-known references to male–male desire (Antinous, Winckelmann, Michelangelo, to name but a few), it remains hard to adduce any palpable evidence that would point, once and for all, to the fact that same-sex desire lies at the root of Dorian's crimes. Jeff Nunokawa grasps this paradox perfectly when he remarks that although the 'love that dare not speak its name has never been less at a loss for words' than in this novel, the 'expression of homosexual desire cancels, rather than clarifies the definition of the character through whom it is conducted'.[27] So even if the narrative provides an extremely rich repertoire of coded allusions that metonymise homoeroticism, at no point does the story make Dorian's desire for other men indubitably visible. Indeed, by using a picture to portray the young man's unseen sins, the narrative foregrounds the idea that representations may hide as much as disclose the truth. It goes without saying that had the novel depicted homosexual acts in 1890, when it first appeared in the American *Lippincott's Magazine*, then Wilde could well have been prosecuted in the courts. (That is why the pornographic novel, *Teleny* – with which Wilde's name has rightly or wrongly been associated – was produced in clandestine circumstances.[28]) But the suggestiveness of *The Picture of Dorian Gray* was certainly enough to provoke the Tory *Scots Observer* to declare that it dealt 'with matters only fitted for the Criminal Investigation Department or a hearing *in camera*'; it was, according to the anonymous reviewer, 'false art – for its interest is medico-legal'.[29] Such comments prompted W. H. Smith to remove all copies from its news-stands. Thereafter, Wilde carefully revised and augmented his manuscript for book publication the following year.

In court, the novel fared no better. Referring to the magazine version for the defence in 1895, Edward Carson cited the passage where Hallward enthuses he once 'worshipped' Dorian 'with far more romance of feeling than a man usually gives to a friend'. 'I quite admit', adds the painter, 'that I adored you madly, extravagantly, absurdly. I wanted to have you all to myself.' Carson was keen to discover whether this 'passage describes the natural feeling of one man towards another'. 'Have you', Carson pursued, 'ever adored a young man madly?' 'No, not madly', Wilde replied. But this denial was an unthinking admission to the charge that was being made. 'I prefer love,' he protested, 'that is – a higher form.'[30] Only too clearly can one see in this exchange the clash of those divergent paradigms that would consign homophilia to 'medico-legal' criminality, on the one hand, and the 'higher' Socratic ethos, on the other.

But there is a deeper contradiction at stake here. Rather than make an apology for male–male desire, *The Picture of Dorian Gray* in fact castigates aspects of the immorality that Carson detects within it. Indeed, when responding to those critics that deplored the novel in 1890, Wilde repeatedly insisted that it contained 'a terrible moral', one that would be revealed, not to the 'prurient', but 'to all whose minds are healthy'.[31] The court, however, was not convinced. Seeking to literalise Hallward's effusive longings for Dorian as expressive signs of Wilde's own homoerotic desires, Carson failed to register the highly moralistic thrust of the narrative, one that barely offers a confident image of *paiderastia* in the modern age. Once the 'Hellenic ideal' upheld by Lord Henry Wotton inspires Dorian to enjoy unabated pleasures (CW 28), every turn the young man takes in his life is definitely for the worse. Why? The answer lies in how the novel addresses the most pressing problems that emerged from Pater's writing, not least the controversial 'Conclusion' to the first edition of *The Renaissance*. There Pater exhorted his readers 'to be for ever curiously testing new opinions and courting new impressions, never acquiescing in a facile orthodoxy', and such a view was considered highly irresponsible by some of his contemporaries.[32] By exposing the damaging consequences of Lord Henry Wotton's desire for Dorian to become the 'visible symbol' of a new 'Hedonism' (CW 31), Wilde is satirising Pater's emphasis upon 'getting as many pulsations as possible into the given time' we are allotted in life.[33] Throughout the novel, one is constantly struck by the gap that opens up between Lord Henry's manipulative theory of pleasure and Dorian's unsuspecting exploration of it, as this passage shows:

> It was clear to [Lord Henry Wotton] that the experimental method was the only method by which one could arrive at any scientific analysis of the passions; and certainly Dorian Gray was a subject made to his hand and seemed to promise rich and fruitful results. His sudden mad love for Sibyl Vane was a psychological phenomenon of no small interest. There was no

doubt that curiosity had much to do with it, curiosity and the desire for new experiences; yet it was not a simple but a very complex passion. What there was in it of the purely sensuous instinct of boyhood had been transformed by the workings of the imagination, changed into something that seemed to the lad himself to be remote from sense, and was for that very reason all the more dangerous. (CW 54)

By repeatedly encouraging Dorian to court new impressions, Lord Henry dangerously remains – as Wilde himself remarked – a 'spectator of life', disregarding the moral consequences of the influence he exercises. Nothing could be more distant from the democratic spirit enshrined in the Socratic ethos that sought to strengthen emotional and physical bonds between men. Little wonder the picture of Dorian Gray undergoes the most appalling kinds of disfiguration, as he becomes tyrannised by passions that need to be disciplined – not exploited – by the care and affection constituting *paider-astia*.

Yet that is not to argue that *The Picture of Dorian Gray* censures sensual and aesthetic pleasure in itself. Although he is led towards nothing less than brutal murder by his intense passions, Dorian learns a valuable lesson, if at an appalling price. Setting the protagonist's 'frank debonair manner, his charming boyish smile, and the infinite grace of that wonderful youth' against the many 'calumnies ... that seemed never to leave him', the narrator seizes on the opportunity to ask: 'Is insincerity a terrible thing? I think not. It is merely a method by which we can multiply our personalities' (CW 107). This assertion is entirely consistent with the maxim published in 'Phrases and Philosophies for the Use of the Young' (1894) where Wilde declares that in 'all important matters, style, not sincerity, is the essential'. There too we read: 'Pleasure is the only thing one should live for' (CW 1244). Only Dorian has the prerogative to enjoy the many-sidedness of the human personality:

> He used to wonder at the shallow psychology of those who conceive the Ego in man as a thing simple, permanent, reliable, and of one essence. To him, man was a being with myriad lives and myriad sensations, a complex multiform creature that bore within itself strange legacies of thought and passion, and whose very flesh was tainted with the monstrous maladies of the dead. (CW 107)

No sooner have we read these words than Dorian wanders through the portrait gallery of his country home, casting his eye across the likes of George Willoughby ('with his powdered hair and fantastic patches') and Lord Beckenham (who 'led the orgies at Carlton House'). Dorian, to be sure, embodies a rich genealogy that can be traced back to a distant past where 'strange terrible figures ... had passed across the stage of the world and made sin so marvellous, and evil so full of subtlety' (*CW* 108). There is no doubt that such emphatically 'strange' passions, in all their complexity and multiformity, have been relished for centuries. But the problem for Dorian lies in how he falls prey to his passions. Violently split between perfect beauty and sordid ugliness, Dorian's divided life makes it patently clear – to cite Wilde's own words – that 'all excess, as well as all renunciation, brings its punishment'.[34] In a different society – one presumably trained by the 'Dorian' ethos encoded in his name – this beautiful youth would be able to explore his vibrant being as a 'complex, multiform creature', free from the puritanical strictures of late-Victorian England.

IV

I will close with a few more words about Platonic friendship, this time by shifting the focus to those of Wilde's writings that are rarely – if ever – associated with the Hellenic ideal. Although it must be remembered that Wilde's Society comedies were produced with altogether different ends in mind from 'The Portrait of Mr W. H.' and *The Picture of Dorian Gray*, they share a special interest in those who dissent from expressing love within marriage. Here, too, there are Socratic inflections to the ways in which Wilde shows how Society treats anyone seeking friendship with the opposite sex as the object of scandal and gossip. Especially vulnerable are single men. In *An Ideal Husband*, for example, Lord Caversham declares to his son: 'Every man of position is married nowadays. Bachelors are not fashionable any more. They are a damaged lot. Too much is known about them' (*CW* 556). Only in wedded bliss, it seems, can one be safe from the perpetual surveillance of one's personal life.

But not only is the bachelor – often portrayed in the dazzling figure of the dandy – the voice of exceptional discontent in Society. Repeatedly, the plays focus our attention on female characters who threaten to disrupt carefully policed codes of conduct. Just think how *A Woman of No Importance* pays such regard to Hester Worsley's *faux-pas*. Admitted to Society solely on account of her wealth, this New England Puritan embodies a set of bourgeois values that are in many respects alien to the round of superficial parties hosted by the English aristocracy. Hester's spontaneous interest in Gerald Arbuthnot – to whom, by the close of the play, she is engaged – unsettles her companions. 'It is not customary in England', remarks Lady Caroline Pontefract, 'for a young lady to speak with such enthusiasm of any person of the opposite sex. English women conceal their feelings till after they are married. They show them then.' But Hester is rarely discouraged by such condescension. 'Do you', she asks, 'allow no friendship to exist between a young man and a young girl?' To which she is told: 'We think it very inadvisable' (*CW* 466). Once their conversation is over, Lady Caroline turns her attention to Lord Illingworth's ambitions to become a diplomat. 'I don't think', she informs her host, Lady Hunstanton, 'that England should be represented abroad by an unmarried man, Jane. It might lead to complications.' Indeed, much of what proceeds in this act turns over many of the 'complications' that beset married life, culminating in Mrs Allonby's characteristically witty remark that her husband 'is a sort of promissory note' (*CW* 479). But Lady Hunstanton insists: 'I believe you are really very happy in your married life.' No amount of protest can make Mrs Allonby's dissatisfactions understood.

Everywhere we look married life inhibits the kind of friendship that promises to harmonise the soul and body. Lord Darlington brings this point to our attention in *Lady Windermere's Fan* when Lady Windermere turns to him when it appears that her husband is conducting an adulterous affair with Mrs Erlynne. Prepared even to leave her small child – a feature of the play that was the source of outrage in the press – she implores him: 'You said you would be my friend, Lord Darlington. – Tell me, what am I to do? Be my friend now.' His reply exposes the limit within which all social and sexual relations in the comedies are entrammelled. 'Between men and women', he declares, 'there is no friendship possible. There is passion, enmity, worship, love, but no friendship. I love you –' (*CW* 439). Although these lines demand to be read as Darlington's ploy to seduce her, they reveal that relations between the sexes must always be impassioned. No other form of intimacy is imaginable.

So great is the imperative to conform that by the end of *An Ideal Husband*, Gertrude Chiltern compromises herself to married life with a man whose successful career she knows rests on a terrible act of parliamentary corruption. If each of these plays is driven towards comic resolution in marriage, then the conciliatory endings are not entirely consoling.[35] Even in *The Importance of Being Earnest* – the farce that has tempted modern readers to delve deeply into its 'homosexual' subtext – the delightful mockery of family relationships, where patrilineage figures as nothing less than a railway line, finally ends with each young bachelor becoming the obligatory husband that Society desperately wants him to be. Such is the fate of the Bunburyist whose unnamed pleasures are terminated once the Army Lists are pulled off the shelves. But that is not to claim that he was ever at any point the 'homosexual' that Wilde, in our confused modern age, was for decades thought to embody.

NOTES

1 On Philip Prowse's memorable productions of Wilde's Society comedies in the 1980s, see Joel H. Kaplan, 'Staging Wilde's Society Plays: A Conversation with Philip Prowse (Glasgow Citizens Theatre)', *Modern Drama* 37:1 (1994), 192–205.

2 'The love that dare not speak its name' is the phrase that concludes Alfred Douglas's 'Two Loves', that first appeared in the Oxford undergraduate magazine, *The Chameleon*, in December 1894. Wilde's 'Phrases and Philosophies for the Use of the Young' were published in the same issue. Both of these works were cited as evidence of Wilde's sexual immorality by the prosecution during the second trial of 1895.

3 Christopher Craft, 'Alias Bunbury', in Craft, *Another Kind of Love: Male Homosexual Desire in English Discourse, 1850–1920* (Berkeley: University of California Press, 1994), pp. 118–19. Craft's analysis builds on the salient points established in Joel Fineman, 'The Significance of Literature: *The Importance of Being Earnest*', October 15 (1980), 79–80, reprinted in Fineman, *The Subjectivity Effect in Western Literary Tradition: Essays toward the Release of Shakespeare's Will* (Cambridge, MA: MIT Press, 1991), pp. 30–42.

4 John Gambril Nicholson's collection of poems, *Love in Earnest*, was published in 1892. The significance of this volume in relation to the large corpus of boy-loving and pederastic poetry produce in the late nineteenth and early twentieth centuries is discussed comprehensively in Timothy d'Arch Smith, *Love in Earnest: Some Notes on the Lives and Writings of English 'Uranian' Poets from 1889 to 1930* (London: Routledge and Kegan Paul, 1970).

5 In June 1969, the New York City police raided the Stonewall Inn, a bar frequented by gay men in Greenwich Village. The resulting riots, which lasted for several days, marked the birth of the Gay Liberation Front.

6 Michel Foucault, *The History of Sexuality – Volume 1: An Introduction*, trans. Robert Hurley (Harmondsworth: Penguin, 1981), p. 43.

7 Oscar Wilde, 'To Leonard Smithers', 11 Dec. 1897 (*E* 695). Hart-Davis notes that Wilde is quoting from Virgil's *Aeneid*, II, 274; the Latin translates as 'How changed'.

8 David M. Halperin, *One Hundred Years of Homosexuality and Other Essays on Greek Love* (New York: Routledge, 1990), p. 18.

9 Alan Sinfield, *The Wilde Century: Effeminacy, Oscar Wilde, and the Queer Moment* (London: Cassell, 1994), pp. vi–vii.

10 Ed Cohen, *Talk on the Wilde Side: Toward a Genealogy of a Discourse on Male Sexualities* (New York: Routledge, 1993), p. 131. Subsequent references to the newspaper reports cited by Cohen appear on pp. 139–42.

11 Sarony's photographs are reproduced in Richard Ellmann, *Oscar Wilde* (London: Hamish Hamilton, 1987), between pp. 226 and 227.

12 I discuss the controversy over conflicting styles of masculinity in late-Victorian culture in *Effeminate England: Homoerotic Writing since 1885* (Buckingham: Open University Press, 1995); see especially pp. 59–62.

13 Gary Schmidgall, *The Stranger Wilde: Interpreting Oscar* (London: Abacus, 1994), p. 46.

14 The photograph in question is reproduced in this volume as figure 2.

15 Merlin Holland, 'Wilde as Salome?', *Times Literary Supplement*, 22 July 1994, p. 14. The photograph of Alice Guszalewicz is taken from her performance in *Salome* in Cologne, 2 July 1906. Holland reminds us that the photograph has been taken up as a focus for discussions of Wilde's sexuality in two recent studies: Elaine Showalter, *Sexual Anarchy: Gender and Culture at the* Fin de Siècle (New York: Viking, 1990), p. 156; and Marjorie Garber, *Vested Interests: Cross-Dressing and Cultural Anxiety* (New York: Routledge, 1992), pp. 342–45.

16 Eve Kosofsky Sedgwick, *Tendencies* (London: Routledge, 1994), 55–6.

17 Plato, *Symposium*, trans. Robin Waterfield, World's Classics (Oxford: Oxford University Press, 1994), p. 16. Numbers and letters in parentheses are the standard forms of reference to passages in Plato's works; these are the pages and sections of pages of the edition of Plato by Stephanus (Henri Estienne), published in Geneva, 1578.

18 Brian Reade (ed.), *Sexual Heretics: Male Homosexuality in English Literature from 1850 to 1900* (London: Routledge and Kegan Paul, 1970).

19 For the details surrounding Pater's and Symonds's withdrawal of their candidacy from the elections for the Professorship of Poetry at the University of Oxford in 1877, see Richard Dellamora, *Masculine Desire: The Sexual Politics of Victorian Aestheticism* (Chapel Hill, NC: University of North Carolina Press, 1990), pp. 158–66. The attack on homophile scholarship at Oxford was made in Richard St John Tyrwhitt, 'The Greek Spirit in Modern Literature', *Contemporary Review*, 29 (1877), 552–66. For further discussion on this see Linda Dowling, *Hellenism and Homosexuality in Victorian Oxford* (Ithaca, NY: Cornell University Press, 1994), pp. 90–2.

20 Henry Hallam, *Introduction to the Literature of Europe* (1839), cited in Alfred Tennyson, *The Poems*, ed. Christopher Ricks (London: Longman, 1969), p. 861.

21 Innumerable twentieth-century studies have sought to define the compelling mysteries held by Shakespeare's Sonnets. There has been much recent debate about the appropriateness of employing the term 'homosexual' to define the desire articulated by the sonneteer for the 'man in hews all *Hews* in his controwling'. One detailed study that employs the idea of homosexuality anachronistically is Joseph Pequigney, *Such is My Love* (Chicago: University of Chicago Press, 1985). For a considered approach to the advisability of the term of 'homosexual' in relation to Shakespeare's works, including the Sonnets, see Bruce C. Smith, *Homosexual Desire in Shakespeare's England: A Cultural Poetics* (Chicago: University of Chicago Press, 1991).

22 Lawrence Danson, 'Oscar Wilde, W. H., and the Unspoken Name of Love', *ELH* 58 (1991), 997.

23 Sinfield, *The Wilde Century*, pp. 20–1.

24 Dowling, *Hellenism and Homosexuality in Victorian Oxford*, pp. 125–7.

25 H. Montgomery Hyde, *The Trials of Oscar Wilde*, 2nd edn (New York: Dover, 1973), p. 201.

26 Joseph Bristow, 'Wilde, *Dorian Gray*, and Gross Indecency', in Bristow (ed.), *Sexual Sameness: Textual Differences in Lesbian and Gay Writing* (London: Routledge, 1992), pp. 44–63.

27 Jeff Nunokawa, 'Homosexual Desire and the Effacement of the Self in *The Picture of Dorian Gray*', *American Imago*, 49:3 (1992), 311, 313,

28 It remains questionable whether Wilde wrote some or any of the sections of

Teleny. On the available evidence, see John McRae, Introduction, to Oscar Wilde and Others, *Teleny* (London: GMP, 1986), pp. 7–24.

29 Unsigned notice, *Scots Observer*, 5 July 1890, p. 181, reprinted in Karl Beckson (ed.), *Oscar Wilde: The Critical Heritage* (London: Routledge and Kegan Paul, 1970), p. 75.

30 Hyde, *The Trials of Oscar Wilde*, pp. 111–12.

31 'To the Editor of the *St James's Gazette*', 26 June 1890, L 259. The succeeding comment on *Dorian Gray* by Wilde is taken from this page.

32 Walter Pater, *The Renaissance*, World's Classics, (Oxford: Oxford University Press, 1986), p. 152.

33 Pater, *The Renaissance*, p. 153.

34 Wilde, 'To the Editor of the *Daily Chronicle*', 30 June 1890, L 263.

35 On the critical treatment of the marital ideal in Wilde's comedies, see Bristow, 'Dowdies and Dandies: Oscar Wilde and the Refashioning of Society Comedy', *Modern Drama* 37:1 (1994), 53–70.

13

RICHARD ALLEN CAVE

Wilde's plays: some lines of influence

I would like to begin by commenting on two recent full-length critical works on Wilde's plays to help define the parameters of my subsequent argument. In 1990 Kerry Powell, in *Oscar Wilde and the Theatre of the 1890s*, examined the extent to which the dramatist must be seen to be a man of his times and moulded to some degree by those times.[1] He showed how aware Wilde was of both popular and less conventional drama in performance on the London stages: current developments in melodrama and comedy were potent influences (Gilbert, Jones, Pinero and Sardou), but so too, crucially, was Ibsen. The opening chapter of Powell's study is significantly entitled: 'Rewriting the Past' and his subsequent thesis in analysing the sources of the major plays extensively documents Wilde's borrowings, 'quotings' and manipulations of situations, dramatic climaxes, visual effects that he could rely on his audience quickly recognising. (Another chapter is pointedly entitled 'Algernon's Other Brothers'.) Wilde was sufficiently ardent and perceptive a theatregoer, as Powell shows, to be capable of devising roles to suit the performance-style of particular actors: Beerbohm Tree, George Alexander, Sarah Bernhardt. This view sees Wilde as both innovatory and Victorian, but the emphasis is chiefly on the second epithet.

An earlier publication by Katharine Worth makes rather different claims.[2] Her study was issued within Macmillan's series, *Modern Dramatists*, and appropriately her concern is to establish Wilde's modernity. What steadily emerges here is an image of Wilde as a transitional figure whose interest, for example, in Wagner and the symbolists shaped in *Salome* a play that anticipated developments in poetic drama to be made by playwrights such as W. B. Yeats. In part Worth is seeking to account for the enduring popularity of Wilde's social comedies in the twentieth-century theatre and consequently she continually stresses their potential for actor, designer, director. She does not ignore the nineteenth-century material that played so creative a part in Wilde's inspiration, but she *places* it differently. She acknowledges that material as influential but in her conclusion argues that 'it is time to forget the nineteenth century idea of them [Wilde's plays] which has lingered on into our era: in any case, it fell far short of Wilde's more modern thought'.[3] For Katharine Worth, innovatory and Victorian would also be fitting epithets for Wilde; but here the emphasis falls firmly on the first not the second term.

There is a potential danger in these points of emphasis, I would argue, since (if one were disposed to carry them to an extreme) they risk inviting an adverse and reductive reaction to Wilde's dramatic artistry, though I quickly add that that is one which neither critic would wish to cultivate. Too great a stress on Wilde as Victorian risks making him appear a subtle plagiarist, 'a snapper-up of unconsidered trifles',[4] a re-shaper of the all-too-familiar with enough touches of the sensational to win a quick popularity. Wilde's recycling of even his own favoured epigrams helps support such a view. This is Wilde as decadent, acting at being a dramatist to relieve his own tedium and titillate the jaded appetites of an equally bored audience. A kind of artistic lethargy insinuates its way between playwright, characters and spectators. (This is the mood that pervades many revivals of Wilde's comedies which offer the plays to us as costume drama and as an excuse for superficial exercises in aristocratic mannerism; such performances are merely indulging in nostalgia for a long-vanished time of leisured elegance and lack the edginess and danger that should underlie much of the action in consequence of Wilde's careful blending of melodrama with comedy of manners.)

But can one as a spectator today altogether afford to 'forget', as Katharine Worth advises us to do, Wilde's historical status as Victorian? To lay too great a stress on the innovatory aspects of his work risks (paradoxically) making Wilde seem deficient in the intellectual rigour and creative stamina that would have been necessary for him to make a complete breakthrough and forge a genuinely modernist drama. Both critical approaches, when pushed like this to an extreme, judge Wilde as artistically lazy. Yet both critics write quite properly of Wilde's consummate energy as a dramatist; and one's experience of the plays in performance is that, though a certain languor may at times afflict one or more of the characters in a scene, torpor never settles detrimentally on the dramatic action; not even in *Salome*, for all its incantatory repetitions and its ritualistic mode. So whence precisely does this vitality derive? The answer would appear to lie in the meticulous poise Wilde sustains between the Victorian and the innovatory. The emphasis needs placing on that all-important connecting 'and': which is to imply that, while Wilde had a vision of where theatre might be progressing, he nonetheless saw the need to provide his audience of the present with some bridge into new kinds of awareness.[5] Recent developments in colonial/postcolonial and in postmodernist critical theory offer ways of reading the plays that show how this poise, this balance, operates and to what effect. This will in turn help distinguish two different kinds of influence that Wilde has exerted over subsequent generations of dramatists.

At first glance Wilde's career appears like that of numerous Irish playwrights, theatre practitioners and men of letters, who quickly abandoned Ireland on maturity to pursue fame in the metropolis. Reading Classics at Oxford won him speedy access to the privileged, and in London with surprising alacrity he found himself becoming a welcome presence in the society of certain titled women. Through being Irish and covertly homosexual he was cast at birth (from a colonial English standpoint) in the role of the despised 'other'; conscious of this, he donned a mask with bravura skill and remade himself after a more acceptable fashion.[6] It is instructive to compare Wilde in this respect with his fellow-Irishman and playwright, Boucicault, another ardent self-fashioner and publicist, who pursued a similar metropolitan acclaim in the middle decades of the century (though Wilde aimed far higher in terms of social acceptability and could never be accused, as Boucicault was, of sheer vulgarity in his pursuit of material well-being). Boucicault evolved a new style of melodrama by blending a sensational plot with scenes that might in a special sense be described as comedy of manners. What is *special* about plays like *The Shaughraun* (1875) is that the manners being subjected to scrutiny and ultimate approval are Irish; and English characters are brought to perceive that these manners, though 'other' and different, demonstrate a fine scruple, delicacy of conscience, taste, personal sense of honour, loyalty and generous intent.[7] Here are Irish characters from a wide social range who are not designed to excite patronising or dismissive laughter but genial acceptance. Boucicault's Irish melodramas abound in strategies to bring English audiences into an open and flexible response to representations of Irish village life.[8] If today his manipulating of the conventions of sentiment in melodrama to give his audiences lessons in feeling have an overly sentimental ring, that is because subsequent historical fact and political circumstance have revealed such aspirations to be naive, however well intentioned. Boucicault was, however, conceiving these plays at the time when the British government in the aftermath of the Catholic Emancipation Act of 1829 was beginning seriously to consider the question of Home Rule for Ireland, despite the aggressive activities of the Fenian Movement; progress was slow and in July 1874 (a year before the opening of *The Shaughraun* at Drury Lane) a motion concerning Home Rule put to the House of Commons by Isaac Butts was massively defeated by 458 votes to 61. However, when viewed within this larger context, the implied political agenda within the plays has some point in presenting Irish individuals as wholly civilised (as distinct from the conventional epithet, *wild*) and worthy of respect. Boucicault's stance was not ridiculous, even if it was not sophisticated.

Wilde's short-lived career as a dramatist coincided with a turbulent period in Anglo-Irish relations. *Lady Windermere's Fan* opened at the St James's four months after the disgraced Parnell, one-time hope of Irish radical politics, who alone had seemed capable of uniting the varying Irish interests represented in the Commons, had died at Brighton; later in 1892 the Irish National Literary Society had been founded and in November Douglas Hyde had given a rousing, much reported address, 'On the Necessity for De-Anglicising the Irish People'. His clarion call resulted in July 1893 in the founding of the Gaelic League, three months after the opening of *A Woman of No Importance* at the Haymarket. In September of that year a second Home Rule Bill, while passed by the Commons, was rejected in the Lords. The following April (1894) saw the founding of both the Irish Agricultural Organisation Society and the Irish Trades Union Congress, shortly after Wilde completed *An Ideal Husband*.

What the rehearsal of these facts shows is that the plays were written at a time when the Irish intelligentsia were reacting against an apparent stalemate in Irish affairs at governmental level by establishing a number of independent organisations, clearly demonstrating that the Irish were capable of ordering their own lives to suit their own needs as they recognised them (by 1898 Yeats, Lady Gregory and Martyn were planning to add the establishing of an Irish National Theatre to the list of achievements). These were optimistic moves, creating the foundations of an autonomous state in preparation for Ireland's eventual emancipation. Wilde is not usually seen as playing any part in this cultural renaissance. But Wilde had infiltrated the British establishment at this date more securely than any of the shapers of the Irish renaissance, and played the required role there to perfection till Lord Queensberry publicly attacked his pose and the ensuing trials showed an astonished public the extent to which Wilde's life was a series of clever and ironic games with masks. There is a point of resemblance here: the wearer of masks holds two or more distinct personalities in a tense balance; the wielder of irony holds two or more distinct levels of meaning in an equally tense juxtaposition. Wilde concluded his essay, 'The Truth of Masks', with the telling observation: 'A Truth in art is that whose contradictory is also true.'

Edward Said in his pioneering study, *Culture and Imperialism*, is at pains to distinguish between independence and emancipation.[9] He argues that a once-subject people are only fully emancipated when they have learned to resist not only decades of indoctrination by the colonisers to the effect that the master race's ways of life, culture, values, habits and manners are superior, but also the tenets of a romantic nationalism, which it had been necessary to pursue in order to achieve political freedom. What he seems to be advocating and what he sees as the strength of Yeats's postcolonial work is the cultivation of an enlightened scepticism, a refusal to take any value on absolute trust without first investigating its 'contradictory'. Irony is clearly a necessary pursuit in such a context.[10] Wilde had found such an emancipated mind-set long before it became an imperative for Irish intellectuals and politicians; his oddly alienated yet privileged position in English society both required and refined it. While Hyde, Yeats and their compatriots pursued overtly nationalist enterprises motivated by the need to restore dignity to Ireland, Wilde would attack the bastions of the English establishment from within. Cultural imperialism thrives by promoting the belief in the subject race that their conquerors have achieved a more advanced state of civilisation than themselves which it is well worth emulating (this is usually rhetorical sleight of hand to disguise the actual state of affairs where might is convinced it is right). Wilde's comedies systematically challenge such arrogance: where Hyde sought to 'de-Anglicise' the Irish, Wilde set about deconstructing Englishness. It could be argued that colonialism forces duplicity onto the subject people, particularly those intent on preserving some measure of nationalist feeling: they must adopt a public manner of adherence to the imposed canons of behaviour, while privately, covertly sustaining a belief in the enduring value of their own outwardly suppressed cultural inheritance. This is consciously to play with masks; and truth to self lies at the tense intersection of these public and private identities. Declan Kiberd recently claimed that 'Wilde was the first major artist to discredit the romantic ideal of sincerity and to replace it with the darker imperative of authenticity: he saw that in being true to a single self, a sincere man may be false to half a dozen other selves.'[11] What the comedies repeatedly show is that English imperialist claiming of the high moral ground on the basis of an absolute integrity is wholly fraudulent. The setting and policing of establishment standards are shown repeatedly to be ridiculous: sincerity in the Society of the plays is but affectation, a façade. What truly counts is a shrewd pragmatism: in *An Ideal Husband* any number of compromises, moral and emotional, are made in the characters' private lives so that it will be with a stable united front that they face the public. Wilde, the consummate manipulator of masks, can readily detect the same proclivity in the establishment that has deigned to admit him as a permitted guest to its ranks.

Mask-wearers must constantly be alert to the likelihood of detection and evolve careful strategies to avoid that happening; and Wilde devised an array of dramatic methods to define or intimate this complexity. Peter Hall admits to a dissatisfaction with many productions of the comedies because they seem little more than competitions of wit between the actors (the implication is that 'character' has been ignored); rehearsing *The Importance of Being Earnest* helped him discover that 'the epigrams are not produced by the author's desire to be clever, but because they are satirising the tradition of the English stiff upper-lip. The more intensely a character feels and the greater his passions the more outrageous the epigrams become in an attempt to control and mask those passions.'[12] Such a rich subtextual life, brought to an audience's awareness by his actors' attention to tone and body-language, was a notable feature of his later production of *An Ideal Husband*. Language itself is being used here as a mask displaying an outward equanimity and nonchalance that is designed to hide inner turmoil and desperation from close investigation. More central to my immediate purpose, however, are Wilde's strategies involving the dramatic conventions currently defining particular *types* of character. As Said and other theorists of colonialism have shown, imperialist rhetoric invariably deploys binary oppositions: good and evil; conqueror and subject; and, since they are relevant to my purpose here, self and other; and the manly man and the womanly woman. Insofar as these categories are to do with mores, they extend their reference and, more importantly, influence from the political to the personal. As a professed individualist, Wilde's adult life was devoted to resisting such contaminating categorisation; and many of the celebrated inversions and subversions that characterised his wit were calculated to explode such absolutism. But the conventions for representing character on the Victorian stage, be it in melodrama or comedy, subscribed to such rigid typing and allowed for few variations on the set patterns (which is why Ibsen's newly arriving drama so terrified traditionalists and caused them to attack his enthusiasts as 'womanly men' and 'manly women', ironically thereby admitting to the existence of those psychological complexities they were seeking to deny[13]).

To create complexity, the subtle differences that define individuality, Wilde evolved a remarkable technique: he set about calculatedly fracturing the conventions he had initially established in a play respecting the various characters, changing tracks (often mid-scene) to develop a particular individual according to a type quite at variance with the type to which that individual originally seemed to be conforming; plays that begin by securely observing the stylistic conditions of one dramatic genre, usually comedy of manners, are surprisingly invaded by features indicative of a radically different genre. *Meaning* in Wilde's plays begins to be determined by these fractures, stylistic shifts, challenging dislocations; they are the moments that lead an alert spectator to engage with subtextual implication. Wilde displays a masterly command of the whole panoply of conventions but deploys them as if to show their uselessness in meeting his needs; repeatedly his usage defines the restricting, limited ineptitude of the methods available to a *serious* dramatist intent on a realistic portrayal of upper-class life. The conventions stand revealed as a kind of subtly sophisticated censorship, allowing that class to be portrayed only on the terms in which it chooses to be portrayed, whereas Wilde wishes to examine that class for what it is. Cleverly he allows those conventions their place in his drama, but in a way that exposes the extent to which they are part of the establishment's misguided tactic to enforce conformity of behaviour. Wilde's strategies with convention are cunningly subversive.

The issue of the mixing of genres, especially where elements of melodrama are concerned, is one that sometimes irritates modern commentators and theatre directors whose preoccupation is chiefly with witty dialogue. Yet melodrama is crucial to Wilde's strategy: it underpins all his plays to intimate how slender a hold the society he depicts has on its professed stability and decorum; a fear of public exposure prevails and gives an edge of desperation to the characters' actions and speech; in each play the central figures are discovered to have good reason for such a fear, as past indiscretions, passionate impulses or longstanding suave duplicities threaten their present composure. But what of the characters on the periphery of the main action? The bored Lady Basildon and Mrs Marchmont lament their marriage to safe, compliant husbands and pitch into an immediate flirtation with any man who chances upon them at the Chilterns' reception (in the opening act of *An Ideal Husband*) as if longing to be indiscreet with no thought for any possible consequence (though the audience have just watched Chiltern learning painfully from Mrs Cheveley how rash it is to dismiss any moment of one's past conduct as incapable of damaging one's present reputation; and there is always the possibility that apparently *safe* husbands might turn disobliging, as O'Shea had done within recent memory with devastating effect on Parnell's career[14]). Mrs Allonby can keep pace with every arabesque of Lord Illingworth's badinage with a decided brio that suggests she is a very *knowing* woman; we never learn whether her forthrightness is the outcome of clever cerebration or the fruit of direct experience. Is it all an artful pose or shameless daring? As the current focus of Lord Illingworth's attentions, she seems a foil to his discarded mistress, Mrs Arbuthnot, who as a woman with a past is dogged by melodramatic suffering. Does Mrs Allonby too have a past which only her apparently *safe* marriage and her skilfully contrived manner shield from investigation? Is that manner the product of an otherwise bored intelligence, or a cunning ruse to pretend to be *louche* to fend off any suspicion that she could be so in fact (working on the assumption that no one would believe her capable of such outspokenness if actually possessed of a guilty conscience). In both these instances there is a fruitful ambiguity (and one that actresses should not presume to resolve), since it brings an intricacy of tone to the wit that shapes the speeches. To treat the melodramatic dimensions of the comedies seriously and give them due weight in performance endows the brilliant wit with a rich psychological vitality: the verbal poise of the characters is then experienced by an audience as at once a dangerously thin and brittle mask (in that they are all in varying degrees vulnerable) and a mark of consider-able courage (in putting up such a confidently brave front to the world). The threat of melodrama invading the world of comedy is fundamental to the dynamic of Wilde's social purpose.

Equally potent is the threat in several of the plays that high comedy might degenerate into farce. When Lord Goring in the penultimate act of *An Ideal Husband* receives a note from Lady Chiltern announcing that she will call during the evening to seek his help, he appreciates that it is a situation that requires great delicacy of scruple and privacy and he makes careful plans for her reception; but all his tact is set at hazard by the untimely arrival in quick succession of Goring's annoyingly interfering father, Caversham, of Sir Robert Chiltern and of Mrs Cheveley. Doors are constantly opening to admit the very people that Goring in the circumstances least wishes to see; the wrong woman is shown by his servant into the seclusion of an inner room. This is the stuff of farce (and was excellently played as such in Sir Peter Hall's recent production at the Globe Theatre, 1992.)[15] The tone shifts precariously to and fro between the hilarious and the anguished as Caversham's boorish interruptions give place to Chiltern's agonised soul-searching, while Goring's debonair self-possession is punctured by Chiltern's accusations of treachery and Mrs Cheveley's blackmailing tactics. It is difficult to determine what would be the appropriate tone since decorum, here emblematised by Goring, is continually being compromised. Wilde is perfectly in control of his dramatic artistry: what he is depicting is a society that is all *surface* in respect of its manners and mores; there are no secure values for coping with what lies behind the façade. The tonal insecurity has a precise satirical purpose. How is one to judge the antics of these characters? Whether one views them as comic, melodramatic or farcical is all a question of one's own perspective. The technique provoca-tively challenges degrees of self-awareness in the engaged spectator.

The Importance of Being Earnest takes this technique to even subtler lengths. From the opening remarks of Algernon's manservant, Lane, we gauge we are in the company of individuals with a highly developed sense of their self-importance. Ideally they wish to conduct themselves with a due

226

decorum, as people conscious of the significance of a good sense of tone and appropriate manner. But everyone has a secret life: Algernon pursues the sport of 'Bunburying'; Jack has invented a necessary *doppelgänger*, Ernest; Gwendolen appears submissive to her mother's dictate but has a will of iron and a determination to get her way; demure, charming Cecily hides a romantic temperament and passionate intensities of feeling; Prism and Chasuble nurse a longstanding affection for each other, which neither dares to express for fear of compromising the authority that accompanies their status as governess and cleric; and the seemingly redoubtable Lady Bracknell is a woman with a past (her energetic efforts to police everyone else's behaviour is a clever cover for the fact that she is a parvenu in aristocratic circles, having 'had no fortune of any kind' till she married into the peerage). The play is undeniably the funniest Wilde created, but what in truth we are laughing at are the struggles of a particular social group to avoid being exposed for what they really are: they yearn for the grace and social ease of characters in high comedy but the complexities of their make-up constantly pitch them into farce. It is by means of the fractures Wilde opens up between the two styles of comic theatre that we penetrate behind the masks these figures adopt to protect themselves from close scrutiny. Again the dramatic technique is subversive. If even Lady Bracknell is an outsider figure, then precisely *who* in this society is not alienated? Wilde has devised a technique to show how all his characters without exception have an *other* hidden within, which they are trying to keep distinct from the concept they possess of their individual identities. Yet as Wilde knew: 'Modern life is complex and relative' (*CW* 1012).

Wilde opined that 'the supreme vice is shallowness' (*CW* 1002). Type figures in drama are inevitably shallow – because determined by convention; they are predictable and immediately recognisable. The characters of *The Importance of Being Earnest* hope to achieve such simplicity, though evidently their desire is for a vanished Eden; and they speak of *modern* life with noticeable anxiety. But which Jack is playing true to type: the pillar of respectability at Woolton or his alias, Ernest, the man about town in London? Which persona is the mask? To be shallow in this way is to be *known*; and Wilde often shows how cruelly gossip can constrict a rich individuality to the limitations of a type. Just how cruel and exacting this can be is particularly revealed by his deconstruction of the conventions underpinning the presentation of the woman with a past in *Lady Windermere's Fan*. Mrs Erlynne is a woman whom it is difficult to *place*: she is introduced to us as a scarlet woman, an object of malice and scorn; but on her entrance into Act II she is seen to be possessed of remarkable intelligence, daring, wit and, crucially in the circumstances, insight into how best to induce others to find her charming.[16] We next see her as the type of adventuress, blackmailing Lord Windermere to gain entrance and position in high Society. Yet when it comes to revealing the motive for her actions, Wilde depicts her as firstly a woman with a past, then as a repentant, suffering mother. Windermere takes the expected response to each of the changing perspectives, refusing to engage with her situation imaginatively or charitably; and noticeably she does not seek to disillusion him. After Lady Windermere rashly attempts to elope, Mrs Erlynne, in pursuing her, effects what is perhaps her most surprising transformation into fervent upholder of the traditional moral code, arguing for propriety and convention. When they are trapped together in Darlington's rooms by the men returning from their club, she is forced to overhear their scandalous talk of her before the situation requires that she bravely enact the very role they have cast her in, so that Lady Windermere can escape such abusive denigration herself. Mrs Erlynne is the consummate actress: she can play effortlessly but exactingly a range of types as each suits her purpose of the moment; but always there is the sense that she is in complete control of herself, that her every change of role is a conscious decision. Where everyone else on stage acts predictably, she – the one figure the rest endeavour to define by type – remains a mystery because her actions are not open to being readily categorised.

The final act shows her skill to perfection in a bravura display of shape-changing. To Lady Windermere she plays the solicitous affectionate friend, engaging in sentimental talk of babies and the need to exchange photographs; with Lord Windermere she hits a note of hard-edged effrontery to leave him with the impression that she is utterly heartless. She plays up to the image each has of her: the wife sees her as 'very good'; the husband as just 'clever'. That Mrs Erlynne is calculating is true, but for a definite purpose. She acts to safeguard the future of the Windermeres' marriage: he must not know of his wife's indiscretion and she must never know Mrs Erlynne's true identity. The game with masks is not duplicitous (in the conventional sense of that word) but a generous moral act tempered by an astute social and psychological insight. Mrs Erlynne knows she must quit this society at the close of the play; she will always be an outsider; yet Wilde's dramatic technique has invested her as outsider with far greater depth, moral stature, presence, intelligence and personal dignity than any other character on stage.[17] He manipulates theatrical styles and dramatic conventions with considerable expertise to represent how she assumes at will her range of personae. Within the format of contemporary Victorian drama Wilde has found the means of showing how outdated its devices of representation are where the staging of modern life is concerned. In the process he continually throws spectators back on their guard, rendering them self-conscious about their responses to current dramatic conventions. If modern life is indeed 'complex' and 'relative' and Mrs Erlynne is its representative in this play, then how one judges her by the end of the action is entirely subjective, as the last act brilliantly demonstrates. It is all a question of perspective; and throughout the play the focus has been continually shifting.

At this point I would like to consider the question of Wilde's influence. It is not my intention to trace the ways that the traits of certain of his characters (especially Lady Bracknell) or the verbal mannerisms of his aristocrats have been imitated by the likes of St John Ervine, Somerset Maugham or Frederick Lonsdale.[18] Nor do I wish to examine how Noel Coward cleverly transposed Wilde's morally ambiguous way of presenting the leisured classes to the world of the bright young things of the inter-war years in plays like *Design for Living* or the world of theatre folk in *Hay Fever* and *Relative Values*, where the grand inflated manner, the egocentric flourish, are masks by which the characters hide from themselves their emotional insecurity, spiritual emptiness or debilitatingly ordinary existence. As Alan Sinfield has shown, the Wildean echo is often deployed by Coward to signal covertly that a character is gay/homosexual, but that interpretation is available only to an élite who can read the signs. Coward does not, on Sinfield's showing, extend an audience's awareness or challenge the very basis of their judgement through such figures in the subtle fashion that Wilde effects through Mrs Erlynne or Lord Goring.[19] These writers tend to toy with the witty, epigrammatic surface of Wilde's drama rather than seeking to develop his experiments with technique to broaden his means of subverting audience expectation. Two contemporary dramatists have come far closer to this method while attempting a critique of Wildean comedy.

Mrs Rafi in Edward Bond's *The Sea* (1973) is immediately recognisable as a pastiche of Lady Bracknell; she is formidable, tyrannical, overbearing, ruling her household and the local community as absolute arbiter of all conduct. We have moved down the social scale from Belgravia to an East Anglian borough and Mrs Rafi's diktats have more immediately apparent social and political consequences; her concern is less with preserving a proper decorum than with keeping people firmly in their place. She has considerable wit and intelligence but they are deployed to refine her speech to a pointed cruelty ('Jessica, stop trying to sound like a woman with an interesting past. Nothing has ever happened to you. That is a tragedy. But it hardly qualifies you to give advice'[20]). Late in the play Bond gives her a long confessional speech in which she reviews her life and sees its likely end in dotage when she will become a prey to her one-time subordinates' revenge

('I'll grow old and shout at them from a wheel-chair. That's what they're waiting for. They get their own back for all the years I bullied them ... There you are: old, ugly, whimpering, dirty, pushed about on wheels and threatened'[21]). Bond has shifted the perspective here and changed his style to complement the shift. But we have seen Mrs Rafi running the local amateur dramatic society; and we are not sure how much this musing is role-play; there is a degree of insight, but no charity either for herself or others. Almost immediately afterwards Bond shifts the perspective again when Rose, Mrs Rafi's niece, viewing her dispassionately, dismisses her as a 'coward' because 'it's safer to stay in the garden and shout over the wall'.[22] Mrs Rafi in Rose's view lacks the courage required either to leave or to shape her life to a pattern different from that prescribed by the type in which she has chosen to cast herself.

Mrs Erlynne's games with masks had great creative potential; Mrs Rafi's assumption of but one mask is indicative of her cynicism and defeatism. When she puts the mask momentarily aside, she stands revealed as arid, loveless and, as such, a source of social corruption ('The town's full of her cripples. They're the ones she's nicest to'[23]). When she first appears, Mrs Rafi excites a predictable kind of laughter as audiences recognise the Wildean allusion; by the end of the play Bond has redeemed the Wildean prototype from such predictability by devising a means of allowing us to see behind the mask and its accompanying social mannerisms. It is less Wilde as playwright that Bond is satirising through Mrs Rafi than the way his drama has been simplified and travestied in the popular imagination to the point where it has lost under the weight of performance-traditions its one-time subversive force. Bond salvages Wilde's artistry on moral and social grounds by making audiences investigate the motives and the mechanisms whereby they welcome Mrs Rafi's arrival in the action with a particular quality of amusement. Bond's representation of Mrs Rafi perfectly exemplifies Wilde's maxim: 'Those who want a mask have to wear it' (*CW* 1038).

Tom Stoppard's *Travesties* (1974) engages in what at first appears to be a deconstruction of Wilde's *The Importance of Being Earnest*. The play is preoccupied with the mind-life, the stream of consciousness of the elderly Henry Carr, who in youth chanced to play Algernon in a production staged in Zurich during the Great War by James Joyce. Carr, a minor official in the English consulate, in real life took Joyce to court over payment of his expenses incurred in the purchase of trousers appropriate for his role (Algernon does after all claim that being 'over-dressed' is preferable to being 'over-educated'). As *Travesties* evolves we see that Stoppard is setting Wilde up in opposition to Joyce (and with him Tristan Tzara and Lenin, who were both also resident in Zurich at this time). They, Stoppard's argument runs, were the great shapers of how modern life was to find expression; they determined the new, dominant modes of representation. As such they startle Carr for the challenge they pose for him as an embodiment of conservative values and conventions. For Carr the world of Wilde's comedy is how life should be: leisured, graceful, effortless because secure in a sense of class and, above all, arrogantly confident where values and their felicitous expression are concerned. Because he detests all that they represent, Carr's imagination totally travesties Joyce, Tzara and Lenin: the first becomes a shifty skinflint whose *Ulysses* is dismissed as sorting 'language into hands for contract bridge'; the second is just an 'over-excited little man with a need for self-expression far beyond the scope of your natural gifts'; while Lenin is to him an incomprehensible, ponderous bore.[24]

But though Carr idealises Wilde, the playwright has undergone the process of being travestied too. Noticeably Carr's efforts at transforming the experiences he recalls from 1916 into scenes from *The Importance of Being Earnest* are constantly disrupted; he can never sustain for long either the mode or the manner. But he never questions why even his daydreaming is fractured so relentlessly. And he tries hard to suppress the fact that Wilde is both Irish like the hated Joyce and (what's worse) as he prissily puts it, 'a Gomorrahist'.[25] It is a sanitised image of Wilde that Carr is fostering (the Wilde that high Society *thought* it was welcoming into its ranks) and in the play that his consciousness is endlessly composing the three outsider figures are decidedly 'other' and out of place. On a closer view, Stoppard seems not to be deconstructing Wilde's comedy so much as scrutinising the impulse to nostalgia, the creating of idylls from carefully selected images of the past to ease a crying need for social and emotional security.[26] Carr is engaging with the surface of Wilde's comedy, wanting the drama played out by clear-cut stereotypes – the very kind of play that Wilde is actually determined subtly but subversively to deconstruct. Carr's need is to be *someone* of note, which, because it is not possible *now*, he imagines might have been possible in some fantasised *then* of yesteryear. The unrelenting impulse of his mind is to elude any acknowledgement of himself as the nonentity that he is.

Yet it is not this fantasy projection of Carr as Wildean exquisite which excites our interest in *Travesties*, but the complex individual that emerges as a consequence of the fracturing of the dramatic action, depicting a psyche torn by conflicting impulses and too riddled with anxiety about maintaining a dapper appearance to know the equanimity it yearns for. Taking his inspiration from Joyce's breaking up of conventional techniques of fiction to create the mind-life of Leopold Bloom, Stoppard plays endless games with dramatic technique to explore the consciousness of Henry Carr. What he succeeds in doing in the process is to bring out into the open that whole subtext of evasions, dreads, anarchic urges, cunning duplicities, social unease, calculated nastiness and sexual disquiet that Peter Hall and his cast discovered lying beneath the surface of Wilde's dialogue when they began to rehearse *The Importance of Being Earnest*. The more Carr struggles to make Wilde comfortably Victorian, the more Stoppard shows Wilde to be irredeemably modern. *Travesties* offers a reading of Wilde's most famous play that positions it exactly at a point of cultural transition; it is a notable reclamation in that Stoppard celebrates openly what Wilde in his comedies could only dare to intimate: the rich potential of the destabilised self which resists all possibility of categorisation or reduction to the quintessential. Carr's absurdity rests in his refusal to embrace that richness.

I would like to conclude by looking at Wilde's influence on three avowedly gay playwrights: Joe Orton, Frank McGuinness and Neil Bartlett. It is Alan Sinfield's contention that Orton's effectiveness as a *gay* dramatist was short-lived, that his provocative stance helped create the milieu in which gay liberation might steadily evolve but that he needed the age of censorship and homophobic censoriousness to stimulate his creativity since his prime ambition and delight was to shock.[27] He does not see the plays as having much potential for revival; and yet there has been a steady recurrence of productions of Orton's plays since his untimely death, including a whole season of his full-length works at the Royal Court in the seventies, West End productions of *Loot* and *What the Butler Saw*, while that last work was revived at the National Theatre in 1995. An adverse critic might be disposed to interpret this as the characteristic British cultural ploy of taking the sting out of a radical talent by absorbing it into the mainstream. But the crucial fact is that Orton's career was predominantly focused on the West End: *Entertaining Mr Sloane*, *Loot* and *What the Butler Saw* were all initially staged by the theatrical establishment (the latter with Sir Ralph Richardson as Dr Rance). The parallel with Wilde, whose plays were all staged by the theatrical establishment of *his* day (Tree, Alexander and the young Lewis Waller, who chose *An Ideal Husband* as his first attempt at actor-management) is remarkable. In both cases we see rebels welcomed into the cultural power-centre.

On what terms was that access granted? Given their propensity to provoke laughter, were they admitted merely as all-licensed fools? The greatest of such fools in our theatrical tradition, however, have slyly but deftly touched their hearers to the quick. It was part of my argument earlier to suggest that Wilde's comedies as satirical attacks by an Irishman on the shortcomings of the British establishment can be read as having a conscious anti-colonial agenda. Orton's agenda as practising queer would seem to be to expose the sexual duplicities which lurk behind and are encouraged by assertions that heterosexuality is the only proper norm. It seems to me remarkable that Wilde's work and Orton's both achieved large-scale popularity shortly before a considerable liberalisation of hegemonic attitudes to the causes they espoused. Were they admitted to the establishment because their plays spoke directly (if wittily) to manifestly troubled consciences, highlighting prevalent anxieties of some magnitude? (The Wolfenden Report on homosexuality published in 1957 preceded the staging of *Entertaining Mr Sloane* by six years; it took till 1967, however, before male homosexual acts were legalised under certain limiting conditions.)

Both Wilde and Orton make language the site of their interrogations and it is here that the relationship between them as dramatists seems strongest. Seemingly insouciant wit in Wilde's plays often covers, keeps tightly in place, a wealth of emotional nuances. When Mrs Erlynne admits to Lord Windermere that she 'lost one illusion last night. I thought I had no heart. I find I have, and a heart doesn't suit me ... Somehow it doesn't go with modern dress' (*CW* 460), she is being anything but heartless; but she has an objective in wanting him to consider her cold, cruel and shameless; and only the audience are privileged to know her motive. We share her awareness of her own complexity and know that this is not deviousness in the conventional pejorative meaning of the word. Her wish is to protect her daughter's marriage and she is prepared to have Windermere think ill of her, to prevent him ever having cause to doubt what he believes to be the innocence and fidelity of his wife. She flatters his wish to play the protecting patriarch at the cost not only of her own feelings but of her reputation. With a slight phrase about clothes, she reduces the momentous to the trivial as if she were quite devoid of moral sense or decorum. As audience we register both the surface and the subtext of the language and recall Lady Windermere's troubled observation that precedes Mrs Erlynne's arrival in the scene: 'There is a bitter irony in things, a bitter irony in the way we talk of good and bad women ... Words are merciless ...' (*CW* 455). Our scruple, perception and powers of discrimination are being challenged here on every level.

Words are merciless in Orton's plays too; but their effects are louder, brasher, and the attack is directly on the institutions which police the boundaries of what the establishment chooses to define as acceptable or sane behaviour. Orton is the first dramatist of those I have been considering who demonstrates how values are constructs and as such are capable of infinite manipulation. When Hal in the closing moments of *Loot* says, 'It's comforting to know that the police can still be relied upon when we're in trouble', he is mouthing what the dramatic action has just shown to be a bogus platitude.[28] Hal has just watched his father being arrested, despite his claims of being a law-abiding citizen, simply because his Catholic sense of morality won't let him acquiesce in the corruption that he has discovered is going on in his household. The police want him out of the way so that they can get their share of the spoils. Mr McLeavy has been framed and his attempts at defence ('The police are for the protection of ordinary people') are ridiculed by the very officer, Truscott, whose protection he seeks ('I don't know where you pick up these slogans, sir. You must read them on hoardings'[29]). Characters who consider themselves law-abiding assert their social and moral rights, only to have their words derided for falling preposterously wide of actual social and moral norms.

Orton is fascinated by the way individuals find ways to claim and justify their authority over others. Where one could in part excuse Lady Bracknell's overbearing manner on the grounds that she does have her daughter's future to protect, there is no such excuse for Dr Rance's insatiable curiosity or the self-importance that allows him to consider only the worst possible interpretation that can be put on circumstances as the right one. Where Lady Bracknell dreads any intimation of the sensational, Rance positively thrives on it because, in the world of tabloid journalism that he inhabits, it will bring him a fortune and a quick reputation. *What the Butler Saw* takes as its groundbase the conventions of bedroom farce (familiar enough territory for the West End audiences who first watched it at the Queen's Theatre in 1969) but the familiar is rapidly transmuted into the strange. An attempt at an adulterous flirtation with a secretary (the stable stuff of sex farce) get interrupted by an angry wife (another stereotype of the genre); but the man caught in the act is in this instance the director of a psychiatric clinic and his efforts at explaining himself plunge everyone involved into a Freudian nightmare. This is that dangerous side of Bunburying that over-took Wilde when his private life was made public knowledge to devastating effect. It is this threat of going public which Rance holds over the other characters that is the source of his power. ('Rance' is an aptly chosen name, implying, through a series of half-puns, the words 'rancid' and 'rank' both in the sense of titled position and of odious smell.) With great resourceful-ness the rest resist his desire to categorise them as monstrous or perverted. Before his gaze they change clothes and appear to change gender in the process with consummate ease, allowing him to suppose they have explored every possible form of sexual relationship.

Critics, such as Katharine Worth, have argued that this dynamic resource-fulness brings to the play in performance a wonderful sense of liberation[30] and see in this the likely influence of Wilde's *The Importance of Being Earnest*. But *What the Butler Saw* is a far darker and more manic play. There is always that ever-threatening presence of Dr Rance, voicing a rabid conservatism based on beliefs in what constitutes the sexual norm which the world of the play shows are outdated and uncharitable; and he has medical and governmental authority on his side. Liberalism is being watchfully, almost vengefully, policed. And at the end of the play that authority is not overthrown: Rance's wildest Oedipal-fixated imaginings are proved true, since the Prentices are the parents of Nicholas and Geraldine. The ironies here are particularly bitter, since what the audience began by genially and permissively watching as an adulterous flirtation such as they might expect in farce now in retrospect carries intimations of incest. The play admits to powerful forces of curtailment within the establishment and (given Rance's constant devising of headlines for the tabloid exposures he is planning) the press. The strength of the play lies in Orton's refusal to resolve this tension between the liberal and the reactionary; indeed the damning attack on the establishment is the stronger in consequence. Orton's debt in this play to Wilde is profound, but less to Wilde as playwright than to the man whose life in becoming a case-history set a firm seal on the policing of intimate relations in British society. Orton in private suffered from that policing; brilliantly as a playwright he took the norm as accepted unquestioningly in bedroom farce (the heterosexual adulterous liaison) and subjected it to a relentless harassment. Would-be adulterers in conventional farce often face some lengthy explaining, but not, as here, such prolonged interrogation. Heterosexuality is cast by Orton firmly in the role of *other* by a daringly witty inversion, and made to suffer experience of the consequences. As long as the binary oppositions survive and perpetuate constructions of the *other*, then there will be ample justification for reviving *What the Butler Saw*.[31]

I argued earlier in this essay that Wilde created a space to define an original approach to the representation of characters in his plays by frequently breaking with the dramatic conventions to which initially he appeared to be adhering. He suggests well-known situations or types and then begins to play with his audience's expectations in the interests of surprising (or sometimes shocking) them into new, more flexible kinds of awareness. In this way he is both at one with the theatre of his time and directly opposed to it: it is as difficult to write in the context of Wilde's drama of influences, inspirations or debts as to write of plagiarism, since what he borrowed he intended to make wholly his own. It is like one composer working a set of variations on a popular theme by a near contemporary (Beethoven even wittily so translated the English national anthem). Such a degree of intertextuality is at work in *What the Butler Saw* in the ways Orton keeps his audience alert to the traditional form, setting and stereotypes of bedroom farce, the better to discriminate his creative purpose in deviating from that norm. But Wilde's intertextual reference in any one play ranges far wider than one specific genre; his strategies involving an ironic deployment of familiar material have an intricacy that sustains an audience at a pitch of attentiveness. It is here that Wilde's technique begins to shade into a dramatic method akin to that of the postmodernist playwright, where a sophisticated but teasing quotation of numerous styles (placed often in ironic juxtaposition) demands that specta- tors shape their own individual interpretations from the experience, since the dramatist refuses wholeheartedly to follow the dictates and conventions of any one particular style lest by so doing she or he would appear to endorse one set of meanings as definitive. The intertextual games here convey a distinctive philosophical purpose: this is the relativity of the modern art-work, which Wilde prized, carried to an extreme. I am not arguing that Wilde is postmodernist, but that he was a significant precursor, anticipating the means and the seriously motivated playfulness of late twentieth-century dramatists; that his innovations have had far-reaching consequences; and that amongst late nineteenth-century dramatists, he is decidedly in tune with our contemporary modes of expression. It is more fitting, perhaps, to write of Wilde's creative relation with (rather than influence on) McGuinness and Bartlett.

Frank McGuinness recently published a superb essay entitled 'The Spirit of Play in Oscar Wilde's *De Profundis*',[32] in which he argues that what saves Wilde's apologia for his life from self-pity and sentimentalism is the sense that it is all performance, consummate play-acting by Wilde for a single spectator, the luckless Bosie. He changes masks with such rapidity and skill, that (for all the evident pain) one is not sure where the truth lies, or what the heart is of Wilde's mystery. The key to McGuinness's reading of *De Profundis* lies in the subtle revision Wilde made 'at the letter's beginning [where] he had written, "an artist as I was". This he altered to "an artist as I am".'[33] Even from the depths of his humiliation Wilde acknowledges that he never ceases to be the artist and performer. The preoccupation with personal and private relativities here disarms any adverse criticism of Wilde as egocentric. Everything about Wilde in one sense by the date of his release from Reading Gaol was *known*; he had been labelled publicly as homo- sexual, decadent, criminal, grossly indecent, and had been jeered and spat at in consequence. But now he chooses to assert his own preferred label for what it is worth: artist.

The essay is valuable not only for its insights into Wilde, but also as a commentary on one of McGuinness's own plays, *Carthaginians* (1988), which centres on the modes of protest devised by a character who is homosexual with transvestite (*queenly*) proclivities, Catholic and Irish. Dido, as he calls himself (his name like much else about him is carefully constructed and self-determined), from an imperialist British standpoint is marginalised to an extreme: he is rendered *other* at every level of his being, social and private, by such a canon of judgement; but he creates a life for himself within the world of the play as artist and player, often being simultaneously both creator and his own creation. This is seen to be his defence against being ostracised. He ministers to a group of outcasts living in a Derry graveyard who are all victims of the colonial process: women from the peace movement whose faith and conviction were shattered by the events of Bloody Sunday and who congregate in the cemetery on its anniversary in a fragile hope that in answer to their visions the thirteen men killed then will rise from the dead; and men who are mentally disturbed as a direct consequence of their involvement with the IRA and paramilitary protest. Traditional forms of protest, pacifist and rebellious, have left all the characters with the exception of Dido psychologically injured; they all choose to live with death in the graveyard, being themselves spiritually dead. If our last view of them, however, is of a group sleeping peacefully, it is because Dido has effected a healing; and he does so through *play*. He encourages them to transcend their immediate lives in time by following his example and adopting masks, playing games, refusing to be categorised as abject.

How Dido will next appear is a constant source of surprise: now in football gear; now in flowing skirt and wig. Equally surprising are McGuinness's shifts of dramatic style: the dialogue of the opening scenes is austerely naturalistic but the setting with its graves that resemble the prehistoric chambers at Knowth intimates a latent symbolism; as Dido's games begin, so the play moves through witty pastiche of agit-prop theatre, bizarrely placed echoes of O'Casey, and quiz shows, or suddenly encompasses direct quotation of a whole poem ('The Listeners' by De la Mare). Moreover, what one might have supposed at first to be background music (Dido's Lament from Purcell's opera; one of Mendelssohn's 'Songs Without Words') takes on an increasingly metaphorical intensity. Dido's agit-prop play, *The Burning Balaclava* (written typically under the pseudonym of Fionnuala McGonigle) is a savage digest of a whole host of plays about the Troubles, and Dido makes its performance bizarrely distanced by having the men play all the women's parts and the women the men's roles (the female characters are invariably long-suffering and the males aggressive and brutish; all are described by Dido as 'tormented'); Dido himself appropriately plays both one Doreen O'Doherty who is found mourning her pet dog *and* the British soldier who kills it; the spectacle ends with a mass shoot-out with waterpistols that leaves every character dead. The mode of black farce at once admits to the horror of the Troubles with its seemingly endless proliferating divisions between Catholic and Protestant and the fact that its terrible longevity has exhausted all modes of dramatic expression to the point where any attempt on such a subject traps the playwright into predictability and cliché. The way Dido has two of his women characters at wildly inappropriate moments resort to the culturally enshrined lament of O'Casey's Mrs Tancred and Juno for their dead sons shocks an audience into such awareness. The deliberate cultural impiety is not mocking O'Casey, but rather the enshrining process that has made an icon of the two mothers as *great art* but ignores O'Casey's artistic and social purpose in shaping words into such a threnody of maternal despair.

And it is in this context that all the references to Dido, Queen of Carthage, come into sharpest focus. Dido is celebrated as a *necessary* victim in Virgil's *Aeneid*, her body and her status are colonised by Aeneas as the means of furthering his ambition to found Rome. Christopher Marlowe in his tragedy about the fated lovers deconstructed Virgil's triumphalist ideology (Virgil was eulogising Augustus through his epic as consolidator of the Empire), reducing Aeneas by emphasising his irresponsibility and investing Dido in her desolation by contrast with an absolute tragic dignity and stature. (Marlowe's Dido would significantly have been played by a boy-actor.) Purcell's opera is an uncompromising tragedy too, its best-known aria being Dido's dying lament at Aeneas's betrayal with its plangent refrain, 'Remember me.' Ironically the opera dates from the first year of William and Mary's reign,[34] shortly before William's invasion of Ireland. *Carthaginians* begins with Purcell's Dido urging the audience to *remember*. Again the ensuing action calls the process of creating cultural icons into question as, despite the tragedy of Dido of Carthage, we confront yet more victims of colonial rule. These are more daring dislocations of style and technique than any Wilde attempted, but the effect is similar in making the audience conscious of their place and function both within the theatrical event and within larger cultural and political processes. The drama, whether by Wilde or McGuinness, situates them precisely where they must question their own values and understanding in what is being defined as a manifest opposition between politics and art within the historical continuum.

McGuinness's Dido, though alert to the possibility of tragedy, is no defeatist. Staging his farcical dance of death acts as a release of anger and frustration that begins to cohere the rest of the group; and Dido quickly builds on that achievement by encouraging them to engage in a pub-style quiz, an innocent pastime which several of them excelled at in the past. This now is a contest devoid of aggressive pressures, seemingly pointless except that its genial tone steadily instils a sense of community within the group. Dido's game has unobtrusively distanced each of them from their private grief with its complex of self-pity, bitterness and sentimentality; each comes to talk openly of that grief with a quiet, dispassionate frankness. When they next meet it is in a circle on the night of the anniversary of Bloody Sunday; ritually they declaim in turn the names, ages and addresses of the men killed that day. Seeking to prolong the unity that prevails amongst them, they speak together a poem they all remember learning at school. 'The Listeners' delicately evokes a sense of spiritual communion between the living and the dead, while respecting an irrevocable material division between them. In a final brief scene, Dido watches over the sleeping group; having effected his healing, he chooses to leave Derry. His last word is an injunction: 'Play'.

Play in the context might seem a gesture of camp extravagance, irresponsible and trivial, but for McGuinness's control in showing what play can achieve within a torn and fractured society. The artist, Dido, cannot affect the political world directly (any more than Wilde for all his wit in the witness box could halt the progress of a social and legal system determined to make him an object-lesson); but through *play* Dido shows a way of achieving a beneficial measure of distance from political circumstance through which to discover possibilities of social integration. *Carthaginians* is a bold defence of the homosexual as artist and dramatist, that could not have been written without Wilde's example on a creative, emotional, intellectual, sexual and political level. McGuinness's essay on *De Profundis* defines with clarity and a precise reference to Wilde's life and work what that example *means* for the postmodern artist; his play demonstrates the inspiration of that example for him as another gay, Irish playwright.

The cover of Neil Bartlett's *Who Was that Man? (A Present for Mr Oscar Wilde)* has a silhouette of a patently 1980s gay male head aligned alongside a portrait photograph of the young Wilde: it is almost as if the one is seeking to impose itself on the other.[35] The cover admirably evokes the postmodernist approach to history that one reads within: late nineteenth-century legal and social research jostles there with literary criticism, authorial autobiography, evocations of Victorian and modern London (its geography; its nightlife; its underworld), enigmatically captioned photographs whose meaning is discovered only through a careful perusal of the footnotes rather than the text. Fragmenting his investigation of Wilde's life as homosexual and continually shifting the focus in this way between the 1890s and the present day, Bartlett attempts to define Oscar's significance for the modern gay sensibility by deftly drawing parallels, discriminations, contrasts between then and now. But there is no through-line of argument; sympathetic readers have to shape that for themselves by defining their own relation to the material. Bartlett completed this book on Wilde over a period when he was also working as a performance-artist with his company,

Gloria, on *A Vision of Love Revealed in Sleep* – a dramatised account of Barlett's 'fascination with the life and work of Simeon Solomon', another homosexual late-Victorian artist, mystic and rebel. 'The piece', Bartlett writes, 'is about many different kinds of inspiration, many different kinds of "survival"'; and he concludes by way of defending the complex mixture of the autobiographical with the historical with the assertion that 'it is always better to tell your own story by telling someone else's. In dark times, which ours surely are, then you turn to the unlikeliest heroes for moral and spiritual support.'[36] Always in Bartlett's works there is a dense texture of implication defining the subtle sexual politics that shape his preoccupation with the role of the homosexual artist in society and his concern to place that role within its particular tradition. Wilde exists as a necessary *presence* in all Bartlett's performance-texts. (It is significant, given my argument about the importance of *play* in recent gay drama, that one has to write of Bartlett's works as *performance-texts*, since the actors are required continually to shift between the roles they are playing, the stage personae they have each cultivated during their careers, and sudden glimpses of their private selves. As audience, we are throughout conscious of the art of acting as a Wildean game with masks. But the resulting theatricality is deeply purposeful: as in Wilde, Pirandello or Genet, the game has the wit and the intensity of a metaphysical conceit.)

Bartlett's technique was to be seen at its most brilliant in *Sarrasine*.[37] Balzac's short story tells of the innocent love, never consummated, between Monsieur Sarrasine and La Zambinella, an opera singer he believes is a woman but whom he discovers to his fatal cost is a *castrato*, kept under the patronage of an eminent, jealous Cardinal with a taste for assassinating his rivals; the main narrative is framed within another in which a Madame de Rochefide is told of La Zambinella's actual nature and of Sarrasine after she has glimpsed the singer now in extreme age, fabulously wealthy and still meticulously guarded. The tale had been subjected to a ruthlessly exacting deconstruction by Barthes in *S/Z* (1973) to define how an author deploys rhetorical devices in an attempt to control subsequent readings; for Bartlett the story becomes the starting-point for an equally exacting deconstruction of the relationship between the drag artist and her/his public. In the play it is now Mme de Rochefide who, as a wealthy connoisseur, is prepared to pay any price to hear La Zambinella sing for one last time; the singer compels her to participate in a re-enactment of Sarrasine's infatuation and its consequences. La Zambinella was played by three performers: an elderly but highly sophisticated drag artist, Bette Bourne, whose artistry allows the feminine and the masculine within his personality to exist in a delicate balance (his definition of feminity was not crude, pantomimic or patronising, as can often be the case with drag artists); a chanteuse, Beverley Klein, whose technique embraces opera as easily as emotional songs in the manner of Piaf and whose vocal range like that of any fine alto encompasses masculine timbres; and an androgynous, elphin-like dancer-singer, François Testory, whose range varies from counter-tenor to baritone and whose artistry can shift between the archly, extravagantly camp and a fragile, tragic vulnerability (he was a one-time pupil with Lindsay Kemp's troupe). The three perform together, facets of one identity.

It is as if Bartlett is inviting us to imagine what an audience actually perceived when they watched a *castrato*: one moment a woman (Klein) sings with a fierce baritone; the next a pouting young man (Testory) in obvious spangled drag serenades us in a seductive counter-tenor but within seconds, transformed by more serious garb, is convincingly voicing a woman's passion in a lyrical tenor; Bourne speaks of one-time lovers with dulcet nostalgia as she fingers the rings each gave her as a memento before launching with great élan into a set-piece from music-hall advising women to be clever, take what they can get and 'give nothing away' to admirers. (The intertextual references in this piece are all musical: it is as much a chamber opera as a play, though the references are as frequently to popular music as opera.) What did audiences choose to *see* in La Zambinella: a freak, a manly woman, an effeminised man, a fetish, a fantasy, an object of fascination or loathing? Was the perceived singer *gendered* at all or as neutered to the perceiver's psyche as in physical fact? Was La Zambinella ever viewed simply as an artist? Given the circumstances of this twentieth-century performance, what does an audience *see* when watching the drag artist or the gay performer (Sir Peter Pears, say, in the role of The Mother in Britten's *Curlew River*) and how gender-conditioned is that reaction? The *castrato* had the most terrible of genders imposed on him by others for their pleasure and aesthetic delight; his identity was precisely and definitively shaped to become a theatrical spectacle. How far can the contemporary extension of the analogy Bartlett is drawing be pushed? At once estranged from society (except as entertainment) yet privately coveted and patronised, La Zambinella's response is to be nothing but a bewildering array of masks that defy any lasting construction.[38] It is a form of revenge. Circumstance has made this the only possible reality. Is the like mode of self-defence the one means of expression available to the gay artist and, as such, the only lasting and profound inheritance from Wilde? The theatricality of *Sarrasine* is invested with an aggressive sexual politics.

Sarrasine is considerably more than a stage adaptation of a work of fiction; Bartlett's *reading* (in Derrida's sense of the term) filters Balzac's narrative through a precisely defined modern sensibility and its attendant experience. What is dramatised is the way in which in the postmodernist view reading is inevitably self-reflexive and, therefore, wholly self-revealing; and this continually challenges a spectator's own perception and means of interpretation. Bartlett carried this structure and technique to yet subtler lengths in his subsequent staging of Wilde's *The Picture of Dorian Gray*.[39] This was no conventional dramatisation or costume drama. Instead we were to suppose we were present at a commemorative reading of the novel at a party presided over by Wilde's 'Sphinx', Ada Leverson, to which she has invited a group of Wilde's other friends: Robert Ross, Reggie Turner, Sidney Mavor (better known as 'Jenny', one of the rent-boys who gave evidence at the trials); and there is her maid and a guardsman-associate of Ross's (a *quality* rent-boy, as we discover) brought there to read Sybil's and Dorian's parts. It is 13 November 1924: the twenty-ninth anniversary of Wilde's public humiliation on Clapham Junction Station. We are in a suite of rooms at the Savoy Hotel, where Wilde reputedly took the likes of 'Jenny'. Ada hopes that this ritual will act as an exorcism after which 'perhaps we will all be able to forget'. What it is they might each wish to forget is the subject of the play.

They embark on a reading, interspersed with comments, anecdotes and reminiscences of their several relations with Wilde; as the narrative takes hold of their imaginations, so they begin increasingly to act crucial episodes. What starts as random recitation becomes more obviously characterised as Ross takes on the role of Basil Hallward, Turner that of Lord Henry, and the guardsman, left silent at first as simply the object of the other men's gaze, finally impersonates Dorian. The choice of roles is in the first two cases felt to be appropriate (Ross is himself quiescent, attentive, long-suffering; Turner has a certain faded style and charisma); the guardsman acts an imposed role for a set fee. It is noticeable that in undertaking the necessary process of selecting and reducing Wilde's narrative, Bartlett has chosen to keep, and thereby highlight, the passages of commentary and dialogue which are preoccupied with time and its effects. Twenty-nine years have passed since Wilde's disgrace and twenty-four since his death but he is still a vital presence in his friends' lives. All his glittering promise came to nothing when, released from prison, he took on the mask of Melmoth the Wanderer and drifted round Italy and France before dying miserably in Paris. And what of his friends? Ada is setting forth herself as a wanderer abroad in the hope of finding the congenial artistic milieu she once presided over in London; Ross is a grey, pedantic civil servant, 'rummaging among the works of the dead'; Turner apes Wilde's (and Lord Henry's) dandified philosophy but he cannot foresee that (as Ada tartly puts it) 'the marvellous doctrine of living for pleasure would come in the end to consist almost entirely of second class railway carriages and other people's parties and Italian waiters whose names he cannot quite bring himself to remember';[40] Mavor sees himself as 'imprisoned' as a bank clerk in West Croydon and unable to accept that all that men like Wilde, Ross and Turner saw in him was his youth ('As you said, Mr Mavor, you were seventeen'[41]). It is the gay fixation with youth that Wilde makes his subject in *Dorian Gray*, analysing his own proclivities with a rare precision: he recognises the lure, the dangerous fetishising, the cruel use of the young, and shapes his fable to encompass that complex psychological and moral insight.

So powerfully is Dorian's beauty described in its effects on Basil and his initial hedonism characterised as it is tutored in him by Lord Henry, that one forgets the extent to which they share responsibility for constructing his identity, just as in retrospect one tends perhaps to forget the terrible consequences when that identity begins to manifest its actual nature. The prospect of eternal youth is as perennially fascinating in Dorian's story as its renewal is in the myth of Faust; both attempts at transcending time are disastrous. In a departure from the novel, Bartlett shows Sibyl preparing to act Imogen (rather than Juliet or Rosalind), which enables him to stage her breakdown after Dorian's desertion through her plaintive singing of the dirge for Fidele from Shakespeare's play with its haunting refrain bidding all men remember that they 'must come to dust'. Her contribution to the reading over, the Maid calculates that Dorian by the close of the novel must be forty and muses rationally: 'Well, if he is forty then he ought to know it can't go on for ever. He must know what's going to happen.' And Ross quietly replies: 'But you don't. We didn't. No one ever does.'[42] That final sentence challengingly encompasses the audience in its reference. None of these friends who have made a cult of the novel and its author recognised its tight and inexorable moral structure; they chose to read selectively; and their present selves are the consequence. But even while recognising their inadequacy they still hanker after the dream: the pathetically servile Mavor has a momentary insight which feeds rather than subverts his desperate longing: 'he [Dorian] can never look any older than on the day he was ... written.'[43] That pause before the final participle intimates that Mavor recognises the absurdity of his observation, but he forcefully concludes his statement nonetheless, the victim of his own dream.

What Bartlett's mode of adaptation restores to the novel is its darker dimensions, most particularly the way that the cult of youth requires its victims. The way that Mavor, the maid and the guardsman are marginalised to the edge of the stage until the plot, Ada as stage-manager or the two gentlemen have a use for them intimates a larger moral issue, of which the cultured characters on stage are quite unaware. When Mavor tries to speak

Figure 12 Benedick Bates as Dorian Gray and Tim Pigott-Smith as Robbie Ross/Basil
Hallward in Neil Bartlett's production and adaptation of *The Picture of Dorian Gray* at the
Lyric, Hammersmith, 1994

as at least their homosexual equal, Ross and Turner immediately make him
feel his place. It is eventually the guardsman (he is never graced with a
name) who speaks out against the abuse of being *used*, objectified,
constructed as a type, and then all-too-readily discarded. He has clearly
been Ross's 'boy', and throughout the action Turner surreptitiously attempts a conquest. But the boy is out of his depth in this educated circle
with their strange charade and their self-deluding fantasies. He coldly
asserts what he has learned from experience of their like ('Look, these men
that come to me, do you think I teach them anything they don't already
know?'[44]), but Ada, Ross and Turner choose to ignore the threatening tone.
When what is by now more a play than a reading demands that, as Dorian,
the guardsman should murder Basil, he attacks Ross with a venom in which
all his pent-up rage against his client's superiority and wealth find release.
The rest sustain a shocked silence, unsure whether the killing is actual, till
Ross finally moves. This is more than the recreation of an episode in a
novel; the casual brutality of Dorian's action, which is all the more
disturbing within the hotel setting and that genteel gathering, is properly
registered. So too is the moment when Dorian meets his fate. Throughout

the production the portrait was represented by a large mirror, which reflected the characters who confronted it. The guardsman in playing Dorian, therefore, gazed at his own immediate reflection, while the others read of Wilde's character viewing the portrait for the last time; the boy saw in the mirror the beauty, framed now and so objectified, which attracted the clients he had grown to despise; and he savaged his face with a knife.

In Bartlett's adaptation, Wilde's novel and in part his career became subject to those postmodernist techniques of deconstruction and intertextual referencing which I have argued can be traced back to features of Wilde's own plays. But where Wilde exposed the limitations of conventions and dramatic stereotypes to bring new insights into familiar material, Bartlett deploys Wilde's text to examine what constitutes a *reading*. The novel emerges from the play as larger than the interpretations that Wilde's associates choose to extract from it. In his Preface to the novel, Wilde opined that 'it is the spectator, and not life, that art really mirrors' and Bartlett seems to be both illustrating that premise and, through the agency of that significant mirror as stage property, pushing it into areas of moral and social analysis which the novel intimates rather than wholly endorses. Liberated gay awareness allows Bartlett to question as dated the suppositions about gay sensibility on which the novel as fable is constructed and, by holding the tale at a critical distance, to sharpen an audience's perception of the ethical scruple which shapes the conclusion. Act I of his play concludes with Lord Henry giving Dorian the seductively clever book, the mesmerised reading of which is to be his undoing. Significantly in performance Turner passed to the guardsman a copy of Wilde's novel. Identical copies were to be seen in the hands of all the *readers* at Ada's memorial. Within Bartlett's scheme, it was a symbolic moment and a justification of his dramatic method. Bartlett was frankly admitting that influences which are venerated and not meticulously deconstructed in ways that respect the historical continuum are likely to prove overly dominant and dangerous. Wilde's novel is reclaimed from potential misreading but in the process a necessary limit to Wilde's influence is carefully determined.

NOTES

1 Kerry Powell, *Oscar Wilde and the Theatre of the 1890s* (Cambridge: Cambridge University Press, 1990).
2 Katharine Worth, *Oscar Wilde* (London and Basingstoke: Macmillan, 1983).
3 Ibid., p. 188.
4 The phrase belongs to Autolycus in Shakespeare's *The Winter's Tale* (IV. iii.),
5 It is noticeable that in Wilde's finest and most challenging critical essay, 'The Critic as Artist', the argument is conducted in the form of a dialogue, where

Gilbert acts as Socratic guide firmly leading the intellectually conventional Ernest (and any hesitant reader) towards more open and flexible ways of thinking.

6 I have taken the idea of remaking the self from Yeats (see, for example, the poem 'An Acre of Grass', in *Collected Poems* (London: Macmillan, 1960), pp. 346–7. Yeats several times performed this feat in the course of his lifetime and may have been influenced in developing this idea by his reading of Wilde's works and observation of the man.

7 *The O'Dowd* (1880) shows the O'Dowd family feeling dreadfully out of place amongst English society in the opening acts; later the aristocratic English characters visit the O'Dowds, improbably, in Ireland where they learn to admire the Irish way of life and the true character of the chief of the clan, Daddy O'Dowd. This is a broader and less sophisticated version of the strategies Boucicault deploys in *Arrah na Pogue* and *The Shaughraun*.

8 For a full discussion of Boucicault's strategies see my article, 'Staging The Irishman', in *Acts of Supremacy: The British Empire and the Stage, 1790–1930*, ed. J. S. Bratton (Manchester: Manchester University Press, 1991), pp. 62–128. Shaw was quick to point out the absurdity of assuming that the English ever act directly out of their sentiments with his portrayal of Broadbent in *John Bull's Other Island*.

9 Edward W. Said, *Culture and Imperialism* (London: Chatto and Windus, 1993). See in particular the chapter, 'Resistance and Opposition', pp. 230–340, during which he analyses the later work of W. B. Yeats as that of a 'decolonised poet'.

10 The early plays of Denis Johnston are a notable example of such irony being directed against a limiting concept of nationalism, while O'Casey's later work, such as *Cock-A-Doodle Dandy*, levels a scathing irony at the Catholic Church for its processes of cultural indoctrination.

11 Declan Kiberd, 'Wilde and the English Question', *Times Literary Supplement*, 16 Dec. 1994, p. 13.

12 Sir Peter Hall, *Making an Exhibition of Myself* (London: Sinclair-Stevenson, 1993), pp. 317–18.

13 See the Introduction to Henrik Ibsen, *Four Main Plays: A Doll's House; Ghosts; Hedda Gabler; The Master Builder*, trans. J. MacFarlane and J. Arupu (Oxford: Oxford University Press, 1981), p. xi.

14 O'Shea had for some ten years connived at his wife Kitty's relationship with Parnell (even acknowledging three of their children as his own) before he filed a petition for divorce on Christmas Eve, 1889. Parnell wielded considerable political power over the decade of the 1880s, but was destroyed as a public figure of authority once his private life was exposed in the law courts.

15 For a detailed appraisal of this production and of the use of a farce-type setting for this particular scene, see my article, 'Wilde Designs: Some Thoughts about Recent British Productions of his Plays', *Modern Drama* 37.1 (Spring, 1994), 175–91.

16 For a detailed analysis of this entrance and the theatrical devices by which Wilde builds up Mrs Erlynne's stature and power in the play, see my article, 'Power Structuring: The Presentation of Outsider Figures in Wilde's Plays', in *Rediscovering Oscar Wilde*, ed. C. George Sandulescu (Gerrards Cross: Colin Smythe, 1994), pp. 37–51.

17 Interestingly Wilde in *An Ideal Husband* shows the morally upright Lady

Chiltern as so blinkered by her concept of integrity, so fixed within the limitations of the type which she has elected to shape her life, that she is virtually incapable of human compassion, because she sees such a feeling as compromising her rectitude. When circumstance requires that she forgive her husband for not living up to the high ideals she expects of him, it is so new a role which she must now play that she has to be taught what to say in it by Lord Goring. The characterisation of Lady Chiltern is a searching indictment of the inflexibility, the lack of a creative imagination, that comes of being totally conventional.

18 Among Yeats's many debts to Wilde, *Calvary*, for example, was initially inspired by a story Yeats recalled Wilde once telling about humankind rejecting Christ's kindness and charity because His generosity placed on them the burden of responsibility for their lives; and throughout the composition of both *The King of the Great Clock Tower* and *A Full Moon in March*, he was anxious lest either play be judged as simply a re-working of *Salome*. Wilde influenced Yeats's concern with masks, both metaphorical and (in the context of the staging of his plays) actual, as is evident from even as early a work as the poem, 'The Mask', first published in 1910.

19 See Alan Sinfield, 'Private Lives/Public Theatre: Noel Coward and the Politics of Homosexual Representation', *Representations*, 36 (Fall 1991), 43–63.

20 Edward Bond, *The Sea* (London: Eyre Methuen, 1973), p. 18.

21 Ibid., p. 57.

22 Ibid., p. 58.

23 Ibid., p. 58.

24 Tom Stoppard, *Travesties* (London: Faber and Faber, 1975), pp. 42 and 62 respectively.

25 Ibid., p. 51.

26 It is of note here that the OED defines nostalgia as 'a form of melancholia caused by prolonged absence from one's country or home'. Carr is psychologically without a centre, and that is the source of his unappeasable anguish and the motive for his urge to inhabit the society of Wilde's plays as if it were his natural milieu. He is moulding fictions out of fictions.

27 See Alan Sinfield, 'Who Was Afraid of Joe Orton?', in Joseph Bristow (ed.), *Sexual Sameness: Textual Differences in Lesbian and Gay Writing* (London: Routledge, 1992), pp. 170–86.

28 Joe Orton, *Loot* (London: Methuen, 1967), p. 87.

29 Ibid., p. 86.

30 See Katharine Worth, *Revolutions in Modern English Drama* (London: Bell and Sons, 1972), pp. 151–6.

31 Much of this analysis is indebted to Phyllida Lloyd's excellent revival of *What the Butler Saw* at the Lyttelton Theatre that played throughout the summer of 1995. In a final image worthy of Orton himself, she contrived that the cast should not climb out of the clinic by means of a rope ladder, 'weary, bleeding, drugged and drunk' as directed in the text (Joe Orton, *What the Butler Saw* (London: Eyre Methuen, 1976), p.92), but were hoisted aloft together into a dazzling sky of impeccable Tory blue accompanied by a flurry and crescendo of patriotic music. Lloyd situated her production in the immediate present, not in the period (late 1960s) of the play's conception and initial staging.

32 The essay is included in Chris Morash (ed.), *Creativity and its Contexts* (Dublin: The Lilliput Press, 1995), pp. 51–9.

33 Ibid., p. 59.

34 The precise date of composition is currently disputed, but the first recorded performance is in 1689 with a known professional revival in 1700. William and Mary acceded to the throne in 1689. William invaded Ireland in 1690 and defeated the Stuart (Catholic) armies at the Battle of the Boyne in July that year; King James subsequently fled to France.

35 Neil Bartlett, *Who Was that Man? (A Present for Mr Oscar Wilde)*, (London: Serpent's Tail, 1988). The cover design is by Ray Trevelion.

36 Neil Bartlett, *A Vision of Love Revealed in Sleep*, in Michael Wilcox (ed.), *Gay Plays: Four* (London: Methuen, 1990), p. 84.

37 The production opened at the Traverse, Edinburgh during the 1990 Fringe Festival. It subsequently played at the Drill Hall, London, before touring nationally and internationally.

38 The tragic absurdity of traditional gender constructions is disturbingly evoked in one climactic scene where we see Leah Hausman as Rochefide (a woman) playing Sarrasine (a man) reach out despairingly towards Testory (a gay man) playing La Zambinella (a eunuch): 'If you were not a woman ... Would I love you, if you were not a woman? Would I love you, if I did not think you know how a woman feels? Would I ask you to sing, if I did not think you know how I feel?' (The text is not available in print.)

39 The production was staged as a collaboration between the Lyric Theatre, Hammersmith and the Nottingham Playhouse, opening in London in September, 1994.

40 The text of Neil Bartlett's adaptation of *The Picture of Dorian Gray* has not been published to date. The quotations are all taken from the prompt copy, p. 127.

41 Ibid., p. 45.

42 Ibid., p. 124.

43 Ibid., p. 93.

44 Ibid., p. 97.

14

JOEL KAPLAN

Wilde on the stage

I

The history of Oscar Wilde's plays in performance is closely linked to the larger history of their author's social and cultural reception.[1] During the 1890s Wilde's dramas helped to inaugurate a series of aesthetic and commercial transactions in which up-market viewers found their worlds both celebrated and mocked on West End stages. They also formed part of Wilde's personal campaign to secure a place in 'best circles' Society. Consequently, although he talked with Shaw about founding a 'great Celtic' school of drama (L 339), and promised to aid Ibsen actress Elizabeth Robins in bringing about a 'theatre of the future',[2] Wilde's career as a professional playwright more closely resembled that of commercially minded rivals like Arthur Pinero and Henry Arthur Jones. Contemptuous of London's avant-garde theatres and makeshift theatre clubs (natural venues for a Shaw or Robins), Wilde turned exclusively to the West End's most fashionable playhouses and flamboyant actor–managers, building upon and responding to the sensibilities of their public. *Lady Windermere's Fan*, Wilde's first stage success, received its première at George Alexander's St James's Theatre in February 1892. Alexander, newly installed at the St James's, believed that a play by Wilde would draw to his theatre the carriage-trade crowd in which Wilde himself was just beginning to move. Wilde, for his part, determined to use the occasion to query the aesthetic and moral values of Alexander's viewers. The result was a production that drew upon the stage conventions of drawing-room melodrama and the goods of an emerging consumer society to challenge the world it seemed to endorse. Wilde's correspondence with Alexander shows how completely the playwright relied upon the textures and commodities of Society life to make his points, as well as the extent to which he intruded himself into every aspect of performance, from minute details of stage business and *mise-en-scène* to the seasonal lines of Alexander's dressmakers, Mesdames Savage and Purdue.[3] Marion Terry, who created the role of Mrs Erlynne, Wilde's

woman-with-a-past, and Lily Hanbury, in the *ingénue* part of Lady Windermere, were, in their confrontations with one another, manoeuvred into
outfits of almost identical colour and cut. The effect was to underscore by
sartorial means what Wilde had proclaimed to be the theme of his play, the
impossibility of dividing the world into opposing camps of 'good' and 'bad'
(see figure 8). On one point Wilde had to give ground. Through rehearsals
he had quarrelled with Alexander about when to let audiences in upon his
play's central secret, the revelation that Mrs Erlynne is, in fact, Lady
Windermere's mother. Wilde wished to place the moment in the play's final
scene, unsettling spectators for three acts with Mrs Erlynne's apparently
unmotivated self-sacrifice. Alexander (in the ungrateful role of Windermere)
had argued that such mystification violated both aesthetic and social
canons. In the end Wilde capitulated. After an initial performance on 20
February, the revelation was moved to Acts I and II, where it would remain
until Philip Prowse's 1988 Glasgow revival. Wilde did, however, reclaim
some of his intended provocation with a mischievous curtain call speech in
which he applauded Alexander's patrons for the success of their 'performance' in appreciating 'a charming rendering of a delightful play'.[4]

Such a double-edged attitude towards audience and actors would inform
the premières of Wilde's two succeeding Society dramas, *A Woman of No
Importance* (1893) and *An Ideal Husband* (1895), staged at the Haymarket
under the respective managements of Herbert Beerbohm Tree and Lewis
Waller. In each case surviving manuscripts and production materials belie
the aloof, careless pose Wilde continued to strike in public. Multiple drafts
of both plays show Wilde writing and rewriting with painstaking care, often
working into final drafts characters and dialogue dropped from earlier
versions. Of particular interest are the actors' parts and prompt books that
record in gratifying detail the progress of each play in rehearsal. Tree's
performance scripts for *A Woman of No Importance*, now housed at the
University of Bristol, and Waller's newly discovered prompt book for *An
Ideal Husband*, held by Princeton University, offer stage texts of each work
interlined and overwritten by author and actor–manager. Each provides
blocking diagrams, set sketches, lighting cues and property lists that enable
us to establish with some confidence the look and feel of these plays during
their first runs. What strikes one at the outset is the sheer opulence of both
stagings, in which Tree and Waller sought to reproduce on the Haymarket
stage an acceptable mock-up of smart Society. *A Woman of No Importance*,
with four lavish sets, was stylishly dressed by West End silk-mercers Lewis
and Allenby, while *An Ideal Husband* featured among its couturières the
ultra-modish Mary Elizabeth Humble. Once again, however, Wilde used
such smartness to confound as well as confirm the prejudices of his public.

Figure 13   Florence West (Mrs Lewis Waller) as the gauche Mrs Cheveley in Waller's 1895
Haymarket première of *An Ideal Husband* (*The Sketch*, 13 February 1895)

In *A Woman of No Importance* the sensuous but severe black gown worn
by Mrs Bernard Beere as the reprobate Mrs Arbuthnot offered (as fashion
critics were quick to note) measured relief from the frills and fripperies of
the play's Society dames (see figure 9). Similarly, the sophistication of Mrs
Cheveley, the continental adventuress of *An Ideal Husband*, was compromised by a succession of outfits calculated to strike contemporaries as
gauche and barbaric (see figure 10). In each instance Wilde sought to use the

market forces of luxury dressmaking to comment upon the worlds of his Haymarket patrons. It was a ploy that allowed him to enjoy their custom while constructing from the products and rituals of their society new fables for an increasingly troubled *fin de siècle*. Audiences in the stalls and boxes continued to be both flattered and vexed by the antics of their on-stage doubles, while viewers in the upper galleries enjoyed the additional spectacle of fashionable Society catching its likeness in Wilde's cunningly set mirrors.

In February 1895 Wilde had two plays running simultaneously on West End stages. Waller's Haymarket production of *An Ideal Husband*, much praised in the popular press, had opened on 3 January. Six weeks later it was joined by Alexander's St James's première of *The Importance of Being Earnest*. The route by which Wilde's 'trivial comedy for serious people' reached the St James's was circuitous.[5] At one point a four-act drama destined for Charles Wyndham's Criterion, the play had been passed to Alexander to help him through the crisis caused by the failure of Henry James's *Guy Domville*. Alexander, whom Wilde felt lacked the requisite flair for comedy, had Wilde reduce the play to its present three acts, largely by conflating its original Acts II and III. As was the case with *Lady Windermere's Fan*, the alteration helped to accommodate Alexander's clientèle, moving Wilde's work from the four-act format of Society drama to the three acts expected of late-Victorian farce. If, however, the piece gained from such compression, its new status as farcical comedy or melodramatic farce led some to underestimate Wilde's achievement. While the play was applauded by audiences and critics – with the signal exception of Shaw who found it mechanically heartless (*Saturday Review*, 23 Feb. 1895) – most threw up their hands at the prospect of extracting meaning from so genial an exercise. For Archer it was 'a sort of *rondo capriccioso*, in which the artist's fingers [ran] with crisp irresponsibility up and down the keyboard of life' (*World*, 20 Feb. 1895), for A. B. Walkley an entertainment that excited laughter 'absolutely free from bitter afterthought' (*Spectator*, 23 Feb. 1895). During the run audiences cheered Wilde's verbal fireworks, but reserved their heartiest laughter for a brilliantly prepared sight gag, Jack's long Act II entrance in mourning attire, complete with black cane and funereal hand-kerchief, for the non-existent Ernest who has just arrived as his house guest. While the episode underscores Wilde's sure grasp of stage effect, it needs to be tempered by the 'contemporaneity' that, for first-run audiences, still constituted much of the play's significance. Society melodrama had, in fact, been recycled as farce, with many of that form's barbed critiques veiled by a flippancy that allowed them to creep round the defences of their viewers. The première of *The Importance of Being Earnest* also contained the seeds of Wilde's demise. The Marquess of Queensberry, who had prowled about the St James's for some three hours, leaving for Wilde an insulting bouquet of root vegetables when his plans for disrupting the production were foiled, would, four days later, present his infamous calling card at the Albemarle Club. By the beginning of May, with Wilde's conviction imminent, both *The Importance of Being Earnest* and *An Ideal Husband* had been taken off. Wilde's fables of men with 'shameful' secrets or alter egos that took them Bunburying away from respectability had acquired for the patrons of the Haymarket and St James's unpalatable resonances. A programme dating from the end of the *Earnest* run, after Wilde's name had been removed from the bill, has scrawled in its margins an account of the 'sense of oppression' that seemed to afflict the enterprise.[6] There would be no further West End productions of Wilde's plays during their author's life.

Salome, which was not staged in England until 1906 – and not publicly there until 1931 – seems, at first glance, an exception to Wilde's penchant for fashionable venues and high-profile performers. Yet although the play became a flagship for Europe's budget-minded little theatre movement, it is well to keep in mind the glossy, almost cinematic production Wilde first envisioned for the piece. Plans for a projected Parisian première were recalled years later by Charles Ricketts, who, on more limited means, oversaw the play's 1906 London staging:

> I proposed a black floor – upon which Salome's white feet would show; this statement was meant to capture Wilde. The sky was to be a rich turquoise blue, cut across by the perpendicular fall of strips of gilt matting, which should not touch the ground, and form an aerial tent. Did Wilde actually suggest the division of the actors into masses of colour, to-day the idea seems mine! His was the suggestion, however, that the Jews should be in yellow, the Romans were to be in purple, and John in white. Over the dress of Salome the discussions were endless: should she be black like the night? or – here the suggestion is Wilde's – 'green like a curious and poisonous lizard'? I desired that the moonlight should fall upon the ground, the source not being seen; Wilde hugged the idea of some 'strange dim pattern in the sky.'[7]

Ricketts's account may be read in the light of surviving set sketches, by Ricketts and Wilde himself, which depict as both material and 'symbolic' Iokanaan's cistern (enclosed by its 'wall of green bronze') and the grand staircase leading to Herod's palace (figure 14).[8] Similar ambitions informed Wilde's efforts to have *Salomé* staged in England (in French) by Sarah Bernhardt in 1892, a project aborted by the decision of the Examiner of Plays to invoke legislation prohibiting the depiction on stage of biblical characters. Bernhardt's production at the Palace was to have been a major West End event, rivalling in splendour Alexander's *Lady Windermere's Fan*

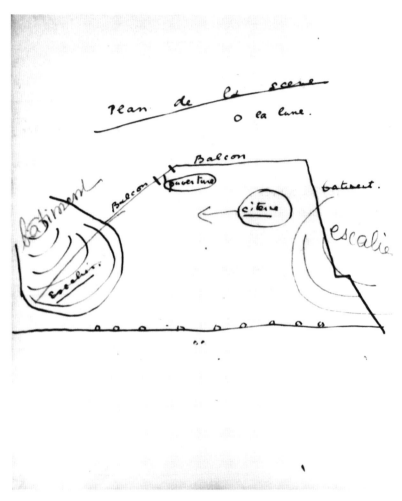

Figure 14   Wilde's sketch for a proposed staging of *Salome*

playing at the St James's that same season. Incorporating costumes and
properties from Sardou's *Cléopâtre*, designer Graham Robertson had
created for Bernhardt 'a golden robe with long fringes of gold, sustained on
the shoulders by bands of gilt and painted leather which also held in place a
golden breastplate set with jewels'. Suggested by 'the sacerdotal robes of
Aaron', the gown was accompanied by 'a triple crown of gold and jewels'
which Bernhardt intended to wear over flowing, powdered-blue hair. In his
memoirs Robertson recounts Wilde's attempt to champion an elaborate
plan to have 'every costume of some shade of yellow from clearest lemon to
deep orange, with here and there just a hint of black ... all upon a great
empty sky of deepest violet' – a conceit extended by Wilde's wish to have 'in

place of an orchestra, braziers of perfume ... [with] scented clouds rising and partly veiling the stage from time to time – a new perfume for each emotion!'.[9] When, under the Censor's prohibition, Bernhardt's production had to be withdrawn, *Salome* was effectively captured by Europe's avant-garde – first, and perhaps most notably, in Aurélien Lugné-Poe's minimalist première at the Théâtre de l'Œuvre in Paris in 1896. The shift meant, with few exceptions, the abandonment of the spectacular, celebrity dimension Wilde had seen to be part of the play's meaning. Its reclamation some eighty years later would constitute a major rediscovery of the play.

II

Wilde's death in 1900 had the effect of making him safely historical, an unsettling but remote figure contained by the old century while being patronised by the new. His plays, from shortly after the time of his arrest, had languished on tour or in suburban venues, his name conspicuously struck from the bills. With his demise, they returned, one by one, to the West End stages and up-scale consumer markets for which they had first been written. The exception, again, was *Salome*, a piece whose 'depravity' was confirmed in English minds by its growing popularity on the Continent. Lugné-Poe's 1896 première had been followed in 1902 and 1903 by Max Reinhardt's Berlin productions, which attracted the attention of composer Richard Strauss and dancer Maud Allan.[10] Strauss's operatic *Salome*, set to a literal translation by Hedwig Lachmann, opened in Dresden two years later. By the end of 1907 it had been performed in more than fifty European cities. Between 1906 and 1908 Allan's balletic 'Vision of Salome', likewise inspired by Reinhardt's stagings, had been danced in Vienna, Budapest, Munich, Paris and Marienbad, where in September 1907 it was applauded by the visiting Edward VII.[11] By 1910 both opera and dance had come to London, participating in an outbreak of what one critic dubbed 'Salomania'. Yet while Strauss's and Allan's adaptations were 'publicly' performed at Covent Garden and the Palace Theatre of Varieties, Wilde's original, still under the Examiner's ban, made its English début in 'private' matinées at makeshift venues. To make matters worse, the play's first London performances, by the New Stage Club at the Bijou (10 May 1905), and the Literary Theatre Society at King's Hall and the National Sporting Club (10 and 20 June 1906), were boycotted by the press. Between them, ban and boycotts enabled the avant-garde to complete its appropriation of the work. Ricketts, in designing the Literary Theatre revival (on a double bill with Wilde's *Florentine Tragedy*), made a virtue of the economies dictated by the resources of a small dramatic club: 'I ... placed dim cypress-like curtains against a star-lit sky; the actors were clothed in every shade of blue, deepening into dark violet and green, and relieved by the red lances of the soldiers' (*Fortnightly Review*, Dec. 1912). Max Beerbohm, one of the few critics to have braved both boycotts, remained unconvinced. Impressed by the dark, brooding Herod of Robert Farquharson ('a terrible being, half-dotard, half-child'), he wondered whether an English Salome could push beyond the drawing-room naughtiness conveyed at the Bijou by Miss Millicent Murby: 'To think that a young English lady in the twentieth century could have been so badly brought up as to behave in so outrageous a manner!' (*Saturday Review*, 13 May 1905).[12]

An answer of sorts was provided in 1911, when Adeline Bourne, a prominent suffrage supporter, organised the first English *Salome* to appear on a proper stage (Court 27 and 28 Feb.). Directed by Harcourt Williams, the production, which played to 'a large audience, mostly [of] women' (*Referee*, 5 Mar.), featured Bourne as a blatantly political princess. Dressed with pointed restraint, a riposte to the scanty costumes of Maud Allan, and a tradition that would give us the screen Salomes of Theda Bara (1918), Nazimova (1923) and Rita Hayworth (1953), Bourne's portrayal of an emancipated virago put viewers in mind of 'a twentieth-century Suffragette attempting an entrance into the House of Commons or asking for Mr Winston Churchill's head on a charge sheet' (*Bystander*, 8 Mar. 1911). It was, the critic for the *Penny Illustrated Paper* shuddered, 'a sorry spectacle, fit only for sexless women and "pussy cat" men' (11 Mar.). The gender anxieties registered in such responses helped to explain the hysteria that greeted J. T. Grein's wartime *Salome* of 1918. Recruiting Maud Allan to appear for the first time in a staged version of Wilde's play, Grein hoped to use two matinées at the Court (7 and 14 Apr.) as a springboard for a production that his War Players might bring to English troupes. The conjunction, however, of Allan's sensuality, recent losses on the Western front, and Grein's Dutchness – which to myopic eyes looked suspiciously German – enabled critics to lay the unmanning of England's youth directly at Wilde's door. What followed was a much publicised libel trial, in which, to borrow a phrase from Robert Ross, the British public 'enjoyed ... kicking Oscar's corpse to make up for the failure of the Fifth Army'.[13]

If, however, *Salome* proved too transgressive for wartime sensibilities, a clean bill of health was given to *The Importance of Being Earnest* and the Society plays, a verdict that marked the rise of Wilde as Apollonian craftsman, a figure as secure in his niche as Goldsmith and Sheridan to whom he was often compared. In 1902 *The Importance of Being Earnest*, after a provincial tour and a tentative run at the Coronet in Notting Hill Gate, was given a triumphant West End re-entry by its initial producer,

George Alexander. This was followed by Alexander's revivals of *Lady Windermere's Fan* in 1904 and 1911, and further productions of *The Importance of Being Earnest* in 1909, 1911 and 1913, the first of which (with Wilde's name back on the bill) ran for an unprecedented 316 nights. Beerbohm Tree, who had staged *A Woman of No Importance* at the Haymarket in 1893, restaged it at his second and more opulent theatre, His Majesty's, in 1907, himself resuming his original role of Lord Illingworth, while Alexander joined Robert Ross in preparing a new text of *An Ideal Husband* that played in the shadow of the Great War into the summer of 1914. In each instance what Wilde called his 'plays of modern life' were routinely updated. Moving to protect their increasingly valuable properties, Tree and Alexander altered frocks, furniture and topical allusions, so that the mirror held for Edwardian spectators reflected not the surfaces of the *fin de siècle* but those of 1904, 1907 and 1914. Such modernisations, however, did not entail a corresponding shift in the values or sensibilities that underpinned Wilde's materiality. As a result, *The Importance of Being Earnest* and the Society plays, 'classics' though they were, presented Edwardian audiences with a succession of disquieting misalignments in which viewers found themselves confronted with worlds that were neither unequivocally 'us' (as they had been in the 1890s) nor quite comfortably 'them' (as they would become in post-war period revivals).

One topic particularly problematic was the meaning of Wilde's dandy philosophers. Figures like Lords Darlington, Illingworth and Goring – even Jack and Algy – had acquired new meanings in the light of what Michael Hurley has called 'the discourses which circulated in the *post-trial* figure of Wilde'.[14] By 1907, when Tree revived *A Woman of No Importance*, spectators aware of an emerging 'queer' consciousness freely juxtaposed Illingworth's Wildean wit with his interest in young Gerald. Tree responded by substituting for his character's now coded effeminacy a more manly, casual demeanour[15] – although even this did not prevent Lytton Strachey from reading Tree's production as a coded fable of subcultural criminality:

> Mr Tree is a wicked Lord, staying in a country house, who has made up his mind to bugger one of the other guests – a handsome young man of twenty. The handsome young man is delighted; when his mother enters, sees his Lordship and recognises him as having copulated with her twenty years before the result of which was – the handsome young man. She appeals to Lord Tree not to bugger his own son. He replies that that is an additional reason for doing it (oh! he's a *very* wicked Lord!).[16]

It is, no doubt, true, as Alan Sinfield has observed, that if the play had been read generally in this way it could not have been performed, in 1907 or, initially in 1893.[17] It is equally true that a reading that in 1893 dared not speak its name had become possible for some spectators by 1907.

In the 1890s Wilde's impatience with Victorian earnestness had led him to underestimate both the force and intelligence of early feminism. In the Society dramas his condescension was bodied forth in a generation of stage Puritans – Lady Windermere, Hester Worsley, Mrs Arbuthnot, Lady Chiltern – whose attempts to preach moral reform collapse into priggish naivety. Lady Chiltern, the last and least palatable of the breed, is, we are told, a member of the Women's Liberal Association and a champion of progressive causes. Yet this feminist free-thinker is, by the play's close, made to endorse a 'separate spheres' ideology that would have heartened the most rock-ribbed reactionary:

> A man's life is of more value than a woman's. It has larger issues, wider scope, greater ambitions. Our lives revolve in curves of emotion. It is upon lines of intellect that a man's life progresses.

The passage was already awkward in 1895, when Ada Leverson wrote a good-natured parody of it for *Punch* (23 May). Delivered in 1914 by a Lady Chiltern whose gowns proclaimed her a contemporary of Asquith and the Pankhursts, it was met with open derision. Indeed if the faultlines apparent in Tree's 1907 *Woman of No Importance* worked to generate our first gay critique of Wilde on stage, those of Alexander's 1914 *Ideal Husband* helped to produce our first feminist one. Damning what she called 'the fatuousness' of Lady Chiltern's 'new wisdom', the critic for *Votes for Women*, a militant suffrage weekly, condemned Wilde's 'picture of male-organized society' with its helpless, 'parasitic' females. Recalling her enjoyment of the play's 1895 début, she articulated the problems faced by modern rejiggings: 'a play of this precise age is not old enough, not remote enough to be a presentment of the past and a little too old to be one of the present'. Convinced that 'had Wilde lived to see the great awakening of women he might have grasped its true inwardness' she proposed, on his behalf, a heroine appropriate to Lady Chiltern's new-century look, a woman 'leading a life of her own, capable of forming her own views, and *with reason* inspiring her husband with the deep respect he feels for her' (3 June). It was the kind of observation that would sound the death knell for Wilde in modern dress.

III

In 1923 Allan Aynesworth, who had played Algernon in the 1895 première of *The Importance of Being Earnest*, directed an important revival of that play at the Haymarket. With the boyish, shingled-headed Cecily of Nancy Atkins, and the 'young dude' Algy of John Deverell, it was an attempt to

Figure 15   Muffin eating in 1923: Leslie Faber (Jack) and John Deverell (Algy) in the last professional 'modern dress' staging of *The Importance of Being Earnest* (Haymarket 1923)

push Wilde into a post-war era of flappers, motor-bikes, and telephones (figure 15). To this end it was dressed 'as though it had been written last week' (*Sunday Pictorial*, 25 Nov.) with wardrobes by Curzon Street fashion house Christabel Russell reflecting vogues that had become popular only in the preceding month. Even Lady Bracknell's Act I cloak incorporated trends

Queen Mary had championed at two recent royal receptions (*Westminster Gazette*, 19 Nov.). By 1923, however, such topicality only served to trigger an extensive debate about the 'dangerous age' Wilde's plays had finally reached. For most, Victorian manners in post-war garb created anachronisms too glaring to overlook. The *Evening Standard*, enumerating the 'ludicrous' compromises that had to be struck merely to preserve the play's action, called particular attention to Deverell's 'ultra modern Algy' condemned to wear 1890s shirt cuffs for the sole purpose of jotting upon them Jack Worthing's country address. What the press described as a crisis of style was also a crisis of meaning. Ivor Brown, writing for the *Saturday Review* (1 Dec.), reflected upon the play's decline as 'a bourgeois-baiting instrument', while 'Tarn' of the *Spectator* (1 Dec.) insisted that Wilde's ahistorical 'fantasticality' could best be achieved through the distance imposed by 'period' costumes and 'period' delivery. Indeed, the need to replace Wilde the transgressive jester with Wilde the producer of chiselled artificial plays 'in the hard, cynical manner of Restoration comedy' seems to have motivated much of the prevailing sentiment for Wilde in original dress. Even what purported to be the shade of Wilde himself, viewing Aynesworth's revival through the eyes of medium Hester Travers Smith, declared that he would have preferred to have seen his work in 'costumes ... [of] my own period' (*Sunday Express*, 2 Dec.).

Yet returning Wilde to something resembling his own era was not the only option. In the summer of 1920 the *Observer* offered its readers an account of an avant-garde *Earnest* staged at Berlin's tiny Tribune Theatre. Interiors were minimal, actors abjured make-up, and 'the ladies [were] dressed in such a way that Strindberg might confess himself satisfied'. Lady Bracknell was a fearsome 'chemical blonde', while Cecily sat down 'upon the topmost of the three steps that led up to the stage and read out her diary in the very ears of the front row'. Impressed by the actors, but baffled by the *mise-en-scène*, the *Observer* critic dismissed most of what he had seen as 'badly mounted' (8 Aug.). A second option was to rejuvenate the practice of 'modern dress' by making corresponding adjustments to Wilde's stage worlds. This was the route taken by Ernst Lubitsch in a remarkably successful 1925 (silent) cinematic adaptation of *Lady Windermere's Fan*. Assisted by a medium that freed him from all obligation to Wilde's text – none of Wilde's epigrams were used as screen titles – Lubitsch was able to dovetail 1920s fashions with the pictorial language of contemporary filmmaking, creating a luminous world of high-ceilinged drawing-rooms and formal hedgerows that played directly to the sensibilities of his public.[18] A third possibility was scouted by Nigel Playfair who in 1930 presented an abstract *Earnest* at the Lyric Theatre, Hammersmith. Working with

Figure 16   John Gielgud (Jack) and Mabel Terry-Lewis (Lady Bracknell) in Nigel Playfair's
experimental 'black and white' *Earnest* (Lyric, Hammersmith 1930)

designer Michael Weight, Playfair aimed to convey what he called in his
programme notes 'an impression, not an archaeological reproduction, of the
wicked 1890s' (figure 16). His set and costumes, based, he acknowledged,
upon designs by Beardsley, were entirely in black, grey and white, a device
that made 'the faces and hands of the players ... look obscenely pink'.
Although some complained that the conceit robbed the play of its visual
coup de théâtre – Jack had to make his Act II mourning entrance into 'a
garden in which even the rose bushes [were] already in funereal black'
(*Nation*, 19 July) – Playfair's production offered a bold, otherworldly
challenge to the earthbound realisms of modern and historical dress.

That 'period' Wilde did, in the end, prevail is due, in large measure, to the influence of two figures who would come to dominate the staging of Wilde's comedies for the next quarter-century. John Gielgud had played John Worthing (to the Lady Bracknell of his aunt Mabel Terry-Lewis) in Playfair's 'black and white' *Earnest*. Praising the production's direction as 'clean-cut, fresh, and incisive', Gielgud, nevertheless, felt that Playfair's staging lacked 'the opulent stuffiness which the snobbish atmosphere of the Wilde text seems to demand'. Gielgud's corrective came in his own Globe production of 1939 (revived 1939, 1941; Phoenix 1942; Royale, New York 1947), an important and much imitated event that introduced the Lady Bracknell of Edith Evans and the Miss Prism of Margaret Rutherford. Working with the design team Motley, Gielgud, who both produced and (again) took the role of John Worthing, argued that the play must be set 'either in the correct period, 1895, or, at the producer's discretion, in a slightly later year – but not ... later than 1906'. In the event, Gielgud struck a compromise, prompted by Motley's conviction that Lady Bracknell would 'look more imposing in the great hats of the early Edwardian era than in the small bonnets worn by the older generation in the nineties'. The decision, to which the look of the entire production was keyed, was of a piece with Gielgud's account of how he felt the laughter provoked by Wilde's work had changed over the previous half-century: '[*Earnest*] must originally have been thought funny because it tilted so brilliantly at contemporary society. The people who laughed at it were, many of them, laughing at themselves ... Today we laugh at the very idea that such types could ever have existed; at the whole system – the leaving of cards, chaperons, official proposals of marriage, the ceremony of meals, the ridiculously exaggerated values of birth, rank and fashion.'[19] It was an interpretation that abandoned Wilde as social critic, while shifting stage centre (in her Edwardian hat) the most formidable exemplar of what Gielgud had termed 'the whole system'. Indeed, Gielgud's reading, together with Edith Evans's magisterial performance (preserved in Anthony Asquith's 1952 film adaptation), helped to create for Lady Bracknell a centrality she has enjoyed ever since.

In the forties Gielgud's 'agreeable' Wilde, formal, distanced and reassuring, was joined by the sumptuous, escapist Wilde of designer Cecil Beaton. Initially inspired by Rex Whistler's sets for Jack Minter's *An Ideal Husband* (Westminster 1943), Beaton created for Gielgud's 1945 Haymarket revival of *Lady Windermere's Fan* a forced, hot-house environment Beaton himself spoke of as 'overcharged, richly stuffed and upholstered' (figure 17).[20] *The Times* (22 Aug.) objected that, between them, Gielgud and Beaton had replaced Wilde's 'audacity' with 'period glitter', likening the effect of their music-box world to 'a ballet of brilliant great butterflies dryly

Figure 17   The decorative approach: John Gielgud's 1945 revival of *Lady Windermere's Fan* (Haymarket) designed by Cecil Beaton; centre right Isabel Jeans (Mrs Erlynne) and Michael Shepley (Lord Augustus), in doorway Dorothy Hyson (Lady Windermere) and Griffith Jones (Lord Darlington), seated left Athene Seyler (Duchess of Berwick) (*The Sketch*, 3 October 1945)

parodying the manners of the nineties'. Yet for many their historicised opulence offered a kind of comfort. 'In times of rapid and violent change', the *New Statesman* (1 Sept.) noted, 'people often enjoy pictures of times more confidently stable.' The *Tatler* (29 Aug.), more to the point, argued that, amid the deprivations of post-war rationing, 'to let the eye wander about [Beaton's] couponless world in which boudoirs are vast canopies of flowers and drawing-rooms sparkle in the light of diamonds is ... a welcome refreshment of spirit'. Such observations marked the arrival of a safe, establishment Wilde, a figure fast becoming part of the confident, Tory élite John Osborne's Jimmy Porter would later denounce as 'the old Edwardian brigade'. They also helped to forge a Wilde–Beaton axis that sought to perpetuate such readings. Its high points would include Beaton's designs for Jack Minter's North American tour of *Lady Windermere's Fan* (Curran Theatre, San Francisco 1946; Cort, New York 1947), a staging in which Beaton himself took the role of the dandy Cecil Graham, and the lavish 'technicolour' wardrobes Beaton built for Alexander Korda's 1947 film of *An Ideal Husband*. Not until the late sixties would critics begin to take a more jaundiced view of Beaton's lush, celebratory style. Indeed, when the *Spectator*, reviewing Anthony Quayle's 1966 (Phoenix) restaging of *Lady Windermere*, suggested that 'Beaton's designs – dingy silk dresses, bulging with puffs and pads in all the colours of a fleshy, well-ripened bruise – struck precisely the note of Wilde's glamorous, worldly, tarnished and materialistic society', it was edging towards the kind of counter-reading that would come to characterise Wilde's reception in the post-Beaton era (*Spectator*, 21 Oct.).

While Wilde's comedies were being made palatable to middle-class sensibilities, *Salome* had to make its own pact with respectability. In the latter case, however, respectability was inadvertent – largely a consequence of the lifting, in 1931, of the Examiner's ban. Accounts of the play's last 'private' performance have a familiar ring. In May 1931 the Gate Theatre Studio offered the work on a double bill with Ninette de Valois's *Danses Divertissements*.[21] Press reports dwelt upon the savagery of the event. Herod's passage about 'masks and mirrors', delivered by Robert Speaight in 'gilt sack-cloth and a scarlet wig', seemed to 'strike deep' as 'a fragment of Wilde's everlasting autobiography', while Salome's dance, choreographed by de Valois and executed by Margaret Rawlings 'in no prudish spirit', evoked 'a chill feline evil' that recalled Beardsley and the 1890s. The *Daily Telegraph* (28 May) found it all 'creepily impressive', especially 'the moment when Salome speaks to the head, and the silver bowl throws in her face a reflected, horrible pallor'. The removal of the Examiner's ban later that same year had the effect of dissipating such morbidity. Little of the forbidden remained in the mother–daughter production of Nancy Price (Herodias) and Joan Maude (Salome) that opened at the Savoy four months later. Promoted as the first 'public' showing of a 'long banned' play, it boasted Robert Farquharson's resumption of his 1906 role of Herod, authentic Dervish music for Salome's dance, and, in place of the euphemistic 'covered dish' that in earlier productions had stood for Iokanaan's head, a plaster cast whose features closely resembled those of actor Lawrence Anderson (*Daily Telegraph*, 6 Oct.). Horror, however, seemed to hesitate in the glare of state approval. Maude's Salome, the *Illustrated London News* (17 Oct.) observed, was neither 'voluptuary' nor 'virago', but rather 'a nice little High School girl slightly offended because John the Baptist refused to partner her in a tennis tournament'. The *Telegraph* (6 Oct.) dismissed her dance as the ill-advised calisthenics of 'a personable young woman in scanty draperies'. Even Farquharson, terrifying in the premières of 1905 and 1906, put one critic in mind of music-hall comic Dan Leno. Alan Parsons summed up much of the contemporary response in expressing his relief that 'now that it has been allowed and performed ... [no one] will want to repeat the experiment'. Gone modest and middle-class, the play would not be seen in London for another quarter-century.[22]

IV

The emergence of Wilde as a playwright for our own time began with Lindsay Kemp's staging of *Salome* in the 1970s. Actor, mime, dancer and choreographer, Kemp presented the play as a homoerotic spectacle, half-danced, half-acted, at London's Round House in the winter of 1977.[23] Incorporating about a third of Wilde's text, with an all-male company performing both in English and French, Kemp constructed a free variation upon the work that began with Herod's archers shooting down a winged Iokanaan, and closed with the dying prophet (unbeheaded) being 'slowly enveloped in Salome's cloak, until she presse[d] a pomegranate kiss on his bloody mouth to the strains of Tristan's Liebestod' (*Observer*, 27 Feb.). The production's rationale lay in its celebration of Wilde's outlaw sexuality, a point underscored by Kemp's decision to alternate performances with his own balletic adaptation of Genet's *Our Lady of the Flowers*. While initial reviews were mixed, critics were impressed by the sheer theatricality of the event – rhythmic drumming, live snakes, incense and blood – as well as by the vulnerable Salome of Kemp himself, 'a bald little gnome [who] really does suggest a depraved waif of 16'. Indeed Kemp's performance of the Dance of the Seven Veils in his own person, abandoning Salome's make-up, wig and headdress, was applauded for replacing the expected strip-tease with the kind of 'inner transformation and self-revelation with which Wilde was fundamentally concerned'.[24] A like passion for inventive decadence characterized Ken Russell's 1987 film *Salome's Last Dance*. Russell, however, chose to stage Wilde's play, virtually uncut, within a pseudo-historical 1890s frame drama, in which brothel-keeper Alfred Taylor (Stratford Johns) surprises Wilde (Nickolas Grace) with a private showing of his newly banned work. As the action, performed by Taylor's 'rough trade', spills from stage to drawing-room, Wilde begins to see himself as Iokanaan, self-destructively drawn to the figure of Alfred Douglas. Film critic Vincent Canby, who dismissed the conceit as 'a perfumed comic stunt' found that beneath Russell's self-indulgent wit lurked a serious work 'in which vice and virtue become so intertwined as to be indistinguishable'

Figure 18   Steven Berkoff (Herod) and Katherine Schlesinger (Salome) in Berkoff's 1989
National Theatre production of *Salome*

(*New York Times*, 4 May). Russell's response, suitably Wildean, was to
expand his scenario, making it the basis for a 1993 Bonn production of
Strauss's opera, in which Salome shoots her way out of the brothel with a
pistol hidden in Iokanaan's severed head.

To such barnstorming meta-theatrics actor–director Steven Berkoff
opposed an austere, tightly controlled reading that shifted the play from the

realm of sexual cabaret to that of power politics. First seen at Dublin's Gate Theatre in April 1988 (with silver-throated Alan Stanford in the role of Herod), then at the Edinburgh Festival, and, in the autumn of 1989, at London's Royal National Theatre (with Berkoff himself as Herod) Berkoff's *Salome* (figure 18) sought to focus attention upon the physicality of Wilde's words. 'So much was the perfume and tapestry in the language', Berkoff explained, 'that I decided that the stage should be bare and allow the words to bounce off the hard surfaces without being softened or cushioned.' To this end a minimal set was constructed, consisting of a dais with banqueting table, a backdrop of night sky, and a large expanse of marbled floor. Here, in 1920s dress, to the tinklings of a cocktail piano, the smart things of Herod's court mimed their way through a fatal Society feast. The elimination of stage properties – Berkoff had indicated that he would admit to the production 'nothing whose physical laws were subject to gravity, accident, or wilfulness' – extended to Iokanaan's head, and, above all, Salome's dance, a pantomime undressing in which Salome (Katherine Schlesinger) removed nothing at all. The point, Berkoff noted, was to insist upon the power of the converting imagination. 'We decided that like everything else [Salome's dance] had to be an illusion … Herod sees her naked fulsome young limbs as the actress "acts" the dance.' Both the stylised gestures of Herod's court, a seething centipede of bodies, and the slow, studied utterance of Herod himself (this was as much Herod's production, as Kemp's had been Salome's) set the pace for a staging that eschewed sexuality in order to explore 'the ways that power manifests itself when divorced from a proper authority'.[25] It was a compelling production, that, in the words of Michael Billington, seemed to overturn 'everything we prize in the British theatre', from the autonomy of the actor, to representational staging, to 'swift, light speaking' (*Country Life*, 16 Nov. 1989).

Perhaps, however, the most surprising development of recent years has been the rediscovery of Wilde's three Society plays as complex theatre pieces worth serious attention. In 1984 director–designer Philip Prowse initiated a watershed series of revivals at the Glasgow Citizens' Theatre with *A Woman of No Importance*.[26] The least performed of Wilde's major works, the piece had since the fifties been played largely in a bowdlerised stage-script by Paul Dehn.[27] Prowse began by restoring Wilde's text, seizing upon its stylistic excesses to create a 'camp' sensibility less at home with Sheridan or Goldsmith than with the 'machine-gun dandyism' of Genet, Orton and Noel Coward. Prowse's richly textured sets and costumes were, likewise, a response to the slick pictorialism of Beaton and Rex Whistler, using opulence to unsettle rather than reassure his viewers. A first act, set on the lawn at Hunstanton Chase, offered a walled garden of brushed gold, with

Figure 19   Nichola McAuliffe (Mrs Allonby) with 'framed landscape' in Act I of Philip
Prowse's 1991 RSC production of *A Woman of No Importance*

ornamental urns, daffodil banks and a large circular carp pond. It was,
Irving Wardle would later note, a pastoral from which nature had been
painted out. (When the production was restaged for the Royal Shakespeare
Company in 1991 Prowse made the effect literal by placing upstage an
enormous gilt frame with two panels from a Fragonard landscape; see
figure 19.) Here to the strains of Elgar's cello concerto Wilde's dowagers
policed the niceties of 'best circles' manners with the rigour of a hanging

court. The effect was to create a kind of Wildean meta-world, a triumph of art over nature complete enough to admit a complex of visual puns and allusions to Wilde's life and previous work. In such a world, aesthetically playful, intertextual and self-referential, the puritanism of Mrs Arbuthnot became a pose as studied as the rest. Its very artificiality, however, gave it an authority that enabled it to hold its own with the play's epigrammatic point-scoring. It was a decision that allowed Prowse to present Wilde's wit and sentiment with equal measures of earnestness and triviality, inviting viewers to detect beneath the glittering surfaces of his décor a 'crazed and ossified' old order panicked at the prospect of its own extinction. Sheridan Morley pronounced the effect 'as markedly end of era as Chekhov's *Cherry Orchard*' (*International Herald Tribune*, 9 Oct. 91).[28]

Prowse's success with *A Woman of No Importance* was followed at Glasgow by equally inventive stagings of *An Ideal Husband* (1986) and *Lady Windermere's Fan* (1988) – the latter with the revelation of Mrs Erlynne's identity shifted to the fourth act where Wilde had initially placed it – as well as by Prowse's own adaptation of *The Picture of Dorian Gray* (1993). His, however, has not been the only voice. An alternative approach to the Society plays, through 'character' rather than 'style', was offered by Peter Hall in his 1992 Globe revival of *An Ideal Husband*. In a pre-production interview Hall had argued for the 'surprisingly good-hearted' nature of Wilde's plays, maintaining that it was their 'warmth' that would ensure them a continued popularity. Hall's staging was an attempt to explore what he had maintained was 'the intense emotional reality' Wilde's characters consciously mask beneath their witticisms (*Guardian*, 11 Nov.). Critics, for the most part, took him at his word. Michael Billington praised the Sir Robert and Lady Chiltern of David Yelland and Hannah Gordon as 'a quasi-Ibsenite couple whose married life is founded on a lie', and the Goring of Martin Shaw for seeming to suggest beneath his 'mask of flippancy ... infinite reserves of charity and shrewdness' (*Guardian*, 13 Nov.). Goring's wit, John Peter concurred, was 'only a cover' to mask his increasing disappointment with life (*Sunday Times*, 15 Nov.). Reinforced by the sets of Carl Toms – the Chilterns' splendid drawing-room was calculated to keep viewers in mind of the play's 'terrible gospel of gold' – Hall's production, thematically and stylistically, argued for tolerance rather than judgement.[29] A more politicised alternative appeared in the Wilde revivals of Mike Alfreds's Cambridge Theatre Company (now Method and Madness), whose 1991 staging of *Lady Windermere's Fan* featured an induction in which, to the applause of a masked on-stage audience, Lord and Lady Windermere were ritually dressed by their servants. As the opposing silhouettes of 1890s manliness and womanhood emerged before them, spectators were asked to concede both the socially constructed nature of gender and Alfreds's larger view of society as a site of constant performance. As a means of integrating Wilde's epigrammatic wit with the play's melodramatic plot line the device won high praise from London's *Evening Standard* which favourably compared it to Prowse's *A Woman of No Importance* on offer at the RSC during that same season.

The Importance of Being Earnest has, thus far, eluded the kind of wholesale rediscovery that has characterised recent stagings of *Salome* and the Society dramas. In part the play has remained hostage to the success of its Gielgud revivals, and the expectations shaped by Asquith's 1952 film. The grace and elegance of Wilde's young men, the solidity of their world, and the elevation of Lady Bracknell to the status of 'star turn' – Edith Evans's delivery of 'hand-bag' must make it the most memorably inflected single word in British stage history – have all become potential traps for any producer hoping to put an individual stamp upon the work. A number of notable post-Asquith revivals have, nevertheless, made the attempt. Jonathan Miller's 1975 Greenwich Theatre production battled memories of Edith Evans with a Lady Bracknell (Irene Handl) who spoke with a thick German accent. Canada's Stratford Festival and Humberside's Great Eastern Stage Company followed suit with male Lady Bracknells (William Hutt and Desmond Barrit), and, in the latter instance, a sinister Pinteresque Lane oddly intimate with his master. Peter Hall's 1982 National Theatre revival[30] chose to undermine the glossy materialism of period productions by having the 'solid opulent furnishings' of Algy's rooms give way in Act II to a transparently artificial Manor House. John Bury's garden set, a 'shimmering blue stage floor backed with a cut-out landscape and panto-mime tree', offered a looking-glass world that allowed Hall to display Wilde's characters at a 'slight tangent to normality' (*Guardian*, 17 Sept.). The few dissenters who longed for Asquith's 'real lawns' were also distressed by the slim sensual Lady Bracknell of Judi Dench, 'a credible picture of a woman young enough to be competitive with her daughter' (*Sunday Times*, 19 Sept.). A like concern with scenery, Lady Bracknell and the sexuality of Wilde's men, characterised Nicholas Hytner's 1993 Aldwych staging. Critics were particularly struck by the Lady Bracknell of Maggie Smith, a predatory parvenu 'turned beady-eyed expert at border-control' (*Independent*, 12 Mar.), and Bob Crowley's Half-Moon Street set, a skewed-perspective sitting-room in lurid reds and greens, dominated by a towering reproduction of Sargent's portrait of 'dandy-boy' Graham Robertson. The complaint was that nothing in the play lived up to the danger of its opening set, or to the mouth-to-mouth kiss with which Jack and Algy first greeted one another.

Figure 20   Sean Kearns as the Duchess of Berwick in Rough Magic's production of *Lady Windermere's Fan* (Tricycle Theatre 1994)

As we rapidly approach our own *fin de siècle* Wilde's plays on stage have never been more popular or more profitable. The 'centennial' year of 1995, which opened with John Gielgud's unveiling of a plaque at the Haymarket Theatre to mark the hundredth anniversary of *An Ideal Husband*, and the presentation of an Oscar Wilde window in Westminster Abbey on the hundredth anniversary of the opening of *The Importance of Being Earnest*, has, not surprisingly, brought in its wake a host of new stagings. Among the most notable have been the *Earnest*s of Nicholas Wright for the English Touring Theatre and Terry Hands for the Birmingham Rep. In the former, Algy's flat, replete with silk cushions, oriental hangings, leather trunks and a hookah – the Indian trophies of General Moncrieff – was made to articulate the gay subtext hinted at in Hytner's 1993 revival. Commenting upon the casual bisexuality of both Jack and Algy, critic John Peter noted that 'it is simply understood that marrying enchanting young ladies need only be part of a young gentleman's social and erotic career' (*Sunday Times*, 2 Apr.). Hands's Birmingham production, which settled into a comfortable London run, took a very different tack, harping unapologetically upon the play's roots in late-Victorian farce. With a keen eye for social detail and razor-sharp timing it managed to return a sense of ensemble fun to the Lady Bracknell scenes, playing them boldly as group efforts rather than vehicles for a star performer. Indeed, the twin concepts of danger and fun would seem to augur well for the future of Wilde on stage, a future whose possibilities may be glimpsed in the work of troupes like Dublin's Rough Magic, which in the spring of 1994 brought a radically readjusted *Lady Windermere* to London's Tricycle Theatre. Making an end run round the massive sets – and budgets – of Prowse, Hall, Hytner and Hands, producer Lynne Parker used cross-dressing, the doubling of roles, direct (and sometimes improvised) audience address and a reduced Palm Court Orchestra to achieve what John Stokes recognised as 'a post-modern juxtaposition of performance styles' nicely calculated to catch the play's straddling of genres (figure 20). When Sean Kearns's drag Duchess of Berwick changes before our eyes into Lord Augustus (outrageously on the line 'None of us men do look what we really are') we find ourselves, Stokes observed, in the presence of 'a passionate, Irish Wilde challenging with robust vitality established notions of sex, gender, and social order' (*Times Literary Supplement*, 13 May 94). It is the kind of moment that in its rich, self-conscious topicality brings us full circle back to the paradoxes of problem play-making with which Wilde greeted his first audiences over a century ago.

NOTES

1 This essay draws freely upon two works I have co-authored with Sheila Stowell, *Theatre and Fashion: Oscar Wilde to the Suffragettes* (Cambridge: Cambridge University Press, 1994) and *Wilde on Stage: A Cultural and Performance History* (Cambridge University Press, 1997). For reasons of space, discussion has been confined largely to British productions, and to plays by Wilde himself, rather than stage adaptations of Wilde's non-dramatic work or the considerable body of dramatic material that takes Wilde as its subject. I am grateful to William Tydeman and Steven Price for permitting me to see in typescript sections of their *Salome* volume in Cambridge University Press's Plays in Production series.

2 Kerry Powell, 'Oscar Wilde, Elizabeth Robins, and the Theatre of the Future', *Modern Drama* 37:1 (1994), 220–37.

3 The costuming of Wilde's Society plays is discussed at length in *Theatre and Fashion*, pp. 12–33.

4 Joel Kaplan, 'A Puppet's Power: George Alexander, Clement Scott, and the Replotting of *Lady Windermere's Fan*', *Theatre Notebook* 46:2 (1992), 59–73.

5 For a full account of the process see Peter Raby, *The Importance of Being Earnest: A Reader's Companion* (New York: Twayne, 1995) and Joseph Donohue, *The Importance of Being Earnest: A Reconstructive Critical Edition of the First Production* (Gerrards Cross: Colin Smythe, 1995).

6 Donohue, *The Importance of Being Earnest*, pp. 68–9.

7 'Stage Decoration', *Fortnightly Review* (Dec. 1912), 1088–9. The essay was reprinted, with minor variants, in Ricketts's *Pages of Art* (London: Constable, 1913).

8 For a discussion of these sketches as well as Ricketts's extended involvement with the play see Richard Cave, *Charles Ricketts' Stage Designs* (Cambridge: Chadwyck-Healey, 1987), pp. 23–30, and the same author's 'Wilde Designs: Some Thoughts about Recent British Productions of His Plays', *Modern Drama* 37:1 (1994), 175–83.

9 Graham Robertson, *Time Was* (London: Hamish Hamilton, 1931), pp. 126–7.

10 Reviews, photos, playbills and posters from Reinhardt's stagings at the Kleines and Neues Theaters are now housed in the Max Reinhardt Archives at the State University of New York at Binghamton. I am grateful to Jeanne Eichelberger, Head of Special Collections, for making this material available to me.

11 For an account of Allan's performance and later career see Maud Allan, *My Life and Dancing* (London: Everett, 1908) and Felix Cherniavsky, *The Salome Dancer: The Life and Times of Maud Allan* (Toronto: McClelland and Stuart, 1991).

12 For an excellent account of the play's early stage history see Graham Good, 'Early Productions of Oscar Wilde's *Salome*', *Nineteenth-Century Theatre Research* 11:2 (1983), 77–92. Good calls particular attention to the centrality of Herod in English productions. John Stokes's *Oscar Wilde: Myths, Miracles, and Imitations* (Cambridge: Cambridge University Press, 1996) discusses Farquharson's 'camp' delivery, apparently modelled upon Wilde's own vocal mannerisms, pp. 9–10.

13 Charles de Sousy Ricketts, *Self Portrait. taken from the Letters and Journals of Charles Ricketts, R.A.*, collected T. Sturge Moore, ed. Cecil Lewis (London: Peter Davies, 1939), p. 297. For an account of the trial, citing testimony directly concerned with the performance and its reception, see Michael Kettle, *Salome's Last Veil* (London: Hart-Davis MacGibbon, 1977). Much additional information is contained in the Millard Clipping Books at the Clark Memorial Library at UCLA. I am grateful to Susan Tatian at the Clark Library for guiding me through this material.

14 'Homosexualities: Fiction, Reading and Moral Training', in T. Threadgold and A. Cranny-Francis (eds.), *Feminine, Masculine and Representations* (Sydney: Allen & Unwin, 1990), pp. 162–3.

15 In Alexander's 1914 production of *An Ideal Husband*, Lord Goring (played by Alexander) was similarly divested of dandaical trappings, turning a figure Wilde had dubbed 'the first well-dressed philosopher in the history of thought' into a po-faced *raisonneur*.

16 Michael Holroyd, *Lytton Strachey: The Unknown Years* (London: Heinemann, 1967), p. 319.

17 ' "Effeminacy" and "Femininity": Sexual Politics in Wilde's Comedies', *Modern Drama* 37:1 (1994), 34. For a more extended discussion see Sinfield's *The Wilde*

Century: Effeminacy, Oscar Wilde and the Queer Moment (London: Cassell, 1994).

18 The considerable literature on Lubitsch's adaptation includes Herman G. Weinberg, *The Lubitsch Touch* (New York: Dutton 1971), pp. 86–90; Leland A. Poague, *The Cinema of Ernst Lubitsch: The Hollywood Films* (New Brunswick, NJ: A. S. Barnes, 1978), pp. 41–50; William Paul, *Ernst Lubitsch's American Comedy* (New York: Columbia University Press, 1983), pp. 139–40; Neil D. Isaacs, 'Lubitsch and the Filmed-Play Syndrome', *Literature/Film Quarterly* 3:4 (1975), 299–308; and David Davidson, 'The Importance of Being Ernst: Lubitsch's Adaptation of *Lady Windermere's Fan*', *Literature/Film Quarterly* 11:2 (1983), 120–31.

19 John Gielgud, *Stage Directions* (London: Heinemann, 1963), pp. 69–70, 78–84.

20 Cecil Beaton, *Self Portrait with Friends: The Selected Diaries of Cecil Beaton*, ed. Richard Buckle (London: Pimlico 1981), pp. 166–67.

21 Limitations of space do not permit discussion here of the remarkable production staged by de Valois's brother, Terence Gray, at the Cambridge Festival Theatre during the summer of 1929. An early instance of full-blown director's theatre it featured an abstract architectural set, a score by Constant Lambert and choreography by de Valois. A revival in November 1931 introduced the Herod of Robert Morley. See Richard Cave, *Terence Gray and the Cambridge Festival Theatre* (Cambridge: Chadwyck-Healey, 1980) and Norman Marshall, *The Other Theatre* (London: John Lehmann, 1947), pp. 53–71.

22 The play's next London revival, on a double bill with J.-P. Sartre's *Respectable Prostitute*, served largely as a vehicle for Australian actor Frank Thring (Q and St Martin's Theatres, 1954).

23 In an earlier guise the production had enjoyed a successful run at New York's Fortune Theatre.

24 Katharine Worth, *Oscar Wilde* (London: Macmillan, 1983), pp. 67, 72.

25 Richard Cave, 'Wilde Designs', 182–3.

26 For an account of Prowse's ground-breaking Wilde productions see Michael Coveney, *The Citz: 21 Years of the Glasgow Citizens Theatre* (London: Hern, 1990); John Stokes, 'Wilde Interpretations', *Modern Drama* 37:1 (1994), 157–61; Richard Cave, 'Wilde Designs', 183–6; Robert Gordon, 'Wilde's "Plays of Modern Life" on the Contemporary British Stage', in *Rediscovering Oscar Wilde*, ed. C. George Sandulescu (Gerrards Cross: Colin Smythe, 1994), 156–66; and Joel Kaplan, 'Staging Wilde's Society Plays: A Conversation with Philip Prowse', *Modern Drama* 37:1 (1994), 192–205 and 'Wilde in the Gorbals: Society Drama and Citizens Theatre', in *Rediscovering Oscar Wilde*, pp. 214–23.

27 Dehn's three-act adaptation, which excises much of the play's 'seriousness' and completely rewrites its last act, was first seen at the Savoy in 1953. It was still in use when the play was revived at the Vaudeville in 1967. In 1960 it was the form in which Wilde's comedy was broadcast by Independent Television as a Play-of-the-Week.

28 Another route to 'end of era' Wilde was taken by director Ben Barnes in his 1996 staging of *A Woman of No Importance* at Dublin's Abbey Theatre. Set on the eve of the Great War the production's garden scenes (Acts I and III) were made to echo the prescient close of Shaw's *Heartbreak House*.

29 The production was successfully revived in 1996 in both London and New York.
30 See Russell Jackson 'A Classic Without Danger: The National Theatre's *Importance of Being Earnest*', *Critical Quarterly* 25:2 (1983), 73–80.

15

DECLAN KIBERD

Oscar Wilde: the resurgence of lying

Wilde once said that people are good until they learn how to talk. He was born into an age when philosophers were coming to the conclusion that language itself is a dubious, slippery commodity and that to talk is to learn how to tell lies. In consequence, many modern artists have distrusted fluency and eloquence, admiring hesitation and even inarticulacy as marks of the honesty of a speaker. Their ultimate guarantee of sincerity is not even a broken sentence but absolute, unqualified silence. Playwrights such as Harold Pinter and Samuel Beckett have constructed their work around moments of shared silence or painful, pregnant pauses. For them language is a mere babble used to frame these epiphanies, or else a device to occlude the truth (as when one of Beckett's characters laments to a girlfriend that words are inadequate to conceal what he feels). Indeed, Beckett went so far as to characterise literature as 'the foul convention whereby you either lie or hold your peace'.[1]

Commentators see this distrust of language as a fairly recent phenomenon, but, like so much else in modern theatre, that tradition has important origins in the work of Oscar Wilde. At the close of the first act of *The Importance of Being Earnest* Jack says 'Algy, you never talk anything but nonsense.' His companion has a deep reply: 'Nobody ever does.' That is to say, no matter how hard a person tries to prattle meaninglessly, there is always some tiny flicker of substance to it all. That residue of meaning may simply lie in the use of words to kill time and ward off boredom:

ALGERNON What shall we do?
JACK Nothing.
ALGERNON It's awfully hard work doing nothing. However, I don't mind hard work where there is no definite object of any kind.[2]

The work in their case is the exacting effort to be trivial in idle conversation. That banal exchange has become a sort of leitmotif in modern literature, heard again in T. S. Eliot's *The Waste Land* ('What shall we do tomorrow? /

What shall we ever do?'[3]) and in F. Scott Fitzgerald's *The Great Gatsby* (where Daisy Fay asks 'What'll we do with ourselves this afternoon? and the day after that, and the next thirty years?')[4]

The tone established by Wilde is one of overbred boredom, of elegant desperation among a leisure class at its wits' end. Its members are all exponents of a glittering style, but without any inner substance. It is no surprise that Wildean paradoxes and one-liners resurface so often in the works of Beckett, who once described style as a bow-tie worn over a throat cancer. In matters of grave importance style – not sincerity – is the crucial element: but without some substance style becomes a mere decoration, a redundancy, a vanity.

The modern distrust of styles and disenchantment with language itself are both strong in Irish writing, if only because of the artists' awareness that whenever they use English they are not writing in their own language. Irish people, whether hesitant students or outright masters of English, are keenly aware that certain words and phrases have one meaning in Ireland and another in England: a further case of countries divided by a common language. This was famously pointed out in James Joyce's *A Portrait of the Artist as a Young Man* in a scene where the young student Stephen contemplates the cultural gap between himself and the Englishman who teaches him at university:

> The language in which we are speaking is his before it is mine. How different are the words *home*, *Christ*, *ale*, *master*, on his lips and on mine! I cannot speak or write these words without unrest of spirit. His language, so familiar and so foreign, will always be for me an acquired speech. I have not made or accepted its words. My voice holds them at bay. My soul frets in the shadow of his language.[5]

An Irish person often uses English with a hesitation which is soon admired by the English as 'a lilting charm'; and suddenly the Irish have a style which is a result of their first awkwardness in grappling with English idioms. Before they know it, the English phrases which they employ are saying things which they never intended. Because English is a naturally rhetorical language, full of tricks of speech, they find themselves all too often borne forward on a tide of baroque eloquence. Beckett's eventual solution to this problem was to switch from English to French ('c'est plus facile d'écrire sans style'[6]), because this was a language in which he might find *le mot juste* and one which he could write with all the slow, cautious exactitude of the learner. In that way he might escape the fatal tendency of so many Irish exponents of English to indulge in torrents of blarney.

An earlier playwright found a way of coping with this problem not by avoiding blarney, but by the opposite strategy. Wilde could resist everything except temptation and so he didn't just yield to flowery and exaggerated language: he made it the central element in his most famous play, which suggests that the highest morality of all might be the noble art of lying. His success was not lost on John Millington Synge, for in a similar fashion the hero of *The Playboy of the Western World* admits to becoming a mighty man by the power of a lie. Both classic dramas form part of an ancient Irish tradition with roots in many previous centuries. In Dion Boucicault's mid-nineteenth-century melodrama *Conn the Shaughraun* the peasant hero praises lying as his only defence against respectable people who try to implant in him habits of Anglo-Saxon dullness: and, in truth, the Shaughraun's wild antics offered Victorian audiences a popular and vicarious release from the strict standards by which they generally lived.

The Irish Question had always been the problem of a dull-witted people trying to govern a quick-witted one. In a countryside oppressed by foreign misrule, lying to government officials had long been seen as a genuinely alternatively morality. The Irishman's reputation for deceit, guile and word-play is not only one result of the distrust by the natives of the coloniser: it is also, more directly, the inevitable outcome of a life under martial law. Sir John Davies, the man who presided over the Plantation of Ulster in the early seventeenth century, admitted this openly when he said: 'This oppression did of force and necessity make the Irish a craftie people; for such as are oppressed and live in slavery are ever put to their shifts.'[7] In a land where words are the sole weapons of the disarmed, irony, ambiguity and deceit flourish as modes of self-protection rather than as graces of literary style. Natives would give false directions to the scouts of the British army knowing that such white lies were both functional and moral, perhaps saving the lands and lives of entire communities.

Even when the British did get a foothold in an area and proclaim the new laws, these laws were seen as lies, not just by the dispossessed but often by the makers of the laws themselves. For instance, through much of the eighteenth century the ferocity of the Penal Laws was more verbal than real, for the good reason that those who framed them knew that they could seldom be applied in full rigour. Roman Catholics were compelled to work on their own church holidays, but justices and constables who refused to apply the law were to be jailed. In other words, the makers themselves wrote into the law their accurate enough suspicion that many of those appointed to implement it might take a contrary view. Another Penal Law decreed that maidens who married Papists were to be deemed dead (although doubtless most of them continued to breathe freely after its passing).[8] The statute book was a pathetic attempt to substitute moral authority for physical power. The very harshness of such measures was a reflection of their inoperability in a land which lacked a comprehensive police force or an adequate system of prisons.[9] The contrast between the official pretence – that the British ruled every valley and hill – and the reality – that they didn't – gave rise to that bifocal vision to be found in most of the great Anglo-Irish writers.

They belonged indeed to a spiritually hyphenated race, forever English in Ireland, forever Irish in England, and nobody could be more aware than they that there are two sides to every story. In Ireland it was not so much a case of the official versus the unofficial as of the unofficial versus the unofficial*er*. No wonder that Oscar Wilde could assert that a truth in art is that whose opposite may also be true, for he grew up in a country where things both could and could not be so. If the law itself was in the eyes of militant nationalists (like his mother 'Speranza') a tissue of lies, then lying itself might be a surprisingly moral, not to say, moralistic activity. And Ireland was simply an extreme case of a universal phenomenon – that all laws *are* lies in the sense that they represent ideal aspirations rather than describing actual practice.

No matter how far back one goes in Irish history, even to times well before the arrival of the invading Normans, one finds official regimes devoted to the ratification of the lie. The poets of ancient Ireland were celebrated for two basic functions: they kept a record of the laws and they told fluent, magnificent lies. The functions of *file* (poet) and *breitheamh* (judge) overlapped in a fashion which suggests that Irish cynicism about law has a long and honourable pedigree. Nobody was more cynical than the lawmakers themselves.[10] They told wild, poetic stories of the sagas; and the men of Ulster, being acerbic Ulstermen, were not easily fooled. Nonetheless, they gave their final assent when they told the first Irish poet Aimhirgín: 'What you say is of course incredible – but we believe you because you are a poet. If a poet says something is true, then it is indeed a fact.' That can be interpreted as meaning that the poets had the power to change reality by their magic words, or that they were simply facile liars.

This is the tradition which Wilde updates in his essays and plays. In 'The Decay of Lying' he asks 'After all, what is a fine lie?' and answers 'Simply that which is its own evidence'.[11] A fiction, colourfully told, acquires an autonomy and vitality of its own so compelling that only a pedant would want to check the story against the facts. A really good tale, however, possesses an inner emotional logic which permits the facts to be forgotten: this is based on a view of art as a matter of internal coherence rather than external correspondence to a knowable, concrete world.

So in Synge's *The Playboy of the Western World* the village girls are never really fooled by Christy Mahon's claim to have killed his father: they are far more impressed by his tale than by his reported deed. 'That's a grand story', they marvel, and 'He tells it lovely.'[12] Christy is accordingly celebrated for his 'poet's talking'[13] by his new love Pegeen Mike.

Wilde observed somewhat laconically in his essay that 'as one knows the poet by his fine music, so one can recognise the liar by his rich rhythmic utterance'.[14] The liars in *The Importance of Being Earnest*, therefore, speak on occasion in iambic pentameter. Algy remarks that the recently widowed Lady Harbury is now living entirely for pleasure and says

> I hear her hair has turned quite gold from grief.[15]

The artificial beauty of the alliteration, along with the pentameter rhythm, suggests that his remark may be about as sincere as the widow's mourning. Similarly, in *The Playboy of the Western World*, Christy Mahon as poet and liar is given many lines which unmistakably take the form of iambic pentameter. When he secures Pegeen's love he says

> That God in glory may be thanked for that!

– and when he takes the gifts of the village girls he cries out to his admirers

> I'm very thankful to you all today.[16]

He is, of course, 'the champion playboy of the western world'. It is no accident that the last of Christy's prizes is a three-thorned blackthorn stick of a type commonly carried by the travelling *spailpín* poets of eighteenth-century Ireland such as Eoghan Rua Ó Súilleabháin. That stick was intended to recall the wand given to the *file* on his ceremonial investiture in ancient Ireland.

It has been pointed out that the underlying conceit of *The Playboy of the Western World* may have been suggested to Synge by a short passage in Wilde's essay on lying:

> Many a young man starts in life with a natural gift for exaggeration which, if nurtured in congenial and sympathetic surroundings, or by the imitation of the best models, might grow into something really great and wonderful. But as a rule, he comes to nothing. He either falls into careless habits of accuracy ...[17]

In Wilde's foremost comedy Jack lies that he is Ernest, but does it so well that the truth conforms to his fiction. Like the village girls in Synge's drama, Cecily is more interested in the story than the facts. Gwendolen asks whether she believes Algy only to be told: 'I don't. But that does not affect the wonderful beauty of his answer'[18] because style, not sincerity, is what counts. She implies that she cares nothing for his actions, having fallen in love with the beautiful imagination of a man who could create such a story in the midst of such a dull and literal-minded age. He, for his part, has already been captivated by her, not by what she has done so much as by what she can imagine. Their fictions acquire the density of truth, as Cecily initiates Jack retrospectively in the touching details of a courtship which existed previously only in her head. And he has enough imagination to understand her game and to play along with it:

> CECILY ... The next day I bought this ring in your name, and this is the little bangle with the true lovers' knot I promised you always to wear.
>
> ALGERNON Did I give you this? It's very pretty, isn't it?
>
> CECILY Yes, you've wonderfully good taste, Ernest. It's the excuse I've always given for your leading such a bad life.[19]

At this point Algy realises that all he has to do is stand back and listen, while Cecily talks herself into a lifelong romance with him.

This is precisely what happens in Act I of *The Playboy of the Western World*, when it is the villagers and Pegeen who fantasise many exotic backgrounds for the silent newcomer. They prefer to speculate endlessly about the nature of his crime rather than hear a blunt and early report from his lips: such a report would spoil all the fun which they derive from feeding their starved imaginations. They, also, are compelled to lead a drab, insipid life; and these girls, just like Cecily, are therefore fascinated by the arrival of a 'wicked' man in an area where the chances of committing a mortal sin are virtually nil. Even as Cecily quailed under the regime of Miss Prism, they groan under the grim rule of Father Reilly, and bemoan the fact that they must 'go up winter and summer with nothing worthwhile to confess at all'.[20] To sin in such a community would be a moral act insofar as it would challenge the prevailing apathy. For this is a community of venial sinners, of apple-lickers (persons who, if tempted in the Garden of Eden, would have licked rather than bitten the apple). Synge knows what Wilde taught: that venial sins are ignoble but that it takes a person of some vision and courage to commit a 'mortaler'. The sinful act has a vitality undreamt of by the cautious peasants and publicans of *The Playboy of the Western World* or by the repressed governesses and canons of *The Importance of Being Earnest*. Both playwrights anticipate Eliot in proposing that it is better to do evil than to do nothing at all, because those who do evil at least prove that they exist.[21]

The ruling regime in both plays sets its face against the life of the imagination: religious and educational institutions conspire in the attempt to suppress the young. Synge's Father Reilly doesn't even have to appear in order to terrorise Shawn Keogh; and Wilde's Canon Chasuble is a weak-kneed old lecher. His spirituality is of such a kind that he gives the same sermon no matter what the occasion, as if to illustrate Wilde's complaint that 'in the English Church a man succeeds, not through his capacity for belief, but through his capacity for disbelief'.[22] Wilde's deathbed conversion to Roman Catholicism is a matter of some dispute; but it may have been his characteristic desire to explore his own opposite that led to the introduction of certain 'Catholic' elements in his writing. It is telling that Joyce chose to see Wilde as a profoundly Catholic writer: one who thought himself a pagan but who put his Irish qualities in service to a theory of beauty that lies at the centre of Catholicism: the notion that man cannot achieve divine truth except through the sense of separation and loss inherent in sin.[23] The *felix culpa*, the fall, may be 'fortunate' because, once confessed, it opens the way back to God. In essence that is the morality of Bunburying: based on a theory that only those who go wrong at first will subsequently learn how to go right, and correspondingly only those who confront lies will learn to know what truth is. Experience may be the name that a man gives to his mistakes but experience is educative, for the man who knows how to make a mistake may still be saved.

In that crucial sense Wilde redefined the nineteenth-century ideas of *innocence*. For him it did not evoke a cloistered inexperience, such as Cecily's, but its very opposite – an openness to experience to be achieved through Bunburying. Innocence was not some precious commodity lost in a careless half-hour at the age of eighteen: rather it was an attribute which people either possessed or lacked, and those who had it almost never lost it. His Bunburyists might immerse themselves in all kinds of questionable activity and yet emerge with a kind of indestructable innocence, open to experience, while on the other end of the spectrum could be found the Miss Prisms, who preached inexperience as a virtue because their minds really were closed and corrupt, incapable of growth or development. 'In England', wrote Wilde, 'everybody who is incapable of learning has taken to teaching';[24] or, as Sören Kierkegaard had already put it, 'There are two ways. One is to suffer. The other is to become a professor of the fact that somebody else has suffered.'[25]

At the root of Miss Prism's theory of education is a suspicion of the imagination. In studying her political economy Cecily must omit the chapter on the fall of the rupee, because it is somewhat too sensational. Miss Prism implies that ideas always come from books, whereas Cecily (like the mother of all creation) has all of her most promising thoughts in a garden. Wilde thus distinguishes between education, which should cultivate the individual, and schooling, which suppresses the individual in a process of socialisation.

The university extension scheme attended by Gwendolen is an example of the latter: Gwendolen cannot come away without having been 'excessively admired'. Academics themselves are hardly more honourable, however, for, as Wilde complained, in examinations the foolish ask questions which the wise cannot answer.

Cecily can hardly be blamed, therefore, for feeling quite plain after her German lesson, for 'People never think of cultivating a girl's imagination. That is the great defect of modern education' (CW 390). It is Lady Bracknell who, somewhat surprisingly, completes Wilde's critique of modern schooling. Honest enough to admit that what most people call innocence is really ignorance, she expresses disapproval of anything that tampers with natural ignorance. Education, which is intended to cure people's ignorance, is something which Lady Bracknell finds positively dangerous. 'Fortunately, in England, at any rate, education produces no effect whatsoever', she opines: 'If it did, it would prove a serious danger to the upper classes, and probably leads to acts of violence in Grovesnor Square.'[26] Behind those lines is Wilde's reminder that a true education teaches the young to rebel against their elders and to consider most critically the society which they are asked to inherit. The ultimate sign of a good teacher may even be a dissenting pupil – but not in Wilde's time, when education seemed a conspiracy against critical thought. 'Thinking is the most unhealthy thing in the world', he observed ironically in 'The Decay of Lying', 'and people die of it just as they die of any other disease. Fortunately, in England at any rate, thought is not catching.'[27] This is because the old-fashioned respect for the young is dying out, as Gwendolen laments. In such a context, disobedience is the only hope of growth.

The defects of nineteenth-century schooling had become, towards the end of the century, the features of its art. This was the Age of Realism, of literal-minded fidelity to social surfaces, as novelists like Emile Zola and – to some degree – playwrights like Henrik Ibsen sought to describe the lives of coal-miners or the problems of the urban poor with a photographic exactitude that verged on documentary journalism. Both Synge and Wilde opposed this trend. In his preface to *The Playboy of the Western World* Synge objected to 'the joyless and pallid words' of Ibsen and Zola.[28] He insisted that in a work of art it was not enough to have reality: one must also know joy. In countries where the imagination of the rural people was still vital, he said, a writer could find words both real and beautiful, whereas the joyless literature of towns had lost this beauty, retaining only a bleak realism. This was an endorsement of what Wilde had written in 'The Decay of Lying', where he had condemned modern novelists such as Zola who presented dull facts under the guise of fiction – hence his particular mockery of Miss Prism who has written a three-volume novel of revolting sentimentality. Zola and Maupassant were guilty of stripping life of the few rags that still covered her, regretted Wilde, who contended that the realists had all sold their birthrights for a mess of pottage. Even newspapers had degenerated and could now be absolutely relied upon.[29]

The capital importance of Wilde and Synge in the history of modern drama is that they represent the end of realism and the rise of a more abstract form of art. For them the artist is advised to abandon the attempt at surface realism, since he or she can never hope to compete in that area with the journalist or the photographer. The spread of photography and of electronic recording has freed the artist from the dreary obligation of realism, allowing him or her to tell the lies and cultivate the distortions which are the basis of art. 'Art is art because it is not nature', said the German Goethe in a phrase beloved of Irish writers, for whom art was not so much a mirror as a veil.

Life is the mirror, said Wilde who loved inversions, but art is the higher reality. Thus the real life is not the one we lead so much as the one which we create in our imaginations. In 'The Decay of Lying' he rejects Shakespeare's image of art as a mirror held up to life, suggesting that the mirror is now a cracked looking-glass, thoroughly discredited. It is remarkable that the same image is used by Joyce at the start of *Ulysses*, where Stephen Dedalus describes the cracked looking-glass of a servant as a symbol of Irish art. What he means to suggest is that the folk-plays of the Abbey Theatre do not project an adequate image of modern Ireland: they merely perpetuate the stereotype of the Irish as a primitive and servile race. There is, however, an even deeper meaning to the image, at a level where its meanings are shared by Joyce and Wilde: and that is the notion that the cracked looking-glass no longer depicts a single image, but instead of a multiplicity of broken images, much like a modernist painting. Wilde held that the only way to intensify personality was to multiply it: his play, like the cracked mirror, renders a multiple self, showing characters who experiment with various personalities in order to try them for size. In the final analysis, however, it becomes clear that that multiple self is Wilde's own and that the stage space contains the field of force that is the Wildean mind. All of the characters in *The Importance of Being Earnest* talk alike, which is to say like Wilde. What the play asks us to endorse in the end is not so much this person or that as an attitude of mind – the morality of the fluid or multiple self. In particular, ratification is sought for the attempt by young people to become the opposite of all that they are by training and inheritance, to put on the anti-self.

So it is also in Synge's *The Playboy of the Western World*. There, Christy cultivates the art of becoming his own opposite. At the outset he is timid and frightened, a result of the low self-esteem induced in him by a stunted education and tyrannical father. When Pegeen tells him, over and over, that he is handsome and courageous, he believes so passionately in her avowal that it becomes true. Synge's point, of course, is that it was never false. Each image of Christy had a certain validity, but each could be only a partial account of his personality, as remarkable for what it left out as for what it let in. In each environment, at home with his father in the old days or now among the worshipping girls of Mayo, he achieves a different and contrary self-image by permitting his identity to be defined in the distorting-mirror of other people's opinions.

It is no coincidence that Synge places a mirror in Christy's hand at the start of the second act, or that the young hero should reject the evidence of the cracked looking-glass which once he used in his father's home. As he looks now into Pegeen's nicely polished mirror his self-image changes:

> Didn't I know rightly I was handsome, though it was the divil's own mirror we had beyond, would twist a squint across an angel's brow.[30]

So the ugly young fellow with a murderous gob on him (to quote his father) turns into a handsome fellow with a noble brow (to quote Pegeen). *Objectively* Christy hasn't changed: only his circumstances have. The cracked mirror abandoned in his father's home indicates the decay of realism: however, the perfect image in Pegeen's mirror is not a complete picture either. 'Them that kills their fathers is a vain lot surely',[31] quips Sara Tansey when she catches Christy hiding the mirror behind his back at the start of Act II. It will only be in Act III that Christy will learn to do without mirrors and without the distorting-mirror of public adulation. Then he will stand, without props or support from others, on his own two feet. Then his self-image will be entirely of his own making and the passing of 'realism' will be marked by the triumph of the Wildean liar.

In 'The Decay of Lying' Wilde had argued that life imitates art far more often than art imitates life. People only started to feel oppressed by the London fogs *after* it became fashionable for artists to paint them. The energy of life, said Wilde, is the desire for expression; and art invaluably presents the forms through which expression is attained. Nature imitates art in the sense that things 'are' because we see them: fogs appear everywhere once someone has started to paint them, for the eye always sees what it was trained to see. However, each work of art is unique, whereas nature repeats itself once a year with the renewal of seasons.[32]

For Wilde, therefore, art is neither nature nor a mirror held to nature, but a deliberate improvement on it. Nature may have good intentions: only art can carry them out. So a green flower must be worn as a protest against nature's limitations and self-plagiarism, and also against English earnestness and dullness. Precisely the same aesthetic pretensions underlie Synge's notorious use of Hiberno-English dialect. In the 1898 notebooks where he recorded passages from 'The Decay of Lying', Synge also wrote a line of his own in which he wondered about the possibilities of creating 'an art more beautiful than nature',[33] that is, a dialect more exotic than everyday Irish speech. So, although he justifiably claims in the preface to *The Playboy of the Western World* that he has used only words and phrases heard in rural Ireland, it must be added that he has intensified the effect, resorting to only the more striking phrases and cramming far more images and elements into a single sentence than any Irish countryman ever would. In the witty words of one critic of the time, Synge exaggerated the coefficient of Hibernicism. His speeches are often undeniably exotic:

> Amn't I after seeing the love-light of the star of knowledge shining from her brow, and hearing words would put you thinking on the holy Brigid speaking to the infant saints, and now she'll be turning again, and speaking hard words to me, like an old woman with a spavindy ass she'd have, urging on a hill.[34]

All this is in keeping with Wilde's protest against Victorian literalism. It may also be Synge's protest against a devout evangelical mother, who taught her son that strong language and exaggerations were sinful, and would have to be accounted for before a vengeful God.[35] Mrs Synge's avowal is in marked contrast with Wilde's happy announcement that 'art itself is really a form of exaggeration; and selection, which is the very spirit of art, is nothing more than an intensified mode of over-emphasis'.[36]

In such a manner might one also explain the stylised nature of Synge's very controversial plot. He repudiated the idea that his play be judged by its fidelity to the sociology of western Ireland: rather it was an account of its 'psychic state'.[37] He saw art not as a criticism of life but as an alternative world with its own terms of reference. He would have concurred with Sir Philip Sidney's aphorism that 'the poet nothing affirmeth, and so he never lieth': making no claim to render the known world, he could not (or should not) be accused of falsifying it. This was not easily understood by those who rioted against *The Playboy of the Western World* in 1907, seeing in it only a travesty of life in the sacred west. Conceding that his plot was strictly incredible – he called it 'an extravaganza'[38] – Synge told a newspaper reporter that it was an abstract version. This, too, was in keeping with Wilde's view that the more imitative art is, the less it represents its age and place, while the more abstract it becomes the better it captures the spirit, the 'psychic state', of its time. Distortion and exaggeration are often necessary to emphasise the peculiarity of a person or an age or a place: otherwise people would not pay thousands of pounds to have a portrait painted when they could have a faithful photograph for a small sum of money. Abstract portraits often probe beneath the surface realism of the human body, capturing some aspect of personality of which the sitter may have been only half aware. And all too often the sitter is quite dissatisfied with what has been revealed in the completed work, for, as Wilde observed, far from being the creation of its own time art is usually in direct opposition to it. This view was also endorsed by Synge who saw it as the artist's duty – in ancient Gaelic tradition – to insult, as well as sometimes to flatter, his compatriots. Yeats summed up this aesthetic principle best of all in saying that the artist of genius is never like a country's idea of itself – and is often accused of villainous lying simply for revealing an underlying truth. Or else the artist is disparaged as an eccentric by those who forget that the eccentric is usually the person with a deeper-than-average understanding of normality.

Wilde concluded 'The Decay of Lying' with the argument that there are many kinds of lie – white lies, black lies, lies told to save face or to gain advantage – but that the highest form is lying for its own sake. Cecily in *The Importance of Being Earnest* had spoken scornfully of 'lying for a moral purpose – for immediate advantage', but in Wilde's mind the highest form of lying was art, 'the telling of beautiful untrue things'.[39] To such a one realism offers only a lower form of truth. When a famous French painter who had just painted his back-garden was reprimanded by a critic for omitting to paint a tree in the centre of the lawn, his response was not to paint in the tree but instead to rush out into the garden, grab an axe and chop the tree down. The lie, if persisted in, acquires its own reality, and may indeed turn out to have been true all along in the world of art. In that world, after all, a truth is that whose opposite might also be true: and so in *The Importance of Being Earnest*, Jack (who really was Ernest all along) pleads for forgiveness:

> Gwendolen, it is a terrible thing for a man to find out suddenly that all his life he has been speaking nothing but the truth. Can you forgive me?[40]

This apology is necessary because the women all along have been cautioning the men against this very fault. Cecily, in particular, expressed the hope that Algy was not leading a double life, 'pretending to be wicked and really good all the time. That would be hypocrisy'.[41]

That is exactly what Christy Mahon has been doing as well: so much so that he becomes 'a mighty man ... by the power of a lie'.[42] He, also, becomes his own opposite. The father whom he hated at the beginning of the play he manages to emulate at the end as 'master of all fights';[43] and the words of amazement which Christy first used to express astonishment at Pegeen's heroic image of him – 'Is it me?'[44] – are now used by the father to register his surprise and delight at the new-found authority of his son. The parallelism is complete, for, like Christy before him, Old Mahon has travelled the countryside winning food and lodging with his amazing tale. So the fiction takes on the contours of truth.

The corollary is obvious: if lies are a higher truth, then what passes as truth may be a form of lower lies. At some point in *The Importance of Being Earnest* everybody seems to tell a lie or commit a falsehood – Lane steals his master's champagne; Lady Bracknell bribes her maid to snoop on her niece; Cecily lies to Gwendolen that her engagement will be announced in a local paper; Algy snoops on the inscription on his friend's cigarette case; Jack tells Gwendolen that he will be in town until Monday and promptly retreats to the country. The end-product of all this fooling is the serious revelation that society is a tissue of lies and couldn't function without them. Algy is right to say that the truth is rarely pure and never simple; and Jack develops the point by saying that 'the truth isn't quite the sort of thing one tells to a nice sweet refined girl'.[45] Since both the men and Miss Prism agree on the need to shelter 'girls' from the brutal facts of life, it is left to the young women to insist on straight talking. Cecily asserts that 'whenever one has anything unpleasant to say, one should always be quite candid';[46] and Gwendolen emphasises the moral duty of speaking one's mind. But these are mere platitudes to justify the bluntness of their impending quarrel. In his heart Wilde knows that the only distinction to be made is between those who lie for pragmatic advantage and those who lie for pleasure and art.

In *The Playboy of the Western World* Synge takes Wilde's idea a stage further to see what happens when a single, monstrous lie is made the basis of a young man's growth and then put to the test. It is at this point that Synge parts company with Wilde for, by showing a massive amount of talk and little real action, he attacks the stage Irish stereotype. He offers indeed a somewhat angular critique of Wilde's theory – of fine words divorced from real action, of gestures struck rather than deeds done. There is, as Pegeen says, 'a great gap between a gallous story and a dirty deed'.[47] In the end Synge is sufficiently sophisticated to mock the very gift for exotic language which is his own trademark: and subtle enough to doubt the very medium through which those doubts are expressed. At bottom he seems to suspect that the mask of the elegant anti-self purveyed by Wilde is perhaps a subtle latter-day version of the ancient blarney. For himself, he is finally less interested in the power of a lie than in that portion of reality which proves resistant to it.

If Synge rewrote the Wildean drama of lying, he also radically revised it. How much survived this critique? Rather more than might seem to have done. The revelation of an apparent opposite as an actual double was to become a central element in the works of many subsequent Irish playwrights. Sean O'Casey, in *The Plough and the Stars*, showed how the Irish and British, though bitter enemies during the 1916 Rising, could nonetheless share certain notions of honour, even to the extent of accusing one another's top brass of breaking the codes of war and 'not playing the game'.[48] Likewise, in the following generation, Brendan Behan discovered that what united British and Irish antagonists in *The Hostage* was far more telling than what divided them: the British colonel back at his depot emerges as a carbon-copy of Monsewer, the IRA leader, and both regard their underlings as expendable pawns.[49] Perhaps because of his ambivalent sexual orientations, Behan proved richly responsive to Wilde's aesthetic doctrine that every force is interpenetrated by its own opposite; and so he saluted his tragic forerunner in a remarkable poem in the Irish language:

> Tar éis gach gleo
> do chuir sé as beo
> le teann anaithe,
> sínte san chlapsholus
> corpán an bheomhaire
> balbh san dorchadas.
> Fé thost, ach coinnle
> an tórraimh na lasracha.
> A cholainn sheang
> 's a shúil daingean ídithe
> I seomra fuar lom
> 's an *concierge* spídeach
> ó an iomarca freastail
> ar phótaire iasachta
> a d'imthigh gan service
> an deich fán gcéad íoctha.
> Aistrith' ón Flore
> do fhásach na naomhthacht,
> ógphrionnsa na bpeacadh
> ina shearbhán aosta,
> seod órdha na drúise
> ina dhiaidh aige fágtha,
> gan *Pernod* ina chabhair aige
> ach uisce na cráifeacht.
> Ógrí na háilleachta'
> ina Narcissus briste,

ach réalt na glanmhaighdine
ina ga ar an uisce.

Ceangal
Dá aoibhne bealach an pheacaidh
is mairg bás gan beannacht
Mo ghraidhn thú, a Oscair,
bhí sé agat gach bealach.

Here is Ulick O'Connor's fine translation:

After all the wit
in a sudden fit
of fear, he skipped it.
Stretched in the twilight
that body once lively
dumb in the darkness.
In a cold empty room
quiet, but for the candles
blazing beside him,
his elegant form
and firm gaze exhausted.
With a spiteful concierge
impatient at waiting
for a foreign master
who left without paying
the ten per cent service.
Exiled now from Flore
to sanctity's desert
the young prince of Sin
broken and withered.
Lust left behind him
gem without lustre
no Pernod for a stiffener
but cold holy water
the young king of beauty
Narcissus broken.
But the pure star of Mary
as a gleam on the ocean.

Envoi
Sweet is the way of the sinner,
sad, death without God's praise.
My life on you, Oscar boy,
yourself had it both ways.[50]

Behan carried the Wildean aesthetic of doubleness or hybridity into new zones, writing with facility in both Irish and English, staging his first nights in both Dublin and London (depending on the language for, of course, *The Hostage* first saw the light of day as *An Giall*). Most of all, perhaps, in his self-appointed role as scourge of British propriety in the 1950s and 1960s, Behan seemed intent on repeating Wilde's performance of doomed, self-destructive genius. Even the magnificent autobiography *Borstal Boy* takes a deserved place in the history of prison literature alongside *De Profundis* and *The Ballad of Reading Gaol*, just as Behan's on-off romance with Roman Catholicism seems to replicate Wilde's spiritual pilgrimage.

However, the strictly *dramatic* tradition initiated by Wilde in Irish theatre had to wait almost a century for the full flowering of Tom Murphy's genius to achieve a spectacular renewal. It would be no exaggeration to describe Murphy's masterpiece *The Gigli Concert* as a further attempt to elevate the lie to the level of magnificent poetic truth. In this study of a successful Irish builder whose riches mean nothing to him unless he can sing tenor like Benimillo Gigli, Murphy has written a play which fully merits the designation 'verbal opera'. The actors in the original Abbey Theatre production in 1983 were rightly encouraged to overplay rather than underplay their roles, to surrender gloriously to the emotional extremism of the piece. So, for instance, the builder's tearful account of a callous and frustrated childhood was his *aria*, his moment to dominate the forestage. In the final scene when his amateur psychiatrist, J. P. W. King, sings another aria, it is from an opera in which a lover is mourning the death of his beloved.[51] In the preceding scene, King's mistress has announced that she is dying of a terminal cancer, a revelation which might seem to be a cheap theatrical shot until we recall that it is out of such blatant emotionalism that opera is always made. As in opera, *The Gigli Concert* is filled with melodramatic reversals, of unmaskers suddenly unmasked.

The term *verbal opera* had, of course, been composed by W. H. Auden to describe Wilde's *The Importance of Being Earnest* as the only pure example of its kind in English. By it Auden intended to denote a drama in which every element is subordinated to the dialogue, existing only for its enhancement:

> Wilde created a verbal universe in which the characters are determined by the kinds of things they say, and the plot is nothing but a succession of opportunities to say them.[52]

Similar subordination of character to verbal energy comes all the more appropriately in *The Gigli Concert* which, like *The Importance of Being Earnest*, evokes the Double. For the Irish builder (who often appears in the outline of a shadow in a window) and the English quack are but two aspects of the same person; and the attempt by the builder to sing like Gigli is the drive to achieve a moment when the mundane and metaphorical might merge into one. That fusion is attained, in Murphy as in Wilde, with a surrender of the ethical imagination to that of pure form, in what amounts to a Faustian pact. If the Anglo-Irish antithesis informed Wilde's world of opposites and doubles, then it may also lie behind Murphy's, with the suggestion that taken together the self and the *doppelgänger* have the makings of a whole person. That is the utopian moment towards which *The Gigli Concert* moves, the future 'not-yet' latent in the present, a future which can be blasted open by a dynamic sense of possibility. Murphy has brilliantly implemented on stage Wilde's thesis that the arts are what mankind may yet become, offering an anticipatory illumination.

Seen against that context the radicalism of Wilde's legacy becomes a little more apparent. In an age when Marxians preached that ownership of the means of production was the key to progress, Wilde correctly sensed that ownership and understanding of the means of expression would be the question of real consequence in the century to come. Subsequent history has proven just how right he was.

NOTES

1 Samuel Beckett, *Molloy Malone Dies The Unnamable* (London: John Calder, 1959), p. 182.
2 Oscar Wilde, *The Importance of Being Earnest*, ed. Russell Jackson (London: Ernest Benn, 1980), pp. 37, 40.
3 T. S. Eliot, 'The Waste Land', *The Complete Poems and Plays of T. S. Eliot* (London: Faber and Faber, 1969), p. 65.
4 F. Scott Fitzgerald, *The Great Gatsby* (New York: Scribner's Sons, 1925), p. 118.
5 James Joyce, *A Portrait of the Artist as a Young Man*, (Harmondsworth: Penguin, 1960), p. 189.
6 Quoted by Martin Esslin, *The Theatre of the Absurd* (Harmondsworth: Penguin, 1968), p. 38.
7 Quoted by Tomás Ó Fiaich, 'The Language and Political History', *A View of the Irish Language*, ed. Brian Ó Cuív (Dublin, 1969), p. 105.
8 Andrew Carpenter, 'Double Vision in Anglo-Irish Literature', in *Place, Personality and the Irish Writer*, ed. A. Carpenter (Gerrards Cross: Colin Smythe, 1977), pp. 182–3.
9 On this see Edith Mary Johnston, *Ireland in the Eighteenth Century* (Dublin: Gill and Macmillan, 1974), pp. 175ff.
10 For more on this see Declan Kiberd, 'Irish Literature and Irish History', *The Oxford Illustrated History of Ireland*, ed. R. F. Foster (Oxford: Oxford University Press, 1989), pp. 280ff.

11 Oscar Wilde, 'Intentions: The Decay of Lying', *The Artist as Critic*, ed. R. Ellmann (London: W. H. Allen, 1970), p. 292.
12 J. M. Synge, 'The Playboy of the Western World', in *Plays* 2, ed. Ann Saddlemyer (Oxford: Oxford University Press, 1968), p. 103.
13 Ibid., p. 149.
14 Wilde, *The Artist as Critic*, ed. Ellmann, p. 294.
15 Wilde, *Earnest*, ed. Jackson, p. 20.
16 Synge, *Plays* 2, p. 99.
17 Wilde, *The Artist as Critic*, ed. Ellmann, p. 294. The connection was first made by the scholar Thomas R. Whitaker.
18 Wilde, *Earnest*, ed. Jackson, p. 83.
19 Ibid., pp. 62–3.
20 Synge, *Plays* 2, p. 97.
21 On this element see Hugh Kenner, *The Invisible Poet: T. S. Eliot* (London: Methuen, 1965), pp. 125–57.
22 Wilde, *The Artist as Critic*, ed. Ellmann, p. 317.
23 James Joyce, *The Critical Writings*, ed. E. Mason and R. Ellmann (London: Faber and Faber, 1959), p. 205.
24 Wilde, *The Artist as Critic*, ed. Ellmann, p. 291.
25 W. H. Auden, *The Kierkegaard Anthology* (New York: Random House, 1957), p. 20.
26 Wilde, *Earnest*, ed. Jackson, p. 27.
27 Wilde, *The Artist as Critic*, ed. Ellmann, p. 291.
28 Synge, *Plays* 2, p. 53.
29 Wilde, *The Artist as Critic*, ed. Ellmann, p. 296ff.
30 Synge, *Plays* 2, p. 95.
31 Ibid., p. 99.
32 Wilde, *The Artist as Critic*, ed. Ellmann, p. 12ff.
33 J. M. Synge, manuscripts TCD 4382, f. 69v.
34 Synge, *Plays* 2, pp. 125–7.
35 David H. Greene and Edward M. Stephens, *J. M. Synge 1871–1909* (New York 1961), p. 26.
36 Wilde, *The Artist as Critic*, ed. Ellmann, p. 302.
37 J. M. Synge, *Collected Letters 1*, ed. Ann Saddlemyer (Oxford: Oxford University Press, 1983), p. 330.
38 Ibid., where Synge regrets using the word.
39 Wilde, *The Artist as Critic*, ed. Ellmann, p. 320.
40 Wilde, *Earnest*, ed. Jackson, p. 104.
41 Ibid., p. 46.
42 Synge, *Plays* 2, p. 165.
43 Ibid., p. 173.
44 Ibid., pp. 79 and 173.
45 Wilde, *Earnest*, ed. Jackson, p. 34.
46 Ibid., p. 68.
47 Synge, *Plays* 2, p. 169.
48 Sean O'Casey, *Three Plays* (London: Macmillan, 1957), pp. 187, 213.
49 Brendan Behan, *The Hostage* (London: Methuen, 1959), p. 61.
50 Gabriel Fitzmaurice and Declan Kiberd eds., *An Crann faoi Bhlath: The*

Flowering Tree – Irish Poetry with Verse Translations (Dublin: Wolfhound Press, 1991), pp. 100–3.

51 Tom Murphy, *The Gigli Concert* (Dublin: Gallery Publications, 1984), pp. 70ff.

52 W, H. Auden, 'An Improbable Life', in *Oscar Wilde: A Collection of Critical Essays*, ed. R. Ellmann (Englewood Cliffs, NJ: Prentice Hall, 1969), p. 136.

SELECT BIBLIOGRAPHY

Wilde's works

Collected Edition of the Works of Oscar Wilde, ed. Robert Ross, 15 vols. (London: Methuen, 1908; reprinted 1969).

Complete Works of Oscar Wilde, introduction by Merlin Holland (London: Collins, 1994).

The Artist as Critic: Critical Writings of Oscar Wilde, ed. Richard Ellmann (New York: Random House, 1969; W. H. Allen: London, 1970).

The Complete Shorter Fiction of Oscar Wilde, ed. Isobel Murray (Oxford: Oxford University Press, 1979).

The Importance of Being Earnest, ed. Russell Jackson (London: Benn, 1980).

Oscar Wilde's 'The Importance of Being Earnest': A Reconstructive Critical Edition of the Text of the First Production, ed. Joseph Donohue and Ruth Berggren (Gerrards Cross: Colin Smythe, 1995).

The Importance of Being Earnest as Originally Written by Oscar Wilde, ed. Sarah Augusta Dickson, 2 vols. (New York: New York Public Library, 1956).

The Definitive Four-Act Version of 'The Importance of Being Earnest', ed. Ruth Berggren (New York: Vanguard, 1987).

The Importance of Being Earnest and other plays, ed. Peter Raby (Oxford: Oxford University Press, 1995).

Lady Windermere's Fan, ed. Ian Small (London: Benn, 1980).

The Picture of Dorian Gray, ed. Isobel Murray (Oxford: Oxford University Press, 1974).

Salomé (Paris and London: Librairie de l'Art Indépendant; Elkin Matthews and John Lane, 1893).

Salome: A Tragedy in One Act: Translated from the French of Oscar Wilde: Pictured by Aubrey Beardsley (London: Elkin Mathews and John Lane, 1894).

Two Society Comedies, ed. Ian Small and Russell Jackson (London: A. and C. Black, 1983).

Bibliographical and works

Fletcher, Ian and Stokes, John, '*Oscar Wilde*', *Anglo-Irish Literature: A Review of Research*, ed. Richard Finnernan (New York: Modern Language Association of America, 1976).

Fletcher, Ian and Stokes, John, '*Oscar Wilde*' in *Recent Research on Anglo-Irish Writers*, ed. Richard Finnernan (New York: Modern Language Association of America, 1983).

Mason, Stuart [Christopher Millard], *A Bibliography of Oscar Wilde* (London: T. Werner Laurie, 1914; reissued, 1967).
Mikhail, E. H., *Oscar Wilde: An Annotated Bibliography of Criticism* (London: Macmillan, 1978).
Small, Ian, *Oscar Wilde Revalued: An Essay on New Materials & Methods of Research* (Greenboro, NC: ELT Press, 1993).

Biographical works

Davis, Coakley, *Oscar Wilde: The Importance of Being Irish* (Dublin: Town House, 1994).
Ellmann, Richard, *Oscar Wilde* (London: Hamish Hamilton, 1987).
Harris, Frank, *Oscar Wilde: His Life and Confessions* (printed and published by the author: New York, 1916; revised edition, London: Constable, 1938).
Hart-Davis, Rupert (ed.), *The Letters of Oscar Wilde* (London: Hart-Davis, 1962).
Selected Letters of Oscar Wilde (Oxford: Oxford University Press, 1979).
More Letters of Oscar Wilde (London: John Murray, 1985).
Holland, Vyvyan, *Son of Oscar Wilde* (London: Hart-Davis, 1954).
Oscar Wilde: A Pictorial Biography (London: Thames and Hudson, 1960).
Hyde, H. Montgomery (ed.), *The Trials of Oscar Wilde* (London: Hodge, 1948).
Oscar Wilde (New York: Farrar, Straus and Giroux, 1975).
Mikhail, E. H. (ed.), *Oscar Wilde: Interviews and Recollections* (London: Macmillan, 1979).
Page, Norman, *An Oscar Wilde Chronology* (London: Macmillan, 1991).
Pearson, Hesketh, *The Life of Oscar Wilde* (London: Methuen, 1946; revised edition, 1954).
Schroeder, Horst, *Additions and Corrections to Richard Ellmann's 'Oscar Wilde'* (Braunschweig: privately printed, 1989).
Sherard, Robert Harborough, *The Life of Oscar Wilde* (London: T. Werner Laurie, 1906).

Criticism

Beckson, Karl, *London in the 1890s: A Cultural History* (New York: Norton, 1992).
The Oscar Wilde Encyclopedia (New York: AMS Press, 1995).
Beckson, Karl (ed.), *Oscar Wilde: The Critical Heritage* (London: Routledge and Kegan Paul, 1970).
Behrendt, Patricia Flangan, *Oscar Wilde: Eros and Aesthetics* (London: Macmillan, 1991).
Bird, Alan, *The Plays of Oscar Wilde* (London: Vision Press, 1977).
Brake, Laurel, *Subjugated Knowledges: Journalism, Gender and Literature in the Nineteenth Century* (London: Macmillan, 1994).
Chamberlin, J. E., *Ripe was the Drowsy Hour: The Age of Oscar Wilde* (New York: Seabury, 1977).
Cohen, Ed, *Talk on the Wilde Side: Toward a Genealogy of a Discourse on Male Sexualities* (New York: Routledge, 1993).
Cohen, Philip K., *The Moral Vision of Oscar Wilde* (London: Associated University Press, 1978) (Rutherford: Fairleigh Dickinson University Press, 1979).
Dellamora, Richard, *Masculine Desire: The Sexual Politics of Victorian Aestheticism* (Chapel Hill: University of North Carolina Press, 1990).

Dijkstra, Bram, *Idols of Perversity: Fantasies of Feminine Evil in Fin-de-Siècle Culture* (Oxford: Oxford University Press, 1986).

Dollimore, Jonathan, *Sexual Dissidence: Augustine to Wilde, Freud to Foucault* (Oxford: Clarendon Press, 1991).

Dowling, Linda, *Language and Decadence in the Victorian Fin de Siècle* (Princeton: Princeton University Press, 1986).

Ellmann, Richard (ed.), *Oscar Wilde: A Collection of Critical Essays* (Englewood Cliffs, NJ: Prentice Hall, 1969).

Eltis, Sos, *Revising Wilde: Society and Subversion in the Plays of Oscar Wilde* (Oxford: Clarendon Press, 1996).

Ericksen, Donald H., *Oscar Wilde* (New York: Twayne, 1977).

Finney, Gail, *Women in Modern Drama: Freud, Feminism, and European Theater at the Turn of the Century* (Ithaca: Cornell University Press, 1989).

Gagnier, Regenia A., *Idylls of the Marketplace: Oscar Wilde and the Victorian Public* (Stanford: Stanford University Press, 1986).

Gagnier, Regenia A. (ed.), *Critical Essays on Oscar Wilde* (New York: Twayne, 1991).

Jackson, Holbrook, *The Eighteen Nineties: A Review of Art and Ideas at the Close of the Nineteenth Century* (London: Grant Richards, 1913).

Kaplan, Joel (ed.), *Modern Drama*, (Special Wilde number), 12:1 (1994).

Kaplan, Joel, and Stowell, Sheila, *Theatre and Fashion: Oscar Wilde to the Suffragettes* (Cambridge: Cambridge University Press, 1994).

Kohl, Norbert, *Oscar Wilde: The Works of a Conformist Rebel* (Cambridge: Cambridge University Press, 1988).

Knox, Melissa, *Oscar Wilde: A Long and Lovely Suicide* (New Haven: Yale University Press, 1994).

Meltzer, Françoise, *Salome and the Dance of Writing: Portraits of Mimesis in Literature* (Chicago: University of Chicago Press, 1987).

Morgan, Margery, *File on Wilde* (London: Methuen, 1990).

Nassaar, Christopher, *Into the Demon Universe: A Literary Exploration of Oscar Wilde* (New Haven: Yale University Press, 1974).

Pine, Richard, *Oscar Wilde* (Dublin: Gill and Macmillan, 1983).

Powell, Kerry, *Oscar Wilde and the Theatre of the 1890s* (Cambridge: Cambridge University Press, 1990).

Raby, Peter, *Oscar Wilde* (Cambridge: Cambridge University Press, 1988).

The Importance of Being Earnest: A Reader's Companion (New York: Twayne, 1995).

Roditi, Edouard, *Oscar Wilde* (Norfolk, CT: New Directions Books, 1947).

San Juan, Epifanio, *The Art of Oscar Wilde* (Princeton: Princeton University Press, 1967).

Sandulescu, C. George (ed.), *Rediscovering Oscar Wilde*, Princess Grace Irish Library Series 8 (Gerrards Cross: Colin Smythe, 1994).

Schmidgall, Gary, *The Stranger Wilde: Interpreting Oscar* (London: Abacus, 1994).

Shewan, Rodney, *Oscar Wilde: Art and Egotism* (London: Macmillan, 1977).

Showalter, Elaine, *Sexual Anarchy: Gender and Culture at the Fin de Siècle* (London: Bloomsbury, 1991).

Sinfield, Alan, *The Wilde Century: Effeminacy, Oscar Wilde and the Queer Movement* (New York: Columbia University Press, 1994).

Smith, Philip E. and Helfand, Michael S., *Oscar Wilde's Oxford Notebooks: A Portrait of Mind in the Making* (New York: Oxford University Press, 1989).

Stokes, John, *Oscar Wilde*, British Council Writers and Their Work Series, (London: Longman, 1978).

In the Nineties (Hemel Hempstead: Harvester Wheatsheaf, 1989).

Oscar Wilde: Myths, Miracles, and Imitations (Cambridge: Cambridge University Press, 1996).

Sullivan, Kevin, *Oscar Wilde* (New York: Columbia University Press, 1972).

Symons, Arthur, *A Study of Oscar Wilde* (London: Charles J. Sawyer, 1930).

Thornton, R. K. R., *The Decadent Dilemma* (London: Edward Arnold, 1983).

Tydeman, William (ed.), *Wilde, Comedies: A Selection of Critical Essays* (London: Macmillan, 1982).

Woodcock, George, *The Paradox of Oscar Wilde* (London: T. V. Boardman, 1949).

Worth, Katharine, *The Irish Drama of Europe from Yeats to Beckett* (London: Athlone Press, 1978).

Oscar Wilde (London: Macmillan, 1980).

Zagona, Helen Grace, *The Legend of Salome and the Principle of Art for Art's Sake* (Geneva: Ambilly-Annemasse, 1960).

Many specialised articles are listed in the endnotes to the essays in this volume. For new listings, and for other aspects of the context of Wilde's work, see bibliographies in, for example, *English Literature in Transition, Modern Drama, Nineteenth Century Theatre, Victorian Newsletter* and *The Year's Work in English Studies.*

The volumes listed above edited by Karl Beckson, Richard Ellmann, Regenia Gagnier and William Tydeman provide an excellent introduction to the range of critical essays and reviews. The collection edited by George Sandulescu reprints the papers given at the Wilde Conference in Monaco in 1993.

For an extensive commentary on the literature about Wilde, see Ian Small, *Oscar Wilde Revalued.*

GENERAL INDEX

INDEX OF WORKS BY OSCAR WILDE